The Essentials of CORPORATION LAW

Second Edition

Leona Beane, B.B.A., M.B.A., M.S., J.D.
Professor of Law
Baruch College
(City University of New York)

KENDALL/HUNT PUBLISHING COMPANY
4050 Westmark Drive   Dubuque, Iowa 52002

Material from Uniform CPA Examination Questions and Unofficial Answers; copyright © 1972–1984 by the American Institute of Certified Public Accountants, Inc., is reprinted with permission.

Copyright © 1984, 1987 by Kendall/Hunt Publishing Company

Library of Congress Catalog Card Number: 87: 82360

ISBN 0-8403-4499-6

All rights reserved. No part of this publication may be reproduced, stored in a retrieval system, or transmitted, in any form or by any means, electronic, mechanical, photocopying, recording, or otherwise, without the prior written permission of the copyright owner.

Printed in the United States of America

Preface

This book is a compilation of text material, cases, problems, and statutes covering the topic of Corporation Law with specific references and emphasis upon the law in effect in New York State, the Business Corporation Law. This has been prepared primarily as a textbook to be used by students studying Corporation Law; the book can also be effectively utilized by the lawyer or accountant reviewing questions and problems involving the Corporation. The materials included are designed primarily to reflect the law of New York State. The text references have been keyed to pertinent sections of the Business Corporation Law (B.C.L.), a copy of which is included in the Appendix.

Representative cases have been included in each Chapter. Portions of the complete court opinions in all instances have not been reproduced for purposes of saving space. Many of the cases and authorities cited by the courts have been omitted, as were purely technical matter and lengthy analysis of the evidence before the courts. However, the author has taken no liberty with any of the language used by the courts. There are discussion questions included at the end of most of the cases for further analysis.

This Second Edition has been updated and expanded to include the more recent corporation problems encountered in Corporation Law.

Representative problems have been included in each Chapter, several of which (28 in number) have been adapted from prior C.P.A. exam questions, each of which has an ** indicated.

Several persons have aided me in the completion of this book, the first edition and the second edition. Special thanks and my utmost appreciation to Professor Abraham Goldstein at Baruch College who took painstaking efforts in reading portions of the manuscript, and who offered numerous suggestions. Special thanks and appreciation to Professor James Sullivan, a retired member of the Baruch College Law Department (who was my first law professor when I was a student) who provided much of my knowledge and appreciation of Corporation Law (many of the examples and problems have been adopted from ones that he used); to Professor Edward Rothman (now deceased) who always gave me encouragement; to several professors in the Law Department at Baruch College who have at various times offered suggestions; several of the problems in the book have been extracted and adapted from problems used by the Baruch College Law Department over the years. My special thanks to Bennet Susser and Tom Friedman, two students who assisted in proofreading portions of the first edition's manuscript, and who offered their comments relating to student comprehension of the material; to Joycelyn Lesfloris a student who assisted in proofing the second edition. This second edition could not have been timely completed without the very able assistance of Sonia Haynes, a secretary in the Baruch College Law Department who did much of the typing of the revised portions.

If there are any errors, omissions or misinterpretations, I take full credit and responsibility.

Contents

Table of Cases	xiii
Table of References to the Business Corporation Law and Other Statutes	xv

1. Introduction   1

    A. Historical Background   1
    B. Development of Corporation Law in the United States   1
    C. What Is a Corporation?   2

2. The Business Corporation in New York State   3

    A. Different Forms of Doing Business   3
        1. The Sole Proprietorship   3
        2. The General Partnership   4
        3. The Limited Partnership   4
        4. The Joint Venture   5
        5. The Joint-Stock Association   5
        6. The Corporation   5
    B. Tax Considerations of a Corporation   5
        1. Comparison with Other Entities   5
        2. The "S" Corporation   6
        3. Other Tax Considerations of the Corporation   7
    C. Classification of Corporations   8
        1. Public Corporations   8
        2. Private Corporations   8
        3. Profit Corporations   8
        4. Non-Profit or Not-for-Profit Corporations   8
        5. Professional Corporations   9
        6. Domestic Corporations   9
        7. Foreign Corporations   9
        8. Closely Held or Close Corporations   10
    D. The Corporation is a Person   10
    E. The Corporation as a Separate Entity   10
    F. Limited Liability and the Corporation   12
        1. Exceptions to Limited Liability   12
    G. Piercing the Corporate Veil   13
    Cases 1, 2   15
    Problems 1–9   19

3. Formation of the Business Corporation — 23
- A. The Shareholders' Agreement — 23
- B. Statutory Requirements for Formation of the Corporation — 23
  1. The Corporate Name — 23
  2. The Incorporator(s) — 24
  3. The Certificate of Incorporation — 24
  4. Filing the Certificate of Incorporation — 25
  5. Defects in Filing — 26
- C. The Role of a Promoter — 26
  1. Who Is a Promoter? — 26
  2. Liabilities of a Promoter for Contracts — 27
  3. Duties of a Promoter — 27
- D. Foreign Corporations — 27
  1. What Is Doing Business in New York? — 28
  2. Licensing Procedure — 28
  3. Names of a Foreign Corporation — 29
  4. Internal Affairs of a Foreign Corporation — 29
  5. Powers of a Foreign Corporation — 29
  6. Enforcement and Penalties Imposed for Non-Compliance — 30
- E. Statutory Requirements for Maintaining Corporate Status — 31
  1. Franchise Taxes — 31
  2. Other Tax Forms — 31
- F. Names Used by a Corporation — 31
  1. Fictitious Names—Filing Requirements — 31
  2. Conflicts with Other Names—Unfair Competition — 32

Cases 3, 4, 5, 6 — 33
Problems 10–20 — 36

4. Corporate Purposes and Powers — 41
- A. Express Purposes — 41
- B. Implied Powers — 42
- C. Ultra Vires Contracts — 43
  1. What Is Ultra Vires? — 43
  2. Illegal Acts Distinguished from Ultra Vires — 43
  3. Legal Status of Ultra Vires Contracts — 43
- D. Incorporators' Organization Meeting — 44
- E. Management of the Corporation — 44
- F. By-Laws — 45
  1. Enactment of By-Laws — 45
  2. Some Typical By-Law Provisions — 45

Problems 21–23 — 46

5. Capital and the Financial Structure of the Corporation — 47
   A. Authority to Issue Shares — 47
   B. Classification of Shares of Stocks and Bonds — 47
      1. Par Value Shares — 48
      2. No Par Value Shares — 48
      3. Common Shares — 48
      4. Preferred Shares — 48
      5. Convertible Shares — 49
      6. Redeemable or Callable Shares — 49
      7. Treasury Shares — 50
      8. Stock Warrants — 50
      9. Corporate Bonds — 50
   C. Stock Subscriptions — 50
      1. Before the Corporation Is Formed — 50
      2. After the Corporation Is Formed — 51
      3. Liability Under Subscription Agreement — 51
   D. Consideration and Payment for Shares — 51
      1. Valid Consideration — 51
      2. Improper Consideration—Liability for Shares — 52
      3. Consideration for Treasury Shares — 52
   E. Issuance of Shares — 52
   F. Stated Capital — 53
   G. Surplus — 54
      1. Capital Surplus — 55
      2. Earned Surplus — 55
      3. Revaluation Surplus — 55
      4. Examples of Surplus on a Corporation's Balance Sheet — 56
   H. Improper Issue of Shares — 58
      1. Remedies Available — 58
   Cases 7, 8, 9 — 59
   Problems 24–32 — 62

6. Shareholders' Rights Regarding Financial Structure of the Corporation — 65
   A. The Stock Certificate — 65
      1. The Form of the Stock Certificate — 65
      2. The Right to a Stock Certificate — 66
      3. Transferring the Certificate — 66
      4. Indorsement of the Certificate — 66
      5. Restrictions on Transfer of Shares — 67
      6. The Buy-Sell Agreement — 67
      7. Shares are *NOT* Corporate Assets — 67
      8. The Stock Record Book — 68

    B. Share Redemption and Reacquisition — 68
        1. Redemption of Shares — 69
        2. Reacquired Shares — 69
        3. Treasury Shares — 69
    C. Rights of Shareholders — 69
        1. Dividends — 69
        2. The Preemptive Right — 74
        3. The Right to Information — 75
        4. Right of Appraisal — 77
        5. Shareholders' Rights After Liquidation — 77
  Cases 10, 11, 12, 13, 14 — 78
  Problems 33–55 — 90

7. Organization and Management of the Corporation — 99

    A. Organizational Structure — 99
    B. The Shareholders — 99
        1. Shareholders' Meetings — 99
        2. Unanimous Written Consent of Shareholders in Lieu of Meeting — 104
        3. Shareholder Voting on Unusual Matters — 104
    C. The Directors — 104
        1. Number of Directors — 104
        2. Qualification of Directors — 104
        3. Term of Office — 104
        4. Removal of Directors — 104
        5. Procedure to Fill Vacancies on the Board of Directors — 105
        6. Meetings of the Board of Directors — 105
        7. Powers of the Board of Directors — 106
        8. Committees of the Board — 107
    D. The Officers — 107
        1. Method of Selection — 107
        2. Term of Office — 108
        3. Titles of Officers — 108
        4. Qualification of Officers — 108
        5. Officers' Authority — 108
        6. Usual and Customary Authority of Particular Officers — 109
        7. Compensation of Officers and the Employment Contract — 110
        8. Removal of Officers — 110
    E. The Close Corporation—Management Structure — 110
        1. The Shareholders' Agreement — 111
        2. Voting Agreements-Abnormal Management Structure — 111
        3. The Voting Trust Agreement — 112
  Cases 15, 16, 17 — 112
  Problems 56–59 — 117

8. The Duties and Liabilities of Directors and Officers — 119

- A. The Duty of Directors and Officers — 119
  - 1. The Duty of Care — 119
  - 2. The Duty of Obedience — 120
  - 3. The Duty of Diligence — 120
  - 4. The Duty of Loyalty — 120
- B. The Liability of Directors and Officers—Generally — 120
  - 1. Conduct Prohibited by B.C.L. — 120
  - 2. The Business Judgment Rule — 121
  - 3. The Liability of Directors and Officers — 122
  - 4. Liability for Contracts — 122
  - 5. Liability for Torts — 122
  - 6. Liability for Crimes — 123
- C. Duties and Liabilities Imposed by Statutes — 123
  - 1. The Securities Laws — 123
  - 2. Foreign Corrupt Practices Act of 1977 — 124
  - 3. R.I.C.O. — 124
  - 4. Other Statutes — 125
- D. Dissenting Directors — 127
- E. The Fiduciary Duty and Conflict of Interest — 128
  - 1. Under Common Law — 128
  - 2. Conflict of Interest — 129
  - 3. The Corporate Opportunity — 129
  - 4. The Duty Not to Compete — 130
  - 5. The Interested Director under B.C.L. §713 — 130
  - 6. The Effect of Ratification by the Shareholders — 131
  - 7. Management Compensation — 132
  - 8. "Insider" Stock Trading — 132
- F. Indemnification of Corporate Directors and Officers — 132
- Cases 18, 19, 20 — 133
- Problems 60–78 — 139

9. Additional Rights, Remedies, and Liabilities of Shareholders — 147

- A. Shareholders' Rights and Remedies for Damage and Loss to the Shareholder — 147
- B. Losses to the Corporation — 147
- C. The Shareholders' Derivative Suit — 148
  - 1. Requirements — 149
  - 2. Special Litigation Committee — 149
  - 3. Security for Expenses — 150
  - 4. The Recovery — 150
- D. Obligations to Minority Shareholders — 150
- E. Extraordinary Business Decisions Requiring Shareholder Approval — 151
  - 1. The Right to Vote — 152
  - 2. Sale, Lease, or Exchange of Substantially All Corporate Assets — 152
  - 3. Mergers and Consolidations — 152

  4. Amendments to the Certificate of Incorporation   152
  5. Corporate Guarantees   152
  6. Mortgaging Corporate Property   152
  7. Loans to Directors   153
  8. Dissolution   153
  9. Abolishment of Abnormal Management Structure   153
  10. Sale of Assets after Dissolution   153
  11. Purchase by the Corporation of Its Own Shares   153
  12. Approving Other Acts of the Board of Directors   153
 F. Liability of Shareholders   154
  1. Stock Subscriptions   154
  2. Watered Stock   154
  3. Illegal Dividends   154
  4. Defective Incorporation   155
  5. Disregard of the Corporate Entity—Piercing the Corporate Veil   155
  6. Wages and Salaries to Employees   155
Cases 21, 22, 23   155
Problems 79–82   162

10. Amendments, Mergers, Consolidations, Acquisitions, and Sale of the Corporate Assets   163

 A. Amendments to the Certificate of Incorporation   163
  1. Authorization Required   163
  2. Amendments Regarding Stated Capital   164
  3. Filing with the Secretary of State   164
 B. Mergers   164
  1. Authorization Required   164
  2. Filing with the Secretary of State   165
  3. Effect of the Merger   165
  4. The Subsidiary Merger   165
  5. Merger of Domestic and Foreign Corporation   166
 C. Consolidations   166
  1. Authorization Required   166
  2. Filing with the Secretary of State   166
  3. Effect of the Consolidation   167
  4. Consolidation of Domestic and Foreign Corporation   167
 D. Acquisitions   167
 E. Acquisition of Shares of Stock   167
  1. Tender Offers   168
 F. Acquisition of Corporate Assets   169
  1. Authorization Required   169
  2. Effect of the Sale   169
  3. The Rights of Creditors   169
 G. Mergers, Consolidations, Acquisitions, and the U.S. Government   170

H. The Rights of a Shareholder Who Objects	171
1. Circumstances Giving Rise to the Right	171
2. How the Right Is Exercised	172
I. Takeovers and the Fiduciary Duty	173
1. The Closely Held Corporation—"Freeze Outs"	173
2. Public Corporations—Defensive Measures	173
Cases 24, 25, 26	175
Problems 83–90	183

11. Dissolution of the Corporation   187

A. Voluntary Dissolution	187
1. Which Circumstances	187
2. Filing with the Secretary of State	187
B. Dissolution by Court Decree	188
1. Who May File the Petition?	188
2. Procedure in Court	190
C. "Winding Up" and Liquidation of the Corporation	190
1. Filing of Claims by Creditors	191
2. Distribution—Priority of Creditors	191
3. Distribution to Shareholders	191
4. Court Supervision of Liquidation	192
D. Receivership	192
1. Which Circumstances	192
2. Procedure	192
Cases 27, 28, 29	193
Problems 91–96	201

Appendix 1—New York Business Corporation Law	**203**
Appendix 2—Other Relevant Statutes	**318**
Index	**323**

Table of Cases

	Case Number	Page Number
Alpert v. 28 Williams St. Corp.	25	177
Aronoff v. Albanese	19	135
Billy v. Consolidated Machine Tool Corp. et al	24	175
Buffalo Forge Co. v. Ogden Corp.	26	181
Crane Co. v. Anaconda Co.	11	81
Dodge v. Ford Motor Co.	10	78
Frankowski v. Palermo et al	7	59
Independent Investor Protective League v. Time, Inc.	27	193
Joseph Polchinski Co. v. Cemetery Floral Co. Inc.	16	114
Kemp & Beatley, Inc., In the Matter of	29	197
Lewis v. Dansker	8	59
Lewis v. S. L. & E. Inc.	21	155
Lorisa Capital Corp. v. Gallo	28	194
Meredith v. Camp Hill Estates Inc.	23	160
Nakano v. Nakano McGlone Nightingale Advertising, Inc.	13	85
Parkoff v. General Telephone & Electronics Corp. et al	22	159
Rafe v. Hindin	14	88
Randall v. Bailey	9	61

	Case Number	Page Number
Rapoport v. Schneider	18	133
Rockwell v. SCM Corp.	12	83
Rye Psychiatric Hosp. Center v. Schoenholtz	17	115
Schacter v. Kulik	20	138
Shigoto International Corp. et al, Application of v. Secretary of State	6	35
Triggs v. Triggs	15	112
Universal Industries Corp. v. Lindstrom et al	4	33
Vantage Careers, Inc. v. Vantage Agency, Inc.	3	33
Von Arx, A. G. v. C. J. Breitenstein	5	34
Walkovzsky v. Carlton, et al	1	15
We're Associates v. Cohen, Stracher & Bloom P.C.	2	18

Table of References to the Business Corporation Law (B.C.L.) in New York State and Other Statutes

The Business Corporation Law

B.C.L. Section	Pages
102	50, 53, 54, 55, 169, 164
201(a)	41
202	41–42
202(a)	41–42, 152
202(b)	31
203	43, 121
301	24, 29, 31, 35–36
302	29–31
303	24
304	25
305	25
306	25
401	23
402	24–25, 43
402(a)(2)	25, 42
403	25–26
404	44, 104
501	47, 70, 152
501(c)	9
502	47
503	50–51, 154
504	51–58, 59
504(a)	51–53, 154
504(b)	51–53, 59–61, 154
504(c)	48, 51–53, 154

B.C.L. Section	Pages
504(d)	48
504(e)	52
504(h)	52
504(i)	51–52, 65
505	53
506	53–54
506(a)	53
506(b)	48, 53, 55
506(c)	54
507	53
508	53, 65–67
510	61, 70–74, 120, 127–28, 154
510(a)	73
510(b)	73
510(c)	55, 70, 73
511	71, 74
512	69
513	67, 69, 85–87, 120, 127–28, 153
513(a)	68
513(b)	68
514	68, 69, 85–87
515	68, 69
516	54, 107
517	55, 69
518	50
518(c)	50, 77
519	49–50
520	74, 77
601	107
601(c)	45
602	99
603	100, 115–17
604	101
605	100
606	100
607	100
608	100, 115–17
608(b)	100
609	100, 106, 112
609(f)	100
610	101
612	101
613	101, 152
614	102
615	104, 106

B.C.L. Section	Pages
616	111
616(a)(1)	100
616(b)	163
616(c)	100, 102, 111
618	102
619	103
620	110–111, 153
620(b)	111, 163
620(d)	111
620(f)	111
621	112
622	74–75
622(a)	74
622(b)	74
622(e)	74
623	68, 77, 171–173, 191
623(a)	172
623(e)	172
623(i)	173
623(j)	172
623(k)	151, 173
624	75, 81–85
624(a)	68, 75
624(b)	75, 77
624(c)	77
624(d)	77
626	147–150, 193–94
626(a)	149
626(b)	149
626(c)	149
626(d)	150
626(e)	150
627	150
628	52, 58
628(a)	52, 154
628(b)	52
630	12, 77, 155
701	44, 104, 106, 108
702	10, 23, 115–117
703	104
704	104
705	105, 153
706	104–5, 153
707	105
708	106

B.C.L. Section	Pages
708(a)	105
708(b)	106
708(c)	106
708(d)	106
709	105, 106
709(b)	163
709(c)	111
710	105
711	105
712	107
713	129–131
713(a)	130, 153
713(b)	130
713(c)	130, 133–35
713(d)	133
713(e)	107, 132
714	120, 127–28, 153
715	10, 107–108
715(a)	107
715(e)	107
715(g)	108
715(h)	119, 122
716	110
717	74, 119, 121–123, 138–39
718	77
719	29, 120–123, 155
719(a)	74, 121–22, 127–28, 191
719(b)	127–28
719(c)	121
719(d)	121
719(e)	74, 121–22
720	29, 120–122, 133–35
720(a)	120–122, 147–148
720(b)	120–122, 147–148
721	132–133
722	132–133, 150
723	132–133
724–726	132–33, 150
801	163
802	163
803	152
804	164, 171
805	164
805-A	164

B.C.L. Section	Pages
806	164, 171
902	165, 166
903	165, 166
904	165, 166
904(b)	165
905	165, 171
906	165, 166–67, 170, 175–77
907	166, 167
908	152
909	152, 169, 171
910	171
911	152
912	168
1001	153, 187
1002	187
1003	187
1004	187
1005	153, 190, 191, 194–97
1006	190, 193–94
1006(a)(4)	187
1007	191
1008	190–92
1101	188
1102	188
1103	188
1104	188–89
1104(a)	188–89
1104(b)	188–89
1104(c)	189
1104–a	189, 197–201
1106	190
1111	190
1113	190
1118	189, 197–201
1201–1217	192
1301	28–30
1303	30
1304	29
1305	29
1306	29
1312	30, 34–35
1505	9, 18–19
1510	9
1600–1612	123, 168–69

Other New York State Statutes	*Pages*
Cooperative Corporation Law	9
General Business Law 130	3–4, 31
132	3
352	123
General Construction Law	8
Election Law 14–116	127
Labor Law 197	125
198–a,b,c.	125
Not-For-Profit Corporation Law (N.P.C.)	8–9
Partnership Law	4–5
Penal Law 190.35	123
Tax Law 180	26
203–a	31, 188, 194–97
275–a	31
675	13, 126
685	13, 126
1085	126

Other Statutes	
Foreign Corrupt Practices Act of 1977	124
R.I.C.O.	124–25
Securities Act of 1933	123–24, 170
Securities Exchange Act of 1934	123–24, 170
Uniform Commercial Code (U.C.C.) Article 6	170
Article 8	66–67
Uniform Limited Partnership Act (U.L.P.A.)	4–5
Uniform Partnership Act (U.P.A.)	4–5
Williams Act	168

CHAPTER 1

Introduction

A corporation is a legal entity created by statute, existing as a separate "legal person"; it is an artificial person, with its own corporate name; it issues shares of stock which are owned by "shareholders". The corporation has a legal existence which is completely separate and apart from that of its shareholders.

The corporation is a fictitious being and separate entity, independent of its owners or investors (the shareholders); it conducts business in its own name, and can sue and be sued as though it were a person. It may have perpetual existence, and is a legal entity on its own, with rights and liabilities entirely different from those of its shareholders. A corporation may enter into contracts with other parties and may enter into contracts with one or more of its shareholders; the transfer of shares of stock from one person to another has no effect upon the legal existence of the corporation. The corporation's property is owned by the corporation, and not by the shareholders. Even if one person owns all the corporation's shares of stock, the shareholder and the corporation are not the same, but each has a separate and distinct existence.

A. HISTORICAL BACKGROUND*

The concept of the corporation goes back to Roman Law, whereby a corporation could be formed by express permission from the Emperor.

In England, ecclesiastical, charitable, and municipal corporations developed as early as the 14th Century, whereby a Crown charter was granted by the King. In the 16th and 17th Centuries the trading corporations were chartered by the King for foreign trade.

B. DEVELOPMENT OF CORPORATION LAW IN THE UNITED STATES*

Beginning about 1780, the corporation began to be used in the United States, whereby a corporation could be chartered by a special state legislative act to operate businesses of a public nature, such as toll road, toll bridge, or water system.

In 1811, New York State enacted the first general corporation-for-profit statute for the manufacture of textiles, glass, metals, and paints whereby five or more persons could incorporate with

---

*See, generally, Henn, *Laws of Corporations and Other Enterprises* Ch. 1 (3rd ed. 1983) for historical background and development of corporation law in the U.S.

certain restrictions. In 1866, New York enacted corporation laws for the formation of a corporation for any lawful purpose.

By the late 19th Century, most of the states had enacted statutes which permitted formation of corporations. Today, all states have corporation laws in operation.

A large majority of the states have adopted all or portions of the Model Business Corporation Act, commonly known as the "Model Act" or M.B.C.A., first published in 1946; this was proposed by the American Bar Association as a drafting guide to the various states, and is constantly being reviewed and revised; the last revision was in 1984.

In 1963, New York State enacted the New York Business Corporation Law (the B.C.L.), many of its sections having been modeled after the Model Act. New York has revised several sections of the B.C.L. since its enactment in 1963, and its sections are constantly being reviewed by several Bar Association Committees in New York with proposals for revision.

C. WHAT IS A CORPORATION?

A corporation is a creature of statute; its existence depends upon a law (either state or federal) which authorizes it to be formed and to exist. The corporation is recognized as a "person" for most purposes, and enjoys many but not all, of the same rights and privileges that U.S. citizens enjoy. A corporation has the same rights as a natural person to equal protection of the laws under the 14th Amendment; it also has the right of access to the courts; it can sue and be sued (although it must be represented by an attorney in court); it has the right of due process before denial of life, liberty, or property; freedom from unreasonable search and seizure, and freedom from double jeopardy; however, a corporation cannot invoke the 5th Amendment right against self incrimination to protect corporate records.*

When one thinks of a corporation's advantages, the aspect of limited liability of its shareholders is immediately emphasized; liability of the shareholders is limited to the amount of their investment; shareholders are not personally responsible for the liabilities of the corporation. Thus (as a general rule), if one invests $1,000 in a corporation, that is the limit of the shareholder's financial risk no matter how extensive the liabilities of the corporation may be; if the corporation becomes insolvent, the creditors of the corporation may sue the corporation; even if the creditors are not able to collect from the corporation, the creditors may *not* sue the shareholders, because shareholders have limited liability.

In order to form a corporation, one needs permission from the State. Since each of the state's corporation laws differ as to requirements for incorporation and internal operation, a factor to consider is in which state to incorporate. Beginning in the early 20th Century, some of the states eliminated restrictions in order to attract more corporations. In prior years, many corporations were incorporated in the State of Delaware, as Delaware had enacted effective and very flexible corporation laws. Of the 1,565 corporations listed on the New York Stock Exchange, over 40% are incorporated in the State of Delaware: of the 500 largest corporations, more than 1/3 are likewise incorporated in Delaware. However, there are presently fewer relative advantages in seeking incorporation in Delaware, particularly for the small closely held corporation.**

---

*See, generally, Henn, *Laws of Corporations* 80 et al. (3rd ed., 1983).
**See, *The New York Corporate Handbook,* pp. 12–15 (N.Y.S. Bar Assoc. 1983) for comparative advantages of New York and Delaware incorporation. For comparison by sections, see Israels, *On Corporate Practice,* pp. 690–771 (P.L.I. 1983) for New York B.C.L., Delaware G.C.L., and the Model Act (1979) comparisons; see also *Delaware/New York Comparisons* (CT Corporation System) June 1, 1986.

CHAPTER 2

The Business Corporation in New York State

Since a corporation is a creature of statute, it is necessary to read and study the statute in effect. Constant reference will be made to the Business Corporation Law (B.C.L.), the corporation statute in effect in N.Y.S. The reader is advised to read the corresponding sections of the B.C.L. (located in the Appendix) in relation to the text.

In order to fully understand the corporation and how it operates, it is necessary to see how the corporation compares with other forms of doing business.

A. DIFFERENT FORMS OF DOING BUSINESS

A sole proprietorship is a business owned by an individual person who has the sole right to manage, is entitled to all the profits, and has full liability for the debts of the business. A partnership is the simplest form of organization involving two or more persons, and is formed merely by agreement of the partners, who share the right to manage and the right to participate in the profits. Each partner has unlimited liability to answer personally for all the liabilities of the business. A limited partnership is a partnership of two or more persons in which there are one or more general partners who have unlimited liability for the debts of the business with general powers of management, and one or more limited partners who have no personal liability for the debts of the business (except to the extent of their capital contributions) and no management authority or power.

1. The Sole Proprietorship

The sole proprietorship is the simplest form of business enterprise. An individual trading in his or her own name may operate in New York State as a sole proprietor without any formality or expense of organization.* A sole proprietor retains all profits and is subject to unlimited personal

---

*If the proprietor wishes to do business under an assumed or fictitious name, then he or she must file a Certificate in the County Clerk's office in each county in which such business is conducted; the Certificate must contain the business name and address and his or her own full name and address. Gen. Bus. Law §130. Failure to file such certificate constitutes a misdemeanor but does not affect the person's liability to third persons. If the sole proprietor wishes to open a bank account under an assumed or fictitious name, a certified copy of the certificate must be supplied to the bank. Use of the name "and Company" or "& Co." for a sole proprietorship is expressly prohibited in New York. Gen. Bus. Law §132.

liability for acts committed by employees within the scope of their employment. The proprietorship ends on the proprietor's death or retirement and the business is an asset of the estate.

2. The General Partnership*

A partnership is an association of two or more persons to carry on as co-owners a business for profit. For this purpose, a "person" may be a corporation, and thus, a corporation may be a member of a partnership. Partnership law in New York has been codified, in the N.Y. Partnership Law, based on the Uniform Partnership Act (U.P.A.). A general partnership may be formed without any formality or expense, and may arise by an express or implied agreement among the partners to associate themselves in business for purposes of a profit.**

The major disadvantage of a general partnership is unlimited personal liability. Each partner stands not only to lose the capital contribution invested in the partnership, but all personal assets as well. Each partner is jointly liable for all partnership debts and obligations and is jointly and severally liable for any torts or other wrongful acts of the co-partners, employees and agents of the partnership committed within the scope of the partnership business. Each general partner has an equal voice in the management and control of the enterprise; important actions such as admission of a new partner or amendment of the partnership agreement require unanimous consent; ordinary matters within the scope of the partnership business require a majority vote. The partnership agreement may, of course, alter these rules.

A general partnership does not have perpetual life, and the partnership is legally dissolved upon the death, bankruptcy, or withdrawal of any partner, followed by winding up and termination of the partnership. This can be another disadvantage of a partnership.

3. The Limited Partnership

A limited partnership consists of one or more general partners who each have unlimited liability for all obligations incurred by the partnership and one or more limited partners whose liability is limited to the extent of that partner's capital contribution. A limited partnership can be formed only by a writing pursuant to the New York Partnership Law, a requirement derived from the Uniform Limited Partnership Act (U.L.P.A.).***

A limited partnership offers the advantages of a general partnership with the added advantage of limited liability for the limited partners. A limited partner retains limited liability so long as

---

*For discussion of Partnership Law, the reader is referred to Beane, *The Essentials of Partnership Law* (Kendall/Hunt Pub. Co. 1982); also, *The Partnership Handbook* (N.Y.S. Bar Assoc. 1986).

**N.Y.S. requires that a general partnership file, in every county in which it does business, a Certificate indicating the name and address of the partnership and the full name and address of each partner. Gen. Bus. Law §130. If the partners or the address of any of the partners changes, an Amended Certificate must also be filed. Gen. Bus. Law §130(3). Failure to comply with these filing provisions constitutes a misdemeanor and precludes the partnership from maintaining any action or proceeding in the courts of New York State, but does not affect the contractual rights, duties and liabilities of the partners. Gen. Bus. Law §130(8),(9).

The filing requirement does not apply to a partnership of attorneys. Gen. Bus. L. §130(7).

***The certificate must be filed, detailing the names and addresses of all partners, their respective contributions and profit shares, the duration of the partnership and other information regarding the partners' respective rights and duties. The certificate together with any amendments must be filed in the Clerk's Office in the county where the partnership has its principal place of business and a copy published once a week for six weeks in two newspapers of general circulation in the county where the partnership has its principal place of business. See U.L.P.A.§2; N.Y. Part. L.§91.

New York State requires the publication in the two newspapers, although not contained in the U.L.P.A.

he does not take an active part in managing the business and does not allow his surname to appear in the partnership name. The limited partnership will be dissolved upon the death of all the general partners or at the expiration of the term stated in the certificate.

4. *The Joint Venture*

A joint venture (sometimes called joint adventure) is very similar to a general partnership but differs in that a joint venture is more limited in its purpose, scope and duration. Very often a joint venture is formed for a single undertaking. Because of its similarity to general partnerships, courts will usually apply the rules governing partnerships to joint ventures (although there are several differences).

5. *The Joint-Stock Association*

A joint-stock company or association is an unincorporated business enterprise with ownership interests represented by shares of stock pooled in a common fund, and is very often referred to as an unincorporated association. It is not an artificial person and has no existence independent of its members. New York specifically recognizes joint-stock associations as legal entities, imposes certain regulations and grants them the privilege of operating as a corporation in virtually every respect except that its members are personally liable for the debts of the company. The unincorporated association may sue and be sued in the name of its president or treasurer and is a form commonly used by labor unions. See N.Y. Gen. Ass'n. L. §2 et al.

6. *The Corporation*

A corporation is a legal entity created by statute and exists as a legal person, separate and distinct from its individual owners or shareholders. A corporation may be formed by one or more natural persons, 18 years of age or older. It is the only form of business enterprise that combines the elements of limited liability, perpetual existence, and free transferability of interests.

B. TAX CONSIDERATIONS OF A CORPORATION

For income tax purposes, the corporation is a separate taxable entity. One of the disadvantages of the corporate form of doing business is that shareholders of a corporation face "double taxation" of dividends received.

1. *Comparison with Other Entities*

A sole proprietor's income is reported on Schedule C of the individual tax return and all expenses related to the business are deducted from gross income. Losses may be used to offset other income and thus reduce total tax liability.

In 1976, a Revised Uniform Limited Partnership Act (R.U.L.P.A.) was presented; approximately 30 states so far have adopted (with some modification) some version of R.U.L.P.A.; in 1985, the Commissioners on Uniform Laws presented a Revised version of R.U.L.P.A.

As of this date, N.Y.S. has not yet adopted any version of R.U.L.P.A., although a Draft has been prepared and presented by the N.Y.S. Bar Association. (This author has been and is a member of the Sub-Committee working on the Draft of New York's version of R.U.L.P.A.; the Committee hopes R.U.L.P.A. will be adopted by the N.Y.S. legislature very shortly).

A partnership is not a separate taxable entity, and the partnership pays no federal income tax. The partnership must file an information return (Form 1065), but only to report the amount of income earned by the partnership. Each partner is then taxed on his or her share of the partnership income, whether or not the income is actually distributed to the partner that year.

Corporate shareholders are subject to so-called "double-taxation". The corporation itself pays tax on the income it earns, and if distributed to the shareholders in the form of dividends, the dividends are again taxed when received by the shareholder. If corporate earnings are retained and not distributed as dividends, the corporation may be subject to an additional undistributed accumulated profits tax.

A partnership is treated as a conduit, with the character of income earned in the hands of the partnership passing through to the partners; in a corporation, income distributed to shareholders as dividends loses its original tax character. For example, income which is received tax free by a corporation when distributed as a dividend, is taxable to the shareholders as ordinary income. Partners are able to offset their share of partnership losses against their other sources of income. Corporate losses are deducted by the corporation, and not by the shareholders. For full consideration of the tax advantages in each particular case, the tax expert and accountant should be consulted.

2. The "S" Corporation

A corporation may, under certain circumstances, elect to be treated for tax purposes similar to a partnership. A corporation electing to do this is referred to as a Subchapter S corporation, or an "S" corporation. An S corporation is a regular business corporation, which after it has been formed, makes an election and qualifies to take advantage of special income tax treatment.* If the corporation does not elect "S" tax treatment it is referred to as a "C" corporation.

A corporation who elects to be an S corporation, elects not to be taxed at the corporate level, but to have its income, whether distributed or not, passed through and taxed pro rata to its shareholders. All shareholders must consent to the election. The election may be terminated by shareholder revocation and is terminated by the loss of eligibility of the corporation. To be eligible, a corporation must meet the following requirements among others: it must be a domestic corporation; have no more than 35 shareholders; each shareholder must be an individual, a decedent's estate, or certain type of trust, but no shareholder may be a nonresident alien; it may have only one class of stock outstanding.

An S corporation is a true corporation with all attributes of a corporation other than its tax treatment. The S corporation, as an entity, pays no federal income tax. Shareholders thus do not have the double-tax burden on corporate dividends. There are many technical requirements to achieve and maintain this tax status. For example, if a shareholder sells his stock to several other persons, causing the corporation to have more than 35 shareholders, or sells to a nonresident alien, the S status will automatically terminate. In addition, if the corporation receives more than 25% of its gross receipts in "passive investment income" (e.g. royalties, rents, dividends, interest) for more than 3 consecutive years, its S tax status will be terminated. In general, there is a five-year waiting period after the termination of an S election before another such election can be made.

---

*See 26 U.S.C. §1361 et al.; the election is made by the corporation on Form 2553.

3. Other Tax Considerations of the Corporation

The corporation as an entity is entitled to deductions from Income for items such as reasonable salaries, interest on loans, rents and royalties, contributions to pension and profit-sharing plans and other employee fringe benefits even when made to persons who are also shareholders.

(a) Salary Paid to Shareholders

If earnings are distributed to shareholders in the form of salary for employment services rendered, they are taxed to the recipient, and deducted as an expense by the corporation as salary is a deductible expense. Thus, it is theoretically possible for shareholders of a corporation to distribute the entire amount of the firm's earnings as salaries to themselves, if in fact they are employed by the corporation, so that the corporation would pay no tax because it made no profit.

However, the I.R.S. limits deductions for salaries to a reasonable amount, and generally disallows deductions for salaries that are unreasonable and exceed the fair market value of an employee's services to the corporation. Where the employee is a shareholder or relative of a shareholder, such salaries are looked at with close scrutiny. If the I.R.S. deems the salary paid to be unreasonable compensation, the excess payment would constitute a dividend to the shareholder (thus double-taxation on said amount), whereas reasonable compensation paid is subject to a single tax.

Consideration should be made regarding the various employment taxes that will have to be paid even though the employee is a shareholder. For example, the cost of payment of the following taxes has to be considered as an additional cost factor: unemployment insurance taxes; employer's contribution to social security—even if a person is a salaried employee of some other entity and even though the only employee of the corporation, the corporation (as employer) must pay the employer's "contribution" to social security. This "contribution" is nonrefundable, and is an additional expense to the corporation.

(b) Interest on Loans to Shareholders

Interest paid to shareholders on a bond, note or other loan is taxable to the shareholder, and is a deductible expense of the corporation. However, the I.R.S. may challenge what the corporation has labeled as a "debt" to be in reality "equity", so that repayment of ostensible "loans" may be treated as dividends, and would thus be taxable to the shareholder and nondeductible by the corporation. Large loans made by shareholders to the corporation may be looked at with close scrutiny by I.R.S., particularly if the corporation is deemed to be undercapitalized, i.e., "thin capitalization".

Loans made by a shareholder to the corporation should be evidenced by a note, which provides for annual interest payments and the repayment of principal. The loan should be reflected and documented in the Minutes of the Directors and/or Shareholders meetings.

(c) Payment of Rent to Shareholders

If a shareholder owns the corporation's plant or equipment, or leases assets to the corporation, rental payments can be deducted by the corporation as an expense of operation in the same manner as salary or interest. However, if the rental payments are unreasonably high, the I.R.S. may disregard the lease, and tax the payments as dividends.

(d) Pension and Profit-Sharing Plans and Other Fringe Benefits

Employee-shareholders of corporations are allowed to participate in pension and profit-sharing plans. The contributions made by the corporation are tax-deductible to the corporation and are not immediately taxed to the individual employee.

In addition, other fringe benefits provided by the corporation could be deducted by the corporation as an expense, and would not be taxable to the recipient. The use of a company car if it can be substantiated is needed for conducting corporate business, would be an example of other fringe benefits; also provisions for medical insurance and life insurance.

(e) "Section 1244" Stock

Another election under the Internal Revenue Code that should be considered is the issuance of "Section 1244" stock. Section 1244 of the Code permits a shareholder of a "small business corporation" as defined (capital not exceeding $1 million) who realizes a loss on the sale or exchange of one's stock (or if the stock becomes worthless) to deduct the loss as an ordinary business loss, rather than as a capital loss; such loss for any taxable year cannot exceed $50,000.

C. CLASSIFICATION OF CORPORATIONS

Corporations may be described and/or classified by several different classifications. Some of these will be briefly described by general description and explanation.*

1. Public Corporations

A public corporation is one organized by a government to administer government affairs or to construct or operate a public improvement (public benefit corporation). Cities and towns may incorporate as municipal public corporations, e.g., the City of New York. The U.S. Postal Service, the Triborough Bridge Authority, N.Y.S. Urban Development Corp., school districts or fire districts are all examples of public corporations.

2. Private Corporations

A private corporation is created by private parties and may be formed for a profit or non-profit purpose, but not a governmental function. Private corporations may also serve a public purpose, such as a public utility, but are owned by private persons.

3. Profit Corporations

These include a business corporation (the subject of this book), a moneyed corporation (banking or insurance), a railroad corporation, or a transportation corporation.**

Profits are distributed to the shareholders in the form of dividends.

The business corporation is the subject of this book, and is governed by the Business Corporation Law in N.Y. (B.C.L.); business corporations may be either publicly held or "closely held".

4. Non-Profit or Not-for-Profit Corporations

A non-profit or not-for-profit corporation is generally organized for charitable, religious, or educational purposes, but is not a public corporation. Examples are: religious corporations such as an incorporated church; membership corporations; an incorporated lodge or club; a school or college; and other corporations organized for a non-profit purpose. Not-for-profit corporations are governed by the Not-for-Profit Corporation Law in N.Y.S. (N.P.C. Law). An educational institution would also be governed by the Education Law.

---

*In New York State, see General Construction Law §65, 66 for classifications and definitions.

**In N.Y.S. a moneyed corporation is governed by the Banking Law or Insurance Law; a railroad corporation by the Railroad Law; and a transportation corporation by the Transportation Corporation Law. These corporations are subject to more government regulation, and not governed by the B.C.L., and will thus not be covered in this book.

A non-profit corporation includes every corporation other than a corporation formed for profit or a public corporation.

Also included is a cooperative corporation which is governed by the Cooperative Corporation Law in N.Y.S.* Several cases in recent years involving cooperative corporations have referred to and have been decided by the courts by reference to applicable sections of the B.C.L. as to the corporation's governance regarding its By-laws, directors meetings, and authority.**

5. *Professional Corporations*

State legislatures, beginning in 1961, have enacted statutes enabling professional persons to form corporations, known as a professional corporation. In New York State, professional corporations are governed by Article 15 of the B.C.L., first enacted in 1970. A professional corporation may use the abbreviation of "P.C."

Shareholders of a professional corporation have limited liability, except for one type of claim: members of a professional corporation do *not* have limited liability relating to all malpractice claims. By statute, any shareholder of a professional corporation who commits malpractice while performing professional services is personally liable for the damage caused; in addition, the professional person is personally liable for the negligent or wrongful professional acts performed by employees and other professionals under their supervision and control. See, B.C.L.§1505. However, shareholders in a professional corporation have the benefit of limited liability as to all other types of claims, the same as shareholders in other corporations.***

The tax benefits of the professional corporation are basically those that apply to all corporations. One of the major benefits is that pension and profit-sharing plans may be set up. In New York State, professional corporations apply to all professions licensed to practice in the state, such as accountants, architects, attorneys, chiropractors, dentists, optometrists, pharmacists, physicians, podiatrists, surgeons, surveyors, and veterinarians. Share ownership is limited to duly-licensed professional persons in that profession. In the event of death or other disability of a licensed professional, provision is made for the purchase of that person's shares within 6 months. See B.C.L.§1510.

6. *Domestic Corporations*

A corporation is domestic in the State in which it is incorporated. Any corporation organized and incorporated in New York State is called a domestic corporation in N.Y.S.

7. *Foreign Corporations*

A corporation is a foreign corporation in every State, other than where it is incorporated. For example, a corporation incorporated in California or New Jersey is a foreign corporation in N.Y.S.

---

*Pursuant to Cooperative Corporations Law §3(d), a cooperative corporation is classified as a non-profit corporation, since its primary object is *not* to make profits for itself or to pay dividends. However, Coop. Corp. Law §5, provides that the B.C.L. applies, but if any provision of the B.C.L. conflicts, then the conflicting provision of the B.C.L. shall not apply.

**See, e.g., Fe Bland v. Two Trees Management Co., 66 N.Y.2d 556, 498 N.Y.S.2d 336(1985) regarding authority for imposing transfer fee or "flip tax". Because of these decisions, B.C.L.§501(c) was amended.

***See, We're Associates Co. v. Cohen, Stracher & Bloom, P. C., 65 N.Y.2d 148, 490 N.Y.S.2d 743(1985) (case #2).

8. Closely Held or Close Corporations

It is a common misconception that all corporations involve "big business"; many small businesses operate as corporations. In general, there are no specific set of rules for "small" corporations as opposed to "large" corporations. Reference to a "small" corporation generally means a corporation with a relatively small number of shareholders, whose shares are not publicly held; the word "small" is not an indication as to the size of its assets or resources. It is often also referred to as a "close" or "closely-held" corporation.

In a closely held corporation, the stock may be owned by one individual, a family, or a relatively small number of shareholders; generally, most, if not all of the shareholders are actively involved as employees and officers in the day-to-day operation of the business.

New York and many other state statutes authorize one person to incorporate, own all the shares of stock, and serve as the sole director and as president. See B.C.L. §702 and §715(e).

Some states have specific statutes relating to "Close" corporations, such as California and Delaware.* New York has no specific Close Corporation Act, but several B.C.L. sections make provision for a corporation with a relatively small number of shareholders. This will be explained in the later Chapters of this book.

D. THE CORPORATION IS A PERSON

A corporation is considered a legal person, separate and distinct from its shareholders. The word "person" includes a corporation. Thus, a corporation has been held to be a "client" for purposes of the attorney-client privilege, and a corporation may be responsible for committing a crime or tort. As a legal person it has the constitutional right to protect itself from arbitrary governmental intervention. The corporation can have perpetual existence; thus its continued existence does not depend on any changes among the shareholders, nor on the life of any of its shareholders.

A corporation may sue for defamation, but not for invasion of privacy. For purposes of federal diversity jurisdiction, a corporation is a "citizen" of the state in which it is incorporated, and of the one state in which it is deemed to have its principal place of business.

E. THE CORPORATION AS A SEPARATE ENTITY

The corporation is a separate distinct entity, even if all of its shares are owned by one person or by another corporation. Even if one or two persons own all the shares of stock in the corporation, the corporation is considered a separate entity, completely separate and apart from its shareholders.

When one enters into a contract with a corporation (whether for goods or services, lending of money, transferring or leasing property, or any other contract), it should be realized and fully recognized that if the corporation breaches the contract and does not pay the amount agreed to, there is a possibility the creditor may not be able to receive its full payment since payment can only be enforced against the corporation, and not against the shareholders or officers. The creditor has the right to be repaid the amount due, but only from the assets of the corporation; the creditor cannot seek repayment from the assets of the shareholders. If the corporation has suffered large

---

*There is a supplement to the Model Act, called the Model Close Corporation Act (providing corporate governance structure where there are fewer than 30 shareholders). This has been adopted in California and Delaware and several other states. As of this date, N.Y.S. has not adopted a Close Corporation Act.

losses so that the corporation has no assets left, there is nothing out of which the creditor may be paid, no matter how many shareholders and how wealthy the shareholders may be. The corporation is responsible for the debt, and *not* the shareholder(s). This is a risk which the creditor should have considered in advance.

If the claim against the corporation is based upon a tort or any other type of claim, the result is the same; the claim may be enforced and pursued against the corporation, but *not* against the shareholders.

Examples:

   (1) Jones is struck by a delivery truck, owned by Able Corp., which was negligently driven by Dick, a corporate employee; Jones has the right to be compensated for the injuries he sustained; but the judgment can only be rendered against Dick, the driver who may be judgment proof (has very little assets or resources) and against Able Corp.
   If the corporate assets are sufficient to pay, Jones will receive full payment. If the corporate assets are not sufficient, Jones may not be able to receive full payment. The shareholders of Able Corp. are immune no matter how wealthy they may be.

The law permits a natural person who may be very wealthy and prosperous to incorporate, thus providing the shareholder (investor) with limited liability so that the shareholder's other assets are safe and secure from creditors of the corporation; also, the law permits a corporation to operate parts of its business by use of subsidiary corporations; if the claim is against a subsidiary corporation, the subsidiary is the one responsible; the creditor of the subsidiary corporation may enforce its claim against the subsidiary corporation only, not against the parent corporation. The parent corporation's assets may thus be insulated from the claims of the subsidiary corporation's creditors.

   (2) Alex Murray, a prosperous newspaper owner, forms a corporation, Alex News Inc.; the corporation owns and operates the newspaper. Alex Murray owns all the shares of stock in the corporation. If Alex News Inc. suffers losses and has unpaid creditors, the creditors will be able to sue only the corporation, Alex News Inc. and not Alex Murray, the sole shareholder, as Alex Murray has limited liability, and is not responsible for the debts of the corporation.

   (3) Assume in (2 above), the corporation, Alex News Inc. regards its delivery department as presenting extreme hazards it does not wish to be subject to. An additional corporation could be organized, Safe Delivery Corp. to operate the delivery business; Alex News Inc. would transfer to Safe Delivery Corp. the delivery trucks in exchange for shares of stock in Safe Delivery Corp. Two separate corporations are in existence.
   Safe Delivery Corp. would contract to deliver the newspapers for Alex News Inc. and would be paid for its services; Safe Delivery Corp. would want to be assured that the periodic payments are sufficient to pay the drivers, maintain the trucks, make payments on the equipment, and cover the other expenses of Safe Delivery Corp.
   The delivery business has been isolated, so that Alex News Inc. has no liability for any claim of the injured pedestrian. Alex Murray is a shareholder and owns all the shares of stock of Alex News Inc.; Alex News Inc. is a shareholder and owns all the shares of stock of Safe Delivery Corp. Both Alex Murray and Alex News Inc. are immune from payment of any claims against Safe Delivery Corp.

Safe Delivery Corp. will be responsible for amounts due under any of its contracts and for any damages sustained by any injured persons.

If Safe Delivery Corp. does not have sufficient assets to pay the pedestrian's damages, the injured person will not be able to collect in full. Alex Murray is not *responsible and Alex News Inc., a corporation is also* not *responsible for any claim against Safe Delivery Corp.*

F. LIMITED LIABILITY AND THE CORPORATION

Shareholders of a corporation have limited liability. If the corporation has amassed huge debts with little resources to pay, the creditors of the corporation may sue, with only the corporation being responsible; the shareholders, no matter how few there may be (even if only one shareholder), and no matter how much assets the shareholders may have, are not personally responsible and do *not* have to pay the creditors of the corporation.

1. *Exceptions to Limited Liability*

(a) *Voluntary Personal Guarantees*

Realizing the problem of limited liability, creditors, particularly the more experienced ones, will frequently demand a personal guarantee of the corporate debt by the shareholders and/or the officers, before credit will be extended to the corporation. In that way, the creditor is protected; if the corporation does not pay, the creditor will still be able to sue the person(s) who have personally guaranteed the corporate obligation. The shareholder, even though he has limited liability for corporate debts, will find that as a practical matter, most creditors (particularly banks and other lenders) will request a personal guarantee, and thus the shareholder will lose limited liability to that creditor. By guaranteeing the debt, the shareholder is taking on a new responsibility, and in effect the creditor now has two claims: against the corporation on the original debt, and against the shareholder on the guarantee. If a shareholder guarantees the corporate obligation, it is a voluntary undertaking, but as a practical matter, a shareholder will find the corporation will not be extended very much credit without any personal guarantees.

(b) *Wages Claims*

Even though a shareholder has the advantages of limited liability, there are specific instances when a shareholder will still be responsible for liabilities relating to the corporation. By statute, in N.Y.S., the ten largest shareholders of a corporation (whose shares are not traded on a national exchange) are personally responsible for unpaid wage claims. If the corporation does not pay its employees, they may have the right under certain circumstances to sue the 10 largest shareholders personally for this claim. See B.C.L. §630 for requirements and procedure involved. In addition, caution should be had in reading B.C.L. §630 carefully, as salary and unpaid wages also include vacation pay, union benefits to be paid by the employer, and payments to the union welfare fund, etc.*

---

*It is believed that N.Y.S. is the only state with such a provision; it is not provided for in the Model Act. The N.Y. Court of Appeals has upheld B.C.L. §630 in Sasso v. Vachris, 66 N.Y.2d 28, 494 N.Y.S.2d 856 (1985).

(c) Claims Regarding Payment of Shares

A shareholder may be held responsible to pay for the unpaid amount of capital which was agreed to but has not in fact been contributed to the corporate capital, and to pay for the full amount of par value stock. This will be discussed in more detail in subsequent Chapters.

(d) Certain Taxes*

In a small (closely held) corporation, where some of the shareholders may also be directors and the controlling officers, they may be responsible for certain taxes, such as withholding and social security taxes withheld and deducted by the corporation from the salary of the corporation's employees, and sales taxes in a retail business on retail sales collected from its customers. These items, although corporate obligations, are considered by the taxing authorities and the courts as being in the nature of trust funds; therefore the law imposes a duty upon the persons responsible for seeing that these funds are in fact paid, and in many instances, various persons involved in the corporation have been held personally responsible when the corporation does not pay.

G. PIERCING THE CORPORATE VEIL

The most important advantage of the corporate form of business organization is the shareholders's limited liability. Corporations are formed for the express purpose of limiting one's financial risk and exposure to the amount of the investment.

If the corporation does not have sufficient funds to pay its creditors, a creditor may attempt to claim that the shareholders are responsible for the obligations of the corporation, or claim a parent corporation responsible for the debt of a subsidiary. This is an attempt to "pierce the corporate veil" or "attack the corporate shield", whereby a Court is asked to disregard the corporate entity and allow the action to proceed against the shareholder(s) as though no separate corporate entity existed. Courts very rarely pierce the corporate veil.

A corporation may plan to risk only a portion of its assets by forming a subsidiary corporation. If the creditor proves an "alter ego" relationship exists between the parent corporation and its subsidiary, whereby the parent dominates (so that the subsidiary has no real existence of its own and the subsidiary is deemed to be a mere instrumentality of the parent corporation) the Court may disregard the separate corporate identity of the subsidiary, and decide the parent corporation responsible for the obligations of the subsidiary corporation.

As a general rule, courts will recognize the separateness of the two corporations even though one corporation owns all the shares of stock of the other, and the two corporations have common directors and officers and operate out of the same premises.

If the formalities of the separate corporations are not observed, or each is not represented to the public and creditors as separate enterprises, or the funds of the corporations are comingled, the courts may pierce the corporate veil and treat them as one entity.

Courts generally will respect the corporate entity so long as shareholders segregate the corporate assets from their own assets, maintain separate corporate books and records, maintain separate corporate bank accounts, hold shareholders and directors meetings, and observe the legal formalities of the corporation's existence and operation.

---

*See, e.g. Tax Law 675–685 et al. (withholding taxes); Tax Law §1145 (sales tax); I.R.C.§7343, 6672, et al.

Some of the factors considered significant in justifying disregard of the corporate entity are: failure to observe corporate formalities such as annual meetings and maintaining separate corporate books and records; siphoning or comingling corporate funds by the dominant shareholders; use of the corporation as a facade; and use of the corporate entity in promoting injustice or fraud. However, no one factor may be fully determining. Even if it is clear that a corporation has been formed to avoid taxes or to prevent creditors from reaching one's personal assets, the court will not ignore the corporate entity.

Some courts have also looked at the question of whether the corporation has adequate capitalization. Although this may be a strong factor for courts to pierce the corporate veil in other states, this is not a major deciding factor by the N.Y. courts, and is merely one factor to be considered. Theoretically, in N.Y., a corporation may be formed with a limited amount of capital, even as little as $1, and that would not be grounds in and of itself to pierce the corporate veil.*

In *Walter E. Heller & Co.* v. *Video Innovations, Inc.,* 730 F. 2d 50, 53 (2nd Cir. 1984), the Court indicated criteria to be considered whether the corporate veil should be pierced:

(1) the absence of the formalities which are part and parcel of normal corporate existence, i.e. the issuance of stock, the election of directors, the keeping of corporate records, etc.,

(2) inadequate capitalization,

(3) personal use of corporate funds, and

(4) the perpetration of fraud by means of the corporate vehicle.

In *Establishment Tomis* v. *Shearson Hayden Stone,* 459 F. Supp. 1355 (S.D.N.Y. 1978), the court listed various factors to consider:

(1) gross undercapitalization of the corporation

(2) disregard of corporate formalities

(3) corporate insolvency at the time in question

(4) lack of corporate records

(5) non-payment of dividends

(6) siphoning of corporate funds by the dominant shareholder

(7) non-function of directors and officers, and

(8) an inquiry as to whether the stockholders used the corporation merely as a facade for their own operations.

Courts will pierce the corporate veil only in extreme situations of fraud; it is a remedy that is not very often granted. The law permits incorporation of a business for the very purpose of enabling the shareholders to escape personal liability.

However, in *Farm Stores Inc.* v. *School Feeding Corp.* 102 A.D. 2d 249, 477 N.Y.S.2d 374 (1984), *aff'd,* 64 N.Y.2d 1065, 489 N.Y.S.2d 877 (1985), the court set aside the transfer of funds from the corporation to its shareholders as a fraudulent conveyance, and entered judgment against the shareholders individually for the sums each of the shareholders wrongfully received.

---

*See, Gardner v. Snyder, 607 F.2d 582 (2nd Cir. 1979).

CASE 1
WALKOVSZKY v. CARLTON, et al
(Court of Appeals of New York, 18 N.Y. 2d 414, 276 N.Y.S.2d 585) (1966)

FULD, Judge.

This case involves what appears to be a rather common practice in the taxicab industry of vesting the ownership of a taxi fleet in many corporations, each owning only one or two cabs.

The complaint alleges that the plaintiff was severely injured four years ago in New York City when he was run down by a taxicab owned by the defendant Seon Cab Corporation and negligently operated at the time by the defendant Marchese. The individual defendant, Carlton, is claimed to be a stockholder of 10 corporations, including Seon, each of which has but two cabs registered in its name, and it is implied that only the minimum automobile liability insurance required by law (in the amout of $10,000) is carried on any one cab. Although seemingly independent of one another, these corporations are alleged to be "operated . . . as a single entity unit and enterprise" with regard to financing, supplies, repairs, employees and garaging, and all are named as defendants.[1] The plaintiff asserts that he is also entitled to hold their stockholders personally liable for the damages sought because the multiple corporate structure constitutes an unlawful attempt "to defraud members of the general public" who might be injured by the cabs.

The defendant Carlton has moved . . . to dismiss the complaint on the ground that as to him it "fails to state a cause of action". The court at Special Term granted the motion but the Appellate Division reversed, holding that a valid cause of action was sufficiently stated. The defendant Carlton appeals. . . .

The law permits the incorporation of a business for the very purpose of enabling its proprietors to escape personal liability (see, e.g., Bartle v. Home Owners Co-op., 309 N.Y. 103, 106 . . .) but, manifestly, the privilege is not without its limits. Broadly speaking, the courts will disregard the corporate form, or, to use accepted terminology, "pierce the corporate veil", whenever necessary "to prevent fraud or to achieve equity". (International Aircraft Trading Co. v. Manufacturers Trust Co., 297 N.Y. 285, 292). In determining whether liability should be extended to reach assets beyond those belonging to the corporation, we are guided, as Judge Cardozo noted, by "general rules of agency". (Berkey v. Third Ave. Ry. Co., 244 N.Y. 84, 95, 50 A.L.R. 599). In other words, whenever anyone uses control of the corporation to further his own rather than the corporation's business, he will be liable for the corporation's acts "upon the principle of respondeat superior applicable even where the agent is a natural person". (Rapid Tr. Subway Constr. Co. v. City of New York, 259 N.Y. 472, 488). Such liability, moreover, extends not only to the corporation's commercial dealings. . . .

• • • •

In Mangan v. Terminal Transp. Sys. (247 A.D. 853, 286 N.Y.S. 666) . . . the plaintiff was injured as a result of the negligent operation of a cab owned and operated by one of four corporations affiliated with the defendant Terminal. Although the defendant was not a stockholder of any of the operating companies, both the defendant and the operating companies were owned, for the most part, by the same parties. The defendant's name (Terminal) was conspicuously displayed on the sides of all of the taxis used in the enterprise and, in point of fact, the defendant actually

---

[1]. The corporate owner of a garage is also included as a defendant.

serviced, inspected, repaired and dispatched them. These facts were deemed to provide sufficient cause for piercing the corporate veil of the operating company—the nominal owner of the cab which injured the plaintiff—and holding the defendant liable. The operating companies were simply instrumentalities for carrying on the business of the defendant without imposing upon it financial and other liabilities incident to the actual ownership and operation of the cabs. . . .

In the case before us, the plaintiff has explicitly alleged that none of the corporations "had a separate existence of their own" and, as indicated above, all are named as defendants. However, it is one thing to assert that a corporation is a fragment of a larger corporate combine which actually conducts the business. . . . It is quite another to claim that the corporation is a "dummy" for its individual stockholders who are in reality carrying on the business in their personal capacities for purely personal rather than corporate ends. (See African Metals Corp. v. Bullowa, 288 N.Y. 78, 85). Either circumstance would justify treating the corporation as an agent and piercing the corporate veil to reach the principal but a different result would follow in each case. In the first, only a larger corporate entity would be held financially responsible (see, e.g., Mangan v. Terminal Transp. System, 247 A.D. 853, 286 N.Y.S. 666, . . . Luckenbach S.S. Co. v. Grace & Co., 267 F.2d 676, 881) while, in the other, the stockholder would be personally liable. (See, e.g., Natelson v. A.B.L. Holding Co., 260 N.Y. 233; Quaid v. Ratkowsky, 224 N.Y. 624; Weisser v. Mursam Shoe Corp., 2 Cir., 127 F.2d 344, 145 A.L.R. 467). Either the stockholder is conducting the business in his individual capacity or he is not. If he is, he will be liable; if he is not, then it does not matter—insofar as his personal liability is concerned—that the enterprise is actually being carried on by a larger "enterprise entity". (See Berle, The Theory of Enterprise Entity, 47 Col.L.Rev. 343.)

• • • •

The individual defendant is charged with having "organized, managed, dominated and controlled" a fragmented corporate entity but there are no allegations that he was conducting business in his individual capacity. Had the taxicab fleet been owned by a single corporation, it would be readily apparent that the plaintiff would face formidable barriers in attempting to establish personal liability on the part of the corporation's stockholders. The fact that the fleet ownership has been deliberately split up among many corporations does not ease the plaintiff's burden in that respect. The corporate form may not be disregarded merely because the assets of the corporation, together with the mandatory insurance coverage of the vehicle which struck the plaintiff, are insufficient to assure him the recovery sought. If Carlton were to be held individually liable on those facts alone, the decision would apply equally to the thousands of cabs which are owned by their individual drivers who conduct their businesses through corporations organized pursuant to B.C.L.§401, and carry the minimum insurance required by the Vehicle and Traffic Law §370 (1)(a). These taxi owner-operators are entitled to form such corporations (cf. Elenkrieg v. Siebrecht, 238 N.Y. 254), and we agree with the court at Special Term that, if the insurance coverage required by statute "is inadequate for the protection of the public, the remedy lies not with the courts but with the Legislature." It may very well be sound policy to require that certain corporations must take out liability insurance which will afford adequate compensation to their potential tort victims. However, the responsibility for imposing conditions on the privilege of incorporation has been committed by the Constitution to the Legislature . . . , and it may not be fairly implied, from any statute, that the Legislature intended, without the slightest discussion or debate, to require of taxi corporations that they carry automobile liability insurance over and above that mandated by the Vehicle and Traffic Law.

This is not to say that it is impossible for the plaintiff to state a valid cause of action against the defendant Carlton. However, the simple fact is that the plaintiff has just not done so here. While the complaint alleges that the separate corporations were undercapitalized and that their assets have been intermingled, it is barren of any "sufficiently particular[ized] statements" . . . that the defendant Carlton and his associates are actually doing business in their individual capacities, shuttling their personal funds in and out of the corporations "without regard to formality and to suit their immediate convenience." . . . Such a "perversion of the privilege to do business in a corporate form" . . . would justify imposing personal liability on the individual stockholders. Nothing of the sort has in fact been charged, and it cannot reasonably or logically be inferred from the happenstance that the business of Seon Cab Corporation may actually be carried on by a larger corporate entity composed of many corporations which, under general principles of agency, would be liable to each other's creditors in contract and in tort.

In point of fact, the principle relied upon in the complaint to sustain the imposition of personal liability is not agency but fraud. Such a cause of action cannot withstand analysis. If it is not fraudulent for the owner-operator of a single cab corporation to take out only the minimum required liability insurance, the enterprise does not become either illicit or fraudulent merely because it consists of many such corporations. The plaintiff's injuries are the same regardless of whether the cab which strikes him is owned by a single corporation or part of a fleet with ownership fragmented among many corporations. . . .

In sum, the complaint falls short of adequately stating a cause of action against the defendant Carlton in his individual capacity.

The order of the Appellate Division should be reversed, . . . and the order of the Supreme Court, Richmond County, reinstated, with leave to serve an amended complaint.

Note: In *Port Chester Electrical Constr. Corp. v. Atlas,* 40 N.Y.2d 652, 389 N.Y.S.2d 327 (1976), the Court of Appeals did *not* pierce the corporate veils. However, the court did grant relief to the plaintiff as a judgment creditor of the corporation because the corporation illegally transferred its assets to Atlas and the other corporations while it was insolvent. The facts as stated by the court are: "Until his death in July, 1973 the late Sol G. Atlas was actively engaged in the acquisition and development of real property. Atlas organized his various ownership and construction ventures into a complex network of separate corporations in which he had both a controlling interest and an active leadership role. This case involves the efforts of an independent subcontractor on an Atlas project to collect a money judgment it obtained against an Atlas controlled general contractor. Since the general contractor was virtually judgment proof due to certain financial manipulations, the subcontractor endeavored to enforce its judgment against other corporations allied with Atlas in the venture, as well as against Atlas' estate. . . ."

The court reasoned: "Here, the external indicia of separate corporate identities were at all times maintained. (Bartle v. Home Owners Co-op., 309 N.Y. 103, 106). The fact that Sol Atlas was the controlling principal of these corporations is, by itself, insufficient to justify disregarding the corporate form. Since Atlas himself carefully respected the separate identities of the corporations, and each corporation was pursuing its separate corporate business, rather than the purely personal business of Atlas, we conclude that the corporate veils of the defendant corporation should not be "pierced".

Even though the corporate veils were *not* pierced, relief was given to the plaintiff as a judgment creditor based upon the illegal transfers.

CASE 2
WE'RE ASSOCIATES V. COHEN, STRACHER & BLOOM, P.C.
(Court of Appeals of New York, 65 N.Y.2d 148, 490 N.Y.S.2d 743) (1985)

Wachtler, Chief Judge.

In this action to recover rents due and owing under a commercial lease, ... The issue presented on this appeal, here by leave of our court, is whether the shareholders of a professional service corporation organized under article 15 of the B.C.L. may be held liable in their individual capacities for rents due under a lease naming only the professional service corporation as tenant.

Defendant Cohen, Stracher & Bloom, P.C. a professional service corporation engaged in the practice of law, whose sole officers, directors and shareholders are the individual defendants, entered into a lease agreement with plaintiff. The lease recited that is was between "We're Associates Company * * * as 'landlord' and Cohen, Stracher & Bloom, P.C. * * * as 'Tenant' ". It was signed in the name of the corporate defendant by one of the individual defendants.

The amended complaint alleged, in its first cause of action, that "Defendant C S & B failed to perform its obligations under the Lease, breached the terms thereof and defaulted, . . . that defendant C S & B failed and refused to pay rent . . . in the sum of $13,333.69, as of June 1, 1983, although payment thereof was duly demanded". The second cause of action repeated the allegations of the first, including the corporate defendant's default, and further alleged: "By reason of the foregoing, [the individual] defendants Cohen, Stracher and Bloom are jointly, severally and personally liable to plaintiff in the sum of not less than $13,333.69".

The individual defendants moved to have their names stricken as parties . . . stating that the corporate defendant was the acknowledged tenant and that the demised premises "were occupied by the corporation and that at no time did any of the individuals act in any other capacity other than as officers and directors of the corporation", which plaintiff never denied. . . .

• • • •

The only specific provision relating to shareholder liability in Article 15 of the B.C.L (the article permitting the formation of domestic professional service corporations) is section 1505(a), which states: . . . [Note: See B.C.L.§1505(a)].

The Appellate Division in this case properly interpreted this section to preclude the imposition of personal shareholder liability in instances not involving the direct rendition of professional services. A principal attribute of, and in many cases the major reason for, the corporate form of business association is the elimination of personal shareholder liability (Billy v. Consolidated Mach. Tool Corp., 51 N.Y.2d 152, 163, 432 N.Y.S.2d 879, . . . Rapid Tr. Subway Constr. Co. v. City of New York, 259 N.Y. 472, 487–488, 13A Fletcher, Cyclopedia of Corporations 6213, at 16–17 [1984 Perm ed]). B.C.L.§1513 provides that all articles of the B.C.L. apply to domestic professional service corporations . . . unless there is a specific contrary provision in article 15. The general rule, set forth in the authorities cited above and in B.C.L.§628, is that shareholders are not personally liable for corporate debts (see also, 13A Fletcher, 6213, at 16). Accordingly, there is no basis for extending the limited liability imposed by B.C.L.§1505(a) to situations not unambiguously covered by that provision.

The plain words of the statute, imposing personal liability only in connection with the rendition of professional services on behalf of the professional service corporation, cannot be defeated by a liberal construction which would include ordinary business debts within the definition of professional services. . . .

Even single-person businesses are allowed to incorporate, and, so long as no fraud is committed and the corporate form is respected, no individual liability will result. (Walkovsky v. Carlton, 18 N.Y.2d 414, 419–420, 276 N.Y.S.2d 585, Elenkrieg v. Seibrecht, 238 N.Y. 254, 262, 144 N.E. 519; 1 O'Neal, Close Corporations 1.05). If shareholders of a conventional business corporation may enjoy limited liability under such circumstances, so may those of a professional service corporation except as limited by B.C.L.§1505(a).

The Code of Professional Responsibility provides no basis for the imposition of personal liability in this case. Plaintiff does not suggest, and indeed no authority has been brought to our attention which has held, that an attorney may be held personally liable for the debts of any business corporation of which he is a shareholder simply because he is an attorney and is thus subject to the strictures of the Code.

In light of our holding, based on what we discern to be the clear command of New York law, it is unnecessary to determine whether the Federal tax laws would have precluded our reaching a contrary conclusion. True, one of the motivating forces behind the passage of article 15 of the B.C.L was to "make available . . . Federal tax benefits now accorded to executives and employees in all other business endeavors." . . . However, the provisions of article 15 are clear and do not themselves require any change in their application should the Federal taxing authorities or courts find they do not accomplish their stated purpose. Thus, for the purpose of this appeal, what the Federal tax laws require of a professional service corporation in order to enjoy the tax advantage for which they are created is irrelevant.

Our decision should work no injustice on those who enter into leases or any other contracts with professional service corporations, who are free to seek the personal assurances of the shareholders that the commitments of the professional service corporation will be honored. Nor do we intend to countenance any abuse of the corporate form of doing business, which, if present in a future case, could compel a different result. . . . What we do hold is that, absent any showing of such abuse, the shareholders of a professional service corporation cannot be held personally liable for any ordinary business debt of the corporation. . . .

Note: For cases involving liability for malpractice in a professional corporation, see: *Connell v. Hayden,* 83 A.D.2d 30, 443 N.Y.S.2d 383 (2nd Dept. 1981); *Paciello v. Patel,* 83 A.D.2d 73, 443 N.Y.S.2d 403 (2nd Dept. 1981).

PROBLEMS

1. Benjamin is the sole shareholder of ten corporations, each organized to operate a taxi service. Each corporation owns a single taxicab which is operated by drivers. The corporations each have the minimum required liability insurance coverage in the amount of $10,000/$20,000 for damages to a person or persons injured by the negligent operation of a taxi.

Benjamin is president of each corporation, and Benjamin is the sole director of each corporation.

Paul, a pedestrian, is seriously injured due to the negligence of Davis the driver of a taxi owned by ABC Taxi Corp., one of the ten corporations. In a law suit by Paul against ABC Taxi Corp., the jury awarded Paul a judgment of $100,000.

Paul has collected $10,000 from the insurance, and $800 from ABC Taxi Corp's bank account; ABC Taxi Corp. has no other assets. The Taxi was demolished in the accident.

(a) Has Paul a cause of action against Benjamin to recover the unpaid balance of $89,200 on the judgment?

(b) Paul also sues the other 9 corporations. What would Paul have to prove to try to hold the other 9 corporations responsible for the $89,200?

(c) Would Benjamin be personally liable for Paul's injuries if he had taken Davis' place as driver on the day of the accident? Discuss.

(d) Would Jack, another driver for ABC Taxi Corp., have a cause of action against Benjamin for the unpaid salary due to him for his work as driver prior to the accident? Discuss.

2. A, B, and C partners, formed a corporation ABC Inc. and transferred to the corporation, all the partnership property in exchange for stock. The corporation expressly assumed the partnership liabilities as part of the price paid for the partnership property.

X, a partnership creditor, neither assented to the transfer nor agreed to accept the corporation as debtor in place of the partnership.

(a) Is X a creditor of the corporation?

(b) Are A, B, and C personally liable to X after the transfer of assets to the corporation?

(c) What are the rights of X?

3. Alex, Baker, and Charles are shareholders of a real estate business, ABC Realty Inc., a corporation. They purchased a building for office use and formed a separate corporation, "123 Ave X Corp." to own the building. The real estate office and other tenants pay rent to the 123 Ave X Corp. Paul, a client of ABC Realty Inc. brought suit against ABC Realty Inc. for return of his down payment regarding a real estate purchase, and has attached the building owned by 123 Ave. X Corp. May the court disregard the corporate entity and allow Paul's attachment?

4. Jackson forms a corporation, J. S. Furniture Inc.; Jackson and his wife own all the shares of stock. Jackson subsequently forms another corporation, Jack's Trucking Inc., a trucking service to make deliveries. All the capital stock of Jack's Trucking Inc. is owned by J. S. Furniture Inc.

One of the trucks owned by Jack's Trucking Inc., driven by Mark a driver is involved in an accident, seriously injuring Doris. Doris commences a law suit, suing Jack's Trucking Inc., J. S. Furniture Inc., Jackson and his wife for the injuries sustained. What result? Discuss.

5. Henry owns all the common stock, and Jill owns all the preferred stock of Alpha Corp. which is now insolvent. The creditors are unable to collect anything from Alpha Corp. The creditors sue Henry and Jill personally. Indicate who, if anyone, is liable to the creditor (indicating your reasons) assuming the creditor is:

(a) A, creditor for $2,000 who sold inventory to Alpha Corp.

(b) B, a bookkeeper to whom Alpha Corp. owed $900 for salary.

(c) C, the landlord who is owed rent of $18,000 for the past 6 months.

(d) D Bank, who granted a $20,000 loan to Alpha Corp.; Henry and Jill personally guaranteed the loan.

(e) E, a pedestrian who was injured by Henry, while Henry was driving the corporation car.

(f) F, a pedestrian who was severely injured by Bob (an employee of Alpha Corp.) who was driving the corporation car to make deliveries to customers.

(g) G, the accountant who is owed $1,000 for his accounting services in preparing Alpha Corp's tax returns.

(h) H, who leased office equipment to Alpha Corp.; Henry personally guaranteed the lease. The lease payments for the past 3 months have not been made.

6. Able, Baker, and Clark are doctors. They incorporate as the "Able, Baker, and Clark, M.D., P.C." What will their individual liability be to the following creditors (indicate your reasons):

(a) A patient of the office sues for malpractice committed by Dr. Clark and Dr. Baker while performing an operation.

(b) A pedestrian, while crossing the street, is knocked down by Dr. Clark while Clark was driving the corporation car to visit a patient.

(c) The landlord at the premises sues for rent due.

(d) The secretary whose salary has not been paid the past month sues Able personally for her salary.

(e) A patient in the office slips on the rug in the office, and now has a fractured ankle.

(f) A patient in the office is injected with a dye by a Nurse in preparation of a medical procedure ordered by Dr. Able; the patient collapses and goes into a coma.

(g) The corporation purchases an X-ray machine for $50,000 from X Co.; Able and Baker personally guaranteed the purchase agreement. The corporation does not pay for the machine.

(h) Dr. Baker negligently drives his own car while rushing to visit an office patient in an emergency; Frank is severely injured and Frank's car is completely demolished because of this accident. Frank sues for personal injuries and for the damage to his car.

**7. Charles Meskill has decided to invest $600,000 in a new business venture. Meskill will be joined by two, possibly three, former business associates. He has purchased the patent rights to a revolutionary adhesive substance known as "sticko." In connection with the transaction, he is considering the various forms of business organization he might use in establishing the business. You have been engaged to study the accounting and business problems he should consider in choosing to operate as a general partnership, limited partnership, or corporation. Meskill requests specific advice on the following aspects as they relate to the operation of a business as one of these three forms of business organization: (1) personal liability in the event the venture proves to be a disaster; (2) the borrowing capacity of the entity; (3) requirements for doing a multi-state business; (4) the liability of the entity for the acts of its agents; and (5) the recognition of the entity for income tax purposes and major income tax considerations in selecting one of the three forms of business organization.

Discuss the various legal implications of each specific aspect for which Meskill seeks advice for operating a business in the above mentioned forms of business organization. [AICPA-6a-May 1973].

**8. Selecting the general partnership versus the corporation as a form of business organization requires consideration of (1) the right to compensation for services rendered, (2) the fiduciary duty, and (3) management prerogatives.

Compare and contrast the rights and responsibilities of a common stockholder with a general partner for each of the three areas stated above. [AICPA-6b-May 1973].

**9. Your client, Donaldson Manufacturing, Inc., a family owned corporation, approached the Faber Corporation to purchase raw materials on a credit basis of 2/10, net/60. Faber Corporation insisted that John Donaldson, Donaldson Manufacturing's president and principal stockholder, guarantee payment of the corporation's debt. John Donaldson did so. After 8 months of prompt payments within the 60 days, Donaldson Manufacturing was unable to make payment within 60 days. Consequently, Faber refused to make further deliveries, demanded immediate payment plus interest, and threatened to sue Donaldson Manufacturing and John Donaldson on the debt.

What are the legal implications resulting from Faber's actions in respect to John Donaldson's personal liability? Explain. [Adapted from AICPA-4b-Nov. 1975].

CHAPTER 3

Formation of the Business Corporation

A. THE SHAREHOLDERS' AGREEMENT

If more than one person wishes to form a business corporation, it is strongly advisable that the parties enter into a written shareholders' agreement. Although not mandatory, it is strongly advisable that there be an agreement. Just as every partnership should have a partnership agreement, the shareholders of a closely-held corporation should have a shareholders' agreement. The agreement may include (among others) the following items: the name of the proposed corporation; the business purpose or purposes; the capital structure, including the number and kinds of shares to be issued; what each party agrees to invest, and the number of shares to be issued to each person; any special provisions to be included in the Charter; provision for payment of incorporation expenses such as legal and accounting fees; rights and restrictions regarding transferring shares in case of death, disability, withdrawal, or retirement of any shareholder, including the method of valuation of the shares and manner of payment (commonly referred to as "Buy-Sell" provisions); and the duties and rights of each of the parties regarding employment with the corporation. Very frequently such agreement is entered into by the prospective shareholders prior to incorporation, and then ratified by the corporation once it is formed.

B. STATUTORY REQUIREMENTS FOR FORMATION OF THE CORPORATION

The general policy of New York is that a business corporation may be formed without limitation or restriction, provided it complies with the provisions of the B.C.L. and any other statute in N.Y.S. One-person corporations are permitted and specifically provided for. See B.C.L. §401 and §702.

A corporation exists solely as a result of the grant of a charter by the state, which may issue a charter, or articles or certificate of incorporation. These terms are used interchangeably because various states do not use them uniformly. For example, the Delaware and New York statutes speak of a Certificate of Incorporation, whereas California refers to Articles of Incorporation. In N.Y.S., once the Certificate of Incorporation is filed with the Secretary of State it may be referred to as the Charter.

1. The Corporate Name

There are several restrictions in the selection of the corporate name; the name must indicate it is a corporation and must contain one of the following words or its abbreviation: "corporation", "incorporated", or "limited". B.C.L.§301(1). It should be noted under the Model Act, an additional name would also be permissible, but not under the B.C.L.

The name should not be the same as that of another domestic corporation or an authorized foreign corporation, or be so similar to any such name as to be confusing; it should not contain any word prohibited by statute; the name should not be misleading in the sense of implying powers usually exercised only by regulated corporations such as banks or insurance companies, or implying powers or purposes other than its own, or implying affiliation with well-known organizations of a non-profit nature, or governmental agencies, or contain words which are indecent or obscene or which will ridicule a person or group or indicate unlawful activity. If a name is similar to that of an existing corporation, the Secretary of State may approve it if a consent is obtained from the existing corporation; even the use of one's own name may be disapproved if another corporation has used it first. See B.C.L.§301 for all restrictions and requirements. Pursuant to B.C.L.§301(2), the name of a new corporation "shall be such as to distinguish it" from the names of corporations on file in the index of the Secretary of State.

Once a name has been approved, it may be reserved for a period of 60 days (upon application and payment of a fee, presently $20) so that no one else may use the name during the reserved period. B.C.L.§303.

2. The Incorporator(s)

The incorporator signs the Certificate of Incorporation which is filed with the Secretary of State. A common abbreviation for the term "Certificate of Incorporation" is C/I, which abbreviation will be used hereafter in this book. Pursuant to B.C.L.§401, there shall be one or more incorporators, each must be a natural person, 18 years old or over. Although the incorporator performs a necessary function, such services are perfunctory and short-lived, and end with the organization meeting of the initial board of directors after the filing of the C/I. Very often, the incorporator has nothing further to do with the corporation and does not have to be a shareholder or a director.

3. The Certificate of Incorporation

B.C.L.§402 requires that the Certificate of Incorporation (C/I) include the following items: the name of the corporation; the purpose or purposes for which the corporation is formed; the city, incorporated village or town and the county in New York where the corporation is to be located; the number of shares authorized, the par value, the number authorized per class, and a statement describing the rights and obligations of each class; a designation of the Secretary of State as agent for service of process and the post office address in New York to which such process may be sent; if the corporation is to have a registered agent, the name and address of the registered agent within the state; and the duration of the corporation if other than perpetual. The Certificate (C/I) may also include optional provisions relating to corporate business affairs, and the rights and powers of shareholders, directors and officers not otherwise forbidden by law. B.C.L.§402(b). The C/I must be signed by each incorporator and be acknowledged and delivered to the New York Department of State for filing.

(a) Nature and Purposes

The intended business activities of the corporation must be specified in the C/I, and they must be lawful. A sufficient purpose clause might be "to engage in the manufacture and sale of shoes and shoe products".

Pursuant to B.C.L.§402(a)(2), the C/I shall set forth the purpose or purposes for which it is formed, it being sufficient to state, either alone or with other purposes, that the purpose of the corporation is "to engage in any lawful act or activity for which corporations may be organized", provided it also states "it is not formed to engage in any act or activity requiring the consent or approval of any state official . . . agency or other body without such consent or approval first being obtained". Thus, N.Y. has now adopted an all-purpose clause, which is also in effect in Delaware and is provided for in the Model Act.

(b) Authorized Shares

The C/I must include the total authorized shares, the par value, the various classes of shares with the rights and liabilities of each separate classification. When the C/I is filed, the Secretary of State has given authorization for the corporation to issue these classifications of shares; the corporation would not be authorized to issue any shares other than those authorized in the C/I, and would not be authorized to issue any shares in addition to the maximum authorized, unless the C/I is amended. See Chapter 10.

(c) Designation of Agent for the Corporation

Every domestic corporation and any foreign authorized corporation in New York State must designate the Secretary of State as its duly authorized agent upon whom process (summonses and other legal papers) may be served. The C/I must indicate the address to which the Secretary of State will mail the process to. The listing of the Secretary of State as the authorized agent for the corporation is a mandatory provision. B.C.L.§402(a)(7). This provides a very useful procedure for creditors and other persons attempting to serve the corporation with a summons, which is necessary in order to institute any legal action against the corporation. As a practical matter, it is usually quite difficult to institute law suits against a close corporation since an officer or managing agent must be served with the summons, and in dealing with close corporations, it may be difficult to determine who is an officer and to locate that person. Therefore, as an alternative, the summons may be served upon the Secretary of State in accordance with B.C.L.§306. See B.C.L.§304 and B.C.L.§402(a)(7). In addition, the corporation may also designate any registered agent. B.C.L.§305.

It is necessary that a corporation (after it is formed) keep its address current with the Secretary of State at all times; if lawsuits are instituted by creditors against the corporation and the Secretary of State is served with the summons pursuant to B.C.L.§306, this will be deemed to be effective service of the summons upon the corporation. Thereafter, a Judgment could be entered by a creditor against the corporation (where the corporation did not even know of the pending action). Several cases have arisen in New York whereby the corporation has later sought to vacate the Judgment entered against it.* The courts have not always been willing to do so.

4. Filing the Certificate of Incorporation

The filing of the Certificate of Incorporation(C/I) in the office of the Secretary of State in Albany formally starts the existence of the corporation.** B.C.L.§403. In order for the corporation to be formed, the required filing fees must be paid to the Secretary of State, which include

---

*See, Eugene Di Lorenzo Inc. v. A. C. Dutton Lumber Co. Inc., 67 N.Y.2d 138, 501 N.Y.S.2d 8(1986); Cristo Bros. v. M. Cristo Inc., 91 A.D.2d 807, 458 N.Y.S.2d 50, app. dism. 59 N.Y.2d 760(1983); Union Indem. Ins. Co. v. 10-01 50th Ave. Realty Corp., 102 A.D.2d 727, 476 N.Y.S.2d 563(1984).

**The C/I may also set a date (not to exceed 90 days) upon which corporate existence can begin.

a filing fee of $100, plus the organization tax based upon the authorized shares as follows: 1/20 of 1% of the value of each par value share, plus 5¢ on each no-par value share (Tax Law §180). The minimum tax is $10. Thus, the minimum sum of $110 must be paid and transmitted to the Secretary of State at the time of filing. The filing of the C/I with the Secretary of State is conclusive evidence that all conditions precedent have been fulfilled. B.C.L.§403.

5. Defects in Filing

In order to create a valid corporation one must be careful to comply strictly with the requirements of the B.C.L.

(a) De Jure Corporation

When a corporation is created properly, it is known as a de jure corporation, a corporation by law. Upon the filing of the C/I along with the required fees, the corporate existence begins and the Secretary of State issues its receipt. B.C.L.§403. All mandatory requirements of the statute must be followed for a de jure corporaion to come into existence.

Under certain circumstances, if a de jure corporation does not exist, the law may still treat a business organization as a corporation, known as a "de facto" corporation.

(b) De Facto Corporation

There have been instances whereby formation of the corporation is not perfect. In such case the corporation may qualify as a de facto corporation which means that no one, except the state may question the corporate existence.

The requirements of a de facto corporation are: (1) there must be a law existing under which a de jure corporation may be created; (2) there must be a bona fide good faith attempt to incorporate under the statute, but an inadvertent failure to comply; and (3) there must be actual use of exercise of the corporate powers in the belief that a corporation has been formed. The entity must actually organize itself internally and operate as a corporation. All of these requirements must be met for the courts to recognize the entity as a defacto corporation.

A business organization which does not qualify as a de jure (legally organized) corporation nor as a de facto corporation is not a corporation at all, but may be treated as a sole proprietorship, or partnership, or joint venture.

The concept of a de facto corporation is very rare in modern corporation law today*, as the formalities of formation have been greatly simplified.

C. THE ROLE OF A PROMOTER

In order for a corporation to be formed, some individual(s) will have to undertake the steps necessary for the corporation's formation; they are often referred to as the promoters of the corporation.

1. Who Is a Promoter?

Promoters are the individuals who undertake to get the business started by obtaining necessary capital, initiating the formation, as well as other matters required for the corporation to begin operation.

---

*However, see Bankers Trust Co. v. Zecher, 103 Misc.2d 777, 426 N.Y.S.2d 960 (Monroe Co. 1980).

Before a new business comes into existence, there may be need to obtain surveys, engineering and legal advice, market research studies, contracts for purchase of merchandise, a lease for the premises, capital, hiring managerial personnel, and other negotiations and contracts. The person in charge of such tasks is a promoter, who may be involved in arranging for capital and financing of the corporation's business as well as arranging for the assets, equipment, licenses, personnel, leases, and services; the promoter may also attend to the legal formation of the corporation. Once the corporation is formed, a promoter is no longer needed as the corporation can then contract on its own behalf through its officers.

2. Liabilities of a Promoter for Contracts

Promoters frequently enter into contracts prior to the actual formation of the corporation; the promoter may lease office space and make employment and sales contracts as well as incur other obligations. Although these contracts are made for the benefit of the corporation, it is the promoter who is liable for them. The reason for this rule is that the promoter is not an agent of the corporation because the corporation is not yet in existence when the contracts are made. The promoter is personally liable on these contracts even though made in the name of the corporation.

The corporation will also become liable on these contracts if it expressly adopts the contract, or knowingly accepts its benefits so that the contract is adopted by implication. The promoter remains liable on the contract even if the corporation later adopts it, as adoption in and of itself does not discharge the promoter from contractual liability. Technically, a corporation cannot ratify a pre-incorporation contract, as it was not in existence at the time the contract was made. A promoter may be relieved of liability if the contract provides that adoption shall terminate the promoter's liability, or if the promoter, the third party, and the corporation enter into a novation substituting the corporation for the promoter.

In the usual case, the promoter has no problem regarding contracts entered into, as the promoter is very often in control of the corporation after it is formed. However, there are instances whereby after the corporation is formed, disputes arise between the promoter and director(s) and shareholders(s) before the contracts are adopted.*

3. Duties of a Promoter**

Promoters have a fiduciary duty to the prospective corporation. Thus, the promoter may *not* obtain any benefit or advantage over the corporation or over the shareholders. Promoters of a corporation have a fiduciary relationship among themselves as well as to the corporation, its subscribers, and its shareholders. The promoter(s) must act in utmost good faith and make full disclosure of all material facts relating to their transactions. A promoter cannot purchase property and then sell it to the corporation at a profit; the promoter should not receive a commission from a third party for the sale of property to the corporation. Promoters will be liable to the corporation if they make a secret profit.

D. FOREIGN CORPORATIONS

Corporations may be classified as either domestic or foreign. A N.Y. corporation is a domestic corporation in N.Y.S., whereas a corporation incorporated in Nevada, New Jersey, or California would be a foreign corporation in N.Y.S.

---

*For the various theories regarding the promoter's liability for contacts, see Henn, *The Laws of Corporations* 107–114 (3rd ed. 1983).

**See, Henn, *supra*, 103–106 for duties and liabilities of promoters.

A foreign corporation does not have an automatic right to do business in a state other than its state of incorporation. It must obtain a certificate of authority in any other state where it plans to do business. For example, a corporation organized under the laws of California would need permission from New York State in order to do business in New York.

1. What Is Doing Business in New York?

A foreign corporation is "doing business" when part of its "business" is transacted within a state; a corporation is "not doing business" in N.Y. merely because it is engaged in interstate commerce, or is involved in a single transaction, is prosecuting or defending a lawsuit, collecting debts, has a resident agent, owns property, or has bank accounts in New York.

It is important to distinguish between a foreign corporation doing *intra*state business in New York in which case, it must be licensed, and a corporation doing *inter*state business which does not have to be licensed. A state could *not* require corporations to be licensed to conduct *inter*state business as that would amount to regulation of interstate commerce which is reserved to Congress under the Federal Constitution.

Each state has requirements relating to foreign corporations, and what constitutes doing business in the state, to require the foreign corporation to become licensed. In New York State, a foreign corporation does *not* have to be licensed merely because it is performing certain actions related to doing business, which include maintaining or defending an action or proceeding (i.e. suing or being sued in N.Y. including judicial, administrative or arbitration), holding shareholders or directors meetings in N.Y.S.; maintaining bank accounts in N.Y.S.; maintaining a transfer or registration office for the transfer of its shares. B.C.L.§1301(b). Thus, a foreign corporation may perform any of the above functions in New York, and would still *not* be considered to be doing business in the state. B.C.L.§1301(b).

What constitutes doing business within the state may at times be a very difficult question.*
If the foreign corporation is doing business in N.Y.S., it must obtain a license to do so, and will become subject to franchise tax and other types of regulation, depending upon the type of business.

Examples:

(1) A Florida corporation sells merchandise at retail. It operates a department store in Florida and wants to set up a branch store in New York. It will need authority from the State of New York.

(2) Assume the same corporation as (1) above sells at retail through a mail order system. Customers send in orders from catalogue descriptions to the warehouse in Florida. Goods are shipped from Florida to the customer's home or place of business in N.Y. This corporation does not need authority from the State of New York.

2. Licensing Procedure

In order to become licensed to do business in N.Y., application must be made with the Secretary of State. The application must set forth the corporation's name, the fictitious name of the corporation if any (as per B.C.L.§1301), the date and state of incorporation, the corporate purposes, the location of its New York office, the designation of the Secretary of State as agent for service of legal process against the corporation, and the name and address of any registered agent.

---

*See, *What Constitutes Doing Business* (CT Corp. System 1985) for analysis of the various states requirements of "doing business".

The corporation must also submit a certificate from its state of incorporation indicating it is still an existing corporation. The application must also state the corporation has not engaged in activity in N.Y.S.

If it has done business in New York prior to applying for the license, it will be required to obtain the consent of the N.Y.S. Tax Commission; such consent will be given only if the franchise tax on any prior business conducted in the State is fully paid to date. See B.C.L.§1304 for all details and requirements.

The current fee for filing the application is $200. A license fee upon capital stock employed within the state, similar to the organization tax for domestic corporations must also be paid. (Tax Law §181).

An authorized foreign corporation may amend or change its application for authority by filing a certificate of amendment. (B.C.L.§1308,1309).

3. Names of a Foreign Corporation

A foreign corporation may find that its corporate name is not acceptable (because it conflicts with an existing corporation name on file, or for reasons pursuant to B.C.L.§301,§302); it may thereby submit in its application for authority a fictitious name under which it will do business in N.Y.S. B.C.L.§1301(d). Thus, the authorized foreign corporation would use its fictitious name (authorized) in all of its dealings in N.Y.S.

The use of a fictitious name by a foreign corporation (as per B.C.L.§1301(d)) should not be confused with the filing of an assumed name by a corporation (pursuant to Gen. Bus. Law §130). (See F. Names Used By A Corporation).

4. Internal Affairs of a Foreign Corporation

The internal affairs of the corporation (such as dividends, shareholders' rights, directors' liabilities, shareholders and directors meetings, by-laws, and filing and amending its C/I) are regulated by the state of incorporation—the state in which it is a domestic corporation. The foreign corporation doing business in the state may be subject to some of the restrictions relating to rights of shareholders; in New York, a foreign corporation is subject to some of the restrictions, such as shareholders rights to demand inspection of shareholders lists (B.C.L.§1315); liabilities of directors and officers in certain situations (B.C.L.§1317); liability of corporation to disclose information to shareholders as to dividends and capital (B.C.L.§1318).

Directors and officers of a foreign corporation doing business in New York are subject to the provisions of B.C.L.§719,720 to the same extent as directors and officers of a domestic corporation. These will be explained in subsequent Chapters. However, the foreign corporation may be exempt from these various provisions if its shares are listed on a national securities exchange, or less than half its business income for the last three (3) years is allocable to New York (See B.C.L. §1320).

5. Powers of a Foreign Corporation

Upon filing the application for authority (and payment of the required fees), the foreign corporation is authorized to do business in N.Y.S. as set forth in its application. (B.C.L.§1305). An authorized foreign corporation can exercise the powers permitted by its state of incorporation as long as such powers do not exceed the powers which a domestic corporation may exercise under the laws of New York. (B.C.L.§1306).

6. Enforcement and Penalties Imposed for Non-Compliance

If a foreign corporation does business in New York State without being licensed, the foreign corporation is subject to enforcement by the Attorney General; there is also indirect enforcement by the courts.

(a) Proceedings by the Attorney General

The Attorney General may commence a proceeding to obtain an injunction to restrain an unlicensed foreign corporation from doing business in New York, to restrain a licensed corporation from exceeding its authority, and to annul a license which has been fraudulently obtained. B.C.L. §1303.

(b) Indirect Enforcement by the Courts

In addition to any proceedings by the Attorney General indicated above, an unlicensed foreign corporation doing business in N.Y.S. is denied the legal capacity to sue in New York; it can not maintain any action or proceeding unless and until it has obtained such license. B.C.L.§1312(a).

The failure to obtain the license does not impair the validity of any contract, and does not impair any substantive rights regarding the litigation; it simply denies the unlicensed foreign corporation the right to maintain any action or proceeding (i.e. as a plaintiff or a petitioner) in the N.Y. courts to enforce any of its rights until the license is obtained. B.C.L.§1312.

A corporation doing business in N.Y.S. without a license still subjects itself to the jurisdiction of the New York courts, and it may be sued here whether it has a license or not; it may not use its non-compliance as a defense. B.C.L.§307,§1312(b).

If the corporation subsequently applies for a license, it will first be required to pay the past franchise taxes, fees, and penalties for the years it did business in the state without authority.

Examples:

(1) Alpha Corp., a N.J. corporation doing business in N.Y. (without being licensed) commences an action in N.Y. against Ezra for breach of contract. If Ezra complains to the court that Alpha Corp. is an unlicensed foreign corporation, the court will enter an order, staying the action or dismissing the action, until Alpha Corp. becomes licensed.

If Alpha Corp. later becomes licensed by filing application and paying all back francise taxes, Alpha Corp. will then be able to proceed with the action.

If Alpha Corp. fails to become licensed, it will never be able to proceed with its action against Ezra in New York.

(2) Beta Corp., a Conn. corporation maintains a substantial bank account in N.Y., and has entered into a contract with Gloria in N.Y.; Beta Corp. has no other contacts in New York State.

Gloria breaches the contract with Beta Corp.; Beta Corp. sues Gloria for breach of contract in the New York Supreme Court. Gloria complains to the court that Beta Corp. is an unlicensed foreign corporation, and requests that the court either stay the action or dismiss the action completely.

Beta Corp. is an unlicensed foreign corporation. However, since it is *not doing business in N.Y.*, it is *not required to become licensed*. Therefore, Beta Corp. does *not have to become licensed*; Beta Corp. may still maintain its action against Gloria for breach of contract in the N.Y. Court.

E. STATUTORY REQUIREMENTS FOR MAINTAINING CORPORATE STATUS

1. Franchise Taxes

Every domestic corporation and every foreign corporation doing business in N.Y.S. is required to file and pay an annual franchise tax. In N.Y.S., the current minimum annual franchise tax is $250 per year; if the corporation is located in N.Y.C., there is an additional minimum tax of $125 per year. (N.Y.C. Gen. Corp. Tax)

Even if a corporation earns no profit (and even if it sustains a loss), the corporation is required to file and pay the minimum tax; if it fails to file and pay the required franchise tax for two (2) years, the corporation may be dissolved by proclamation.* See N.Y. Tax Law §203-a for details; see also Tax Law Art. 9-A.

2. Other Tax Forms

A corporation is required to file forms with the Internal Revenue Service (I.R.S.) and the New York State Tax Commission. New York Tax Law §275-a requires that a corporation file, within 10 days of establishing a principal office or place of business in New York, a stock transfer certificate that designates a place for sale, transfer or delivery of the corporation's stock.

The I.R.S. requires that a corporation file an Application for Employer Identification Number (SS-4) regardless of whether the corporation has any employees. There are many other tax forms a corporation must periodically file with I.R.S., the State Tax Commission, and other governmental agencies.**

F. NAMES USED BY A CORPORATION

When a C/I is presented to the Secretary of State for filing, it is checked to see that it complies with the requirements of the B.C.L. and to see whether the name conflicts with any other corporate name on file in that office. See B.C.L.§301 and §302 for all requirements and restrictions. If the corporate name conflicts with any other corporate name on file in the index of the Secretary of State, the name will be rejected.

1. Fictitious Names—Filing Requirements

Very often, corporations may wish to use a trade name or a fictitious or assumed name (which is different from its corporate name). Pursuant to B.C.L.§202(b), a corporation may not do business in New York State under any name, other than that appearing in its C/I, unless it complies with the filing provisions of Gen. Bus. Law§130. If a corporation wishes to use a trade or an assumed name, it may do so by filing a certificate of assumed name with the Secretary of State along with paying the required fee for filing. In addition, the certificate must also be filed in each County Clerk's Office in the State where business will be transacted under the assumed name. If a corporation fails to comply, it is guilty of a misdemeanor, and shall be prohibited from maintaining any action or proceeding in any court in N.Y.S. See. Gen. Bus. Law §130(9).

It is thus possible for a business to have a trade, assumed, or fictitious name, which is quite different from its corporate name, by fully complying with B.C.L.§202(b) and Gen. Bus. Law§130(1)(b), (5).

---

*See case of Igbara Realty Corp. v. N.Y. Property Ins. Underwriting Assn., 94 A.D.2d 79, 80, 463 N.Y.S.2d 211 (1983), and Lorisa Capital Corp. v. Gallo et al. (case #28).

**See, generally, *The New York Corporate Handbook,* Chapter IV (N.Y.S. Bar Assoc. 1983).

In addition to New York, there are approximately 40 states that require or permit a corporation to record or file the fictitious name. The various states differ as to the requirements; the filing requirement in 33 states is mandatory, although the penalties imposed are quite different.* The primary purpose of these statutes is to give notice to the public of the names of the persons or entities using the assumed or fictitious name.

However, this does not provide protection against others using the name. In order to obtain protection, the corporation or business entity could seek trademark protection by registration pursuant to the Federal or State Trademark Laws.**

2. Conflicts With Other Names-Unfair Competition

Sometimes the name selected by a corporation does not conflict with any corporate name on file, but may conflict with another business name such as the name of a partnership, sole proprietorship, or an assumed or fictitious name being used. The mere fact the corporation's name was approved by the Secretary of State does not mean the corporation has an absolute right to use the name. The Secretary of State merely checks to see that the name does not conflict with any other "corporation" name on file; if the corporation name conflicts with another business name being used, the problem would involve the question of "unfair competition".

A business name is a very valuable property right, and is an asset of the business. If a new business is formed using the name of an already established business, or a name so close or similar that the public assumes both are the same, the established business may go to court, requesting an injunction to stop the new entity from using the name. Even if selection of the name was unintentional (where it was not known of the prior established business), the court may still grant an injunction if it is shown the public is and will be misled into thinking it is dealing with the same business entity; damages may be awarded to compensate for the loss of profits during the period of time the name was used. If it can be shown that selection of the name was deliberate, exemplary (punitive) damages may also be granted.***

In such case, where the court is requested to grant an injunction, the court will look into and consider the following: how long has the established business used the name; does the public identify the use of that name with the established business so that the public is being deceived and misled; who, if anyone, has the better right to the use of the name? If the court finds the public is being misled and deceived into thinking both businesses are the same, the court will grant the injunction.†

If an injunction is issued against the continued use of the name, the corporation would then be required to file an Amended Certificate of Incorporation with the Secretary of State in order to amend its name.

---

*See, generally, publications of CT Corporation System, such as: *Corporate Names* (March 1986); Bramson, *Business Names: Problem In their Adoption and Use* (Trademark Serv. Corp. 1984).

**In New York, see Gen. Bus. Law §360 et al.; more than 26 states have adopted the Model State Trademark Law. The Federal Trademark Law is contained in 15 U.S.C. §1051 et al.

New York has an anti-dilution statute; see Gen. Bus. L. §368-d.

See McCarthy, *Trademark and Unfair Competition* (2nd ed. 1984) for thorough treatment of the topic. (2 vol.).

***In New York State, See Gen. Bus. Law §133, whereby it is a misdemeanor if intent to deceive can be shown.

†See, Corning Glass Works v. Corning Cut Glass Co. 197 N.Y. 173 (1910) for rules that court would consider.

CASE 3
VANTAGE CAREERS, INC. v. VANTAGE AGENCY, INC.
(App. Div. 1st Dept., 79 A.D. 2d 912, 434 N.Y.S.2d 428) (1981)

MEMORANDUM DECISION.

Judgment, Supreme Court, New York County entered June 25, 1980, which, permanently enjoined defendant from using the word "Vantage" as part of its corporate name or in its business, is modified, on the law and the facts. . . .

While plaintiff used the word "Vantage" in its corporate name before defendant did, there is little evidence or likelihood of confusion, particularly in view of the essentially different geographical areas in which the parties operate and the somewhat different kinds of service that they specialize in. The name "Vantage" is not so distinctive nor is its use by plaintiff so well established and exclusive as to warrant the relief granted on trial. Further, whatever relief might have been appropriate when defendant first began to use the name "Vantage," intervening events have made it inequitable to forbid defendant to use the name "Vantage" altogether. For some years defendant has been actively conducting its business under that name; and for two and a half years after plaintiff's first motion for a preliminary injunction was denied, plaintiff permitted the action to remain relatively inactive, without even appealing from denial of the temporary injunction, while defendant continued to do business and to be known as "Vantage Agency." In the exercise of our power as a court of equity to mold our decree with due regard to the equities of the situation, we think it will be sufficient to require defendant to use some qualifying word or phrase in conjunction with the use of the word "Vantage" that will clearly distinguish defendant's business from plaintiff's.

On the settlement of the order, the parties may submit suggestions as to such qualifying word or phrase.

CASE 4
UNIVERSAL INDUSTRIES CORP. v. LINDSTROM et al
(App. Div., 4th Dep't, 92 A.D.2d 150, 459 N.Y.S.2d 492) (1983)

This appeal concerns defendants' liability for goods procured from plaintiff by defendant Dana Lindstrom which were, according to the invoices, sold and shipped to "Kimco Warehousing Inc./Dana Lindstrom & Assoc" between August 31, 1979 and December 20, 1979. These transactions occurred prior to the incorporation of corporate-defendants. . . .

Plaintiff claimed that Lindstrom is personally liable for the value of the goods since it dealt with him individually and directed the invoices to the "two corporations" for his convenience. . . .

As a general rule a person contracting in the name of a proposed corporation is personally liable on the contract unless the parties have otherwise agreed (see 13 N.Y. Jur.2d, Business Relationships, §111, p. 380; see, also 1 Fletcher, Cyclopedia of Corporations [1982 Cum. Supp.] §190, p. 104; 3 Cavitch, Bus. Organizations §56.01[2]). Such liability "is based upon the principle that one who assumes to act for a nonexistent principal is himself liable on the contract in the absence of an agreement to the contrary." . . . (See, also, Tarolli Lbr. Co. v. Andreassi, 59 A.D.2d

1011, 1012, 399 N.Y.S.2d 739). Whether a person is personally obligated on a preincorporation transaction depends on the intention of the parties and if it is the intention that he be personally liable, that result will follow. . . .

• • • •

Here, there was no written agreement to absolve Lindstrom and the parties disagree regarding whether it was their intention that Lindstrom be personally bound. Further, no documentary proof was submitted which clearly shows the intention to relieve Lindstrom of liability. Although the invoices indicate that the goods were sold and shipped to "Kimco Warehousing Inc./Dana Lindstrom & Assoc." and it is clear from the other proof that plaintiff knew that Lindstrom acted for those entities, the documentary proof does not unequivocally indicate an agreement that plaintiff would look exclusively to the corporate-defendants for payment. . . .

Further, plaintiff's claim that it "was . . . dealing with Dana Lindstrom personally" does not preclude its cause of action against the corporate-defendants. A corporation may bind itself to the terms of a preincorporation contract if it knowingly accepts the benefits referable to the contract (Matter of Reif [Williams Sportswear], 9 N.Y.2d 387, 392, 214 N.Y.S.2d 395 . . .) and this conduct gives rise to corporate liability in addition to any individual liability. . . . Here, plaintiff's allegation in its complaint that the corporate-defendants accepted delivery of the shipments in question was not challenged by the corporate-defendants in their cross motion. Even if plaintiff dealt with Lindstrom personally, this would not necessarily relieve the corporate-defendants of their alleged contractual liability.

Accordingly, the order and judgment of Special Term, insofar as it granted summary judgment to defendant Lindstrom, should be reversed and the motion denied. . . .

Discussion Questions:
1. What did the court take into consideration regarding Lindstrom's liability as a promoter?
2. What did the court take into consideration regarding the liability of the corporations?

CASE 5
VON ARX, A. G. v. C. J. BREITENSTEIN
(App. Div. 4th Dep't., 52 A.D.2d 1049, 384 N.Y.S.2d 895) (1976)

MEMORANDUM:

• • • •

. . . Whether a foreign corporation is "doing business" within the purview of section 1312 of the B.C.L. so as to foreclose access to our courts depends upon the particular facts of each case with inquiry into the type of business activities being conducted. . . . In connection with such determination it is to be recognized that, while some activities might constitute "doing business" pursuant to CPLR 301 and so subject a foreign corporation to the jurisdiction of New York courts, such a finding would not necessarily render a corporation liable to the qualification requirements of section 1312 of the B.C.L. . . . The purpose of §1312 of the B.C.L. and its predecessor statutory provisions is not to enable defendants to avoid contractual obligations but to regulate such foreign corporations which are in fact conducting business within the state so that they shall not be doing business under more advantageous terms than those allowed a corporation of this state

(Cummer Lumber Co. v. Associated Mfrs. Ins. Co., 67 App.Div. 151, 154, affd., 173 N.Y. 633.) Nor may a state unlawfully interfere with a foreign corporation's right to engage in purely interstate commerce. . . . Denial of access to our courts by such foreign corporations engaged solely in interstate commerce would constitute such unlawful interference.

Plaintiff maintains no office or warehouse in New York; it has no New York bank account; it holds no real estate or personal property here; it sends no officers or employees regularly into the state to perform or oversee services. In essence there is no showing that plaintiff conducted continuous activities essential to its corporate business. Rather, the evidence indicates that plaintiff ships goods into the state from Switzerland for further shipment by defendant within or without the state. Orders of defendant are accepted in Switzerland with no solicitation or advertising taking place in New York State by plaintiff's agents or employees. Clearly, this is not qualifying activity that would or constitutionally could subject plaintiff to New York State regulation and cannot be said to constitute "doing business" in New York State within the context of §1312 of the B.C.L.

• • • •

Note:

This decision was appealed to the Court of Appeals (41 N.Y.2d 958, 394 N.Y.S.2d 876) (1977). The Memorandum Decision of the Court of Appeals follows:

The order of the Appellate Division should be affirmed.

There is no merit to defendant's affirmative defense based on plaintiff's failure to comply with §1312 of the B.C.L. The purpose of that section is to regulate foreign corporations which are "doing business" within the State, not, as defendant would suggest, to enable the avoidance of contractual obligations.

For the reasons noted by the Appellate Division, the plaintiff is not "doing business" within this State as would render it liable to the qualification requirements of section 1312 of the B.C.L. In addition, plaintiff's activity must be classified under the United States Constitution as beyond State interference. (Allenberg Cotton Co. v. Pittman, 419 U.S. 20; Dahnke-Walker Co. v. Bondurant, 257 U.S. 282, 291, International Fuel & Iron Corp. v. Donner Steel Co., 242 N.Y. 224, 229).

CASE 6
APPLICATION OF SHIGOTO INTERNATIONAL CORP. et. al.
v. SECRETARY OF STATE
(Sup. Ct. N.Y. Co., 101 Misc. 2d 646, 421 N.Y.S.2d 784) (1979)

HORTENSE W. GABEL, Justice:

In this Article 78 proceeding Petitioners Shigoto International Corp., Shigoto Industries, Ltd. and Sekai Manufacturing Co., Inc., seek a judgment directing the respondent Secretary of State, to strike the names Shigoto Far East Importers, Ltd., and Sekai Far East Importers, Inc. from the index of authorized foreign corporations.

The Court finds that the Secretary of State has abused his discretion by allowing the challenged names to be placed in the index of foreign corporations authorized to do business in the State of New York. [See B.C.L.§301(a)(2)]. . . .

The Department of State has wide discretion as to whether a name is so similar as to tend to confuse or deceive. However, if the choice of the name is so wanting in logical premise as to be violative of good sense and reason, the choice will be deemed to be an abuse of discretion (American Auto Accessories Stores, Inc. v. Lomenzo, 69 Misc.2d 972, 331 N.Y.S.2d 278).

The respondent had previously disallowed the names Shigoto Far East Ltd. and Sekai Far East Ltd., but had permitted the indexing upon the addition of the word "Importers" to each name.

It is clear that the challenged names, either with or without "Importers" added thereto, tend to confuse and deceive the public, as would the use of the name "Chrysler Importers, Ltd." as opposed to "Chrysler Corporation" or "Sears Roebuck Importers, Ltd." as opposed to "Sears, Roebuck & Co., Inc.".

Furthermore, out of the myriad of names that could have been used, the choice of the names Shigoto Far East (Importers) Ltd. and Sekai Far East (Importers) Ltd., could only have been made with the "intent to deceive". The court has made this determination even though the requirement of such intent is no longer necessary under B.C.L.§301(a)(2).

• • • •

The petition is granted.

PROBLEMS

10. Finley Corp., a N.J. corporation, unlicensed to do business in N.Y., opens a retail store on 57 St. in N.Y.C. Finley Corp. sold merchandise to Thomas on credit. Thomas was supposed to pay last month; Finley Corp. sues Thomas; Thomas' lawyer checks with the Secretary of State and discovers that Finley Corp. is not licensed to do business in N.Y. Thomas now claims he doesn't have to pay because Finley Corp. is unlicensed.
    (a) Explain whether or not Finley Corp. should become licensed.
    (b) Explain how Finley Corp. can become licensed.
    (c) Explain how this affects Finley Corp's law suit against Thomas.

11. Ruth, a promoter, was engaged to organize the Elger Sales Corp. On September 22, on behalf of the proposed corporation, she entered into a contract in writing with Matthews for his services as Controller of the corporation for a period of 6 months beginning October 1 at an annual salary of $80,000. The Elger Sales Corp. was incorporated on October 1, and on that date, Matthews commenced his duties as Controller. No formal action with reference to his employment was taken by the board of directors or by the officers. On October 10, Matthews was discharged without cause.
    (a) Matthews sues Elger Sales Corp. for salary due for the balance of his contract. What result?
    (b) Matthews also sues Ruth, the promoter. What result?
    (c) Matthews sues both Elger Sales Corp. and Ruth for salary due for the 10 days he worked, from October 1–October 10. What result?

12. Paula, a promoter, hired Abe, an accountant to prepare the set of books for Arrow Corp., a corporation to be formed; Paula agreed that Arrow Corp. would issue 20 shares of its $100 par value stock to Abe, in payment for his services.

After Arrow Corp. was formed, Abe set up an entire bookkeeping system. The corporation later refuses to issue the 20 shares of stock to Abe on the ground the corporation had never adopted the contract made by Paula. The corporation, is, however, willing to pay Abe the sum of $2,000, the reasonable value of his services.

(a) What are the rights of Abe against the Corporation?
(b) What are the rights of Abe against Paula, the promoter?

13. Harry and Nat were partners in the dress manufacturing business for the past 30 years in N.Y.C. under the trade name of Boutique Dress Co. In 1984, Jack Smith submits a certificate of incorporation for filing with the Secretary of State to organize a corporation known as Boutique Dress Co., Inc. The Secretary of State approves the name; the corporation, Boutique Dress Co. Inc. is formed, and starts its operation in the dress selling business.

(a) Harry and Nat complain to the Secretary of State, and commence a proceeding against the Secretary of State; what result?
(b) What remedies, if any, do Harry and Nat have regarding this? Explain.

14. Alpha Corp., a corporation organized under the laws of N.J., was not licensed to do business in New York. It did, however, maintain an office in Manhattan for the transfer, exchange and registration of its securities in New York and held meetings of its directors here. Last year, Alpha Corp. defended two actions brought against it by two New York residents in New York Courts based on injuries allegedly sustained due to the negligence of Alpha Corp.'s President while she was driving a car owned by Alpha Corp. in N.Y.C.

On March 1, 1984, Alpha Corp. sold to X Corp. (a New York corporation) 1,000 TV sets to be delivered to X Corp. at its warehouse in the Bronx. The contract was made and signed in New York.

a) X Corp. refuses to pay for the 1,000 TV sets. Is Alpha Corp. permitted to maintain an action against X Corp. for breach of contract in the New York Supreme Court? Explain.

b) Based upon the facts stated, do you think that Alpha Corp. is doing business in New York State? Is Alpha Corp. required to become licensed?

c) Assume Alpha Corp. wishes to become licensed in New York State; describe and explain the procedures involved.

15. A Corp., a Conn. corporation, has been doing systematic business in New York without obtaining a license. It becomes involved in various transactions and law suits.

In each of the actions, the other party to the law suit complains to the court that A Corp. is not licensed. What result in each of the cases? What advice would you give to A Corp? Is A Corp. required to be licensed in New York? The law suits are:

(a) One of A Corp.'s trucks is damaged to the extent of $2,000 by the negligence of B Corp.; A Corp. sues B Corp. for $2,000.

(b) D, a New York resident refuses to take delivery of goods ordered by him from A Corp.'s New York store, causing A Corp. to suffer damages of $500. A Corp. sues D for $500.

(c) C, a New York resident, is damaged to the extent of $1,000 by the refusal of A Corp. to take delivery of goods ordered by A Corp. C sues A Corp. for $1,000.

16. Conway, the plaintiff, entered into a contract with Trend Set Construction Corp. for remodeling work to be done on Conway's home. Samet, the defendant, signed the contract as president of Trend Set Construction Corp. Conway subsequently learned that Trend Set had never filed a certificate of incorporation. Suit was then brought against Samet personally. Samet defended on the ground that her attorney was supposed to have incorporated the business. The attorney told Samet she was incorporated and gave her a corporate seal. The attorney had all the necessary information to incorporate and was paid the incorporation fees. Samet claimed she had a de facto corporation. Discuss.

**17. During the course of your year-end audit for a new client, Otis Corporation, you discover the following facts. Otis was incorporated in 1974 and is owned 94% by James T. Parker, President; 1% by his wife; and 5% by Wilbur Chumley. These three individuals were incorporators and are officers and directors of the corporation.

Otis manufactures and sells telephonic equipment. In 1974 it sold approximately $350,000 of its various products almost exclusively in the state of its incorporation. In 1975 it began to branch out and sold $550,000 of its products in a neighboring state. Otis expanded rapidly, and 1976 was a banner year with sales of $1,250,000 and its profits of $175,000. Otis constructed a small office building on a tract of land it had purchased for expansion purposes in the neighboring state and used the top floor to establish a regional sales office and rented the balance of the building.

During the course of your audit for the year 1976, you discover that Parker commingles his personal funds with those of the corporation, keeps very few records of board and shareholder meetings, and at his convenience disregards corporate law regarding separateness of personal and corporate affairs. The corporation had 1976 sales in excess of $300,000 in the neighboring state. The corporation has not filed any papers with the Secretary of State of that state in connection with these operations.

In light of the above discoveries, it was deemed prudent to examine the original incorporation papers which were filed by Parker in 1974. The following irregularities were discovered. The powers and purposes clause states that the geographical territory in which the newly created corporation was to do business was solely the state of incorporation. Additionally, Mr. Chumley and Mrs. Parker did not sign the articles of incorporation, and prior to the effective date of incorporation, a lease was taken out and a car purchased in the corporate name.

Discuss the legal problems which Otis may face as a result of the above facts. Do not consider any tax implications. [AICPA-6a-Nov. 1977].

**18. Phillips was the principal promoter of the Waterloo Corporation, a corporation which was to have been incorporated not later than July 31, 1981. Among the many things to be accomplished prior to incorporation were the obtaining of capital, the hiring of key executives and securing of adequate office space. In this connection, Phillips obtained written subscriptions for $1.4 million of common stock from 17 individuals. He hired himself as the chief executive officer of Waterloo at $200,000 for five years and leased three floors of office space from Downtown Office Space, Inc. The contract with Downtown was made in the name of the corporation. Phillips had indicated orally that the corporation would be coming into existence shortly. The corporation did not come into existence through no fault of Phillips.

Discuss the legal implications for each of these transactions; what is the liability of Phillips for each? [A.I.C.P.A.-#9-May 1982].

**19. Jim Bold is a promoter for a corporation to be formed and known as Wonda Corp. Bold entered into several supply and service agreements with Servco. These agreements were executed in Wonda's name, expressly contingent upon adoption by Wonda, when formed, and were based solely on Wonda's anticipated financial strength. Within two weeks after the signing of the agreement, Wonda was duly formed and operating. Shortly thereafter, Wonda by its board of directors rejected the preincorporation agreements entered into by Bold and Servco, stating that it could obtain more beneficial contracts elsewhere.

Discuss Wonda's and Bold's liability to Servco on the preincorporation agreements. [Adapted from A.I.C.P.A.-#5-November 1984].

**20. Bixler obtained an option on a building he believed was suitable for use by a corporation he and two other men were organizing. After the corporation was successfully promoted Bixler met with the Board of Directors who agreed to acquire the property for $200,000. Bixler deeded the building to the corporation and the corporation began business in it. Bixler's option contract called for the payment of only $155,000 for the building and he purchased it for that price. When the directors later learned that Bixler paid only $155,000, they demanded the return of Bixler's $45,000 profit. Bixler refused, claiming the building was worth far more than $200,000 both when he secured the option and when he deeded it to the corporation.

What are the legal implications involved? [Adapted from A.I.C.P.A.-23-May 1981].

CHAPTER 4

Corporate Purposes and Powers

A corporation exists as a legal entity by permission of the state; in order for it to function, it must have authority or power. The state is the source of all corporate power and determines what a corporation may and may not do.

A. EXPRESS PURPOSES

The purpose or purposes for which a corporation is formed should be clearly stated in the Certificate of Incorporation (C/I) so that any person dealing with the corporation may ascertain the nature of the business from the C/I on file with the Secretary of State.

The C/I may specify any number of related or unrelated purposes. For example, it may include the following related purposes:

1. to grow fruits and vegetables;
2. to package, sell and process fruits and vegetables;
3. to import and export fruits and vegetables;
4. to operate grocery stores and fruit and vegetable markets.

Also, the corporation may include completely unrelated purposes, such as:

1. to grow fruits and vegetables;
2. to manufacture and sell yachts and airplanes;
3. to operate a laundry;
4. to purchase and manage residential real property.

The objects or purposes for which a corporation is formed are expressly stated in its C/I, which include the type of business activities the corporation proposes to engage in. B.C.L.§201(a) allows a purpose clause authorizing the corporation to engage in any lawful business. A typical purpose clause for a restaurant business may state the purpose is "to engage in the restaurant business and any legal business transactions related thereto."

A corporation's authority is limited to activities included in the purposes stated in the C/I. If the C/I provides the corporation is formed for purposes of manufacturing, buying, selling, and otherwise dealing in toys, then that is all the corporation can do.

Pursuant to B.C.L.§402(a)(2), New York now has a general purpose clause, and thus it is no longer necessary to also include a specific purpose clause except for certain situations. However, most attorneys will still include one or more specific purposes.

The C/I may also include powers of the corporations. B.C.L.§202(a) provides implied powers the corporation may exercise in furtherance of its corporate purposes.

B. IMPLIED POWERS

B.C.L.§202(a) lists general powers (which may be referred to as implied powers) that every corporation has *in furtherance of its corporate purposes*. A corporation has the power to acquire real and personal property, to make contracts, to invest corporate funds, and to engage in business ventures with others, provided same is in furtherance of its corporate purposes. The corporation may not exercise any of these powers unless it furthers the corporate purpose(s) as stated in its C/I. A corporation organized "to buy and sell goods, wares, and merchandise" has implied powers in furtherance of its corporate purposes to purchase or lease store premises, employ salesmen, buy or rent trucks, spend money for advertising, maintain bank accounts, hire employees, pay their salaries and traveling expenses, as well as other powers necessary or incidental to the stated purpose(s).

In N.Y.S. pursuant to B.C.L.§202(a), every C/I includes 16 general implied powers as long as they are not specifically restricted or limited in the C/I. The implied powers are briefly summarized as follows:

1. To have perpetual duration.
2. To sue and be sued in the corporate name.
3. To have and use a corporate seal.
4. To acquire in any manner, and to deal in property, real and personal.
5. To sell, lease, or mortgage its property in any manner.
6. To acquire, deal in, use and sell bonds, other obligations, shares, and securities issued by other corporations or governmental activities.
7. To make contracts, give guarantees, incur liabilities, and to borrow money, with or without security.
8. To lend money and invest funds on terms with or without security.
9. To carry on business anywhere in the world.
10. To elect or appoint officers, employees and other agents, define their duties, fix their compensation and the compensation of directors, and indemnify corporate personnel.
11. To adopt by-laws relating to the corporate business, the conduct of its affairs and the powers of shareholders, directors and officers.
12. To make contributions for charitable purposes, irrespective of corporate benefit.
13. To establish and carry out pension, profit sharing, share purchases, share options and other retirement, incentive and benefit plans for its directors, officers, and employees.
14. To purchase, sell and deal in its own shares.
15. To be a partner, joint venturer, investor or manager in other enterprises.
16. To have all powers necessary or convenient to effect any or all of the purposes for which the corporation is formed.

See B.C.L.§202(a) for details of the general powers of a corporation. It is important to note that the implied powers are only "in furtherance of its corporate purposes."

C. ULTRA VIRES CONTRACTS

A corporation may perform only those acts authorized by its express, implied, or statutory powers. The powers of a corporation are derived from the B.C.L., the C/I, and its implied powers. If it should engage in any unauthorized act, it is ultra vires—that is, beyond the powers of the corporation.

1. What Is Ultra Vires?

The term ultra vires means "beyond the powers"; acts of a corporation that are beyond the authority provided in its C/I or the statute by which it was incorporated are ultra vires.

New York law permits a corporation to be formed for "any lawful business purpose or purposes". B.C.L.§402. The "purpose" clause should be drafted in as broad language as possible so as to encompass every possible corporate activity planned. The corporation should restrict its activities to those stated in the C/I and those which are in furtherance of its stated purposes. Acts which exceed the stated purposes or implied powers are considered to be ultra vires. However, since New York and many other states have adopted a general purpose clause, the problem of ultra vires should occur very rarely today.

2. Illegal Acts Distinguished from Ultra Vires

Any action of the corporation in excess of its authority is ultra vires, but it is not necessarily illegal unless contrary to statute or public policy. Ultra vires acts are not necessarily illegal.

3. Legal Status of Ultra Vires Contracts

The defense of "ultra vires" can no longer be raised as a defense to the enforcement of a contract. The remedies for an ultra vires contract are restricted by statute to an action by the corporation, by the shareholders, or by the attorney general. The three possible remedies for an ultra vires contract are provided in B.C.L.§203 as follows:

(1) An action by a shareholder against the corporation to enjoin the "ultra vires" act. If a contract is involved, the other parties to the contract may be included in the action; the court has discretionary power to set aside and enjoin the performance of the contract, to make allowances for compensation to any party as may be called for to compensate for loss or damage already sustained, but loss of profits cannot be awarded. B.C.L.§203(a)(1).

(2) An action by the corporation (or by the shareholders in a derivative action in the right of the corporation) to procure a judgment against the officers and directors who approved and participated in the ultra vires act for any losses or damages sustained by the corporation. B.C.L.§203(a)(2).

(3) An action by the attorney general of the state to dissolve the corporation or to enjoin it from carrying out unauthorized business. B.C.L.§203(a)(3).

As a general rule, the attorney general would proceed only in extraordinary cases where the public interest was involved.

Although third parties have no right to object to the ultra vires acts of a corporation, any shareholder (even if he or she owns only one share) may bring an action to enjoin the corporation from performing the ultra vires contract; this may be resorted to only if the contract is still executory; if the contract has been fully performed, there is nothing to enjoin. Generally, in an action for an injunction, all parties involved should be parties to the action, and the court may allow such damages as is equitable, but anticipated lost profits can not be awarded.

If the corporation sustains any loss or damage because of the ultra vires transaction, the corporation may recover its damages from the directors and officers who approved the contract. When directors exceed corporate powers, they may be personally liable for the resulting loss. If the corporation does not commence the action against the officers and directors for the damage to the corporation, an action may be maintained by the shareholder(s) on behalf of the corporation (commonly known as a shareholders' derivative suit which is provided for in B.C.L.§626 and will be covered in Chapter 9 of this book).

Examples:

(1) Jones Corp. was organized to operate supermarkets, grocery and other food stores in New York City. On February 1, its board of directors, consisting of D, E, and F approve the purchase of land in upstate New York for speculation purposes from Mighty Sales Corp. for $40,000, the transfer of deed to take place on April 1. Sam, a shareholder who owns one share of stock, finds out about this transaction; Sam (even though he owns only one share) has the right to seek an injunction stopping the corporation from purchasing the land. If Sam commences an action on March 20, he may request that the court grant an injunction, enjoining both Jones Corp. and Mighty Sales Corp. from proceeding with the contract. Sam may apply for the injunction only while the contract is executory, up until April 1; after the contract has been fully performed, the remedy of an injunction would serve no purpose.

(2) The corporation purchases the land in (1) above, and now a year later, the land is worth much less; it is now worth only $2,000; the corporation has thus sustained a loss of $38,000. The corporation has the right to sue the directors personally who approved the ultra vires contract (D, E, and F) for the $38,000 damage to the corporation. If the corporation does not commence the action, the shareholders have the right to commence said action on behalf of and for the benefit of the corporation.

(3) Same facts as (1) above; however, assume Sam does not commence an action for an injunction. Subsequently, Mighty Sales Corp. decides it will not perform because the contract is ultra vires. Mighty Sales Corp. cannot use ultra vires as a defense.

D. INCORPORATORS' ORGANIZATION MEETING

After filing the C/I, the incorporator(s) meet to adopt by-laws and elect directors. B.C.L.§404. At the meeting, directors are elected to hold office until the first annual meeting of shareholders and by-laws are adopted. Other business may, but need not be transacted. Any action required to be taken at the meeting may be taken without a meeting if all incorporators sign a statement which sets forth the action so taken.

E. MANAGEMENT OF THE CORPORATION

The corporation is managed by its board of directors. B.C.L.§701. Directors are elected by the shareholders. Directors are in charge of hiring officers to run the corporation on a day to day basis. The officers obtain their authority from the board of directors and act for the corporation in making contracts. The management of the corporation is subject to the following sources: the

Business Corporation Law; Certificate of Incorporation (C/I); By-Laws; Proceedings of Shareholders; Proceedings of the Board of Directors.

The authority of the corporation for doing any corporate act would be found from the above sources, any of which may refer to the act in question, either authorizing, forbidding, limiting or conditioning the right to so act. It may be necessary to refer to all of these sources of authority before the validity of action of the corporation may be fully determined. Each of these sources of authority for the corporation to act will be covered in the next section and in the following Chapters of this book.

F. BY-LAWS

By-laws are the rules and regulations adopted by the corporation to govern its affairs, its shareholders, directors and officers. By-laws need not be filed with or approved by any New York State official. B.C.L.§601(c) provides that by-laws of a corporation "may contain any provision relating to the business of the corporation, the conduct of its affairs, its rights or powers or the rights or powers of its shareholders, directors or officers" so long as each provision is consistent with New York law and with the C/I. The initial by-laws should be adopted by the incorporators immediately after the corporation is formed.

1. Enactment of By-laws

The initial by-laws are adopted by the incorporators at the organization meeting. Thereafter, they may be added to, amended or repealed by vote of the shareholders. The C/I or the by-laws themselves may delegate this right to the board of directors. B.C.L.§601(a).

2. Some Typical By-Law Provisions

By-laws normally include provisions regarding the time and manner of holding shareholders' meetings; who may call special meetings; quorum and voting requirements for shareholders; proxies; the manner of issuance and transfer of shares of stock; dividends and distributions; qualifications of, rights and powers of directors; manner of election and term of office of the board of directors; quorum and voting requirements at directors' meeting; method of replacing directors; compensation of directors and expense reimbursement; titles of officers, their duties, term of office, and method of removal; amendment of the by-laws; the place for the corporation's bank account; location of the principal office for the corporation; the corporate seal; the fiscal year of the corporation; indemnification of directors and officers, and provisions for insurance; waivers of notices of shareholders or directors meeting; bonding of officers, and other matters relating to the particular corporation. The above are merely representative of typical by-laws that are usually provided for.*

Some items of internal management operation may be included in either the by-laws or in the C/I, whereas some items must be included in the C/I. In order to amend the C/I, an amended certificate has to be filed with the Secretary of State with filing fees, whereas amendment of the by-laws entails an internal operation and no filing with the Secretary of State.

---

*For a very good explanatory set of By-Laws, see, Israels, *On Corporate Practice*, 559–616 (4th ed. 1983) with reference to applicable sections of the B.C.L. and the Del. Gen. Corp. L.; see, also, Sample By-Laws in *The New York Corporate Handbook*, 267–278 (N.Y.S. Bar Assoc. 1983).

PROBLEMS

21. G Corp. was organized to conduct a fruit and vegetable store. A, B, and C are the directors. A, who has just returned from a vacation in Nevada presented to the Board a proposition to buy vacant land in Nevada for speculation. The Board unanimously approved, and the property was purchased from Oster for $80,000. Six months later, the value of the land had fallen to $30,000.

(a) May G Corp. rescind the transaction? Explain.

(b) Assume that instead of attempting to rescind, G Corp. sold the land for $30,000. What are the rights of G Corp. and its shareholders?

(c) X, a shareholder complains and insists that the corporation rescind the transaction, and get back the $80,000. What are the rights of X?

22. The Certificate of Incorporation of Garment Corp. authorizes it to engage in the manufacture of clothing. The Corporation has enjoyed a great deal of success and has a large cash balance. Pursuant to unanimous vote of the Board of Directors, Garment Corp. for purposes of speculation, entered into a contract on May 1, 1978 to purchase gold coins from Green at a price of $100,000, with delivery and payment due June 15, 1978. Sally has been a shareholder of Garment Corp. since its incorporation, and owns 2% of the stock.

(a) Could Sally on May 10, 1978 prevent the corporation from carrying out the contract? Explain.

(b) Assume that Green tendered the gold coins to Garment Corp. pursuant to the contract, and that Garment refused to accept or pay for them. Green sues Garment Corp. What result? Explain.

(c) Assume that Garment Corp. and Green fully performed the contract; a year later, Garment Corp. subsequently sold the gold coins for $70,000. Does Sally have a basis for recovering the $30,000 loss? Explain fully what this right is, and the mechanics involved.

23. Harvey Tool Inc., was chartered under New York law as a tool company located in N.Y.C. with 100 shares of stock, authorized and outstanding. Nowhere in its certificate of incorporation was it authorized to acquire real estate. At a Board of Directors meeting on May 1, 1980, the Board voted to purchase two parcels of real property (both for $100,000 each), an old building on 20th Street to be used to expand their tool company, and some land upstate New York for purposes of speculation, both purchases to be made on June 1, 1980.

On May 15, 1980, Jack, a shareholder of Harvey Tool Inc. with one share of stock, finds out about both contracts and complains to the Board of Directors. They ignore his complaints.

a) Does Jack have any rights on May 15th?

b) Assume that both parcels of real property are purchased and now several months later (in 1981) both parcels are worth less than the $100,000 purchase price. The building on 20th St. is worth only $85,000 and the land upstate is now worth only $50,000. Jack again complains, claiming he lost $15,000 on one building and $50,000 on the land upstate. Indicate all of Jack's rights, if any, relating to both purchases.

CHAPTER 5

Capital and the Financial Structure of the Corporation

The Certificate of Incorporation (C/I) specifies the total number of shares the corporation is authorized to issue, together with a description of their attributes. Authorized shares are the total maximum number of shares the corporation will be authorized to issue. Not all authorized shares have to be issued.

A. AUTHORITY TO ISSUE SHARES

The authority for a corporation to issue its own shares is derived from B.C.L.§501 whereby the corporation has the power to issue the number of shares stated in its C/I. B.C.L.§501 provides that shares may be all one class or may be divided into two or more classes, with or without par value, having such relative voting, dividend, liquidation and other rights, preferences and limitations as indicated in the C/I. If the corporation has authority to issue more than one class of shares, at least one class of outstanding shares must be entitled to unlimited dividend and liquidation rights. A corporation is limited in issuing only the total number of shares authorized in the C/I; this number cannot be increased or decreased unless the C/I is amended authorizing same.

B. CLASSIFICATION OF SHARES OF STOCKS AND BONDS

The terms "capital stock", "stated capital", and "capital" are treated the same; also the words "stock" and "shares" are used interchangeably. Capital represents the consideration the corporation has received from its shareholders, for which the corporation issues shares of stock.

Two of the principal sources of acquiring funds for use in corporations involve debt and equity. Equity securities represent an ownership interest in the corporation, and include both common and preferred stock. Corporations also finance their operations through debt securities or bonds which do not represent an ownership interest, but rather create a debtor-creditor relationship between the corporation and the bondholders.

1. Par Value Shares

Par value shares are those which have an arbitrary minimum value assigned. For example, "$100 par value" means that $100 is the minimum price the corporation may initially sell each share, B.C.L.§504(c). Thus, the price of the stock intially sold must be greater than or equal to the par value. The consideration received for the par value portion constitutes Stated Capital, and if the stock is sold for an amount greater than par value, the premium above par value is Capital Surplus. The Board of Directors determines the price of the shares, subject to the par value restriction.

2. No Par Value Shares

No par value shares are those whereby no arbitrary minimum value has been assigned; thus the corporation may sell the shares for any price. B.C.L.§504(d). The entire consideration received constitutes Stated Capital. The board of directors is allowed to allocate this consideration between Stated Capital and Capital Surplus. B.C.L.§506(b). No par value stock is issued for any price as determined by the board of directors, unless the C/I reserves the right to the shareholders.

3. Common Shares

The two basic types of shares are common and preferred. The holders of common shares generally have the right to vote at shareholders' meeting, receive dividends, and share in the distribution of corporate assets on liquidation. A common shareholder has no priority or preference over any other class of shareholders unless otherwise specified. There must be at least one class of shares with full voting rights and at least one class with unlimited dividend and liquidation rights. Such shares are usually the common shares.

4. Preferred Shares

Preferred shares have preferences, which means that holders of preferred shares have priority over holders of common shares as to dividends and/or liquidation rights. Usually such shares are preferred in both respects. Preferred shareholders usually do not have the right to vote.

There are a number of different types of preferred shares. For example, "8% Preferred, $50 par value, preferred as to dividends and distribution" means that holders of these shares are entitled to receive a dividend of 8% per year on the par value ($50), namely a dividend of $4, before any dividend may be paid to the common shares, and at liquidation, they are paid back $50 before any payment to the common shares; "$10 Prior Preferred, no par value, preferred as to dividends only" means that holders of these shares are entitled to receive a dividend of $10 per share before any dividend may be paid to the other preferred shareholders or to the common shareholders, and at liquidation, they share on the same basis as the other shareholders.

The holders of preferred shares have a right to a fixed dividend and this dividend is paid before any dividends may be distributed to the common shareholders. Preferred shareholders have no guarantee of receiving a dividend; however, they will be paid before the holders of common shares. Preferred shares may also be designated as "cumulative", "noncumulative", or "participating preferred".

(a) Cumulative Preferred

Cumulative preferred shares entitle the holder to a certain dividend each year, and if it is not paid, it accumulates. If a dividend is declared to any other class of shareholder, it cannot be paid until all prior accumulations on the cumulative preferred are paid first.

Example:

Baker Corp. is a N.Y. corporation; in 1978 it issued 1,000 shares of 5% Cumulative Preferred $100 par value; 1,000 shares of 8% Preferred $100 par value, and 5,000 shares of common no par value. It has not paid any dividends during 1978, 1979, 1980, 1981, and 1982.

In 1983, the corporation by its Board of Directors declares a dividend. In order to declare a dividend, the corporation must first declare and pay dividends to the cumulative preferred shareholders for 1978, 1979, 1980, 1981, and 1982, and also for the year 1983; therefore the corporation will be required to pay $30 per share or $30,000 to the cumulative preferred shareholders before paying any dividends to the other shareholders.

In addition Baker Corp. will also be required to pay $8 per share or $8,000 in dividends to the other preferred shareholders before paying any dividends to the common shareholders.

After paying $30,000 to the cumulative preferred shareholders and $8,000 to the other preferred shareholders, any additional dividends may be paid to the common shareholders.

(b) Noncumulative Preferred

If shares are noncumulative preferred, the dividends do not accumulate; if the board does not declare a dividend, rights to the dividends for the period omitted are gone forever. However, noncumulative preferred shareholders have priority to dividends over the common shareholders.

(c) Participating Preferred

Preferred shares may also be participating. A participating preferred shareholder can share in additional dividends; such shares entitle the holder to participate with the holders of common shares in any dividend distribution remaining after dividends are first paid on the preferred shares. The preferred shareholders would be paid their dividends, for example, $4 per share (the dividend preference), and then the common shareholders would be paid an equal amount, after which any additional dividends declared by the board of directors are distributed among the participating preferred and the common shareholders, so that the preferred shareholders "participate."

5. Convertible Shares

Convertible preferred shares are convertible into common shares at a stated ratio which is specified in the C/I and on the stock certificate.

6. Redeemable or Callable Shares

Redeemable or callable shares are issued by a corporation under the express provision that the corporation has the right to buy back the shares from the shareholders at some future time. The terms of the buy-back arrangement are specified in the C/I and on the certificate.

7. Treasury Shares

These are the corporation's own shares which have been issued to shareholders and then reacquired by the corporation. During the time the corporation holds its own reacquired shares, they are called treasury shares. See B.C.L.§102(a)(14).

8. Stock Warrants

A stock warrant is a certificate that gives its holder the right to subscribe for or purchase a given number of shares of the corporation at a stated price. They are also called "rights". They are usually issued in connection with the sale of other shares of stocks or bonds; they are transferable, have value, and can readily be sold on the market in the same manner as other securities.

9. Corporate Bonds

A bondholder is a creditor. B.C.L.§518 provides rules governing issuance of bonds; the consideration to be received shall be money or other property, tangible or intangible, or labor or services actually received by or performed for the corporation or for its benefit or in its formation or reorganization, or a combination thereof.

B.C.L.§518(c) specifically permits the C/I to grant bondholders the right to inspect the corporate books and records and the right to vote in the election of directors and on any other matters on which shareholders of the corporation may vote. Unsecured bondholders, usually called debentures, are unsecured creditors and rank equally with other general creditors. In order to protect the unsecured bondholders, debenture agreements frequently impose limitations upon the corporation's borrowing, payment of dividends, as well as its redemption and reacquisition of its own shares. Secured bondholders have the security of specific corporate property in addition to the general obligation of the corporation.

C. STOCK SUBSCRIPTIONS

Prospective shareholders may agree to buy shares of stock from the corporation. Such agreement (called a stock subscription) whether made before or after the corporation is formed, must be in writing and signed by the subscriber to be enforceable. B.C.L.§503(b). The person signing the stock subscription (the prospective shareholder) is the offeror; the corporation is the offeree to the contract to be formed.

1. Before the Corporation Is Formed

When a subscription is signed before the corporation is formed, it is an offer by the prospective shareholder to buy, which by statute, can not be revoked for a period of three months, unless consent of all other subscribers or the corporation is obtained. B.C.L.§503(a). The subscription may also be revoked if so permitted by its terms.

When the corporation is formed (usually within the three-month period) the subscription (offer) may be accepted by the board of directors at which time the subscription becomes a fully enforceable contract, enforceable by both the corporation and the subscriber. The pre-incorporation stock subscription is binding on the subscriber during the three-month period so that the corporation to be formed has sufficient time to come into existence and avail itself of the capital commitments agreed to by its subscribers.

2. After the Corporation Is Formed

A subscription signed after the corporation is formed is immediately available for acceptance by the corporation, and upon acceptance it becomes a fully binding contract.

A stock subscription executed after the corporation is formed is governed by general rules of contract law. The subscription is an offer to buy and is not binding until accepted by the offeree (the corporation); the offeror can revoke the offer anytime prior to acceptance. If the offer is accepted, an enforceable binding contract exists.

3. Liability Under Subscription Agreement

Payment under the subscription agreement shall be paid in full or in installments pursuant to the subscription, and as determined by the board of directors. B.C.L.§503(c). When full payment for the shares is made, the certificate for the shares may be issued marked "fully paid". B.C.L.§504(h). If full payment is not received, the certificate for the shares should not be issued. If payment of any installment or call for payment is not met, the corporation may sue for the money owed, or the corporation may declare a forfeiture of the subscription provided that payment has been demanded in writing and has not been received 30 days thereafter. See B.C.L.§503(d).

D. CONSIDERATION AND PAYMENT FOR SHARES

B.C.L.§504 is explicit in prescribing the nature and amount of consideration required for issuing shares.

1. Valid Consideration

B.C.L.§504(a) provides that consideration for issuance of shares shall consist of (1) money or (2) other property (tangible or intangible), or (3) labor or services actually received by or performed for the corporation, or a combination thereof. Note that only services actually rendered can be exchanged for issuance of shares, and future services is not adequate consideration; the acceptance of a promise to pay or other obligation (such as a note) for future payment is also not permitted. B.C.L.§504(b).

Determining the amount of consideration to be paid to the corporation for its shares will depend, in part, on whether the shares are par value or are no par value. The corporation may issue its par value shares for par value or for a greater amount, but not for less than par value. B.C.L.§504(c). When issued for par value, the amount received is accounted for on the corporation's books as Stated Capital. When more than par value is received, an amount equal to the par value of the shares issued is Stated Capital, and the excess is Capital Surplus which is also known as "Additional Paid In Capital", "Paid In Surplus", or "Premium Above Par". The concept of Surplus will be explained in a subsequent section of this Chapter.

Shares of the corporation may be issued for money, property (tangible or intangible), services actually rendered for the corporation, or any combination thereof. B.C.L.§504(a). With respect to the last two items, a valuation must be placed upon the property or the services. Normally the valuation is made by the board of directors, and in the absence of fraud, such valuation is conclusive. B.C.L.§504(a). Cancellation of a corporate debt is considered the equivalent of a cash payment for the amount of the debt.

Once the consideration has been paid in full, the subscriber becomes a shareholder entitled to all the rights and privileges of a shareholder including the right to receive a certificate to evidence such status. B.C.L.§504(i).

2. Improper Consideration—Liability for Shares

The subscriber for shares has the obligation to pay the unpaid portion of the subscription price, which shall not be less than the consideration for which such shares could be issued lawfully. B.C.L.§628(a). Thus, a subscriber who holds shares obtained by payment of less than the amount of the legal consideration may be held liable for the difference. However, an assignee or transferee of the shares or of the subscription for the shares, who takes in good faith and without knowledge or notice that the full consideration has not been paid, is not personally liable for any unpaid portion of the consideration. The transferor of the shares still remains liable. B.C.L.§628(b).

A corporation is said to have issued "watered" stock if it issues fully paid shares and has received consideration less than the par value of the shares, or if the corporation has not received the full agreed upon consideration. The liability of shareholders on "watered" stock is enforceable by the corporation.

The amount of the consideration depends upon the type of shares being issued. Par value shares may be issued for any price (not less than par value); the par value indicates the minimum price which the corporation must receive. No par value shares may be issued for any price as set by the board of directors (unless the C/I reserves such right to the shareholders).

3. Consideration for Treasury Shares*

Treasury shares are those which have been issued and subsequently reacquired by the corporation. Treasury shares are issued but not outstanding, in contrast to shares owned by shareholders which are deemed issued and outstanding.

Treasury shares, while owned by the corporation, may not be voted, no dividends may be paid upon them, and they do not have any preemptive rights.

B.C.L.§504(e) provides that treasury shares may be disposed of by the corporation on such terms and conditions as fixed from time to time by the board. They may be sold at less than par value, for future services, or a promissory note. Once treasury shares are sold, they are sold with full rights, so that a person purchasing treasury shares has full voting rights, dividend rights, and all other rights of a shareholder.

E. ISSUANCE OF SHARES

The corporation upon receiving the full consideration for the shares may issue a stock certificate representing the shares as being fully paid and nonassessable. B.C.L.§504(h)(i).

When a corporation is authorized to issue shares of more than one class, the front or back of the certificate of each class of stock must set forth a full statement of the designation, relative rights, preferences and limitations of each class of stock authorized to be issued, or must set forth that upon request, a shareholder may receive a full statement thereof. The face of the certificate must also state that the corporation is formed under the laws of the State of New York, the name

---

*See, case of Buffalo Forge Co. v. Ogden Corp., 555 F. Supp. 892 (1983), aff'd, 717 F. 2d 757 (2nd Cir. 1983).

of the person to whom the certificate is issued and the number of shares and the designation of the shares, if any, which the certificate represents. B.C.L.§508(c).

There is a difference between "Authorized Shares", "Issued Shares", and "Outstanding Shares".

"Authorized Shares" are those which the corporation is authorized to issue as stated in the C/I; there generally is no limit on the number of authorized shares, other than what is stated in the C/I.

"Issued Shares" are those which are issued by the corporation to shareholders; they are part of the authorized shares for which certificates have been issued. There is no specific percentage of authorized shares that must be issued. A corporation may issue one share or it may issue all of its authorized shares.

"Outstanding Shares" are those which are owned by the shareholders. Shares reacquired by the corporation are known as "Treasury Shares" which are authorized and issued, but not outstanding; these shares have been reacquired and are in the hands of the corporation. Therefore the number of issued shares does not always equal the number of outstanding shares.

Example:

> A corporate balance sheet might indicate that 100,000 common shares (no par value) have been authorized, 30,000 are issued and outstanding, and 10,000 are treasury shares. Following is an explanation of those items:
>
> If we were to examine the corporation's C/I on file with the Secretary of State, we would see that 100,000 shares of common stock (no par value) have been authorized.
>
> Outstanding shares are 30,000.
>
> Treasury shares are 10,000.
>
> The sum of the outstanding shares and the treasury shares will equal the issued shares. Therefore, in this case, 40,000 shares have been issued, 30,000 are issued and outstanding, and 10,000 are Treasury.

F. STATED CAPITAL

Stated Capital is used to describe the total amount of capital contributed by the shareholders. It is necessary to understand "Stated Capital", since it is a crucial item on the corporation's Balance Sheet, which must be referred to before various decisions are made. The definition and description of "Stated Capital" is contained in B.C.L.§102(a)(12) and §506.

Upon issuance by a corporation of shares with par value, the consideration received shall constitute Stated Capital to the extent of the par value. B.C.L.§506(a). Upon issuance of shares without par value, the entire consideration shall constitute Stated Capital, unless the board of directors within 60 days after issue, allocates to surplus a portion, but not all, of the consideration received for such shares. B.C.L.§506(b). There is no restriction as to which portion must be retained in Stated Capital; however, if the shares have a preference in liquidation, the preferential amount must be allocated to Stated Capital.

Example:
>   *Assume a corporation has $100 par value shares:*
>
>   *(1) If the shares are issued at par ($100 per share), the full par value of $100 is "Stated Capital".*
>
>   *(2) If the shares are issued at a price above par (e.g., $125 per share), the par value of $100 is "Stated Capital", and the Premium Above Par or Capital Surplus is $25 per share.*
>
>   *(3) If the shares are issued below par (e.g., at $90 per share), the full par value of $100 is Stated Capital. Such stock is referred to as "watered" and, of course, illegally issued.*
>
>   *(4) Assume a corporation has no par value shares: The shares are sold for $110 per share. The entire consideration paid of $110 per share constitutes "Stated Capital". The board of directors, if it acts within 60 days, may by resolution allocate a portion of the consideration received to Surplus.*

Generally, Stated Capital means the (1) number of par value shares issued multiplied by the par value, plus (2) the full consideration received for no par value shares, except such part allocated to Surplus (in a manner permitted by law), and (3) such amounts that have been transferred to Stated Capital. See B.C.L.§102(a)(12) and §506. Once the amount of Stated Capital has been determined, there are strict limitations on withdrawing or encroaching upon it. Since shares cannot be issued for less than par value, or for less than the price fixed by the board of directors in the case of no par value stock, the Stated Capital requirements must be satisfied. B.C.L.§516(a) specifies the specific times when the Board of Directors has the authority to reduce Stated Capital. Any other reduction of Stated Capital would require an Amendment to the Certificate of Incorporation. If the Board of Directors has the authority to reduce Stated Capital in the limited situations contained in B.C.L.§516(a), the amount of the reduction must be disclosed to the shareholders on the next financial statement, or within six months of the reduction. The courts view "Stated Capital" as a trust fund or cushion for the protection of creditors and shareholders on liquidation. Therefore, if there is a reduction in Stated Capital, Stated Capital must still be at least the Par Value of the Issued and Outstanding shares, plus the liquidation preference of any shares having liquidation preferences. See B.C.L.§516(b).

Stated Capital may be increased by resolution of the board by transfer of all or part of Surplus to Stated Capital. B.C.L.§506(c).

G. SURPLUS

The term Surplus is a major item that must be investigated on a corporation's balance sheet any time prior to the corporation paying a dividend and prior to the corporation repurchasing its own shares of stock, as payments for these items may be made only from "Surplus".

Surplus is defined as the excess of net assets over "Stated Capital". B.C.L.§102(a)(13). Net assets means the amount by which total assets exceed total liabilities. B.C.L.§102(a)(9). Thus, the following relationships might be considered:

Net Assets = Assets − Liabilities
Assets = Liabilities + Stated Capital + Surplus
Surplus = Net Assets − Stated Capital
Therefore, Surplus = Assets − Liabilities − Stated Capital.

The A.I.C.P.A. has been attempting to abolish the term "Surplus" from its literature and balance sheets; therefore, some of the current graduates and students in accounting may not be familiar with such term. However, it is a very important legal concept as the B.C.L., the Model Act and other statutes use the term "Surplus" and its components as having very important legal significance.

There are several components of Surplus: Capital Surplus, Earned Surplus, and Revaluation Surplus. "Capital Surplus" may also be known as "Additional Paid In Capital", "Paid In Surplus", or the "Premium Above Par". "Earned Surplus" may be referred to as "Retained Earnings". There is also a third source of surplus, known as "Revaluation Surplus", which will be explained in the next sections.

In New York State, a dividend may be legally declared and paid only if there are sufficient amounts in Surplus (any of the components of Surplus or any combination of Surplus). Likewise, if a corporation were to purchase its own shares of stock, that purchase could legally be made only if there were sufficient amounts in Surplus.

1. Capital Surplus

Capital Surplus may be created at the outset by issuing par value shares for more than par value (allocating the par value to Stated Capital and the excess or premium to Capital Surplus), and in addition by allocating part of the consideration received for no par value shares to Capital Surplus, with the balance allocated to Stated Capital. B.C.L.§506(b).

2. Earned Surplus

"Earned Surplus" is defined as "the portion of the surplus that represents net earnings, gains or profits, after deduction of all losses, that have not been distributed to the shareholders as dividends, or transferred to stated capital or capital surplus, or applied to other purposes permitted by law. . . ." B.C.L.§102(a)(6). Earned surplus may also be known as Retained Earnings. It is the most common known source of Surplus; it is generally the source for payment of dividends, and if dividends are paid or distributed from a source other than Earned Surplus, the dividend shall be accompanied by a written notice disclosing the source and its affect on the several components of Surplus. See B.C.L.§510(c). When it is necessary for a corporation to determine the amount of Earned Surplus and Capital Surplus, the rules contained in B.C.L.§517 apply.

3. Revaluation Surplus

Surplus may also consist of Revaluation Surplus, which is the unrealized appreciation of fixed assets, derived from the realistic reappraisal of the corporation's fixed assets. See the case of Randall v. Bailey (Case #9) where Revaluation Surplus has been determined as a legal source for the payment of dividends in New York State. Although the theory of Revaluation Surplus has not been adopted by the A.I.C.P.A. nor by all other states, it is still determined to be a legal source of Surplus in N.Y.S.

4. Examples of Surplus on a Corporation's Balance Sheet

To further illustrate and explain "Surplus" the following example is presented: The A-1 Fan Corp. was formed on January 1, 1985; the corporation was authorized to issue 1,000 shares of $100 par value preferred shares, and 25,000 no par value common shares. One month after its formation, the corporation issued 300 shares of the $100 par value preferred shares at $110 per share for cash ($33,000), and 4,000 shares of no par value common shares for property as follows: 1,500 shares for a factory valued at $90,000; 1,000 shares for a patent valued at $60,000; 200 shares for a Truck valued at $12,000; 1,200 shares for machinery valued at $72,000; and 100 shares for $6,000 cash. The total consideration received for the 4,000 no par value shares was $240,000. There are unpaid liabilities for organization expense of $15,000. The financial position of the A-1 Fan Corp. appears as follows on February 1, 1985:

Assets		Liabilities		
		Organization Expense Payable	$ 15,000	
		Total Liabilities		$ 15,000
		Stated Capital		
Cash	$ 39,000	Preferred Shares:		
Machinery	72,000	($100 Par Value; 1,000 shares authorized)		
Truck	12,000	300 shares Issued and Outstanding	$ 30,000	
Patent	60,000	Common Shares: (no par value; 25,000 shares authorized) 4,000 shares Issued and Outstanding	$240,000	
Real Property (factory)	90,000	Total Stated Capital		270,000
		[Surplus]		[12,000]
Total Assets	$273,000	Total		$273,000

The corporation's assets are less than Stated Capital and Liabilities combined; it has a deficit of $12,000, which is indicated by a negative Surplus.

Assume that during the next several months, it has done considerable business, sold some of its products, and purchased merchandise on credit.

It has not issued any additional shares. Therefore, A-1 Fan Corp.'s Balance Sheet as of November 1, 1985 may appear to be as follows:

Assets		Liabilities		
Cash	$ 10,000	Amounts Due to Creditors for purchase of materials	$ 75,000	
Machinery	72,000			
Truck	12,000			
Patent	60,000	Total Liabilities		$ 75,000
Real Property (factory)	90,000	*Stated Capital*		
		Preferred Shares: ($100 Par Value; 1,000 shares authorized) 300 shares Issued and Outstanding	$ 30,000	
Inventory on hand	100,000			
Accounts Receivable	40,000			
		Common Shares: (no par value; 25,000 shares authorized) 4,000 shares Issued and Outstanding	$240,000	
		Total Stated Capital		270,000
		Surplus		39,000
Total Assets	$384,000	Total		$384,000

The corporation's assets have increased to $384,00; it has less cash, but now has the assets of inventory and accounts receivable.

Stated Capital is still $270,000; there are liabilities owed to creditors of $75,000. Its assets are in excess of its capital and liabilities by $39,000; thus, it has a surplus of $39,000, defined as net assets less capital, which is obtained by subtraction.

It will be noted that when the corporation issued the 300 shares of $100 par value stock at $110 per share, this $10 premium above par ($3,000) in reality should be accounted for as Capital Surplus. Therefore, Surplus as of November 1, 1985 is composed of:

Capital Surplus or Paid-in Surplus	$ 3,000
Earned Surplus	$36,000
Total Surplus	$39,000

In addition, consider the effect of the corporation's realistic reappraisal of its Real Property to be in reality $190,000 (based upon a realistic reappraisal). In such case, Total Assets would then be $484,000; Surplus would then be composed of:

Capital Surplus	$ 3,000
Earned Surplus	$ 36,000
Revaluation Surplus	$100,000
Total Surplus	$139,000

The determination whether at any particular time there is a Surplus and its amount has an important bearing on the legality of the corporation's declaration and payment of dividends and upon the legality of the corporation's repurchase of its own shares, as neither of these can be done when the corporation does not have Surplus sufficient for the transaction.

In the above example, the corporation could legally declare and pay a dividend of up to $39,000, provided it had sufficient cash. It will be noted the corporation only has cash of $10,000; therefore may only pay cash dividends up to $10,000 even though Surplus is in excess of that amount. After the Revaluation Surplus, the corporation could legally declare and pay a dividend of up to $139,000 provided it had sufficient cash. We will see there are additional considerations in declaring dividends which will be discussed in Chapter 6.

H. IMPROPER ISSUE OF SHARES

Shares of stock are improperly issued when (1) the consideration received has been fraudulently overvalued; (2) the agreed consideration has not been received; or (3) the full par value has not been received for par value shares.

1. Remedies Available*

If there is fraudulent overvaluation, the remedies for any fraudulent transaction could apply, to wit: (1) The corporation could rescind the transaction and recover the shares (provided they had not been resold to a bona fide purchaser for value); (2) The directors could be held liable for fraud, the damages being the amount by which the property received had been overvalued in which case the corporation could sue to recover the damages, and most probably, a shareholder's derivative action for the benefit of the corporation could be brought. (See Chapter 9); (3) The shareholders involved in the fraud most probably could also be liable for damages.

If the corporation has not received the agreed-upon consideration and the directors have improperly issued the shares as "fully paid", such issuance is contrary to law; in such case, the corporation or its successor in interest (e.g., a receiver or trustee in bankruptcy) may sue the subscriber to enforce the balance of the subscription agreement. Even if the subscriber resells the shares to a bona fide purchaser, the subscriber's liability on the contract continues until the stock has been fully paid. B.C.L.§628.

If the corporation sells par value shares for less than par value, the stock has been "watered". The corporation could rescind the transaction; this right, of course, would be lost if the shares were resold to a bona fide purchaser. The directors should be held personally liable for waste of corporate assets. B.C.L.§720. In addition, pursuant to an interpretation of B.C.L.§628, the shareholder should be personally responsible for the difference between par value and the price paid.

Shareholders who contract with the corporation for the purchase of shares are obligated to pay to the corporation the full consideration of the shares, which must be at least the par value. B.C.L.§504. Such purchases do *not* render the transaction void, but such transactions are voidable.**

---

*See Henn, *Laws of Corporations* 171 et. al. for different theories.
**See, case of S. & S. Realty Corp. v. Kleer-Vu Ind. Inc., 575 F.2d 1040, 1042 (2nd Cir. 1978) (involving promise by president to make future payments); in Bronsell v. Commissioner, 317 F.2d 61(1963), the court held that watered stock is *not* void; it's still stock.

CASE 7
FRANKOWSKI v. PALERMO et al
(App. Div., 4th Dep't, 47 A.D.2d 579, 363 N.Y.S.2d 159) (1975)

MEMORANDUM:

A cash purchase of par value stock cannot be made under §504 of the B.C.L. for less than par value (Stone v. Young, 210 A.D. 303, 206 N.Y.S. 95; 2 White, New York Corp. 13th Ed., §504.02). In determining whether full par value has been paid for the issuance of par value stock, the cancellation of a corporation debt is considered equivalent to a cash payment in the amount of the debt (Veeder v. Mudgett, 95 N.Y. 295, 315; 2 White, New York Corp.§504.03). At a meeting of the Board of Directors on April 27, 1972 attended by defendants Palermo and Wylegala, the minutes signed by the secretary of D & M Fish Shoppe, Inc. state that a discussion was had concerning the payment of certain loans made by president Palermo to the corporation and a resolution was passed that the corporation issue to Palermo sufficient stock at the present book value to convert Palermo's loan on the books of the corporation into a capital investment. The minutes further state that it was determined that 44 shares of the stock of the corporation be issued to Palermo and that the sum of $2,726 be added to the capital of the corporation as a capital investment of Palermo. The financial report incorporated into the minutes of the April 27 meeting lists total loans from Palermo to the corporation in the amount of $2,726. It appears from the minutes of the April 27 meeting that 44 shares of the stock of the corporation of the par value of $100 were issued to Palermo in exchange for the cancellation of the corporate debt in the amount of $2,726. Thus the minutes recite that Palermo paid $1,674 less than the $4,400 value of the 44 shares of $100 par value issued to him. Shares issued for less than par value are voidable at the option of other shareholders absent the intervention of third party rights (B. & C. Electrical Constr. Co. v. Owen, 176 A.D.399, 163 N.Y.S. 31, affd, 227 N.Y. 569). . . . Respondents Palermo, et al. do not challenge such consideration as recited in the minutes and in such circumstance they should be bound by the prima facie provisions of §624(g) of the B.C.L. Plaintiff is entitled to judgment directing cancellation of the shares issued to defendant Palermo at less than par value, which judgment should provide that: (1) The action of the Board of Directors in issuing 44 shares of $100 par value stock in D & M Fish Shoppe, Inc. in consideration of the cancellation of the corporate debt to Palermo in the amount of $2,726 be nullified. (2) The directors of the corporation be ordered to record in the books of the corporation the cancellation of the 44 shares. (3) The Board of Directors be directed to call a stockholders meeting forthwith and no new shares be issued by the directors prior to such meeting.

CASE 8
LEWIS v. DANSKER
(U.S. Dist. Court, S.D.N.Y., 357 F. Supp. 636) (1973)

LASKER, District Judge.

This is a stockholder's derivative action brought under The Securities Exchange Act of 1934. Plaintiff alleges that defendants procured shareholder approval at a special meeting of the stockholders for various corporate acts through the use of a proxy statement. . . .

• • • •

Here plaintiff moves for summary judgment on the ground that the third corporate proposal—the outright sale of 15,000 IFC shares to the Danskers evidenced by a series of non-interest bearing promissory notes—is violative of §504 of the N.Y.B.C.L. We agree.

Section 504(b) states in pertinent part:

"(b) Neither obligations of the subscriber for future payments nor future services shall constitute payment or part payment for shares of a corporation."

It is clear the prohibition of section (b) was violated since the promissory notes constitute "obligations of the subscriber for future payments." If there were any doubt about this construction of the statute it is quickly dispelled by an examination of the legislative background of §504 (as set forth in 6 McKinney's. . .) It is indicated there that Para. (b) is derived from Model Business Corp. Act §18 (sic §19) and is consistent with the old Penal Law §664(3). §664(3) of the Penal Law made it a misdemeanor for a director to authorize the corporation. . . .

> "To discount or receive any note or other evidence of debt in payment of an installment of capital stock actually called in, and required to be paid, or with intent to provide the means of making such payment;" [Note: See N.Y. Penal Law §190.35(1)(c)].

See also 2 White on New York Corporations 504.03 (1972) "A mere promise to pay money in the future, such as a promissory note . . . does not constitute payment or part payment for shares of a corporation although it may otherwise constitute good consideration to sustain a contract at common law."

The Danskers would have us limit the prohibition of §504 to newly formed corporations which, they argue, are more in danger of becoming insolvent than established businesses. No authority or legislative material is cited to support this interpretation. On the contrary, the broad reach of the statute suggests that creditors, the public and other stockholders were to be protected at all times during the life of the corporation.

Defendant Grunebaum argues there was no violation of §504 because the stockholders ratified the proposal. However, it is hornbook law that stockholders may only ratify and render valid acts done or authorized by the board of directors, but which were beyond the powers of the directors, *if the stockholders themselves could have authorized such acts.* See Fletcher on Corporations, §764. Since the sale of the stock here was expressly prohibited by §504 the "ratification" was, therefore, ineffective. Furthermore, since the statute is designed, in part, to protect creditors of the corporation, it would defeat its purposes to allow the stockholders to ratify the proposal.

The cases cited by defendant Grunebaum, Kimmel Sales Corp. v. Lauster, 167 Misc. 514, 4 N.Y.S.2d 88 (Sup. Ct., Monroe Co. 1938) and Usher v. Schenectady Mason Supply Corp., 278 A.D. 610, 102 N.Y.S.2d 93 (3d Dept. 1951), though running counter to the principle referred to above, presented exceptional circumstances not here present. In Kimmel the plaintiff, a stockholder, sought to cancel shares of issuance of stock to the defendants on the ground that the shares were transferred for inadequate consideration, in violation of §69 of the Stock Corporation Law, the predecessor statute to §504. The court did not disturb the transaction "[i]nasmuch as [the payments of monies paid out of the corporate treasury] represented personal liabilities of [Kimmel's] and were acquiesced in by all of the stockholders of the corporation and no rights of creditors [were] involved. . . ." (Kimmel, 4 N.Y.S.2d at 93). Here the picture is altogether different. Although the record does not indicate whether IFC had creditors, it can safely be assumed it does since it is a large public corporation. Moreover, defendants have admitted that there were dissenting shareholders.

• • • •

CASE 9
RANDALL v. BAILEY
(Court of Appeals of New York, 288 N.Y. 280) (1942)

CONWAY, J. The Plaintiff, as trustee, seeks in this action to recover from directors and executors of deceased directors dividends declared and paid between 1928 and 1932, alleging that they were paid from capital in violation of §58 of the Stock Corporation Law. [Presently B.C.L.§510].

The corporation involved is the Bush Terminal Company, hereinafter called Terminal, which was organized in 1902. It owns and operates a great ocean terminal. The land in Brooklyn which it and its wholly owned subsidiary, Bush Terminal Buildings Company, hereinafter called Buildings, purchased between 1902 and 1905, increased in value with the passing years. Until 1915 Terminal and Buildings carried that land at its original cost. In 1915 and again in 1919 they committed to their books a portion of the increase in value of that land. It is not since been increased. The trial court found that its value during the years 1928 to 1932 was greater than the value to which it had been increased upon the corporate books. . . . The question presented, therefore, is solely one of law and involves the construction of §58 of the Stock Corp. Law. We are concerned only with the legislative prohibition as evidenced in §58 as enacted in 1923. If the directors of Terminal were permitted to include among the corporate assets the value of the land at the amount at which it was valued on the books from 1919 onward there was a surplus for the payment of dividends and no recovery may be had in this action. If it must be carried at cost then the directors unjustifiably declared and paid the dividends which plaintiff seeks to recover. The question presented, therefore, is, may unrealized appreciation in value of fixed assets held for use in carrying on a corporate enterprise be taken into consideration by directors in determining whether a corporate surplus exists from which cash dividends may be paid to stockholders.

• • • •

The Legislature having declared that dividends may be paid when there is no impairment of capital or capital stock caused thereby and when the value of the corporate assets remaining after the payment of such dividends is at least equal to the aggregate amount of its debts and liabilities including capital or capital stock as the case may be (Stock Corp. Law §58), in other words from its surplus, our inquiry turns to the question whether surplus may consist of increases resulting from a revaluation of fixed assets. Surplus has been well defined as follows in Edwards v. Douglas ([Brandeis, J.] 269 U.S. 204, 214): "The word 'surplus' is a term commonly employed in corporate finance and accounting to designate an account on corporate books. . . . The surplus account represents the net assets of a corporation in excess of all liabilities including its capital stock. This surplus may be 'paid-in surplus', as where the stock is issued at a price above par. It may be 'earned surplus', as where it was derived wholly from undistributed profits. Or it may, among other things, represent the increase in valuation of land or other assets made upon a revaluation of the company's fixed property. See La Bell Iron Works v. United States 256 U.S. 377, 385."

Discussion Questions:

What is Surplus? What is Revaluation Surplus?
Note: For full discussion and explanation of Revaluation Surplus read the opinion of the lower court, 23 N.Y.S.2d 173 (Sup. Ct. N.Y. 1940).

PROBLEMS

24. Davis Corp. issued 7% cumulative $100 par value preferred stock, and $50 par value common stock. In order to induce investors to buy the preferred stock, Davis Corp. offered one free share of common stock to go along with each share of preferred purchased, so that for $100 one could acquire one share of preferred plus one share of common. Some common shareholders claimed this sales device was improper. Was it? Explain.

25. X Corp. issued to shareholders 10,000 shares of $100 par value 8% cumulative preferred stock and 10,000 shares of no-par value common stock. X Corp. commenced business in January 1978. It paid no dividends in 1978. In 1979, it declared a dividend of $8 per share on the preferred stock and $8 per share on the common. X Corp. had sufficient earned surplus and sufficient cash for payment of said dividends. Some preferred shareholders still claimed this was illegal. Were the dividends proper? Discuss.

26. (a) Jim was approached by Sam who was acting as a promoter for ALPHA CORP. a corporation which was to be organized; Jim orally promised and agreed to purchase 10% of the authorized capital which was to consist of 100 shares of $100 par value stock. Based on Jim's promise, which was publicized by Sam, the other 90% of the capital was immediately subscribed for by other investors. Jim later repudiates his agreement and refuses to purchase the 100 shares; ALPHA CORP. is formed, and now institutes an action for breach of contract against Jim. Judgment for whom? Discuss?

(b) Assume Jim's agreement is in writing. May Jim revoke his agreement to purchase the shares? If yes, under what conditions? Discuss.

27. Alice, Betty, and Carole organized a corporation, Suma Corp. which had been authorized to issue 10,000 shares of stock, each share having a par value of $100. At the first Board of Directors meeting, Alice submitted an offer to purchase 1,000 shares by paying $60,000 in cash and by transferring a patent which was worth $80,000. The offer was accepted.

At the same time Betty offered to purchase 1,000 shares for the sum of $100,000, payable $90,000 in cash and the balance by executing her promissory note for $10,000 payable in one year and bearing interest at the rate of 9% per annum. This offer was accepted.

Carole, who was an accountant, offered to purchase 1,000 shares and pay for them by paying $10,000 in cash, and by rendering all the necessary accounting services on behalf of Suma Corp. during the first five (5) years of its existence. This offer was also accepted.

A month later, Alice paid the $60,000 and transferred the patent, Betty paid the $90,000 and delivered her promissory note for $10,000, and Carole paid the $10,000, and started setting up the accounting books. Suma Corp. issues 1,000 shares to Alice, 1,000 shares to Betty, and 1,000 shares to Carole. The other shareholders complain, claiming the consideration for the shares was inadequate. Indicate in each of these instances whether the shares were properly issued, and explain.

28. Alpha Corp. is a corporation organized in N.Y.S. Pursuant to its Certificate of Incorporation which was filed on June 1, 1980, it is authorized to issue 10,000 shares of common stock $5 par value. The following transactions have occurred:

(a) Jones, a promoter has entered into a lease on May 15, 1980 in the name of Alpha Corp. with a landlord, Market Corp., for business premises. Alpha Corp. later objects to the lease. The landlord, Market Corp. sues for the amounts due under the lease. Who is responsible under this lease?

(b) On May 15, 1980, Jones, the promoter hired an accountant for Alpha Corp., and has agreed that the accountant will receive 1,000 shares of stock. The corporation later refuses to issue the stock. What are the accountant's rights?

(c) On May 15, 1980, Mary has signed a subscription to purchase 1,000 shares of stock at $5 per share. Alpha Corp. refuses to issue the 1,000 shares. What are Mary's rights?

On July 1, 1980, the following transactions are entered into:

(d) the sale of 5,000 shares of stock to Barbara for $20,000; Barbara pays the $20,000.

(e) the sale of 1,000 shares of stock to Carol for $8,000. Carol pays $5,000 and gives a promissory note for $3,000 which she never pays.

(f) the sale of 1,000 shares of stock to David in return for David's promise to perform legal services for the corporation.

(g) the sale of 1,000 shares of stock to Frank in return for Frank's delivery of a truck worth $4,000.

All of the above shares of stock in (d), (e), (f), and (g) are issued. Explain and discuss the legal significance of each of these above transactions.

**29. Plimpton subscribed to 1,000 shares of $1 par value Common Stock of the Billiard Ball Corporation at $10 a share. Plimpton paid $1,000 upon the incorporation of Billiard and paid an additional $4,000 at a later time. The corporation subsequently became insolvent and is now in bankruptcy. The creditors of the corporation are seeking to hold Plimpton personally liable.

Discuss. [Adapted from A.I.C.P.A.-16-May 1980].

**30. Franklin Corporation was incorporated in 1970. At that time 150,000 shares of common stock with a par value of $10 per share were sold. Three of the original subscribers who were also the promoters and first directors of the corporation purchased 50,000 shares at $5 per share. The offering price to the public was $15 per share. The three promoters in question sold their shares for $8 per share after they were defeated for re-election as directors three years later. The corporation is now in bankruptcy. All other creditors with the exception of Mabry, Franklin's major creditor, have settled their claims. Mabry had loaned the corporation $500,000. At the time of the loan, Mabry insisted upon audited financial statements before he would extend credit. This was done and the audited financial statements clearly indicated that par value had not been paid by the promoters upon their purchase of the 50,000 shares.

(a) What rights does Mabry have against the three promoters?

(b) What rights does Mabry have against the purchasers who bought from the promoters? [AICPA-4b-Nov. 1976].

**31. Grace Dawson was actively engaged in the promotion of a new corporation to be known as Multifashion Frocks, Inc. On January 3, 1978, she obtained written commitments for the purchase of shares totaling $600,000 from a group of 15 potential investors. She was also assured orally that she would be engaged as the president of the corporation upon the commencement of business. Helen Banks was the principal investor, having subscribed to $300,000 of the shares of Multifashion. Dawson immediately began work on the incorporation of Multifashion, made several contracts for and on its behalf, and made cash expenditures of $1,000 in accomplishing these goals. On February 15, 1978, Banks died and her estate has declined to honor the commitment to purchase the Multifashion shares. At the first shareholders' meeting on April 5, 1978, the day the corporation came into existence, the shareholders elected a board of directors. With shareholder approval, the board took the following actions:
  1. Adopted some but not all of the contracts made by Dawson.
  2. Authorized legal action, if necessary, against the Estate of Banks to enforce Banks' $300,000 commitment.
  3. Declined to engage Dawson in any capacity (Banks had been her main supporter).
  4. Agreed to pay Dawson $750 for those cash outlays which were deemed to be directly beneficial to the corporation and rejected the balance.

Discuss the legal implications of each of the above actions taken by the board of directors of Multifashion. [AICPA-4a-May 1978].

**32. Fairfax Corporation was created on April 2, 1979. Its initial capitalization consisted of (1) 5,000 shares of no-par voting common stock which it sold to subscribers at $20 a share; (2) 1,000 shares of cumulative, non-voting, 8% $100 par value, preferred stock which it sold at $100 per share; and (3) 2,000 20-year debentures with a face value of $1,000 each, interest at 10%, which it sold at a 5% discount. All securities were sold for cash during April 1979. At a meeting on May 15, 1979, the board of directors voted to increase the capital surplus of the corporation by transferring to capital surplus $19 per share of the $20 per share originally credited to stated capital upon the sale of the no-par common stock.

What is the stated capital of the Fairfax Corporation as of May 16, 1979? [AICPA-2a-Nov. 1979].

CHAPTER 6

Shareholders' Rights Regarding Financial Structure of the Corporation

As a general rule, the B.C.L. provides that shareholders have certain rights: to receive a stock certificate; to receive information; to inspect the books and records of the corporation; to attend shareholders' meetings; to vote for directors and for various extraordinary matters such as dissolution, merger, or amendment of the C/I; to share in profits when dividends are declared; to share in the net assets upon dissolution of the corporation after all creditors have been paid; to subscribe for and purchase additional shares of stock of the corporation (called the preemptive right); and to institute shareholders' derivative suits for the benefit of the corporation. Under certain circumstances shareholders may also have a right of appraisal to require the corporation to purchase the shares back from the shareholder(s). Some of these rights are restricted, limited, or expanded by statute or by the C/I; some may apply to only certain classification of shareholders.

Shareholders' voting rights will be discussed in Chapter 7; shareholders' derivative suits are discussed in Chapter 9. Shareholders' rights regarding the financial structure will be covered in subsequent sections of this Chapter.

A. THE STOCK CERTIFICATE

Upon payment of the full consideration, the subscriber is entitled to all the rights and privileges of a shareholder, including the right to have a certificate issued by the corporation, representing the shares.B.C.L.§504(i).

1. The Form of the Stock Certificate

The stock certificate is usually a printed form which certifies the named person(s) as the owner of a stated number of shares, and indicates that the corporation is formed pursuant to the laws of the particular state. The certificate must be signed by two corporate officers. See B.C.L.§508(a) for details. If the corporation is authorized to issue shares of different classes, the front or back of the certificate must state the class and the relative rights and limitations of each class or state that the corporation will supply to the holder a full statement of such rights. B.C.L.§508(b). If the shares are par value, the par value is stated; if no par value, a statement indicating same.

2. The Right to a Stock Certificate

A shareholder of record has the right to receive a stock certificate and the corporation must issue it upon demand. A certificate of stock is physical evidence that the corporation recognizes a certain person as being a shareholder who has the rights of a shareholder. Even if shares of stock are not issued, the person is still a shareholder with all rights of a shareholder.*

A corporation may now also issue uncertificated shares; in such case, the corporation will send a written notice to the registered owner, providing the required information (that would be contained on the Certificate). The rights and obligations of holders of uncertificated shares are the same as those of holders of certificated shares (unless otherwise provided). See B.C.L.§508(f). See also U.C.C.§8–102(1)(b) for definition of an uncertificated security. It should be noted that as of this writing, no cases have been decided on the legal aspect of uncertificated shares, and a noted authority strongly urges against its use.**

3. Transferring the Certificate***

A shareholder has the right to transfer the certificate by sale, gift, or pledge just as one has the right to transfer any other property.

Unless otherwise stated in the Certificate of Incorporation (C/I), shares of stock are freely transferable. According to B.C.L.§508(d) shares shall be transferable in the manner provided by law and as per the corporation's by-laws. The statutory rules applicable to transfer of securities are contained in Article 8 of the Uniform Commercial Code, relating to Investment Securities. Article 8 applies not only to shares but also to bonds, debentures, and voting trust certificates. Transfer of securities is also regulated by the Securities and Exchange Commission (S.E.C.) if the securities are publicly held.

A share of stock is generally transferred by an indorsement and delivery of the certificate of stock.

4. Indorsement of the Certificate

The certificate generally provides a form on the back of it, for use to transfer the shares by written indorsement with space for the signature(s) of the owner(s) (the transferor), and space for filling in the name of the new owner (the transferee). An indorsement may be "in blank" or "special". An indorsement "in blank" does not specify to whom it is being transferred; a "special" indorsement names the person to whom the certificate is to be transferred. Transfers are completed by delivery after all necessary indorsements.

If a certificate is stolen and the owner's indorsement is forged, the owner may recover the certificate from anyone who has possession of it, including a bona fide purchaser for value.

The owner of a certificate who claims it has been lost, stolen, or destroyed is entitled to receive from the corporation a new certificate upon filing with the corporation an indemnity bond. See B.C.L.§508(e). The indemnity bond protects the corporation against the possibility that a bona fide purchaser may also present the old certificate to the corporation with a valid indorsement of the former owner; if this should occur, such purchaser would be entitled to a new certificate also,

---

*See, *Rapaport v. Jileen Security,* 110 A.D.2d 639, 487 N.Y.S.2d 376(1985).
**See, Israels, *On Corporate Practice,* at 116–117 (4th ed. 1983).
***See, generally, *Encyclopedia of Corporate Minutes, Meetings and Resolutions,* Chapters 21 and 22 (3rd ed. 1986).

or if "overissue" would result, its market value. The idemnity bond provides protection to the corporation that the capital will not be imparied in case there is a double issue. U.C.C.§8–405; B.C.L.§508(e).

5. Restrictions on Transfer of Shares

Unless otherwise stated in the C/I, shares of stock are freely transferable. However, the C/I may impose reasonable restrictions upon a shareholder's right to transfer the shares. The shareholders agreement may provide restrictions on transfer of the shares by use of a Buy-Sell provision. Restrictions should be definite, clear and reasonable to ensure their enforcement.* Any absolute prohibition on the transfer of shares or a restriction that requires consent of all directors or the shareholders (to transfer shares) would be held invalid; any unreasonable transfer restrictions will be declared invalid and void as against public policy. Notice of any restriction must appear on each stock certificate issued in order to be effective against a bona fide purchaser. U.C.C.§8–204. The restriction need not be set forth in full on the certificate, but notice of the restriction must be indicated.

6. The Buy-Sell Agreement

Shareholders in a closely-held corporation generally desire veto power over admission of new shareholders, and also to provide for continuation of the control structure in the event one of the shareholders dies or decides to sell or transfer the shares. Shares of stock in a closely held corporation are not readily marketable and are quite difficult to value. However, provision may be made in a Buy-Sell Agreement between the shareholders to provide a ready market for the shares (which would be the other shareholders and/or the corporation) and a method of valuation. A Buy-Sell provision is usually contained within the Shareholders Agreement.

Buy-Sell agreements usually include a "right of first refusal", so that a shareholder must offer his or her shares to the corporation and/or the other shareholders before selling the shares to an outsider, and the shares so offered must be purchased by the corporation or the other shareholders at an agreed-upon price. The typical buy-sell agreement is usually considered by New York courts to be a "reasonable" restraint on alienation and is therefore enforceable.

The price of the shares would be based upon the valuation, as provided for in the agreement. The buy-sell agreement ordinarily provides for the manner of payment of the shares, and may provide in advance for a specific payment plan, which may extend over several years, so there is no immediate drain on the corporation's liquid assets.

It may be advisable for the corporation to obtain life insurance on the shareholders' lives, payable to the corporation, so that if a shareholder dies, the corporation will have sufficient funds with which to purchase the shares from the estate, as this is a repurchase of the corporation's own stock, which may be made only out of "Surplus" (B.C.L.§513). Without available insurance proceeds, the corporation might not have sufficient resources to legally make the purchase possible.

7. Shares are NOT Corporate Assets

Share ownership should *not* be confused with ownership of the corporate assets. Even if all the assets of the corporation are real property, the shares of stock are still personal property. An agreement to sell all of the shares of stock is *not* the same as an agreement to sell all of the cor-

---

*See case of *Allen v. Biltmore Tissue Corp.*, 2 N.Y.2d 534, 161 N.Y.S.2d 418(1957). See, O'Neal & Thompson, *Close Corporations* (3rd ed. 1986), particularly Chapter 7 for thorough explanation.

porate assets, and likewise, an agreement to sell the corporation's assets is *not* the same as selling shares of stock.* It has been held that an agreement to transfer stock in a close corporation may be enforced by specific performance, even if the corporate assets have been destroyed by fire.**

8. The Stock Record Book

A N.Y. corporation is required to keep at its office (or at the office of its transfer agent) in the state a record containing the names and addresses of all shareholders, the number and class of shares, and the dates when they became owners of record. B.C.L.§624(a).

When shares are transferred, an entry should be made in the stock record book to record the transfer, indicating the new owner, and a new certificate should be issued. The owner of shares is entitled to registration of the certificate in order to vote, to receive dividends, notices, and periodic reports from the corporation.

In a small corporation, the secretary of the corporation usually handles all transfers of shares; large corporations frequently employ transfer agents,*** which generally are banks; the transfer agent transfers the shares, cancels old certificates, issues new ones, keeps up-to-date lists of the names and addresses of the shareholders, distributes dividends, and mails out notices to the shareholders.

B. SHARE REDEMPTION AND REACQUISITION

There are statutory restrictions upon redemption and reacquisition of shares; a corporation may not purchase or redeem its redeemable shares when it is insolvent or when the redemption or purchase would render it insolvent; in addition, the purchase or redemption must be made from Surplus. B.C.L.§513(a).

If a corporation purchases its own shares when it does not have sufficient surplus, or when it is insolvent, such purchase would be a violation and the directors could be held guilty of a crime.† If the corporation merely promises to purchase its shares, such promise is not illegal because of the possibility there may or may not be sufficient surplus at the time of performance; the statute is violated if payments are made when the corporation does not have sufficient surplus, whereby payment for the shares would be made out of capital which is not permitted.

A corporation may purchase its own shares out of Stated Capital only under three very specific instances: to eliminate fractions of shares, to collect or compromise indebtedness of the corporation, or to pay shareholders entitled to appraisal rights under B.C.L.§623. However, no such purchase or redemption may be made when the corporation is insolvent or would thereby be made insolvent. See B.C.L.§513(b). If the corporation reacquires or redeems its shares out of Stated Capital, the shares must be cancelled. B.C.L.§515(a).

B.C.L.§514 provides that agreements by a corporation for the purchase of its own shares shall be enforceable by the shareholder and by the corporation; however, this pervails if the corporation

---

*See, Helfand v. Cohen, 110 A.D.2d 751, 487 N.Y.S.2d 836 (1985).

**See, *Fontana D'Oro Foods Inc.,* 65 N.Y.2d 886, 493 N.Y.S.2d 300(1985); see, also, *5303 Realty Corp.* v. *O & Y Equity Corp.,* 64 N.Y.2d 313, 486 N.Y.S.2d 877(1984) for court's distinction between transfer of the shares of corporate stock and transfer of the corporation's real property.

***For explanation of functions of a transfer agent or registrar and for signature requirements on transfer of securities, *see,* C. Israels & E. Guttman, *Modern Securities Transfer,* Ch. VII & VIII (1971 & 1981 Supp).

†See Penal Law §190.35.

is legally permitted at the time to purchase the shares as per B.C.L.§513; the possibility that a corporation may not be able to purchase the shares (because it may not have sufficient surplus or may be insolvent at the time) shall not be grounds to deny either party specific performance of the agreement if at the time for performance the corporation can legally purchase all or part of such shares. B.C.L.§514(b).

If there is a claim that the corporation does not have sufficient surplus at the time, the party claiming same has the burden of proving the corporation's lack of surplus.

1. Redemption of Shares

Preferred shares are frequently made redeemable by the corporation; the power of redemption must be expressly provided for in the C/I. B.C.L.§512 and §513 govern the circumstances under which a corporation may redeem its redeemable shares.

2. Reacquired Shares

A corporation may acquire its own shares by purchase, gift or otherwise. Shares reacquired by the corporation may be retained as treasury shares or may be cancelled. B.C.L.§515(b).

When reacquired shares are cancelled, Stated Capital is reduced. Cancelled shares are restored to the status of authorized but unissued unless the C/I prohibits reissuance; in such event, the board of directors could then amend the C/I reducing the authorized number of shares accordingly. B.C.L.§515(e).

3. Treasury Shares

A corporation may reacquire its own shares from a shareholder by gift or by purchase out of Surplus; they may be purchased for any reasonable amount, which may be unrelated to their par value.

Treasury shares are considered to be "issued" but "not outstanding". (B.C.L.§102(a)(14)).

When the corporation purchases its own shares, Stated Capital is not affected; Surplus is decreased by the amount of the consideration paid. When the corporation sells its treasury shares, again, Stated Capital is not affected.

The retention of treasury shares, or their subsequent distribution to shareholders, or their sale does not affect Stated Capital. If treasury shares are disposed of for consideration, Capital Surplus is increased by the amount of the consideration unless the corporation purchased the treasury shares out of Earned Surplus, and exercises its option to restore to Earned Surplus, pursuant to B.C.L.§517(a)(5). See B.C.L.§515(c).

C. RIGHTS OF SHAREHOLDERS

1. Dividends

A corporation may declare and pay dividends to its shareholders in cash, property, or additional shares of the corporation's stock. There is no absolute right, however, for a shareholder to receive dividends.

Dividends may be paid in the form of:
(1) Cash
(2) Any property owned by the corporation (including shares or bonds of other corporations)
(3) Treasury Shares as a stock dividend
(4) Unissued shares as a stock dividend

(a) When May Dividends Be Declared?

Dividends may be declared or paid (and other distributions may be made) out of Surplus only, so that the net assets of the corporation remaining shall be at least equal to Stated Capital. B.C.L. §501(b). However, corporations engaged in the exploitation of wasting assets (such as coal mines, oil wells, or patents) may declare and pay dividends in excess of Surplus. See B.C.L.§510(b).

If any dividend is paid or any other distribution made from a source other than Earned Surplus, the dividend shall be accompanied by a written notice disclosing how the dividend or distribution affects Stated Capital, Capital Surplus, and Earned Surplus. B.C.L.§510(c).

(b) Discretion of the Board of Directors

A shareholder has the right to share in dividends when declared; however, whether or not a dividend is declared and its amount is within the discretion of the board of directors. Shareholders are not entitled to the payment of dividends simply because Earned Surplus exists. The board of directors may decide to continue the profits in the business for purpose of expansion, to retire bonds, provide for other liabilities or contingencies, or to serve any other corporate purpose, but it must act reasonably and in good faith. Until a dividend is declared by the board of directors, the shareholders have no right to receive one.

(c) Law Suits to Direct Payment of Dividends

After a cash dividend is declared, it becomes a debt of the corporation; shareholders who are entitled to receive such dividend then become creditors of the corporation, and may sue the corporation if they do not receive the dividend declared.

If the Board of Directors refuses to declare a dividend, a shareholder might commence a suit in equity for a mandatory injunction requiring it to declare a dividend. However courts are reluctant to grant such relief which involves substituting the business judgment of the court for that of the directors who were selected by the shareholders. In very unusual circumstances, a court may direct that a corporation declare a dividend after demand has been made, provided there is sufficient surplus available out of which a dividend may be declared, there is sufficient cash to pay the dividend, and the directors have acted unreasonably in withholding dividends so that their conduct clearly amounts to an abuse of discretion. See case of *Dodge v. Ford Motor Co.*, case #10.

(d) Cash Dividends

The most common type of dividend is the cash dividend, usually declared and paid at regular intervals. The amount and frequency of the cash dividend depends on the policy of the Board of Directors and the earnings of the corporation. A corporation may borrow funds to pay a cash dividend—this is within the discretion of the Board of Directors.

In order to determine the legality of a cash dividend, the corporation must have sufficient Surplus, should not be insolvent,* should not be rendered insolvent by the declaration and payment of the cash dividend, and should of course have sufficient cash. See B.C.L.§510.

---

*Insolvent means "being unable to pay debts as they become due in the usual course of the debtor's business". (B.C.L. §102(a)(8)).

(e) Property Dividends

In a few instances dividends may be made to shareholders in the form of property, which has been termed a property dividend. In order to determine the legality of a property dividend, the corporation must have sufficient Surplus, should not be insolvent and should not be rendered insolvent by the distribution of the dividend. B.C.L.§510.

(f) Stock Dividends

A stock dividend is a distribution of additional shares of the capital stock of the corporation to its shareholders. The practical and legal significance of a stock dividend differs greatly from a dividend payable in cash or property. After payment of a stock dividend, the assets of the corporation are no less than they were before, and a shareholder does not have any greater relative interest in the net worth of the corporation than before (except possibly where the dividend is paid in shares of a different class). However, after payment of a cash dividend or property dividend, the assets of the corporation are diminished by the amount of the dividend.

A stock dividend should not be confused with a stock split. With a stock split, each of the issued and outstanding shares is simply broken up into a greater number of shares, each representing a proportionately smaller interest in the corporation. A stock split ordinarily does not require any adjustments to Surplus or to Stated Capital.*

A corporation may declare a stock dividend by using either unissued shares, or by using Treasury Shares, each of which entails a different evaluation.

If a corporation issues a stock dividend using unissued shares, the corporation must be sure it has sufficient Surplus, and the corporation must have sufficient shares authorized not yet issued. B.C.L.§511 deals with distributions of unissued shares to shareholders. Generally, a corporation may make pro rata distributions to holders of any class or series of its outstanding shares, subject to several conditions: with respect to distribution of par value shares, the shares must be issued for at least par value accompanied by a transfer to Stated Capital from Surplus equal to the aggregate par value of the shares distributed; if no par value shares are distributed, the amount of Stated Capital of the distributed shares is fixed by the board of directors (in the absence of a right in the C/I to have such amount fixed by the shareholders), and the appropriate amount is transferred from Surplus to Stated Capital, B.C.L.§511(a).

Every distribution to shareholders which affects the corporation's Stated Capital, Capital Surplus, or Earned Surplus must be accompanied by a notice similar to the notice provided by B.C.L. §510(c) with respect to cash dividends. See B.C.L.§511(f),(g).

If a corporation distributes *treasury shares as a stock dividend, no transfer from Surplus to Stated Capital need be made,* and it is thus not necessary to ascertain the amount of Surplus. See B.C.L.§511(d).

Thus, declaring a stock dividend utilizing unissued shares is quite different from declaring a stock dividend utilizing Treasury shares.

---

*See, FASB Accounting Standards, Original Pronouncements at 25–27 and 140 (AICPA 1982).

Examples:

Corp. X has 100,000 shares $5 par value stock authorized; a total of 12,000 shares have been issued; 10,000 shares are issued and outstanding; and 2,000 are held as Treasury Shares.

Corp. X's Balance Sheet might look as follows:

Assets	Liabilities	$ 25,000
	Stated Capital:	
	100,000 Shares Authorized ($5 par value)	
	12,000 shares are Issued (of which 2,000 are Treasury shares)	60,000
	Surplus:	
	Earned Surplus	5,000
	Capital Surplus	10,000
$100,000	Total	$100,000

Assume Corp. X issues a 10% stock dividend. There are presently 10,000 shares Issued and Outstanding; therefore the stock dividend would be 1,000 shares. Remember, Treasury Shares are not entitled to receive dividends.

(1) Corp. X issues a 10% stock dividend by issuing some of its authorized but unissued shares.

Thus, Corp. X, in issuing 1,000 shares of $5 par value stock, would have to be sure there is at least $5,000 in Surplus, which there is.

After issuing the 1,000 additional shares as a stock dividend, Stated Capital is now $65,000; there would be 13,000 shares Issued (11,000 shares are Issued and Outstanding; 2,000 are Treasury Shares); $5,000 should be deducted from Capital Surplus and therefore, Earned Surplus is now $5,000 and Capital Surplus is also $5,000.

Total Assets are $100,000; Liabilities are $25,000; the total of Liabilities, Stated Capital, and Surplus are $100,000, unchanged.

(2) Instead of (1) above, Corp. X issues a 10% stock dividend by using its Treasury Shares. Therefore, 1,000 Treasury Shares are distributed as a stock dividend to the present shareholders. There would be no changes in any of the Balance Sheet figures, except that now, after the 10% stock dividend, there would be 1,000 Treasury shares, and 11,000 shares issued and outstanding.

There would be no changes in Stated Capital, Liabilities, Surplus, or Assets.

(3) Assume instead of (1) or (2) above, Corp. X intends to issue a 50% stock dividend. There are currently 10,000 shares Issued and Outstanding, and therefore the 50% stock dividend would entail 5,000 shares.

Corp. X cannot issue a 50% stock dividend by issuing authorized but unissued shares, as it does not have sufficient Surplus, because in issuing 5,000 shares of $5 par value stock, Corp. X would have to be sure there is at least $25,000 in Surplus, which there is not.

Corp. X cannot distribute a 50% stock dividend by distributing its Treasury Shares either, as there are only 2,000 Treasury Shares available.

However, Corp. X could distribute a 50% stock dividend, utilizing both its Treasury Shares and some of its Authorized (unissued) shares, as follows: by distributing its 2,000 Treasury Shares, plus distributing 3,000 of its Authorized (unissued) shares, and by transferring $15,000 from Surplus to Stated Capital.

After issuing the 50% stock dividend, Stated Capital is now $75,000; there would be 15,000 shares issued and outstanding (there are no Treasury Shares left); there would be no amounts left in Surplus; Total Assets would still be $100,000, and Total Liabilities and Stated Capital would be $100,000.

Any stock dividend greater than 50% would be unlawful. In addition, if there were no Treasury Shares available, the above 50% stock dividend would also be unlawful.

(4) Assume instead of the stock dividends in (1), (2), or (3) above, Corp. X intends to issue a cash dividend. There is Surplus in the amount of $15,000. Therefore a cash dividend of up to $15,000 could legally be declared, provided there was sufficient cash available. Any cash dividend in excess of $15,000 would be unlawful even if Corp. X had an excess of cash.

(5) Assume in (4) above that Corp. X issues a cash dividend of $10,000; each shareholder would receive a cash dividend of $1 for each share of stock owned.

After payment of the $10,000 cash dividend, Total Assets would now be $90,000; Liabilities would remain $25,000; Stated Capital remains $60,000; Surplus would now be $5,000. In addition, notice as per B.C.L.§510(c) should be given to the shareholders.

(g) Liquidating Dividends

Dividends ordinarily are identified with distribution of profits; however, after dissolution of the corporation, the distribution of the net assets to shareholders (after all creditors are paid) is considered a form of dividend and is referred to as a liquidating dividend. See Chapter 11 for more details.

(h) The Effect of Illegal Dividends

Legal restrictions on payment of dividends are designed to protect creditors and the various classes of shareholders in relation to one another. B.C.L.§510 permits payment of dividends out of Surplus only; although dividends may be declared or paid from Earned Surplus or Capital Surplus (or Revaluation Surplus), dividends may not be paid from Stated Capital as such payment would impair the capital of the corporation. In New York dividends must be paid from Surplus; if dividends are paid from any source other than Earned Surplus, the shareholders must be informed of the type of Surplus from which the dividends are paid, and the status of the Surplus Accounts. B.C.L.§510(c).

B.C.L.§510 governs the declaration and payment of cash or property dividends; the declaration, payment or distribution should not be contrary to any restrictions in the C/I. This applies where there are two or more classes of shares authorized and the relative dividend rights are set forth in the C/I. Also, the corporation may not declare or pay a dividend or make distributions when the corporation is insolvent or will be made insolvent by such declaration, payment, or distribution. B.C.L.§510(a).

All states including New York impose the insolvency test which prohibits payment of any dividend or other distribution when the corporation is insolvent or when payment of the dividend or distribution would render the corporation insolvent. B.C.L.§510.

B.C.L.§511 governs the declaration of stock dividends and share distributions. Any change in issued shares which increases Stated Capital may be made if there is sufficient Surplus to permit the transfer. B.C.L.§511(c).

Any distribution which affects Stated Capital, Capital Surplus, or Earned Surplus shall be accompanied by a notice disclosing same. B.C.L.§511(f),(g). B.C.L.§520 provides that failure of the corporation to comply in good faith with B.C.L.§510(b),(c) or B.C.L.§511(f), (g) notice and disclosure provisions makes the corporation liable for any damage sustained by any shareholder in consequence thereof.

Directors are personally liable for dividends improperly declared in violation of B.C.L.§510. See B.C.L.§719(a)(1) and Penal Law §190.35. Directors of a foreign corporation doing business in New York may also be personally liable if the dividend violates B.C.L.§510, even though it might be proper in its state of incorporation. B.C.L.§1317(a)(1). If the directors declare a dividend in violation of statute, e.g., where the corporation is insolvent or where there is not sufficient Surplus, the illegal dividend may be rescinded. If the dividend has already been paid to the shareholders, the directors may be responsible for the amount of the illegal distribution, unless they acted in good faith and in reliance on the corporate books and financial statements. B.C.L.§719(e), §717.

Pursuant to B.C.L.§719(a)(1), any director who pays to the corporation the amount of any improper dividend shall be subrogated to the rights of the corporation against the shareholders who received the dividend or distribution with knowledge that it was not authorized by B.C.L. §510. A shareholder who receives an improperly declared dividend, may be compelled to return said dividend. If the shareholder did not know the dividend was improper, it is not clear whether the corporation may sue for its return.*

2. The Preemptive Right

In order to allow existing shareholders the opportunity to maintain their proportionate control and interest in the corporation, shareholders may have a preemptive right to subscribe for additional shares before they are offered to others; preemptive rights are governed by B.C.L.§622.

The right belongs to the holders of two kinds of shares: (a) equity shares—those which have unlimited dividend rights (without limitation to current or liquidating dividends), and (b) voting shares—those which have the right to vote for directors. See B.C.L.§622(a), (b), (c). Usually "equity" shares and "voting" shares are the common shares, although the right would also apply to the holders of any voting or participating preferred shares.

Preemptive rights may be specifically limited or excluded by provision in the C/I. B.C.L.§622(b), (c). The rights apply both to shares authorized not yet issued, and to newly authorized shares. However, B.C.L.§622(e) provides that the preemptive right does not apply to shares issued under certain circumstances, to wit:

(1) To effect a merger or consolidation;

(2) For consideration other than cash, (e.g. shares issued in exchange for real or personal property);

---

*See discussion in Israels, *Corporate Practice*, 347–349 (4th ed. 1983); see, also, *Quintal v. Adler*, 146 Misc.300, 262 N.Y.S.126 (Sup. Ct. 1933), *affd*, 239 A.D.775, 263 N.Y.S.943 (1st Dept. 1933), *affd*, 264 N.Y.S.936 (1934) involving innocent shareholders.

(3) Under an employee stock purchase plan;
(4) To satisfy existing conversion rights;
(5) For Treasury Shares;
(6) As part of the authorized shares of the corporation authorized in its original C/I and issued within 2 years of the corporation's existence;
(7) Issued under a corporate reorganization approved proceeding (e.g. reorganization in bankruptcy).

All of the exceptions are contained in B.C.L.§622(e).

The preemptive right generally applies to the corporation's issuance of unissued common shares for cash (except during the first two years of the corporation's existence).

It should be remembered that every New York corporation automatically has preemptive rights for its equity shareholders and its voting shareholders; if the preemptive right is excluded, limited, or modified, it must be so provided in the C/I.

If issuance of shares would adversely affect the unlimited dividend or voting rights of existing shareholders, such shareholders have the right to purchase shares in such proportion as to preserve and maintain their same percent interest. The right to purchase exists at a price not less favorable than the price at which they are offered for sale to outsiders.

If the preemptive right exists, an existing shareholder would have the right to subscribe to a percentage of shares being issued, so that such shareholder may maintain one's relative interest of ownership in the corporation. Of course, a shareholder does not have to exercise the right, and the rights may be sold, transferred, or merely not used.

Example:

Beta Corp. has authorized 10,000 shares; it has issued and outstanding 1,000 shares of stock; shareholder A owns 200 shares; A thus owns 20% of Beta Corp.'s outstanding stock. If Beta Corp. decides to issue 1,000 additional shares, A would need to purchase 200 additional shares to maintain the same 20% interest. The preemptive right would entitle and allow A to do so.

If A did not assert the preemptive right, A's proportionate control and voting power would be diluted from that of a 20% shareholder to a 10% shareholder.

Preemptive rights can be particularly important in closely-held corporations where the majority shareholders attempt to freeze out the minority by issuing a large number of additional shares, thereby diluting the minority's proportionate interest. Preemptive rights allow a shareholder to protect one's pro-rata interest in such instances. However, the preemptive right may not always protect the minority shareholder if the shareholder does not have funds available to subscribe to the additional shares.

3. The Right to Information

Every corporation is required to keep correct complete books and records of accounts, minutes of shareholders' and directors' meetings, records of the names and addresses of shareholders, including the number and the class of shares held by each shareholder and the date each became owner of record. B.C.L.§624(a).

The C/I or by-laws may limit the hours during which inspection may be made and impose other conditions reasonably calculated to prevent undue interference with the corporation's business.

Shareholders in a corporation enjoy both common law and statutory inspection rights. Common law inspection rights exist concurrently with any inspection rights created by statute. It will be seen that B.C.L.§624 provides inspection rights to shareholders provided they have been shareholders for a certain period of time or own a certain percentage of shares. Sometimes, a shareholder may not come within the requirements of B.C.L.§624. Statutory inspection rights are not exclusive. The shareholders could still possibly also have the advantage of common law inspection rights. (See Rockwell v. SCM Corp., Case #12).

If the corporation improperly refuses inspection of the records, the shareholder may proceed in court requesting the court to direct the corporation to permit the inspection.

(a) Common Law Right

Shareholders at common law have a qualified right to inspect the corporate books and records, and to inspect the corporate headquarters. The corporation's directors and the president have the absolute right to inspect the corporate books and records.

The common law grants to a shareholder the qualified right to inspect the corporate books and records if acting in good faith and if for a "proper purpose"; review of the corporate books as a 'fishing expedition' is not permitted.

Since the right of inspection is qualified by the "proper purpose" test, the shareholder must demonstrate lawful and proper motives, and that inspection is needed to advance the welfare of the corporation or the other shareholders.

The right of inspection has been used to a very great extent in proxy contests where a group is attempting to acquire control of a corporation. The inspection is needed so as to obtain names and addresses of shareholders so that shareholders may be contacted. If the corporation is subject to the S.E.C. and if it has made or intends to make its own solicitation to the shareholders, it must, if the outsider so desires, mail the proxy material for the outsider also, but the outsider will pay the mailing costs.

(b) Inspection of Books and Records Under the B.C.L.

Any shareholder of record for more than six (6) months or any shareholder who holds at least five percent (5%) of any class of the outstanding shares may, on five days written notice to the corporation, have the right to examine the shareholders' minutes and record of shareholders. B.C.L.§624(b). Such right also applies to a foreign corporation doing business in N.Y. (B.C.L.§1315). A shareholder will be allowed to make copies, and may also send his or her attorney, accountant, or other authorized agent.

Shareholders are entitled to inspect the list of shareholders so as to permit them to contact others to organize a group to take over management by electing a new slate of directors in a "proxy fight"; also, shareholders are entitled to contact other shareholders regarding commencing a shareholders derivative suit. (Ch. 9). The right of inspection may not be abused for other than corporate purposes, and the court has the power to resolve any question.

A shareholder is also entitled to an annual balance sheet and profit and loss statement; the corporation must mail to the shareholder its most recent financial statements showing in reasonable detail its Assets and Liabilities and Income Statements. The S.E.C. and the national stock exchanges require all listed corporations to issue periodic financial reports to their shareholders; in addition, large publicly held corporations, whose stock is traded over the counter, are also required by the S.E.C. to make periodic reports to their shareholders. In the case of many closely held corporations, the shareholder's right of inspection is very important since it may be the only way to obtain financial information about the corporation.

The B.C.L. imposes various requirements on a shareholder's inspection right. The shareholder may be required to submit an affidavit that such inspection is not desired for a purpose which is in the interest of another business and that he has not within 5 years sold any shareholder lists. See B.C.L.§624(c). A shareholder may properly be denied access to corporate records to prevent harassment or to protect trade secrets or other confidential corporate information.

If the corporation refuses to comply with a proper request, the person making the demand may apply to the court for an Order directing the corporation to comply. B.C.L.§624(d).

(c) Other Rights to Information Under the B.C.L.

The B.C.L. also requires a corporation to give notice to its shareholders of information in connection with corporate action relating to dividends, share distributions, reacquired shares, reduction of Stated Capital, Earned Surplus, Capital Surplus, Surplus and reserves, and convertible shares and bonds. See B.C.L.§520.

Also, a shareholder or creditor of a New York corporation may demand in writing to inspect a list of the officers and directors and their residence address; the corporation must within two (2) days after receiving the demand make the list available for inspection at its office during usual business hours. B.C.L.§718.

An unpaid wage-earner, before instituting suit against the ten largest shareholders, may have access to the list of shareholders. See B.C.L.§624(b); B.C.L.§630.

While creditors in general do not have the right to inspect corporate books and records, a corporation may by provision in its C/I, give bondholders the right to inspect books and records. B.C.L.§518(c).

4. Right of Appraisal

Shareholders, in certain specific extraordinary instances, may require that the corporation buy back its shares of stock; the specific instances and the procedure to determine the value of the shares to be purchased by the corporation is known as the shareholder's right of appraisal, governed by B.C.L. §623, and covered in Chapter 10 of this book.

5. Shareholders' Rights after Liquidation

When a corporation is dissolved, the assets are used to pay creditors; any remainder is distributed to the shareholders. Certain classes of shares, such as preferred, generally have a preference or priority in the distribution; they share in the distribution after the creditors. See Chapter 11 for details.

CASE 10
DODGE v. FORD MOTOR CO.
(204 Mich. 459, 170 N.W. 668) (1919)

• • • •

The articles of association were executed June 16, 1903, . . . In the articles the capital stock is fixed at the sum of $150,000, with 1,500 shares of the par value of $100 each. It is recited therein that the amount of capital stock subscribed is $100,000, and that said sum is actually paid in, $49,000 in cash and $51,000 in other property. . . . Article 2 of the articles of association reads: "The purpose or purposes of this corporation are as follows: To purchase, manufacture and placing on the market for sale of automobiles or the purchase, manufacture and placing on the market for sale of motors and of devices and appliances incident to their construction and operation."

• • • •

The company began business in the month of June, 1903. In the year 1908, its articles were amended and the capital stock increased from $150,000 to $2,000,000, the number of shares being increased to 20,000. . . . The business of the company continued to expand. The cars it manufactured met a public demand, and were profitably marketed, so that in addition to regular quarterly dividends equal to 5% monthly on the capital stock of $2,000,000, its board of directors declared and the company paid special dividends [from 1911 through 1915]. . . . Originally, the car made by the Ford Motor Company sold for more than $900. From time to time, the selling price was lowered and the car itself improved until in the year ending July 31, 1916, it sold for $440. Up to July 31, 1916, it had sold 1,272,986 cars at a profit of $173,895,416.06. . . . For the year beginning August 1, 1916, the price of the car was reduced to $360. No special dividend having been paid after October, 1915 . . . the plaintiffs who together own 2,000 shares, or one-tenth of the entire capital stock of the Ford Motor Company . . . filed . . . their bill of complaint, [where] they charge that since 1914 they have not been represented on the board of directors of the Ford Motor Company, and that since that time the policy of the board of directors has been dominated and controlled absolutely by Henry Ford, the president of the company, who owns and for several years has owned 58% of the entire capital stock of the company . . . that for a number of years a regular dividend, payable quarterly, equal to 5% monthly upon the authorized capital stock, and the special dividends hereinbefore referred to, had been paid, it is charged that notwithstanding the earnings for the fiscal year ending July 31, 1916, the Ford Motor Company has not since that date declared any special dividends,—and the said Henry Ford, president of the company, has declared it to be the settled policy of the company not to pay in the future any special dividends, but to put back into the business for the future all of the earnings of the company. . . .

It is charged further that Henry Ford stated to plaintiffs personally, in substance, that as all the stockholders had received back in dividends more than they had invested they were not entitled to receive anything additional to the regular dividend of 5% a month, and it was not his policy to have larger dividends declared in the future, and that the profits and earnings of the company would be put back into the business for the purpose of extending its operations and increasing the number of its employees, and that inasmuch as the profits were to be represented by investment in plants and capital investment the stockholders would have no right to complain. . . . Plaintiffs ask for an injunction to restrain the carrying out of the alleged declared policy of Mr. Ford and the company, for a decree requiring the distribution to stockholders of at least 75% of the accumulated cash surplus, and for the future that they be required to distribute all of the earnings of the company except such as may be reasonably required for emergency purposes in the conduct of the business.

• • • •

When plaintiffs made their complaint and demand for further dividends the Ford Motor Company had concluded its most prosperous year of business. The demand for its cars at the price of the preceding year continued. It could make and could market in the year beginning August 1, 1916, more than 500,000 cars. Sales of parts and repairs would necessarily increase. The cost of materials was likely to advance, and perhaps the price of labor, but it reasonably might have expected a profit for the year of upwards of $60,000,000. It had assets of more than $132,000,000, a surplus of almost $112,000,000, and its cash on hand and municipal bonds were nearly $54,000,000. Its total liabilities, including capital stock, was a little over $20,000,000. It had declared no special dividend during the business years except the October 1915, dividend. It had been the practice, under similar circumstances, to declare larger dividends. Considering only the facts, a refusal to declare and pay further dividends appears to be not an exercise of discretion on the part of the directors but an arbitrary refusal to do what the circumstances required to be done. These facts and others call upon the directors to justify their action, or failure or refusal to act. In justification, the defendants have offered testimony tending to prove, and which does prove, the following facts. It had been the policy of the corporation for a considerable time to annually reduce the selling price of cars, while keeping up, or improving their quality. As early as in June, 1915, a general plan for the expansion of the productive capacity of the concern by a practical duplication of its plant had been talked over by the executive officers and directors and agreed upon. . . . The erection of a smelter was considered, and engineering and other data in connection therewith secured. In consequence, it was determined not to reduce the selling price of cars for the year beginning August 1, 1915 but to maintain the price and to accumulate a large surplus to pay for the proposed expansion of plant.

• • • •

A business corporation is organized and carried on primarily for the profit of the stockholders. The powers of the directors are to be employed for that end. . . .

There is committed to the discretion of directors, a discretion to be exercised in good faith, the infinite details of business, including the wages which shall be paid to employees, the number of hours they shall work, the conditions under which labor shall be carried on, and the prices for which products shall be offered to the public. It is said by appellants that the motives of the board members are not material and will not be inquired into by the court so long as their acts are within their lawful powers. As we have pointed out, and the proposition does not require argument to sustain it, it is not within the lawful powers of a board of directors to shape and conduct the affairs of a corporation for the merely incidental benefit of shareholders and for the primary purpose of benefiting others, . . .

We are not, however, persuaded that we should interfere with the proposed expansion of the business of the Ford Motor Company. In view of the fact that the selling price of products may be increased at any time, the ultimate results of the larger business cannot be certainly estimated.

The judges are not business experts. It is recognized that plans must often be made for a long future, for expected competition, for a continuing as well as an immediately profitable venture. The experience of the Ford Motor Company is evidence of capable management of its affairs. It may be noticed, incidentally, that it took from the public the money required for the execution of its plan and that the very considerable salaries paid to Mr. Ford and to certain executive officers and employees were not diminished. We are not satisifed that the alleged motives of the directors, in so far as they are reflected in the conduct of the business, menace the interests of shareholders. It is enough to say, perhaps, that the court of equity is at all times open to complaining shareholders having a just grievance.

Assuming the general plan and policy of expansion and the details of it to have been sufficiently formally approved at the October and November meetings of directors, and assuming further that the plan and policy and the details agreed upon were for the best ultimate interest of the company and therefore of its shareholders, what does it amount to in justification of a refusal to declare and pay a special dividend, or dividends? The Ford Motor Company was able to estimate with nicety its income and profit. It could sell more cars than it could make. Having ascertained what it would cost to produce a car and to sell, the profit upon each car depended upon the selling price. That being fixed, the yearly income and profit was determinable, and, within slight variations, was certain.

There was appropriated—voted—for the smelter $11,325,000. . . . The company was continuing business, at a profit—a cash business. If the total cost of proposed expenditures had been immediately withdrawn in cash from the cash surplus (money and bonds) on hand August 1, 1916, there would have remained nearly $30,000,000.

Defendants say, and it is true, that a considerable cash balance must be at all times carried by such a concern. But, as had been stated, there was a large daily, weekly, monthly receipt of cash. The output was practically continuous and was continuously, and within a few days, turned into cash. Moreover, the contemplated expenditures were not to be immediately made. The large sum appropriated for the smelter plant was payable over a considerable period of time. So that, without going further, it would appear that, accepting and approving the plan of the directors, it was their duty to distribute on or near the first of August, 1916, a very large sum of money to stockholders.

• • • •

The decree of the court below fixing and determining the specific amount to be distributed to stockholders is affirmed.

• • • •

Discussion Questions:

Do you agree with the court's decision?

Do you feel that shareholders are absolutely entitled to receive dividends?

Note: See reasoning of the New York Courts in *Gordon* v. *Elliman,* 306 N.Y. 456(1954); see, also, *Kamin* v. *American Express Co.,* 86 Misc.2d 809, 383 N.Y.S.2d 807 (N.Y. Co. 1976) (Holding that declaring dividends is in the discretion of the Board of Directors).

CASE 11
CRANE CO. v. ANACONDA CO.
(Court of Appeals of New York, 39 N.Y.2d 14, 382 N.Y.S.2d 707) (1976)

WACHTLER, Judge

In August, 1975, respondent Crane Company, an Illinois corporation, publicly announced a proposed offer to exchange up to 100 million dollars in subordinated debentures for as many as 5 million shares of common stock of the appellant Anaconda Company, a Montana corporation. This offer was vigorously opposed by Anaconda's management which sent four letters to shareholders asserting that the exchange offer was not in the best interests of Anaconda. Before the exchange offer could proceed Crane was obligated to file with the Securities and Exchange Commission a registration statement detailing the material facts of the offer in a prospectus. . . .

On November 19, 1975, Crane's registration statement became effective and Crane proceeded to distribute its prospectus to numerous brokers, dealers, commercial banks and trust companies for use in soliciting Anaconda stockholders. The next day Crane requested a copy of Anaconda's list of shareholders claiming that Anaconda had a fiduciary duty to its shareholders to present them with all the information pertinent to the pending tender offer. Crane owned no Anaconda stock at this time and Anaconda refused contending that there was no basis for Crane's request. However, as of December 11, 1975, approximately 2,350,000 Anaconda shares had been tendered to Crane, making Crane Anaconda's largest stockholder. The following day, a formal written demand to produce its stock book for inspection was made by Crane on Anaconda. This demand, accompanied by an affidavit stating that the inspection was "not desired for a purpose which is in the interest of a business or object other than the business of Anaconda", was made pursuant to section 1315 of the B.C.L. and the common-law right to inspect corporate records. Anaconda rejected the demand but offered to mail Crane's prospectus to its shareholders at Crane's expense. Crane responded by commencing this . . . proceeding.

In its petition Crane stated that it held in excess of 11% of Anaconda's common stock and that its request conformed to the requirements of the B.C.L. in that the inspection was not required for a purpose other than the business of Anaconda and that Crane had not participated in the sale of any stockholder list within the last five years (B.C.L.§1315[b]). Crane also stated in substance that it desired to communicate directly with its fellow stockholders to inform them of the terms of both its tender offer and the consent order in the Federal litigation. . . .

* * * *

Succinctly put, the issue here is whether a qualified stockholder may inspect the corporation's stock register to ascertain the identity of fellow stockholders for the avowed purpose of informing them directly of its exchange offer and soliciting tenders of stock? In our view this question should be answered in the affirmative. A shareholder desiring to discuss relevant aspects of a tender offer should be granted access to the shareholder list unless it is sought for a purpose inimical to the corporation or its stockholders—and the manner of communication selected should be within the judgment of the shareholder.

The significance of this appeal is evident in view of the fact that this right is the one most frequently litigated by stockholders . . . and the fact that the tender offer is the primary method of corporate acquisition. . . . The authority to inspect corporate books and records in general is traceable to the right given to partners to ascertain the names of other partners and the condition of the business, and is recognized both at common law . . . as well as by statute (see B.C.L.§§624, 1315; N.P.C.L.§621). The conceptual basis for this right is derived from the shareholder's beneficial ownership of corporate assets and the concomitant right to protect his investment. . . .

At common law, this right is qualified and can only be asserted where the shareholder is acting in good faith . . . and has established that inspection is for a "proper purpose" (Matter of Steinway, 159 N.Y. 250, 258, 53 N.E. 1103, 1105). . . . When asserting a common-law right of access the petitioner must plead and prove that inspection is desired for a "proper purpose". . . .

The statutory right to inspect corporate records was adopted in 1848 and has had a checkered history. The early legislation expanded the common-law right by omitting the "proper purpose" requirement. . . . This absolute right, which was intended to remedy management recalcitrance . . . was not exclusive but supplemented the common law. . . . The present statute (B.C.L.§§1315, 624) was enacted in 1961 and modified the direct mandate . . . by providing that access be permitted to qualified shareholders on written demand, subject to denial if the petitioner refused to furnish an affidavit that the "inspection is not desired for a purpose . . . other than the business" of the corporation and that the petitioner has not been involved in the sale of stock lists within the last five years (B.C.L.§1315[b]; §624 [c]). This was deemed to work no substantive change in the law.

• • • •

In an enforcement proceeding the stockholder must allege compliance with the statute. At this point the bona fides of the shareholder will be assumed . . . and it becomes incumbent on the corporation to justify its refusal by showing an improper purpose or bad faith. . . .

Although everything affecting the shareholders will not affect the corporation, the converse is not true. Whenever the corporation faces a situation having potential substantial effect on its well-being or value, the shareholders are necessarily affected and the business of the corporation is involved within the purview of section 1315 of the B.C.L. This statute should be liberally construed in favor of the stockholder whose welfare as a stockholder or the corporation's welfare may be affected. To say, as Anaconda would, that a pending tender offer involving over one fifth of the corporation's common stock is a purpose other than the business of the corporation is myopic. Since the pendency of such an exchange offer may well affect not only the future direction of the corporation but the continued vitality of the shareholder's investment, inspection of the stock book should be allowed so that qualified shareholders may have the means to independently evaluate the situation. An extant tender offer or abandoned tender offer, or for that matter a successful tender offer, may have dramatic impact on the value of the corporate stock. Consequently, shareholders should be apprised of all aspects surrounding a tender offer.

• • • •

Early in the proceedings Anaconda offered to have the corporation's transfer agent transmit the tender offer prospectus to all the stockholders. This was declined by Crane as much too expensive and not a productive way of soliciting tenders. . . . Obviously then, Crane was and is interested in pursuing a selective and direct approach by other means to stockholders. This is not by itself improper and is due to the pragmatics of soliciting tenders from likely prospects who hold sufficient shares.

Anaconda next raises the specter of the unscrupulous corporate raider as a reason for sustaining its contention that a "proper purpose" should be determined in light of the corporation's business and not the stockholders' interest. This argument is without merit in that it disregards Federal involvement in the area . . . and our consistent rejection of those seeking personal gain completely apart from any benefit to the corporation or its shareholders. As noted in Matter of Ochs v. Washington Hgts. Fed. Sav. & Loan Assn., 17 N.Y.2d 82, 88, 268 N.Y.S.2d 294, 299, "Our case law has uniformly and without hesitation required a bona fide intention on the part of him who seeks such common-law relief." This principle is equally applicable when statutory relief is sought. In addition, the court has the inherent power to consider any and all relevant factors in exercising its sound discretion. Moreover, in requiring the stockholders to hold a substantial amount of stock or to have held stock for six months, the statute provides additional protection. Lastly, the requirement that the statement of no purpose other than a business one, be made under oath is also designed to deter the unscrupulous (Matter of Gottdenker v. Philadelphia & Reading Corp., 31 A.D.2d 152, 295 N.Y.S.2d 683). Accordingly, since it appears that Anaconda has failed to sustain its burden of proving an improper purpose and it cannot be said that the court below abused its discretion, we conclude that inspection should be compelled.

Discussion Questions:

Do you feel that shareholders should be allowed to inspect the corporation's books and records? Under which conditions?

Why did the court refer to B.C.L.§1315(b)?

CASE 12
ROCKWELL v. SCM CORP.
(U.S. District Court, S.D.N.Y., 496 F. Supp. 1123) (1980)

KEVIN THOMAS DUFFY, District Judge:

This diversity action was commenced by the plaintiff, Willard F. Rockwell, Jr., against the SCM Corporation [hereinafter referred to as "SCM"], seeking the production of a list of SCM shareholders and other related material. Plaintiff, himself an SCM shareholder, seeks the information so that he may communicate with his fellow shareholders concerning the shareholder meeting scheduled for October 30, 1980, at which SCM's board of directors will be elected. He charges that he has a statutory as well as common law right to the information he requests under §624 of the B.C.L. and New York Common Law. . . .

The facts which gave rise to the instant suit are not in dispute. On June 16, 1980, the plaintiff became the record holder of 24,000 shares of SCM. For at least six months prior to the June 16th purchase, Rockwell was the beneficial owner of 124,000 shares of SCM.

• • • •

On July 18, 1980, plaintiff served a written demand upon SCM requesting the production of a recent shareholder list and other materials arguably related to the list. In the demand, plaintiff asserted that he had a statutory and common law right to the information. The information was not produced and on July 25th the instant action was commenced.

. . . SCM argued that plaintiff had no common law right with respect to the materials. Rather, §624 provides the sole basis by which a shareholder may gain access to shareholder lists. Defendant concludes that since plaintiff has failed to meet the statutory requirement of §624, he was not entitled to the information in issue. . . .

Although technically the shareholder list and related materials are in issue, there is something much more valuable to plaintiff which is at stake. That is, plaintiff's ability to communicate with the 35,000 record shareholders of SCM and, thereafter, wage an effective proxy fight in an effort to elect plaintiff's slate of directors. Indeed, when stripped of all else, the sole basis for plaintiff's substantial investment into SCM, well in excess of $10,000, was to insure the election of his directors. Thus, when viewed from plaintiff's perspective, there is considerably more than $10,000 at stake. . . .

Section 624 of New York's B.C.L. provides in relevant part: [Note: See B.C.L.§624(b)].

• • • •

There is no question that plaintiff has failed to meet these statutory requirements. He holds only 1.3 percent of the outstanding shares of SCM and has been a shareholder of record only since June 16, 1980. . . . [T]he only argument advanced by plaintiff was that since he has been the beneficial owner of SCM shares for more than six months this constitutes substantial compliance with §624. It is enough to say that substantial compliance is not statutory compliance and plaintiff is not entitled to the requested materials under §624.

The question remains, however, whether a common law right of inspection exists and if so, whether plaintiff is entitled to avail himself of this right. Defendant argues that §624 replaced whatever common law right of inspection existed and now provides the exclusive means by which a shareholder may obtain the materials in issue. Defendant's reasoning, is that if every shareholder was entitled, under the common law, to inspect the corporate materials in issue, this "would render §624(b) absurd." . . . On the contrary, defendant reasons that §624 was intended to replace the common law.

Plaintiff, of course, rejects defendant's argument and urges that it is not every shareholder who has a right of inspection, but only a holder of record who, in good faith, has demonstrated a "proper purpose" in seeking the corporate information.

A review of New York law leads to the inescapable conclusion that the common law right of inspection survived enactment of §624 of the B.C.L. Crane Co. v. Anaconda Co. In Crane the New York Court of Appeals made it abundantly clear that the statutory right of inspection, originally adopted in 1848, was intended to expand the common law right of inspection "by omitting the 'proper purpose' requirement." (39 N.Y.2d at 20, 382 N.Y.S.2d at 710). The statutory right of inspection provides a minimum threshold which a shareholder must meet in order to be entitled to inspect the materials in issue. That is to say, if a shareholder meets these minimum requirements, and requests the information in good faith, the court has no choice but to grant the inspection request. The shareholder has an absolute right to the information. . . . The statutory right of inspection was intended only to supplement rather than replace the common law.

Section 624, the present inspection provision, was not intended to work a substantive change in the law. . . . Thus, the statutory right of inspection emerges as a supplement to the common law right which survives today. . . .

Given that a common law right of inspection exists, there is no question that plaintiff has demonstrated a "proper purpose" for requesting the shareholder information. Indeed, in Crane the Court of Appeals observed that the basis for the right of inspection is to permit a shareholder to protect his investment. This precisely is what plaintiff hopes to do by proposing an independent slate of directors for the SCM shareholders to consider. But in order to do so, he must have access to the list of shareholders entitled to vote. Absent the ability to communicate with his fellow shareholders, plaintiff's attempts to elect an independent slate of directors would truly be futile. In re Lopez, 71 A.D.2d 976, 420 N.Y.S.2d 225 (1st Dep't 1979). . . .

• • • •

The question remains whether plaintiff is entitled to all the materials requested. I think not. Plaintiff is entitled to inspect only insofar as is necessary to ascertain the names of his fellow shareholders who are entitled to vote at the October shareholders' meeting (shareholders of record as of September 11, 1980). This includes the most recent list of SCM shareholders, and transfer sheets reflecting all transfer of SCM stock subsequent to the date of the list up to and including September 11, 1980. Access to the other materials must be denied.

• • • •

Accordingly, defendant is directed to grant plaintiff access to the above materials as soon as possible from which materials plaintiff may copy or extract information, at his own expense.

SO ORDERED.

Discussion Questions:
(1) How does the common law right of inspection differ from the B.C.L. right?
(2) Can a shareholder have both a common law right of inspection and the statutory right?

CASE 13
NAKANO v. NAKANO McGLONE NIGHTINGALE ADVERTISING, INC.
(Sup. Ct. N.Y. Co., 84 Misc. 2d 905, 377 N.Y.S.2d 996) (1975)

ARNOLD L. FINE, J.

• • • •

Plaintiff George Nakano, moves for an order granting summary judgment in lieu of complaint to recover the sum of $44,000 with interest from July 10, 1974, upon a promissory note issued by the corporate defendant. . . .

It appears that the corporation executed and delivered the promissory note to redeem and purchase plaintiff's corporate stock following the alleged discharge of plaintiff from employment.

Plaintiff was one of three stockholders who formed and organized Nakano McGlone Nightingale Advertising, Inc. to engage in the business of an advertising agency. Each of the parties owned a one-third interest in the corporation. The shareholders agreement entered into by the parties provides that, in the event of death, disability, termination of employment or physical relocation away from the New York City area, the stock of said shareholder shall be offered for sale to the corporation for a purchase price to be computed as provided in the agreement.

Following an alleged history of disagreement and hostility among plaintiff and the other shareholders including an alleged assault by Nakano, . . . [defendant] determined that the agency could not continue with plaintiff's presence. Accordingly, the Board of Directors, on May 15, 1974, discharged plaintiff, effective May 20, 1974. Thereafter, on July 10, 1974, defendant issued its promissory note in the sum of $44,000. plus 6% interest, in exchange for Nakano's stock interest. The note was payable in twelve installments, commencing August 10, 1974. Defendant defaulted on the first such installment. Plaintiff thereupon accelerated the balance due in accordance with the terms of the instrument.

Defendant does not deny issuance of the note for the stated purpose, and admits its liability to Nakano for the agreed purchase of his outstanding shares. However, it asserts that shortly before the due date of the first installment, it was advised by its accountant that there was a corporate net worth deficit in excess of $100,000 which legally, did not permit defendant to proceed with the stock redemption. Defendant contends that the stock redemption would constitute a violation of §513 of the B.C.L.

B.C.L.§513(a) and (b) provides that a corporation, subject to any restriction contained in its certificate, may purchase or redeem shares out of surplus, or out of stated capital if the purchase is for one of the enumerated purposes not here relevant, provided the corporation is not insolvent or would not thereby be made insolvent. Insolvency is defined as the corporation's inability to pay debts as they become due in the usual course of business (B.C.L.§102[a][8]). Section 513(c) provides: . . . [Note: See B.C.L.§513].

The law is well settled that except in the well-defined situations prescribed in the statute, a corporation may only purchase or redeem its stock out of surplus. Corporate directors may be held jointly and severally liable to the corporation for the benefit of creditors or shareholders for improper purchases in violation of B.C.L.§513 (1 White on New York Corporations ¶ 100.09[8], pp. I–41 and I–42). The redemption of stock where there is an undisputed deficit in the corporate surplus account would violate both criminal and civil law (Mantell v. Unipak Aviation Corp., 28 A.D.2d 1134, 284 N.Y.S.2d 640; B.C.L.§§513, 514; Penal Law §190.35[1][e]).

The rule is designed to protect creditors who extend credit in reliance upon the corporation's capital structure. Accordingly, where creditors became such with notice of the purchase, and the redemption is in good faith, the purchase does not infringe upon or prejudice creditor's rights (Cross v. Beguelin, 226 A.D. 349, 234 N.Y.S. 336, affd. 252 N.Y. 262; Bolmer Bros v. Bolmer Const. Co., Sup., 114 N.Y.S.2d 530).

Thus, an agreement by a corporation to purchase or redeem its stock is both valid and legal, subject to the stated limitations on its enforceability, requiring the existence of a corporate surplus from which the purchase must be made (Richards v. Ernst Wiener Co., 207 N.Y.598). If a surplus which existed at the time of the agreement disappears, or shrinks to a deficit, the agreement is rendered unenforceable (Cross v. Beguelin; Christie v. Fifth Madison Corp., 123 N.Y.S.2d 795; Mantel v. Unipak Aviation Corp. supra).

• • • •

The burden is on the corporation to establish that, at the time payments were to be made, it lacked the necessary surplus to make the payments called for by the contract.

• • • •

No financial records or proof is submitted to substantiate its claim. No statement of assets and liabilities is furnished. Nor has the court been supplied with a list of creditors and the respective amounts owed to each. All defendant asserts is that a deficit existed at the time that payment under the note was to be made. Defendant does not, however, state whether the asserted deficit was an actual deficit or a book deficit. In this connection, it has been held that the proper test is whether the corporation had an actual deficit or surplus at the appropriate time (Bolmer Bros. v. Bolmer Const. Co., 114 N.Y.S.2d 530, 538). Nor has defendant presented proof as to the non-applicability of §513(c) of the B.C.L. Other than bald assertion, no scintilla of evidence has been submitted which raises even a suggestion of a triable issue.

Accordingly, plaintiff's motion for an order granting summary judgment in lieu of complaint is granted. . . .

Upon motion to reargue (377 N.Y.S.2d 1001):

• • • •

In granting plaintiff's motion for summary judgment, this court held that the defendant had failed to sustain its burden to establish by affirmative proof that it would be illegal to proceed with the reemption. . . .

. . . However, defendant now submits an affidavit of its chief financial officer, with supporting documents and financial statements, including accountants' report evidencing the existence of a corporate deficit. The financial records now submitted appear to establish the non-availability of a corporate surplus from which payment of the purchase price can be made.

Plaintiff has offered no proof as to the existence of available funds and relies solely on defendant's failure to submit proof upon the initial application. However, these documents require reconsideration of the motion, because they amount to controlling material evidence which now stands undisputed. Although such data should have been submitted on the original motion and the explanation of the failure to do so has a hollow ring, the court is constrained to consider it because of its materiality.

Accordingly, defendant's motion is granted only to the extent of directing that summary judgment be entered in favor plaintiff in the sum of $44,000 with interest from July 10, 1974, payments to be made in years in which a surplus is available for that purpose (*Friedman v. Video Television Inc.,* 281 A.D. 815, 118 N.Y.S.2d 844; *Mantell v. Unipak Aviation Corp.,* 23 A.D.2d 1134, 284 N.Y.S.2d 640).

• • • •

Settle Order providing an appropriate vehicle for insuring that payments will be made when a surplus is available.

Discussion Questions:

(1) Will plaintiff be able to require defendant to purchase plaintiff's shares pursuant to their agreement?

(2) What penalties are there if the corporation purchases plaintiff's shares of stock when the corporation does not have a surplus?

Note: The burden of proof is on the party claiming the lack of Surplus. For additional cases, see *Keating v. BBDO,* 438 F.Supp. 676 (S.D.N.Y. 1977); *Spear v. Plaza Sound,* 57 A.D.2d 778, 398 N.Y.S.2d 900 (2nd Dept. 1977). For further discussion on burden, see *Vowteras v. Argo Compressor Serv. Corp.,* 77 A.D.2d 945, 431 N.Y.S.2d 136 (1980), modified, 83 A.D.2d 834, 441 N.Y.S.2d 562 (1981), app. denied, 55 N.Y.2d 605, 447 N.Y.S.2d 1028 (1981).

If Surplus is available for only part of the shares, then the corporation can purchase only that part. See, *Mantell v. Unipak Aviation,* 28 A.D.2d 1134, 284 N.Y.S.2d 640 (2nd Dept. 1967); *Schlaifer v. Kaiser,* 84 Misc.2d 817, 377 N.Y.S.2d 356 (1975) (deferred compensation plan).

See, also, In Re Flying Mailmen Service Inc., 402F. Supp. 790 (S.D. N.Y. 1975), aff'd, 539 F.2d 866 (2nd Cir. 1976).

CASE 14
RAFE v. HINDIN
(App. Div. 2nd Dep't, 29 A.D.2d 481, 288 N.Y.S.2d 662)(1968)

BELDOCK, Presiding Justice.

On November 1, 1963 the plaintiff and the individual defendant organized the corporate defendant for the purpose of purchasing and developing a parcel of real property in Port Jefferson Station, New York. Each owned one certificate for 50% of the outstanding stock. There was a legend on each certificate, signed by the parties, which made it non-transferable except to the other stockholder, and written permission from the other stockholder was required to transfer the stock to a third party on the books of the corporation.

In April, 1967, being in financial difficulties, the plaintiff found a prospective purchaser for his stock for $44,000. The plaintiff offered to sell his stock to the individual defendant at that price. The latter refused to buy the stock and also refused to consent to the sale thereof to the plaintiff's prospective purchaser.

The plaintiff then instituted this action for a judgment declaring void the legend on the certificate, declaring the stock transferable to a third party without the consent of the individual defendant, and granting other incidental relief.

• • • •

The legend on the stock certificate was not contained either in the certificate of incorporation or in the by-laws of the corporation, but was the result of agreement between the parties. That fact is not a sufficient ground for invalidating the restriction. A restriction on the alienation of stock made between all the stockholders of a corporation may be enforced, if reasonable, even though it is not contained in the certificate of incorporation or the by-laws (Reynolds v. Bank of Mt. Vernon, 6 A.D. 62, 39 N.Y.S. 623, aff'd.158 N.Y. 740).

The legend contained two separate restrictions: (a) each stockholder is required to sell to the other stockholder, but no price is stated at which the offeror is required to sell or the offeree to purchase, and no time limit is set for the offeree to exercise his option to purchase; and (b) each stockholder is required to obtain the consent of the other stockholder to a proposed transfer of the stock to a third party, but there is no provision that the second stockholder may not unreasonably withhold his consent. We are concerned on this appeal solely with the validity of the second restriction.

There is a conflict of authority in other States on the subject of the validity of a restriction on the transfer of stock in a close corporation without the consent of either all or a stated percentage of the other stockholders or the board of directors of the corporation.

• • • •

In Tracey v. Franklin, 31 Del. Ch. 477, 67 A.2d 56, 11 A.L.R.2d 990, it was held that a provision whereby two stockholders in a close corporation agreed not to sell their shares, except on the consent of both, was invalid because a restraint on alienation of property is against public policy; and the fact two stockholders wish to solidify ownership in themselves is not a legally sufficient purpose to justify the restraint on alienation. . . .

In New York certificates of stock are regarded as personal property and are subject to the rule that there be no unreasonable restraint on alienation (Allen v. Biltmore Tissue Corp., 2 N.Y.2d 534,540, 161 N.Y.S.2d 418, 4210. In Penthouse Properties v. 1158 Fifth Ave., 256 A.D. 685, 690-691, 11 N.Y.S.2d 417, [quoted with approval in Allen, 2 N.Y.sd at 541-542,161 N.Y.S.2d at 423] the court declared that "[t]he general rule that ownership of property cannot exist in one person and the right of alienation in another . . . has in this State been frequently applied to shares of corporate stock . . . and cognizance has been taken of the principle that 'the right of transfer is a right of property, and if another has the arbitrary power to forbid a transfer of property by the owners that amounts to annihilation of property.' "

* * * *

The legend on the stock certificate at bar contains no provision that the individual defendant's consent may not be unreasonably withheld. Since the individual defendant is thus given the arbitrary power to forbid a transfer of the shares of stock by the plaintiff, the restirction amounts to annihilation of property. The restriction is not only not reasonable, but it is against public policy and, therefore, ilegal. It is an unwarrantable and unlawful restraint on the sale of personal property, the sale and interchange of which the law favors, and in restraint of trade.

* * * *

It is further noted that, because of the individual defendant is given by the legend on the stock certificate the arbitrary right to refuse for any reason or for no reason to consent to the transfer of the plaintiff's stock to a prospective purchaser, and since no price is stated at which the plaintiff must sell to the individual defendant and which the latter is required to pay to the plaintiff for the plaintiff's stock, the legend may be construed as rendering the sale of the plaintiff's stock impossible to anyone except to the individual defendant at whatever price he wishes to pay. This construction makes the restriction illegal (Allen v. Biltmore Tissue Corp., 2 N.Y.2d 534,542, 161 N.Y.S.2d 418, 423).

* * * *

Judgment should be directed to be entered (1) declaring void the legend on the certificate requiring the consent of the individual defendant to the transfer of the plaintiff's stock to a third-party and (2) directing the corporate defendant, upon submission to it of a properly endorsed assignment of the stock and appropriate payment to it on account of any taxes on the transfer, to record the transfer in its stock transfer book, to cancel the plaintiff's stock certificate, to issue a new stock certificate to the plaintiff's transferee, and to record the plaintiff's transferee in its stock book as the present holder of the stock.

Note: This was affirmed by the Court of Apeals, 23 N.Y.2d 759, 296 N.Y.S.2d 955 (1968).

Discussion Questions:

(1) Was the restriction on the transfer of shares proper?

(2) How would you have restricted the transfer of shares?

PROBLEMS

33. ABC Corp. had no profits and no Surplus for a period of 5 years and during that period paid no dividends to either its common or preferred shareholders. Its preferred shares provided for 7% preferred dividends. In the sixth year a 7% dividend was declared for the preferred shareholders, and a dividend was also declared for the common shareholders.

Alex, a preferred shareholder, sued on behalf of himself and other preferred shareholders, to enjoin the payment of any dividend to the common shareholders until the preferred shareholders were paid their dividend of 7% for each of the past 5 years.

(a) How should the court decide?

(b) Would your answer be different if Alex's preferred shares were listed as being cumulative preferred? Discuss.

34. Great Surprise Corp. was formed as a corporation pursuant to the laws of N.Y.S. in 1980; it was authorized to issue 10,000 shares of $10 par value stock. It issues 5,000 shares for $15 per share. In January 1981, its Assets were $175,000; Liabilities were $100,000. On that date, its Board of Directors declares and issues (1) a cash dividend of $2 per share, and (2) a stock dividend of 30%.

(a) Indicate what the Board of Directors must consider and take into account before declaring and paying each of the above two dividends. Indicate if either or both of these dividends are proper.

(b) Assume both dividends are declared and paid. In 1983, it declares a 10% stock dividend. At that time, its Liabilities are $100,000, and its Assets are $150,000. Indicate if this stock dividend has been properly declared.

(c) The shareholders complain that no dividends were paid in 1982. They feel they should receive some dividends each year. What are their rights to receive dividends?

35. The Standard X Corp. had an authorized capital stock of 1,000 shares, $50 par value stock. On May 1, 1985, there are 600 shares Issued and Outstanding. The assets were $120,000; its liabilities were $80,000. On that day, its Board of Directors declared and thereafter distributed a stock dividend of 10% and a cash dividend of $1 per share.

The Corporation continued to do business; on November 1, 1985, its assets were $130,000; liabilities were $95,000. On that day the Board of Directors declared and thereafter distributed a 10% stock dividend, and also a cash dividend of $1 per share.

Indicate whether or not each of these dividends was proper and explain:

(a) was the stock dividend on May 1, 1985 proper?
(b) was the cash dividend on May 1, 1985 proper?
(c) was the cash dividend on November 1, 1985 proper?
(d) was the stock dividend on November 1, 1985 proper?

36. Kim, a shareholder of X Corp. seeks to inspect the shareholders list. X Corp. denies this request on the ground that Kim's application is made in bad faith because she has a grudge against certain individuals who are members of the Board of Directors.

(a) Assume Kim goes to court; should the court order X Corp. to permit inspection?

(b) What would Kim have to show the court to be granted the right to inspect the shareholders list?

37. Sally owned a certificate for 100 shares of X Corp. $100 par value stock, which was worth $150 on the New York Stock Exchange. Bank Trust Co. is the transfer agent for X Corp.

Discuss the rights of the parties in each of the following situations;

(a) Tom stole the certificate, forged Sally's name and indorsed it to himself, and then had a new certificate reissued to himself.

(b) Same as (a) except that Tom reindorsed the certificate to Peter, an innocent purchaser for value, who had a new certificate reissued to himself.

(c) Tom, by fraudulent representations, persuaded Sally to indorse the certificate to Tom. Tom resold and indorsed the certificate to Peter, an innocent purchaser for value. Sally notified Bank Trust Co. who then refused to issue a new certificate to Peter.

(d) Sam, an infant, 17 years old, also owned a certificate for shares of stock in X Corp.; Sam sold the certificate to Paul, an innocent purchaser for value. Sam notified Bank Trust Co. of the sale who then refused to issue a new certificate to Paul.

(e) Sally, an adult, intending to sell the certificate, indorsed it in blank, and mailed it to her broker. Tom stole the certificate from the mails and sold it to Peter, an innocent purchaser for value, without an indorsement. Sally notified Bank Trust Co. that the broker never received the certificate; Bank Trust Co. refuses to issue a new certificate to Peter.

38. The certificate of incorporation of Acme Corp. which was filed three years ago is silent as to preemptive rights. It authorizes the issuance of 15,000 shares of $5 par value common stock. There are now:

5,000 shares of unissued stock; and
8,000 shares of outstanding stock; and
2,000 shares of treasury stock.

In answering the following questions, treat each question as being unrelated to the other questions:

(a) The Corporation presently has a surplus of $8,000, and $50,000 in cash.

(1) May Acme Corp. now distribute its treasury stock as a 25% stock dividend? Explain.

(2) May Acme Corp. now distribute some of its unissued shares as a 25% stock dividend? Explain.

(3) May Acme Corp. now distribute a cash dividend of $2 per share? Explain.

(b) The services of L, a lawyer, are worth $5,000 a year. May the Acme Corp. issue 2,000 shares of unissued stock to L in exchange for L's promise to render legal services to Acme Corp. for the next two years? Explain.

(c) Sara sold and delivered goods to Acme Corp. at the agreed price of $9,000. Payment was due last week, but Sara has not been paid. May Acme Corp. issue 1,000 shares of unissued stock to Sara in full satisfaction of Sara's claim against Acme Corp.? Explain.

(d) May Acme Corp. sell 1,000 shares of treasury stock to the general public at the market price of $4 per share without first offering to sell the shares to its shareholders? Explain.

(e) May Acme Corp. issue 3,000 shares of unissued stock to Peter in exchange for certain patent rights worth $20,000 owned by Peter without first offering to sell the shares to its shareholders? Explain.

39. The Board of Directors of Tina Corp. consisted of four directors, K, L, M, and P. The Corporation has 2,000 shares of authorized capital stock, all of which have been issued. The shareholders of the corporation are as follows:

K: 400 shares
L: 1,000 shares
M: 600 shares

At a meeting of the Board of Directors of Tina Corp. at which a quorum was present, K, M, and P voted for and adopted a resolution for the issuance of 1,000 shares of newly authorized stock, with voting rights, to be offered to K, M, and P only, at the price of $25 per share. L objects and insists that L is entitled to purchase some of the new stock also. The certificate of incorporation of Tina Corp. is totally silent on this point.

a) Does L have a legal right to purchase any of the newly authorized shares? Explain.

b) Assume that L does have a right to purchase the newly authorized stock, how many shares of the new stock, if any, should be offered to K, L, M, and P? Explain.

40. A corporation has realized an operating profit and has a balance in its surplus account, but because of additions to fixed capital assets it has no cash beyond its requirements for working capital.

(a) May this corporation legally declare a dividend?

(b) On the assumption that a dividend can legally be declared, explain what type of dividend this can be.

(c) May the corporation obtain a loan from a Bank in order to pay a cash dividend?

41. Hal went to work for Baker Corp. pursuant to a written contract of employment whereby he was to receive a salary of $150,000 per year for 5 years, and in addition he was to receive 10 shares of the corporation's authorized but unissued no par value stock for each year he worked for the corporation. The agreement provided that upon termination of employment with the corporation, Hal promised to resell his shares to the corporation at book value. The employment contract expired, and Hal did not want to renew it, though the corporation was most eager to renew. Baker Corp. demands that Hal resell his shares to the cororation. Hal refuses and Baker Corp. sues.

Hal defends on the ground that the contract was unenforceable since there was lack of mutuality of obligation at the time the contract was executed since a corporation may purchase its own shares only out of surplus and there was no assurance at the time the contract was executed there would be sufficient surplus for the corporation to meet its obligations when the employment contract terminated. Therefore, Hal says the agreement is unenforceable.

(a) What result? Discuss.

(b) Assume there is not sufficient surplus at the time of termination of the agreement, but that there is a sufficient surplus 2 years later. What result? Discuss.

42. Ann owns 20,000 shares of Sand Corp. Sand Corp. had authorized 200,000 shares and issued all of them during its first six months of operation. Later Sand Corp. reacquired 10,000 of these shares. The following year, Sand Corp. amended its charter so as to authorize and issue an additional 100,000 shares; also, the board of directors voted to reissue the 10,000 shares of treasury stock. There is no provision in the corporate charter dealing with shareholder preemptive rights. Ann claims she has the preemptive right to purchase 10,000 shares of the new issue and 1,000 shares of the treasury stock. Discuss her claims.

43. The minority stockholders of Gale Inc., bring legal action to compel the directors of the corporation to declare a dividend. They claim the failure to pay dividends is the result of a conspiracy of the directors to depreciate the value of the corporation's stock so that the directors might acquire the shares at less than the true value. The directors defend on the ground that their action is in conformity with their policy to build up a large surplus in view of the hazards incident to the type of activity in which the corporation is engaged. What would be the outcome if
   a) the directors prove their defense? What will the directors have to prove to the court?
   b) the stockholders prove their claims?

44. Perry Corp. was duly incorporated in New York State on February 1, 1976 and was authorized to issue 4,000 shares of $50 par value common stock. The certificate contained no provision regarding preemptive rights.

Thomas, Smith, and Jones each purchased 1,000 shares of the common stock for $60 per share. The corporation issued the 3,000 shares and received the $180,000.

On June 1, 1976, the corporation repurchased from Thomas 500 of his shares, and duly paid Thomas the $50 par value, totalling $25,000. On June 1, 1976, just prior to the transaction, the assets of the corporation were $300,000, liabilities were $115,000; earned surplus [retained earnings] was O.

On January 1, 1977, the corporation sells the 500 shares to Frank for $40 per share.

On March 1, 1978 the corporation sells 100 of the authorized but unissued shares to Gary for $40 per share.

Smith, one of the original shareholders, complains about the above three transactions as follows:
   (a) the purchase from Thomas on June 1, 1976 was improper as there was no earned surplus [retained earnings] on that date;
   (b) the sale to Frank was improper as the price was below par value;
   (c) the sale to Frank was in violation of Smith's preemptive right;
   (d) the sale to Gary was improper as the price was below par value;
   (e) the sale to Gary was in violation of Smith's preemptive right.

Discuss each of Smith's complaints and decide whether each transaction was proper or improper, giving legal reasons.

45. Jane has acquired one share of common stock of a corporation that has over 500,000 shareholders. Jane's ownership is so small that she is questioning what her rights are as a shareholder. What are Jane's rights regarding each of the following?
   (a) To attend and vote at shareholders' meetings.
   (b) To inspect the corporate books.
   (c) To receive yearly dividends.

46. (a) Betty owned 10% of A Corp's voting shares for 2 years. She headed a slate of candidates opposing the incumbent directors for election to A Corp's Board at the 1980 annual meeting. Betty asked A Corp. for a list of shareholders so that she could solicit proxies from them. They refused her request. Betty sues to force A Corp. to issue the list. Can she succeed?

(b) Kit had owned 6% of A Corp's shares for 3 years. Kit asked A Corp. for a list of shareholders to be used as a mailing list for advertising material for her personal business which was in competition with A Corp. They denied Kit's request. Kit sues to force them to furnish the requested list. What result?

(c) On July 3, S bought 100 shares of A Corp., which had 1,000,000 shares outstanding. On July 20, after S was registered as a shareholder, S asked to inspect A Corp's books. A Corp. denied the request. Can S force A Corp. to furnish the books for inspection?

(d) Carl owned 25% of the voting shares of B Corp. He also owned 6% of the voting shares of A Corp., a competitor of B Corp. Carl asked to inspect A Corp's books. Knowing that Carl was a director and a large shareholder of B, A Corp. refused to let him inspect. Carl sues to force A Corp. to let him inspect the books. What result? Discuss.

47. (a) Y Corp., organized in 1978, sold 100,000 shares of $10 par value common stock, its only outstanding shares, to shareholders for $15 per share. The corporation was authorized to issue 500,000 shares. Y Corp. began business on January 2, 1978; it lost $200,000 during 1978. In 1979 it lost $25,000. In 1980 it earned a profit of $75,000. In January 1981, the directors voted to declare a 10% stock dividend. Some shareholders thought this was improper. Was it?

(b) Assume Y Corp. had sold the 100,000 $10 par value shares for par value. Could it legally issue the 10% stock dividend? Explain.

(c) Assume Y Corp. sold its 100,000 shares for $12 per share, and, then had re-acquired 10,000 of them; may it now declare and issue the 10% stock dividend? Explain.

**48. Maximum Corporation is a medium sized manufacturing company whose shares are publicly traded. Maximum's capital structure consists of 500,000 shares of common stock and 200,000 shares of 8% non-cumulative preferred. During each of the past five years, Maximum has earned an amount well in excess of the $16,000 which the preferred shareholders would be entitled to if any dividends were declared. The board has stated that it has refrained from declaring any dividends because of the need to expand its operations by construction of new facilities or the acquisition of another corporation. In fact, the real motivation behind the board's dividend policy is to depress the market value of the preferred shares which the board members have been quietly accumulating over the past two years. As a consequence of the foregoing, the accumulated earnings and profits of Maximum are now $130,000. What are the legal implications of the above facts? [AICPA-4a-Nov. 1976].

**49. The Decimile Corporation is a well-established, conservatively-managed, major company. It has consistently maintained a $3 or more per share dividend since 1940 on its only class of stock, which has a $1 par value. Decimile's board of directors is determined to maintain a $3 per share annual dividend distribution to maintain the corporation's image in the financial community, to reassure its shareholders, and to prevent a decline in the price of the corporation's shares which would occur if there were a reduction in the dividend rate. Decimile's current financial position is not encouraging although the corporation is legally solvent. Its cash flow position is not good and the current year's earnings are only $0.87 per share. Retained earnings amount to $17 per share. Decimile owns a substantial block of Integrated Electronic Services stock which it purchased at $1 per share in 1950 and which has a current value of $6.50 per share. Decimile has paid dividends of $1 per share so far this year and contemplates distributing a sufficient number of shares of Integrated to provide an additional $2 per share.

(a) May Decimile legally pay the $2 per share dividend in the stock of Integrated?

(b) As an alternative, could Decimile pay the $2 dividend in its own authorized but unissued shares of stock? What would be the legal effect of this action upon the corporation?

(c) What are the federal income tax consequences to the noncorporate shareholders—

(1) If Decimile distributes the shares of Integrated?

(2) If Decimile distributes its own authorized but unissued stock? [AICPA-3a-May 1979].

**50. The directors of Despard & Company, Inc., are considering several alternatives to their usual declaration of a cash dividend. The cost of borrowing money has become prohibitive and the directors would prefer to retain the cash to further the corporation's expansion plans. The following possibilities have been suggested:

- A dividend to each shareholder consisting of 60% treasury stock and 40% cash.
- A stock dividend declared and paid in its own authorized and unissued $1.00 par value common shares.
- A 2-for-1 split of the issued shares of the $1.00 par value common shares. Par value would be changed from $1.00 to $0.50.

(a) Separately analyze and discuss the legal impact of each of these possibilities from the standpoint of the corporate requirements (ignore accounting entries) that must be met and the effect that each would have upon the stated capital of the corporation.

(b) What is the federal income tax effects or implications to the shareholder as to each of the above possibilities?

(c) What is the federal income tax consequence if the corporation continuously elects not to pay any cash dividends? [AICPA-2b-Nov. 1979]

** 51. The Dexter Corporation has not paid a dividend since 1970 on its 7% non-cumulative preferred stock. In the years 1970–1973 the company had net losses which threatened to impair its financial position. Since 1974 the company has had earnings sufficient to pay the preferred stock dividend. In fact, earnings have gradually increased since 1974, and by 1976 Dexter had recouped all losses which occurred in the years 1970–1973. During the years 1974–1979 the profits were credited to retained earnings.

The funds were neither committed to physical plant or equipment nor did the board indicate that it had long range plans calling for such a commitment. Preferred shareholders had complained at board meetings regarding the repeated passing over of preferred dividends. The board's actions were explained on the grounds of pessimism about the company's and the economy's outlook and therefore, the need to build up adequate additional reserves to provide for the possibility of future losses. The board's outlook during the time in question could properly be categorized as one of pessimism and conservatism.

On January 15, 1980, the board decided to pay the 7% dividend on the preferred stock and a large dividend on the common stock. The preferred shareholders were irate. A group of preferred shareholders have commenced a suit seeking an injunction against Dexter and its board of directors prohibiting the payment of dividends on the common stock unless it first pays dividends on the non-cumulative preferred for previous years to the extent that the corporation had net earnings available for payment. Will the preferred shareholders prevail? [AICPA-2a-Nov. 1980].

** 52. The Kramer Corporation, a closely held company, has 1,000,000 shares of common stock outstanding. The balance of retained earnings and cash accounts are presently $3,000,000 and $4,000,000, respectively. These amounts appear to be in excess of Kramer's historic business needs, having been accumulated during an unusually profitable period which is unlikely to recur. The Kramer Board of Directors recently decided to retain all of the Corporation's earnings for investment in projects which do not appear destined to increase, or even maintain, the Corporation's rate of return on capital. The Board of Directors indicated that it intended to withhold the payment of dividends indefinitely to finance the planned expansion. The Board of Directors had approved the payment of higher salaries and additional bonuses to several officers (who are also directors) as an incentive to administer the expansion program. The prices of Kramer's products are also to be reduced in an effort to expand sales.

A minority stockholder of Kramer, Mr. Moffat, is dissatisfied with the new dividend policy and suspects that the planned expansion program will not be in the best interests of the Corporation. Moffat and Kramer's management have a record of open hostility. You have been retained by Moffat as his accountant to aid his attorney in the determination of the relevant facts for a possible suit.

(a) Can Moffat accompanied by his attorney and accountant inspect the books and records of Kramer in this connection? What are the Corporation's rights in this connection?

(b) Can Moffat compel the payment of a cash dividend by Kramer? State "yes" or "no" and explain.

(c) Discuss the legal means by which Moffat may proceed to redress his grievances. [AICPA-4b-Nov. 1972].

** 53. You have just begun your first examination of the financial statements of Burke Corporation. Your examination is for the year ended December 31, 1974.

You have extracted the following information from Burke's general ledger and the corporation's Articles of Incorporation.

Stockholders' Equity

8%, cumulative, nonvoting preferred stock; par value, $100 per share; authorized, issued, and outstanding, 10,000 shares, liquidation preference, $115 per share aggregating $1,150,000	$1,000,000
Common stock; par value, $10 per share; authorized, 100,000 shares; issued and outstanding 10,000 shares	100,000
Additional paid-in capital	50,000
Retained earnings	110,000
Total	$1,260,000

Your preliminary inquiry has revealed the following information:

No dividends have been declared or paid on the preferred stock for 1973 and 1974. Dividends on the preferred stock had been declared and paid in all prior years. The preferred stock was issued six years ago at par to a group of local investors different from the common stockholders.

Dividends of $20,000 were declared and paid on the common stock in both 1973 and 1974. Annual dividends have been declared and paid on the 10,000 shares of common stock outstanding since Burke's incorporation. The common stock is closely held and most of the common stockholders are members of the board of directors, officers, or employees.

Burke's net income was $50,000 and $40,000 for 1973 and 1974, respectively. The $110,000 balance of retained earnings at December 31, 1974, was after closing the books on that date.

Burke is and has been solvent since its incorporation.

Discuss the legal implications of the above facts to Burke, its directors, and its stockholders. [AICPA-4a-May 1975].

54. Four accountants formed a professional corporation and signed a buy-sell agreement whereby CPA, P.C., agreed to repurchase the shares of each accountant at book value upon death, incapacity, or retirement. Hall, one of the shareholders, retired; his shares had a book value of $200,00. CPA, P.C. had retained earnings of $10,000 and a capital surplus of $120,000 for a total

Surplus of $130,000. CPA, P.C. agrees to buy back Hall's shares by giving Hall a note for $200,000 in exchange for his stock. The shareholders contend that CPA, P.C. cannot lawfully issue a note in excess of $130,000; Hall then claims he will sell the shares worth $130,000 to CPA, P.C. and will sell the remaining $70,000 worth of shares to his sister, who is not an accountant. In addition, Hall does not want a note from the corporation, but insists on cash. Discuss and explain all issues involved.

55. George, the president of G.S. Corp., purchased 400 shares of G.S. Corp. stock and signed a right-of-first-refusal agreement at the time of the purchase. The agreement required George to offer his shares at book value, to the other shareholders or to the corporation before selling the shares to outsiders. A summary of the agreement was printed on the stock certificate. George died and bequeathed his shares to his wife, Mary, who was not a party to the agreement. The other shareholders and G.S. Corp. claim an absolute right to acquire the shares, and G.S. Corp. refuses to transfer the stock to Mary. Mary sues to compel the corporation to do so.

(a) Is Mary entitled to the shares?

(b) Do the shareholders and G.S. Corp. have any rights under the agreement?

(c) Mary insists she is now a Shareholder, owning 400 shares; she attends shareholders meetings and wants to vote the 400 shares. What result?

CHAPTER 7

Organization and Management of the Corporation

A. ORGANIZATIONAL STRUCTURE

Three groups control and/or manage the corporation in different ways: the shareholders, the board of directors, and the officers. The shareholders, through their voting power, elect directors, and thus have *indirect* control over the management of the corporation; shareholders also have control by their voting rights to approve all extraordinary matters. The board of directors is responsible for management of the corporation and thus in effect controls the corporation's operating policy. The officers of the corporation are hired by the board; the officers hire and fire all the necessary employees so as to run the day-to-day affairs of the corporation.

B. THE SHAREHOLDERS

A shareholder is not an agent for the corporation and has no authority to act for the corporation. The corporation is owned by its shareholders, but managed by its board of directors. However, shareholders have ultimate control over management because the shareholders elect the directors, and can approve or veto major corporate decisions.

1. Shareholders' Meetings*

Shareholders act as a group at the annual meeting or at special meetings. The place for the meeting may be held within or without the state, as fixed by the by-laws, and if not so fixed, at the corporate office. B.C.L.§602(a).

(a) Call of Meetings

An annual shareholders' meeting must be held for the election of directors and for the transaction of other business on a date fixed in the by-laws. B.C.L.§602(b). The board is required to call a special shareholders' meeting for the election of directors if there is a failure to elect a sufficient number of directors if no shareholders' meeting is held for a period of one month after the date fixed in the by-laws for the annual meeting of shareholders, or, if no date has been fixed,

---

*See, generally *Encyclopedia of Corporate Meetings, Minutes and Resolutions* (3rd ed. 1986).

for a period of thirteen months after formation of the corporation or after the last annual meeting. B.C.L.§603. In addition, special meetings may be called by the board or by such other person(s) as are authorized by the C/I or the by-laws. B.C.L.§602(c).

(b) Notice of Meetings

Shareholders must be given written notice of the place, date and time of the annual meeting, as well as the purpose of any special meeting. The notice of meeting must be given personally or by mail to each shareholder entitled to vote at the meeting no less than ten nor more than fifty days before the date of the meeting. B.C.L.§605.

Special meeting notices must include a statement of the purpose of the meeting; business transacted at a special meeting is limited to that purpose, and any action taken on other matters will be ineffective.

Failure to give proper notice of a meeting generally invalidates the action taken at the meeting. A shareholder who has not received notice but who attends and participates in a meeting is deemed to waive the notice by his presence if he does not formally object.

(c) Waiver of Notice

A shareholder may waive the notice requirement by submitting a signed waiver of notice before or after the meeting, or by attending the meeting in person or by proxy without protesting the lack of notice. B.C.L.§606.

(d) Quorum of Shareholders

A quorum consisting of the holders of a majority of shares entitled to vote must be present in order to transact any business at a meeting. B.C.L.§608. The C/I or the by-laws may allow for a quorum smaller than a majority, but not less than one-third of the shares entitled to vote. In addition, the C/I may provide for a quorum greater than a majority. See B.C.L.§608(b),§616(a)(1).

Greater-than-majority quorum requirements, sometimes as high as 80% or 100%, are frequently utilized in closely-held corporations. This is designed to protect the minority by ensuring that no shareholder action can be taken without the presence of most or all of the shareholders. If the C/I contains a provision for a higher quorum requirement, such provision must be conspicuously noted on the face or back of each share certificate issued. B.C.L.§616(c).

A quorum that is present to organize a meeting is not broken by the subsequent withdrawal of any of the shareholders. B.C.L.§608(c).

(e) Proxies

A shareholder who is not able to attend a meeting may vote by proxy. A proxy is a written power of attorney granted by a shareholder enabling another to attend the meeting and exercise the shareholder's voting rights at the meeting. Unless the proxy states otherwise, the proxy holder has discretion to vote any way desired.

In New York, a proxy is not valid after eleven months of its issue unless otherwise provided. Every proxy must be in writing and signed by the shareholder, and is revocable at the pleasure of the shareholder unless stated to be "irrevocable". B.C.L.§609. New York allows a proxy to be made irrevocable if coupled with an interest which is provided for under certain circumstances in B.C.L.§609(f).

Without the use of proxies, large public corporations would find it virtually impossible to conduct shareholders' meetings. By use of proxies, management is able to gather a sufficient number of shareholders to satisfy quorum and voting requirements. Solicitation of proxies is regulated by the S.E.C., which requires full disclosure of the purposes and circumstances surrounding the solicitation.

(f) Record Date of Shareholders

Because thousands of shares in large public corporations are traded on a daily basis, it is difficult to determine on any given day the exact identity of the owners of the corporation who are entitled to vote. Therefore, the corporation is authorized to accept votes cast only by persons who are shareholders of record on a date fixed (in the by-laws or by the board of directors) as the determinative date. See B.C.L.§604.

(g) Conduct of the Shareholders' Meeting

A shareholders' meeting is called to order and presided by a Chairman, who is usually the President of the corporation, or Chairman of its Board of Directors. The Secretary of the corporation may make a statement concerning notice of waiver of the meeting, and reads the minutes of the last meeting (a proceeding usually dispensed with). The Chairman usually states the list of shareholders of record is available for inspection, and then announces that any shareholder present may vote in person whether or not one has previously given a proxy (assuming the proxy was revocable); the inspector(s) of elections, if any, are identified to indicate the presence or lack of a quorum. B.C.L.§610. If a quorum exists, nominations for and election of directors proceed.

The meeting may also include voting on other matters, as well as presentation of the President's or management's report on corporate affairs.

(h) Inspector of Elections

Elections at shareholders' meetings in New York should be supervised by inspectors if the by-laws so require and if compliance is requested by a shareholder. B.C.L.§610. Inspectors may be appointed prior to or at the meeting, and must be named upon the request of any shareholder entitled to vote. Usually an inspector is an assistant secretary or assistant treasurer of the corporation, counsel, an independent accountant or auditor, or bank or service company. The inspectors verify the number of shares represented at the meeting, the existence of a quorum, and the validity and effect of proxies. B.C.L.§611. They hear and determine all challenges and questions on voting rights and certify the election results; each inspector is required to sign and take an oath of faithfully executing the duties of inspector with strict impartiality.

(i) Voting of Shareholders

Unless otherwise specified in the C/I, each shareholder of record who has voting rights is entitled to one vote per share. B.C.L.§612(a). The right to vote may be denied in the C/I to the holders of any class of stock, in which event the shareholder has non-voting shares. B.C.L.§613. Voting rights are generally denied to preferred shareholders, and usually the common shareholders have full voting rights.

Treasury shares, which are the corporation's own shares reacquired by the corporation, do not have voting rights while in the corporation's hands.

Directors are elected by a plurality of the votes cast, in person or by proxy at the meeting. B.C.L.§614(a). Thus, if 5 directors are to be elected, and 20 names are placed in nomination, the 5 persons with the highest number of votes among the 20 are declared elected, even though no one person has a majority of the votes cast.

The C/I may specify a higher proportion of votes necessary than would otherwise be required; but such provision must be conspicuously noted on the face or back of every share certificate issued by the corporation. B.C.L.§616(c). The C/I may also provide for a different manner of voting called cumulative voting (B.C.L.§618) to be discussed in the next section.

As a general rule, every shareholder is entitled to as many votes as one owns shares of stock. The shareholder whose name appears upon the corporate records is designated in the by-laws as the person entitled to vote.

If a quorum is present, a majority vote of the shares represented at the meeting would be required to pass resolutions. B.C.L.§614(b).

Example:

Baker Supply, Inc. has 10,000 outstanding shares of voting stock.

(1) At the shareholders' meeting, a quorum of shareholders representing at least 5,001 outstanding shares must be present to conduct business; if there are shareholders present representing 5,001 or more shares, a quorum is obtained; a vote of at least 2,501 of those shares represented at the meeting is needed to pass most resolutions.

(2) If more than 5,001 shares are represented at the meeting, a larger vote will be needed; if 9,000 shares are represented at the meeting, a majority vote needed to pass resolutions would be at least 4,501.

(3) If the minimum quorum were present, the majority vote of 2,501 could pass resolutions, whereas if a much higher number of shares were represented at the meeting (9,000 in the example), the minimum majority vote to pass resolutions would be 4,501.

It can be seen from the above, that varying numbers of shares represented could be sufficient to pass resolutions, all depending upon the quorum represented at the meeting.

(j) Cumulative Voting for Directors

As an alternative to the one share/one vote method of electing directors, the C/I may provide for voting by a method known as cumulative voting for directors. See B.C.L.§618. Its purpose is to enable and assist minority shareholders to elect one or more representatives to the board of directors by cumulating their votes for their candidates. If straight voting were the rule, the holders of the majority of shares could always be in a position to control the election of the entire board of directors.

In electing the board of directors, where cumulative voting rights have been provided, each shareholder is entitled to as many votes as one owns shares of voting stock, multiplied by the number of directors to be elected, and the shareholder may cast the total for a single director or may allocate the total pooled votes in any manner desired.

The effect of cumulative voting is to assist minority shareholders in the opportunity to elect a director more easily.

Examples:

(1) Three directors are to be elected in Jeff Corp. Sam, a shareholder has 300 shares of voting stock; With regular voting, Sam votes for 3 different candidates; in effect he would give 300 votes to each candidate selected. However with cumulative voting, Sam may combine and pool a total of 900 votes all for one candidate. Sam, the shareholder may vote the total 900 votes for one candidate, or may allocate the 900 votes in any manner desired.

(2) Y Corp. has 2 shareholders: A owns 70 shares; B owns 30. The corporation has 100 shares outstanding. Three (3) directors are to be elected. A will cast 70 votes each for G, H, and J; B will cast 30 votes each for K, L, and M.
G, H, and J would always be elected, as they each receive 70 votes (a plurality), and A would always be able to control the Board of Directors.

(3) Assume Y Corp. in (2) above has cumulative voting: A has 70 × 3 or 210 votes; B has 30 × 3 or 90 votes. B will cast all 90 votes for one candidate, K. A can split his 210 votes in any way, but he will not be able to have a plurality for all 3 directors of his choice. If A casts 91 votes for G, and 90 votes for H, he assures the election of G and H. Then G, H, and K are elected. These three have more votes than any other candidate. B has been able to elect one of the three directors instead of none, as would be the case with non-cumulative voting. A no longer controls all three members of the Board; B was able to elect one member of the Board, to wit, K.

Cumulative voting for directors does not always guarantee that a minority shareholder will be able to elect the directors of one's choice, but it does assist and enable minority shareholders a greater opportunity of electing one or more members to the board of directors. Minority shareholders may strategically combine their votes; a formula has been developed so that they may predict their chances of electing one or more candidates of their choice.*

In effect, cumulative voting allows a minority to combine its strength so that it has a better chance of electing at least one or more candidates.

(k) Powers of the Supreme Court Respecting Elections

Pursuant to B.C.L.§619, any shareholder aggrieved by an election may petition the New York State Supreme Court, and, upon notice to the opposing party, the court may hold a hearing on the allegations of the parties to confirm the election or order a new election.

---

*The minimum number of shares that will elect a given number of directors out of a total number of directors to be elected under cumulative voting can be calculated by the following formula:

$$X = \frac{S \times N}{D + 1} + 1$$

where:
X = minimum number of shares required to elect directors;
S = number of shares represented at the meeting;
N = number of directors desired to be elected;
D = total number of directors to be elected.

For example, if the minority group desires to guarantee the election of one representative to a nine-person board, and 1,000 shares will be voted at the meeting, the minority will need 101 shares, since under our formula:

$$X\text{(the minimum number of shares required to elect one Director)} = \frac{1,000 \times 1}{9 + 1} + 1$$

2. Unanimous Written Consent of Shareholders in Lieu of Meeting

Whenever shareholders are required or permitted to take action by a vote, the action may be taken without a meeting upon the unanimous written consent of each shareholder who would have been entitled to vote at the meeting. B.C.L.§615. This is a particularly useful device in the closely-held corporation, as it may be difficult for shareholders who are employed to attend and vote at a formal shareholders' meeting. The unanimous written consent of the shareholders should be kept in the corporation's Minute Book where it has the same effect as the minutes of a shareholders' meeting. If there is less than unanimous consent among the shareholders, a formal shareholders' meeting must be scheduled.

3. Shareholder Voting on Unusual Matters

In addition to voting for directors, shareholders also have the right to vote to amend the by-laws (B.C.L.§601), to remove directors (B.C.L.§706), to amend the C/I (B.C.L.§803), and to vote on mergers and consolidations (B.C.L.§903) and on other unusual management decisions. All of these are covered in detail in this and in subsequent Chapters of this book.

C. THE DIRECTORS

Pursuant to B.C.L.§701, the business of the corporation shall be managed by the board of directors. The directors (who are elected by the shareholders) manage the corporation and establish corporate policy.

1. Number of Directors

The number of directors in a corporation is usually set in the by-laws; there cannot be less than 3, except when there are less than 3 shareholders; in such case, the number of directors may equal or be greater (but not less) than the number of shareholders. For example, if all outstanding shares of a corporation are held by two persons, there must be two or more directors; if there is only one shareholder, one director is sufficient.

2. Qualification of Directors

The only statutory qualification of a director is that each director must be at least 18 years of age. B.C.L.§701. Any other qualifications may be provided for in the C/I or the by-laws.

3. Term of Office

When the corporation is formed, the initial board of directors is elected by the incorporators at an organization meeting, and holds office until the first annual meeting of shareholders. B.C.L.§404(a). Unless it is otherwise provided in the C/I or by-laws, directors serve for one year until the next annual election. A director stays in office and continues until his term expires and until his successor has been elected and qualifies. B.C.L.§703. The C/I or by-laws may provide for classification of directors in classes of at least 3 each, one class being elected in each year. See B.C.L.§704 for details.

4. Removal of Directors

A director may be removed for cause (e.g., commission of a crime, willful misconduct, neglect of duties, or other mismanagement) by (1) vote of the shareholders, or (2) if provided in the C/I or by-laws, by vote of the board of directors. B.C.L.§706(a). A director may be removed without cause by vote of the shareholders, only if provided for in the C/I or the by-laws. B.C.L.§706(b).

In the case of a corporation with cumulative voting, a director cannot be removed (with or without cause) if there are cumulative votes cast against removal that would be sufficient to elect him if voted cumulatively at an election of the full board. B.C.L.§706(c).

In extreme cases, the New York Attorney General or the holders of 10% of all the outstanding shares (voting and non-voting) may bring an action in court to remove a director for cause. B.C.L.§706(d).

5. Procedure to Fill Vacancies on the Board of Directors

The board may fill any vacancies or newly-created positions on the board by a majority vote of the directors then in office, unless the C/I or by-laws requires otherwise. B.C.L.§705(a). If a vacancy is caused by the removal of a director without cause, shareholder vote is required unless the C/I or shareholder-approved by-laws requires otherwise. B.C.L.§705(b). A director elected by the board to fill a vacancy holds office until the next annual shareholders' meeting. B.C.L.§705(c).

6. Meetings of the Board of Directors

The directors may vote on corporate matters only at a legally held board meeting. The by-laws may provide for regular board meetings to be held with or without notice. Special meetings require notice to the directors.

(a) Time and Place of Meetings

Regular meetings of the board are held as specified in the by-laws. Special meetings of the board may be called for as provided in the by-laws. B.C.L.§710. If the by-laws do not so provide, the board may adopt its own regulations as to the time and place for meetings. Meetings may be held at any place either within or outside the state, unless specifically provided for in the C/I or the by-laws. B.C.L.§710.

(b) Notice of Meetings

Regular meetings may be had without notice if the time and place is fixed in the by-laws or by the board. For special meetings, notice is necessary, but the notice of special meeting need not set forth the purpose of the meeting unless the by-laws so provide. Time and method of notice may be set by the by-laws, or if not so set, by procedures adopted by the board itself.

Notice of meeting can be waived by attendance at the meeting without protest or by a written waiver signed before or after the meeting. B.C.L.§711(c).

(c) Quorum

A quorum of the board is a majority of directors in office unless the by-laws or C/I specify a lower number, which cannot be less than one-third. B.C.L.§707. The C/I may provide for a higher quorum up to 100%. B.C.L.§709(a)(1).

(d) Conduct of Meetings

Any action to be taken by the board is defined as action at a meeting of the board of directors. B.C.L.§708(a). Proxies may *not* be used at a Board of Directors meeting. No director shall have more than one vote.

Any action of the board may be taken without a meeting if all directors consent in writing to the action (unanimous written consent of directors), unless restricted in the C/I or by-laws. The resolution and written consents are filed with the Minutes of the proceedings, and have the same effect as if the resolutions were approved at a meeting where all directors were physically present. B.C.L.§708(b). This is similar to the unanimous written consent of shareholders in lieu of a meeting (B.C.L.§615), and is especially convenient and useful in a closely held corporation, where the directors and shareholders may be the same person.

Meetings of the board may also be had by way of a telephone conference or other similar communication device, whereby all persons participating at the meeting hear each other at the same time. However, there must be an authorized provision for such telephone conference call in the C/I or the by-laws. Participation in such telephonic conference shall constitute presence in person at the meeting. B.C.L.§708(c).

Thus, all action must be conducted at a Board of Directors meeting or as otherwise provided by B.C.L.§708.

(e) Voting at Meetings

A vote of a majority of the directors present at the time of the vote, if a quorum is present, shall constitute board action. B.C.L.§708(d). However, the C/I may provide for higher voting percentages. B.C.L.§709. Proxies are not permitted at a board meeting.

(f) No Proxies Permitted

Proxies are *not* permitted at a board of directors meeting. There is *no* common law right for a shareholder or a director to vote by proxy. The right to vote by proxy is a right that is derived from a statute; if permitted by statute, the right to vote by proxy will be in accordance with the C/I or by-laws. In N.Y.S., shareholders have the right to vote by proxy as per B.C.L.§609. However, there is no statutory provision for Directors to vote by proxy and certainly there is no common law right.

By analysis, when a proxy is issued, the shareholder is appointing the proxy holder as an agent, enabling the proxy holder to act on behalf of the shareholder. A director, however, is elected to represent the shareholders; the director was chosen and elected because of the particular expertise and discretion involved based upon the personal qualifications of the director (similar to an agent). An agent selected for one's particular expertise and discretion can *not* delegate authority to a sub-agent (unless specifically authorized to do so). This is based upon the rules of agency law.

7. Powers of the Board of Directors

The business of the corporation is managed by the board of directors, which determines corporate policy and strategy. B.C.L.§701. The by-laws may contain any provision limiting or defining board authority as long as they do not interfere with the directors' duty to use their best judgment, do not violate the B.C.L., nor contradict the C/I. In the exercise of their duties and powers, directors must exercise their authority collectively and not individually.

The board of directors generally appoints corporate officers, specifies the authority and duty of officers to the extent not specified in the by-laws, and supervises all actions of the officers; it delegates authority to the officers. It can adopt or refuse to adopt recommendations of the officers or shareholders; it can accept stock subscriptions; it can adopt or refuse to adopt preincorporation contracts made by the promoters; it declares dividends; it fixes salaries including its own; it can authorize the raising of capital by borrowing funds; it can authorize the commencement of lawsuits in the name of the corporation.

The board of directors may have the power to adopt, amend, or repeal by-laws, if so provided in the C/I or by-laws. B.C.L.§601(a). The Board may reduce Stated Capital as per B.C.L.§516.

In addition, the board may initiate action beyond its powers which requires shareholders approval, such as to amend the C/I, to dissolve the corporation, or to effect a merger, consolidation, or sale or lease of all or substantially all the assets of the corporation other than in the regular course of business. All of these must then be approved by a specified vote of the shareholders to be legally effective.

The board of directors determines the capital structure and financial policy of the corporation; it has the power to: fix the selling price of par value shares (at not less than par value); fix the value and selling price of no par value shares (unless the power to do so is reserved to the shareholders); determine the value of the consideration in the form of property, or labor or services actually performed for the payment of shares issued.

The board of directors declares the amount and type of dividends which is within their discretion, subject to restrictions provided by the B.C.L., the C/I, or other restrictions. The board also provides for closing the stock transfer books and fixes the record date for the purpose of determining the shareholders entitled to receive dividends.

The board of directors determines compensation of officers, and in addition, B.C.L.§713(e) empowers the board to fix the compensation of board members. This will be discussed in more detail in Chapter 8.

8. Committees of the Board*

B.C.L.§712 provides that an executive committee of at least 3 board members may be designated to have the full power of the board as to routine matters except when the full board is in session.

A committee, subject to limitations in the C/I, the by-laws or resolution creating such committee, has all the powers of the board. Committees may *not,* however, submit any action to shareholders that requires their vote, fill vacancies on the board or the committee, determine compensation of directors, amend by-laws, or change any board resolution that by its terms cannot be amended or repealed by committee. B.C.L.§712. Delegation of authority to a committee does *not* relieve the board members of their duty to the corporation.

D. THE OFFICERS

B.C.L.§715 provides that a corporation shall have officers. The officers carry out on a day-to-day basis the policy established by the board. The titles of the various officers along with their duties are provided for in the by-laws.

1. Method of Selection

The board may elect or appoint officers. B.C.L.§715(a); the shareholders may elect some or all officers if authorized in the C/I. B.C.L.§715(b).

---

*See, *The Overview Committees of the Board of Directors,* 35 Bus. Law 1335 (1980) for functions of various committees.

2. Term of Office

Officers are usually elected or appointed by the board; however, officers may be elected by the shareholders (if provided for in the C/I). B.C.L.§715(b).

If elected by the shareholders, they hold office until the next annual meeting of shareholders. B.C.L.§715(c). Officers normally hold office for their term or until a successor has been appointed and qualifies. The C/I or by-laws may provide for longer terms. B.C.L.§715(c).

The board of directors has authority to approve contracts of employment for officers, which, in addition to fixing salary and fringe benefits, may also provide for a specific term of employment.

3. Titles of Officers

There may be a president, one or more vice-presidents, a secretary, and a treasurer. B.C.L.§715(a). There may also be other titles, such as comptroller or cashier, as may be provided for by the board of directors or by-laws. The president and secretary of the corporation cannot be one and the same person, except where all the outstanding shares are held by a single shareholder. B.C.L.§715(e). However, other than this provision, any person may hold two or more offices, and in a corporation with only one shareholder, that person may hold any and all offices.

4. Qualification of Officers

There are no statutory qualifications for officers; the by-laws may prescribe any qualifications.

5. Officers' Authority

The by-laws and the board may delegate as much or as little authority to any of the officers as they choose. B.C.L.§701(g).

An officer is an agent of the corporation; in order for a corporation's contract with a third party to be enforced against the corporation, it must be proven that the officer was authorized to enter into the contract on behalf of the corporation. As agents, their authority depends upon express, implied, or apparent authority, or upon ratification. Actual authority includes both express and implied authority.

(a) Express Authority

Express authority may be granted to the officer by statute, the C/I, the by-laws, or by resolution of the board of directors.

(b) Implied Authority

Implied authority is that authority necessary to carry out express authority, as long as there is no express prohibition. Officers, as agents of the corporation, have implied authority to do what is reasonably necessary to perform their actual delegated authority. The president would have a certain amount of implied authority to bind the corporation in ordinary business transactions. However, any act requiring board approval, such as issuing stock, is clearly beyond the implied authority of the president or any other officer.

(c) Apparent Authority

Apparent authority stems from the equitable doctrine of estoppel. If the corporation or the board creates the appearance of granting an officer authority, e.g., by acquiescing in an officer's act or course of conduct, the corporation may be bound by the officer's acts even though they were beyond the officer's express or implied authority. Apparent authority might arise when a third party relies on the fact that an officer has exercised the same authority in the past with the consent of the board of directors.

Anyone dealing with the corporation, however, is under a duty to ascertain the officer's actual authority where circumstances would put a reasonably prudent person on inquiry; for example, where the corporation's janitor shows up to sign documents at the closing of a securities transaction, it would be difficult to believe he was authorized.

(d) Ratification

Ratification by the corporation of a prior unauthorized act confers authority and has the effect as though the officer were fully authorized at the time. A corporation may ratify the unauthorized acts of its officers and employees. Ratification relates back to the original transaction; it may be express, or implied from the corporation's acceptance of the benefits of the contract with full knowledge of the facts.

6. Usual and Customary Authority of Particular Officers

a) The President

The president is generally responsible for the conduct of corporate affairs, and reports to the Board of Directors. The president is presumed to have authority to make any contract or do any act appropriate to the ordinary course of business; in general the president supervises all the business and affairs of the corporation, presides at all meetings of shareholders, and signs on behalf of the corporation, deeds, mortgages, bonds, contracts, or other instruments which the board of directors has authorized to be executed.

As a general rule, the president of a corporation may have implied authority to hire and fire corporate employees and to fix their compensation; however, the president does *not* have implied authority to execute "unusual or extraordinary" contracts of employment.*

(b) The Vice-President

There may be one or more vice-presidents as provided in the by-laws; this title may be given to heads of departments or divisions within the corporation. In the absence of the president or in the event of death, disability, inability or refusal to act, a vice-president shall perform the duties of president, and, when so acting, shall have all the powers and be subject to all the restrictions of the president.

(c) The Treasurer

The treasurer receives and disburses the corporate funds (under supervision of the directors). The treasurer's signature alone or with another officer is usually required on all corporate checks as provided by the By-laws.

(d) The Secretary

The Secretary keeps the minutes of the proceedings of the shareholders and of the board of directors and sees that all notices are duly given, is custodian of the corporate records and the corporate seal, signs along with the president the certificates of shares of the corporation's stock,

---

*Goldenberg v. Bartell Broadcasting, 262 N.Y.S.2d 274, 279 (1965).

keeps the corporate records and certifies their contents. The secretary is a ministerial officer* whose authority is presumed to extend only to the keeping of corporate records, minutes, and the seal.

7. Compensation of Officers and the Employment Contract

Corporate officers as employees of the corporation receive compensation for their services. All employees of a corporation receive wages in the form of salary; there may in addition be various employee fringe benefits. Top executives and other "key" employees generally negotiate their compensation by means of an employment contract with the corporation for a specified period of time. Generally, there would be included a "covenant not to compete", or restrictive covenant. This provision does two things: it restricts the employee upon the expiration or termination of the employment contract, from taking a position with a competitor in the same geographic area for a certain number of years, and prevents the employee from soliciting customers of the corporation for a number of years after the expiration or termination of the contract. Restrictive convenant agreements may be enforceable so long as they are reasonable as to time and geographic area.

8. Removal of Officers

Officers, if appointed by the board of directors, serve at the pleasure of the board. Accordingly, officers may be removed by the board with or without cause. If elected by the shareholders, officers may be removed with or without cause, by vote of the shareholders.

If the officer has a valid enforceable employment contract for a specified period of time, removal of the officer without cause (before expiration of the contract) constitutes a breach of the employment contract, and the officer will then be able to recover damages from the corporation as removal without cause does not affect any existing contract rights the officer may have. B.C.L.§716(b)

In addition, an action may be brought to remove an officer for cause, by the New York Attorney General or by the holders of ten percent of all outstanding (both voting and non-voting) shares. See B.C.L.§716(c).

E. THE CLOSE CORPORATION—MANAGEMENT STRUCTURE**

A close corporation is one in which there are a relatively small number of shareholders. In N.Y. there is no set number, but several states have referred to close corporations as those having fewer than 30 shareholders. A close corporation is one in which the managers and shareholders are usually the same; the shareholders (or most of them) very often are also officers, directors, and employees of the corporation. The B.C.L. does not expressly distinguish between publicly-held and closely-held or close corporations. The B.C.L. speaks only in general terms of a "corporation".

Shareholders in a close corporation frequently institute procedures that preserve the right to veto admission of new shareholders and veto other major actions. Minority shareholders, fearful of being frozen out in the future, may also want devices locking in some or all of the other share-

---

*See, Landorf v. Glottstein, 500 N.Y.S.2d 494 (N.Y. Sup. Ct. 1986) indicating that duties of treasurer or secretary are ministerial.

**See, generally, Painter, *Corporate and Tax Aspects of Closely Held Corporations,* Chapter III (2nd ed. 1981); O'Neal, *Close Corporations* (3rd ed. 1986), particularly Chapters 4, 5, 6, 7.; O'Neal & Thompson, *Oppression of Minority Shareholders* (2nd ed. 1985 & 1986 Supp.), particularly §9.05.

holders to a united course of action. Cumulative voting, high voting and high quorum requirements provide minority shareholders a form of veto power, and are devices used in the closely-held corporation. If there are higher quorum and/or higher voting requirements at shareholders and/or directors meetings, such provisions must be provided for in the C/I, and must be conspicuously noted on the face or back of every stock certificate. B.C.L.§616(c),§709(c).

In addition since there is no ready market for the shares in a closely-held corporation, shareholders usually want to provide for some method of liquidating their shares should they desire to leave the business.

1. The Shareholders' Agreement

Shareholders of a closely-held corporation should have a shareholders' agreement. Usually such agreement is entered into by the prospective shareholders prior to incorporation, and then ratified by the corporation once it is formed.

The agreement usually contains provisions for issuance of the shares and places restrictions on transfer of the shares to limit admission of new shareholders. One major purpose of the agreement is to have the shareholders bind themselves to follow certain specified corporate policies; also to provide for purchase of the shareholder's shares upon the shareholder's death or withdrawal from the corporation. The agreement will generally contain the proposed capital structure of the corporation and the respective shareholders' investment.

The agreement may also contain provisions for the shareholders to vote for certain directors, pool their votes for directors, or grant each other irrevocable proxies for the election of specified directors.

A shareholders agreement in a closely held corporation may provide for unanimous consent of the shareholders for all action. Such provision is enforceable only if provided for in the C/I. B.C.L.§616. However, it has been held that such contractual provision (even though not in the C/I) may still be valid and binding upon the persons signing the agreement.*

Agreements which attempt to bind the parties as directors, however, may run afoul of the rule that directors may not delegate discretion to manage the corporation which is vested in them by statute. Agreements which tie the hands or the authority of present and future directors in such fundamental matters as the selection of officers, payment of salaries, or issuance of dividends, may be held to be void as against public policy.** This may occur despite the fact that such agreements are normally entered into by the parties as shareholders.

2. Voting Agreements-Abnormal Management Structure

Pursuant to B.C.L.§620(b), the C/I may provide that all shareholders may delegate management authority to some person or persons (not the board of directors). Such provision is valid, provided B.C.L.§620(b) is fully complied with. This must be approved by all incorporators or all holders of the stock (voting and non-voting); the shares must not be listed on a national exchange, and subsequent transfer of the shares are only to persons who have knowledge or notice of or who consent in writing to such provision. The effect of such provision as authorized by B.C.L.§620(b) is to relieve the directors of liability for managerial acts, and impose upon the shareholders (authorizing or approving same) the liability for managing or mismanaging the corporate affairs.

---

*See, Adler v. Svingos, 80 A.D.2d 764, 436 N.Y.S.2d 719(1981); Zion v. Kurtz, 50 N.Y.2d 92, 428 N.Y.S.2d 199(1980) (involving a Delaware Corporation)

**See, the case of Triggs v. Triggs, Case #15, and citations contained therein for details. See, also, Zion v. Kurtz, 50 N.Y.2d 92(1980).

B.C.L.§620(f). If the C/I contains such provision as authorized by B.C.L.§620(b), notice shall be conspicuously noted on the face or back of each certificate.

An amendment to strike out such provision must be authorized by vote of 2/3 of the shareholders. See B.C.L.§620(d). In effect, B.C.L.§620 permits shareholders in a closely-held corporation to treat themselves as directors and eliminates the traditional separation of powers between owners and managers.

(a) The Voting Pool Agreement

B.C.L.§620(a) expressly validates agreements between two or more shareholders to vote their shares in a specified manner. Also, B.C.L.§620(a) validates the so-called "voting pool" agreement whereby shareholders agree to pool their votes on certain matters such as the election of named directors.

(b) The Irrevocable Proxy

A voting arrangement among the shareholders can provide further protection by the use of an irrevocable proxy issued to a person designated by or under an agreement pursuant to B.C.L.§620(a). Such an irrevocable proxy would be effective for the duration of the agreement. B.C.L.§609(f)(5).

3. The Voting Trust Agreement

A more complicated method of achieving voting unity among shareholders is the voting trust agreement whereby the shares themselves are transferred to a trustee for a period of up to 10 years, with the trustee having power to vote the shares, all other rights in the shares being reserved to the real owners. The trustee issues voting trust certificates to the real owner to evidence the beneficial ownership of the shares actually held in the name of the trustee. The voting trust agreement is renewable for successive periods of 10 years each. See B.C.L.§621 for details.

CASE 15
TRIGGS v. TRIGGS
(Court of Appeals of New York, 46 N.Y.2d 305, 413 N.Y.S.2d 325) (1978)

JONES, Judge

That an agreement between corporate shareholders includes illegal provisions with respect to the election of corporate officers and the fixation of their compensation does not preclude enforcement of the provision for a stock purchase option contained in the same agreement where it has been found that over the seven-year life of their agreement there was in fact no intrusion on the unfettered management of corporate affairs by the board of directors because the parties ignored and made no attempt to enforce the illegal portions of their agreement and evidence does not show that the parties themselves considered that enforcement of the stock purchase option was contingent on observance of the illegal portions of the agreement.

After a trial without a jury the court granted respondent specific performance of the stock purchase option. A majority at the Appellate Division agreed, and we now affirm. . . .

Appellant contends that because the March 19, 1963 agreement was not executed or approved by all of the corporate shareholders, its provisions requiring the election of respondent and his father as officers and fixing their compensation constituted an impermissible restriction of the rights and obligations of the board of directors to manage the business of the corporation under the doctrine of Manson v. Curtis, 223 N.Y. 313, 119 N.E. 559 . . . No argument is made that the stock purchase option, standing alone would be invalid. . . .

The uncontroverted evidence is that in the years following the signing of the agreement, the assertedly illegal provisions of the agreement were ignored; no attempt was made to observe or enforce them and the management of corporate affairs was in no way restricted in consequence of the 1963 agreement. The evil to which the cited rule of law is addressed was never sought to be achieved nor was it realized. Although Triggs, Sr., and Ransford continued to serve as directors, the record discloses there were also three or four other, independent directors. That Triggs, Sr., continued to be elected chairman of the board (he was also elected corporate treasurer) and Ransford, corporate president and that for several years their salaries were fixed by the board at the figures stated in the March 19, 1963 agreement was in consequence of action freely taken by the entire board of directors and cannot be attributed to the sanction of the March 19, 1963 agreement of which the other directors, constituting a majority of the board, were wholly unaware. Indeed Triggs, Sr., took no exception when, on May 11, 1965, the board reduced his salary from $20,000 (the agreement figure) to $10,800, and when the board later entirely eliminated his salary his complaint in April of 1969 was predicated on the departure from the board's action of May 11, 1965 rather than on any asserted violation of the provisions of the March 19, 1963 agreement.

The legal issue here, too, depends on what is now an affirmed factual determination. The claim of illegality, raised for the first time some 8 years after the agreement had been signed, must fail because, as the trial court concluded, the March 19, 1963 agreement "did not in any way sufficiently stultify the Board of Directors in the operations of this business". . . .

Analytically we are presented with an agreement which in a single document deals with two different sets of obligations. On the one hand, the agreement contains the stock purchase option exercisable on the death of the father as to which, standing alone, there is no claim of illegality. On the other, there are the provisions with respect to the election of corporate officers and the fixation of their salaries, which are of questionable legality. Any illegality exists, however, only to the extent that the agreement operated to restrict the freedom of the board of directors to manage corporate affairs. There was nothing illegal per se in the election of Triggs, Sr., as chairman of the board or his son Ransford as corporate president or in fixing their annual salaries at $20,000 and $18,000, respectively. There would have been illegality only if the election of those officers or the determination of their compensation had been in consequence of the prior agreement and thus in constraint of the freedom of the board of directors to exercise their responsibilities of management. The finding below, however, was that there had been no such stultification. In that circumstance, the fact that the second portion of the 1963 agreement, if it had been enforced, might have involved illegality provides no compulsion not to enforce the other, legal portion of the agreement where, as here, there has been no factual determination that enforcement of the stock purchase option was dependent on enforcement of the terms with respect to corporate management. The fact is that the courts below have enforced only the stock option provisions of the March 19, 1963 agreement.

• • • •

Accordingly, the order of the Appellate Division should be affirmed, with costs. (4 Judges in favor; 3 Judges against; Dissenting opinions).

Discussion Questions

Which provision of the agreement was enforced by the court?

Were any of the provisions of the agreement illegal? Why?

CASE 16
JOSEPH POLCHINSKI CO. v. CEMETERY FLORAL CO. INC.
(App. Div.2nd Dep't, 79 A.D.2d 648, 433 N.Y.S.2d 825) (1980)

MEMORANDUM BY THE COURT:

• • • •

Defendants contend that the commencement of the action solely at the behest of the plaintiff corporation's president was unauthorized. However, it is well-settled that "[a]bsent a provision in the [certificate of incorporation or] by-laws or action by the board of directors prohibiting the president from defending and instituting suit in the name of and in behalf of the corporation, he must be deemed, in the discharge of his duties, to have presumptive authority to so act" (West View Hills v. Lizau Realty Corp., 6 N.Y.2d 344, 348, 189 N.Y.S.2d 863). Since the certificate of incorporation and by-laws of the corporate plaintiff do not restrict this "presumptive" power, it must be concluded that the corporate president possessed the requisite authority to act to protect the corporate interests (see Cicero Ind. Development Corp. v. Roberts, 63 Misc.2d 565, 312 N.Y.S.2d 893), especially where it appears that, by resolution dated April 24, 1980, the board of directors voted to authorize the instant lawsuit (see Byers v. Baxter, 69 A.D.2d 343, 419 N.Y.S.2d 497; see, also, B.C.L.§701). Thus, even if initially unauthorized, it would appear that this subsequent resolution would serve to ratify the action taken by the corporate president.

In the alternative, defendants maintain that a by-law of the corporate plaintiff, which states, inter alia, that "[a]t all meetings of [the] stockholders, all questions . . . shall be determined by a unanimous vote of the stockholders", required the unanimous consent of the plaintiff corporation's shareholders in order to institute this action. We cannot agree. By statute, any restriction on the powers of the board of directors must be placed in the certificate of incorporation (B.C.L.§§701, 620[b]), so that a by-law would be ineffective to shift this managerial prerogative into the hands of the shareholders (B.C.L.§601[c]; Model, Roland & Co. v. Industrial Acoustics Co., 16 N.Y.2d 703, 261 N.Y.S.2d 896). Moreover, it is extremely doubtful whether the cited by-law can be read in the manner which defendants suggest. Finally, but not least importantly, this by-law would appear to be ineffective in any event, as sections 614[b] and 616[a][2] of the B.C.L. prohibit the requirement of a greater than majority vote by the shareholders for the transaction of corporate business unless the certificate of incorporation so provides. Accordingly, since there is no parallel provision in the corporate plaintiff's certificate of incorporation, the statutory norm of majority voting would appear to be applicable herein (B.C.L.§614[b]).

As the corporate president possessed the requisite authority to commence the instant lawsuit, so much of the determination of Special Term as is based upon a contrary conclusion must be reversed. In addition, the complaint adequately states a cause of action for relief. . . .

• • • •

Discussion Questions

Who is authorized to commence an action for the corporation?

What authority does a President have?

Note: For the implied authority of a president, see case of Goldenberg v. Bartell Broadcasting Corp., 47 Misc. 2d 105, 262 N.Y.S.2d 274 (N.Y. Co. 1965). See, also *Inherent Power As A Basis Of A Corporate Officer's Authority to Contract,* 57 Columb. L.R. 868 (1957) for discussion of officer's authority (actual, implied, or apparent).

CASE 17
RYE PSYCHIATRIC HOSP. CENTER V. SCHOENHOLTZ et. al.
(Court of Appeals, 66 N.Y.2d 333, 497 N.Y.S. 2d 317)(1985)

JASON, J.

The issue of first impression presented on this appeal is whether the B.C.L. permits the number of directors constituting a corporate board to be determined by custom, usage and acquiescence, where there is no governing provision in the bylaws. We hold that it does not.

Respondent Rye Psychiatric Hospital Center (Rye Center) is a private psychiatric hospital incorporated in October 1973. At the time of incorporation, Rye Center had five equal shareholders who adopted corporate bylaws but failed to specify the size of the board of directors. In 1977, a sixth individual purchased an equal share in Rye Center. Although the bylaws remained silent on the number of directors, the parties conducted business as though the six of them, as the corporate shareholders, also constituted the board of directors.

In August 1982, petitioners, three of the shareholders, commenced an article 78 proceeding challenging the status of the sixth shareholder as a member of the board. The proceeding was eventually dismissed, but during its pendency, respondents, the remaining three shareholders, decided that the composition of the corporate board for which there had concededly been no election at least since 1977, ought to be settled by a special meeting of the shareholders. One of the respondents formally demanded the special meeting and another, in his capacity as secretary of Rye Center, notified each of the shareholders in writing that such would be held on November 12, 1982, "for the purpose of electing directors". Petitioners initially sought to obtain a temporary restraining order but, ultimately, chose instead simply to boycott the special meeting.

On the scheduled date, the special meeting proceeded in the petitioners' absence. The respondents, all of whom were present, elected themselves as the three directors of Rye Center. Immediately thereafter, the respondents held a meeting of the board of directors and elected themselves to all the corporate offices.

Subsequent to being notified of the results of the meetings held on November 12, 1982, petitioners commenced this proceeding pursuant to B.C.L.§619, seeking to nullify the respondents' election of themselves as directors and then as officers of Rye Center. . . .

• • • •

Pursuant to B.C.L.§603(b), a quorum for the purpose of electing directors at a special meeting called on the demand of one of the shareholders is merely the actual number of "shareholders attending, in person or by proxy, and entitled to vote in an election of directors". But such does not constitute a quorum of shareholders "for the transaction of any other business." For that purpose, B.C.L.§608 requires that, unless otherwise provided in the certificate of incorporation or the bylaws, the "holders of a majority of the shares entitled to vote" must be present. Here it cannot be disputed that the three individual respondents attending the special meeting constituted a quorum of shareholders for the purpose of electing directors under the definition of section 603(b). Whether, however, the three respondents in attendance constituted a quorum of shareholders under section 608 for the transaction of any other corporate business, and whether any such quorum was even necessary, are questions for which resort must be had to other provisions of the B.C.L.

• • • •

[B.C.L.§702(a) provides. . . .]

Pursuant to the unambiguous and unequivocal language of this statute where, as here, the corporate bylaws make no provision whatsoever for the size of the board of directors, "the number shall be three".

This court has previously held that the clear provisions of B.C.L.§702 specifying particular requirements for setting the number of directors on a corporate board must be compiled with strictly. (See, Model, Roland & Co. v. Industrial Acoustics Co, 16 N.Y.2d 703.) In Model, Roland, we held that, in accordance with section 702(b), a change in the number of directors could not be accomplished except "by means of a by-law". . . . [H]ere, the corporation has no governing bylaw whatsoever, a deviation from the number of directors explicitly fixed by the statute could only be effectuated by the proper enactment by the shareholders of a statutorily requisite bylaw.

The sole New York authority relied upon by petitioners and the Appellate Division for the proposition that the size of the board of directors may be established by "custom, usage and acquiescence" is Thistlethwaite v. Thistlethwaite (200 Misc, 64). Although this 1950 case has been cited as authority in some of the commentaries . . . reliance thereupon is misplaced. . . . Such a rule would be wholly incompatible with the clear mandate of section 702 that a board of directors shall consist of three members in the absence of a bylaw provision to the contrary. . . .

Here, Rye Center having never adopted a bylaw provision establishing the size of its board of directors, B.C.L.§702 governs and the board, thereby, comprised three members. Consequently, the three individual respondents, acting as a lawful section 603(b) quorum of shareholders, filled all the directorships at the special meeting of November 12, 1982, when they elected themselves to the corporate board. Further, because the number of directors was already fixed by operation of statutory law at three, no section 608 quorum consisting of the holders of the majority of the shares was necessary to "reduce" the size of the board to that number.

• • • •

. . . [A]n election of directors was properly demanded and scheduled, all the parties were properly notified, a quorum was in attendance at the special meeting, and the statutorily mandated number of directors was elected. No violation of the B.C.L. is alleged.

Finally, having the authority to elect three directors and having elected themselves to those positions, respondents then constituted the entire corporate board. Thereafter, they had the authority to elect corporate officers. Under B.C.L.§707, a majority of the directors constitutes a quorum sufficient for the transaction of corporate business and, under section 715, the election of officers is a proper function of the board. Consequently, respondents, in their capacity as the newly elected board of directors, were empowered to conduct the business of Rye Center following the special meeting of November 12, 1982, and, under such authority, to elect themselves as corporate officers.

Accordingly, the order of the Appellate Division, insofar as appealed from, should be reversed, with costs, and the petition dismissed insofar as it sought to vacate and set aside actions of the board of directors under authority of the election held at the special meeting of November 12, 1982.

••••

PROBLEMS

56. The Able Corp. was organized March 1, 1980. The directors elected by the incorporators for the first year held over and continued in office as directors, since no provision was made for the holding of a stockholders' meeting in March 1981 for the election of directors. In June 1981, the original board of directors hired an accountant, Max under a written contract for two years. At a stockholders' meeting held in August 1981, a new board of directors was elected. This new board rejected the employment contract, discharged Max, and refused to pay him for the services already rendered. Max sues Able Corp. for breach of his employment contract. What are Max's rights?

57. The board of directors of Davis Corp. consists of 5 members. There are 5 shareholders of record. One of the directors hires Peters as Controller at a salary of $95,000 per annum. Two of the other directors send Peters a letter in which they, as directors, approve the employment contract. Another director on a visit to the plant tells Peters that the contract met with her approval. At the next meeting of the board of directors, the remaining director states the employment contract was not properly authorized. She states there is no enforceable employment contract.

(a) What are the rights of Peters?

(b) Is the Davis Corp. responsible for the amounts due to Peters pursuant to the employment contract?

(c) Assume the above voting was done at a regular Board of Directors meeting. Indicate if your answer to (a) and (b) would be any different.

58. (a) On January 8, L a shareholder, in Alex Inc. gave a proxy to P to vote his shares at the January 31 shareholders' meeting. On January 20, L gave K a proxy to vote these same shares. At the meeting, both P and K claim the right to vote L's shares. Who votes them?

(b) On January 20, X, a shareholder, in Alex Inc. gave D a valid proxy to vote his shares at the January 31 shareholders' meeting. X then showed up at the meeting himself. Both X and D claimed the right to vote X's shares. Who votes them?

(c) On January 20, M, who is both a director and shareholder in Alex Inc. gives a proxy to S, to vote her shares at the January 31 shareholders meeting, and also a proxy to S, to vote at the Directors meeting on February 1. Are either or both of these proxies valid? Explain.

59. Alpha Corp is a corporation that has been duly formed and is existing in New York State. The corporation has four shareholders, Andrew, Bill, Carole, and Diane. The four shareholders enter into a Shareholders Agreement whereby they agree to the following:

(a) They agree to vote for each other as members of the Board of Directors for the next ten years.

(b) They agree to vote for each other as President, Vice-President, Secretary, and Treasurer respectively.

(c) They agree never to sell their shares to any outside person unless all of the shareholders agree.

(d) They agree not to enter into any agreements as officers of the corporation or as shareholders unless there is unanimous consent among them.

None of the above provisions are contained in the Certificate of Incorporation. However, all of the above provisions are contained in the By-Laws. Discuss the legal significance of each of the above provisions.

CHAPTER 8

The Duties and Liabilities of Directors and Officers

A. THE DUTY OF DIRECTORS AND OFFICERS*

Directors and officers have the obligation to perform their duties in good faith and with that degree of care which an ordinary prudent person in a like position would use under similar circumstances. See B.C.L.§717 and B.C.L.§715(h) for New York standard. Officers are agents of the corporation and the general rules regarding their duties depend on agency law; directors, although not really agents, are considered trustees of the corporation, and many of the agency rules apply to the performance of their duties. Directors and officers have the duty to comply with the B.C.L., other statutes, the Certificate of Incorporation (C/I), the By-laws, Resolutions of the Board of Directors, and Resolutions of the Shareholders.

1. The Duty of Care

The duty of care refers to the duty to act carefully in fulfilling the tasks as director or officer. The standard may be stated in a variety of ways, but directors must exercise the degree of care and skill that prudent persons would exercise in managing their own affairs. The standard of care varies with the size and type of the corporation; in corporations invested with a public trust—such as insurance companies, banks, and public utilities, more rigid supervision and additional obligations are imposed upon directors, and such directors may be held to a higher standard of care.**

Depending on the nature of the business, directors and officers are expected to act in accordance with their own knowledge and training; they are expected to attend board of directors meetings, and are expected to be informed of corporate matters and understand legal and other professional advice rendered to the board. A director should agree to serve on a Board only when he or she will be able to devote adequate time and attention, be contientious, have sufficient time to review and study all reports, documents, and materials for the meetings, so that the director will be in an informed position to vote intelligently. A director is entitled to rely upon information furnished by competent reliable officers, employees, and professionals such as attorneys and accountants, and also by committees of the board in performing the duty of a director. See B.C.L.§717 for New York standard.

---

*See, generally, *Corporate Director's Guidebook*, 33 Bus. Law. 1595 (A.B.A. 1978).
**See, Hershman, *Libilities and Responsibilities of Corporate Officers and Directors*, 33 Bus. Law 263, 268 (1977).

2. The Duty of Obedience

Directors and officers must act within their respective authority. For any loss resulting to the corporation from unauthorized acts, they may be held personally liable for damages sustained by the corporation if they intentionally exceed their authority.

3. The Duty of Diligence

In the discharge of their duties, directors and officers must exercise that degree of diligence, care and skill which ordinarily prudent persons would exercise under similar circumstances. Directors and officers are permitted to entrust work to others, and if employees have been selected with care, officers and directors are generally not personally liable for the negligent acts or willful wrongs of such employees, but a reasonable amount of supervision is required.

4. The Duty of Loyalty

Officers and directors owe the duty of loyalty known as a fiduciary duty to the corporation and to its shareholders. The essence of the fiduciary duty requires undivided loyalty and the utmost good faith on the part of officers and directors.

B. THE LIABILITY OF DIRECTORS AND OFFICERS—GENERALLY

Directors may be held personally liable if they violate a duty owed which causes financial loss to the corporation.* They are required to be careful, obedient, diligent, and completely loyal. These duties of obedience, diligence, and loyalty are primarily common law duties. B.C.L.§719, §720 and other statutes impose liability upon directors and officers for specific acts.

1. Conduct Prohibited by the B.C.L.

The B.C.L. specifically prohibits certain acts by corporate officers and directors. Directors are jointly and severally liable if they vote or concur in any of the following: the declaration of a dividend or distribution contrary to B.C.L.§510; the distribution of assets after dissolution without adequate provision for known corporate liabilities; the granting of a loan to a director without shareholder approval (B.C.L.§714); the repurchase by the corporation of its own shares in violation of B.C.L.§513. See B.C.L.§719(a).

B.C.L.§714 contains limitations on the granting of loans by a corporation to its directors. In fact, a corporation is prohibited from granting a loan to a director; a loan shall not be granted to any director unless authorized by vote of the shareholders; if the director is also a shareholder, he shall not be permitted to vote in the required shareholder approval. A loan made in violation of B.C.L.§714 is a violation of a duty to the corporation; if the director does not repay the loan, the directors who approved said loan are jointly and severally liable to the corporation for damage to the corporation (i.e. the amount of the unpaid loan). There does not appear to be any limitations on loans to employees or shareholders, as the granting of such loans would be a management decision within the discretion of the board of directors.

---

*For checklist of Director's and Officer's potential liabilities, see Knepper, *Liability of Corporate Officers and Directors*, 558–563 (3rd. ed. 1978).

A director is not liable for any of the acts specified in B.C.L.§719(a) if in assenting to them he acted in good faith and in reliance upon information, reports, or financial statements of the corporation represented to him to be correct by an officer or employee of the corporation having charge of its books of account, or public accountant, or by a board committee. See B.C.L.§719(e); §717. Nor is he liable if in good faith he considered the assets of the corporation to be their book value in determining the amount available for a dividend or other distribution to shareholders. It should be noted that with respect to liabilities based upon B.C.L.§719(a) the directors act as sureties for the beneficiaries of the improper action, so that the directors who are personally liable, have a right to reimbursement if they pay. See B.C.L.§719(c),(d).

Equitable relief is specifically earmarked for particular officer and director misconduct, such as waste and unlawful transfers. B.C.L.§720. Pursuant to B.C.L.§720 an action may be brought against directors and officers of a corporation to compel them to account for their official conduct for the neglect of or failure to perform or for any other violation of duty in the management and disposition of corporate assets, or the acquisition, transfer, loss or waste of corporate assets due to neglect or failure to perform. In addition an action may be brought to set aside or enjoin an unlawful conveyance, assignment or transfer of corporate assets where the transferee knew of its unlawfulness.

Directors and officers may also be responsible for damages for ultra vires activities (B.C.L.§203) previously discussed in Chapter 4.

2. The Business Judgment Rule*

Directors are obligated to be honest and use prudent business judgment in the conduct of corporate affairs. However, directors cannot be required to guarantee the success of every venture the corporation undertakes; directors must exercise the same degree of care that reasonably prudent people use in the conduct of their own personal business affairs.

The business judgment rule bars judicial inquiry into actions of corporate directors taken in good faith and in the exercise of honest judgment in the lawful and legitimate furtherance of corporate purposes.**

Pursuant to the business judgment rule, there is a presumption that in exercising their corporate duties, directors have acted in good faith, reasonably and in the corporation's interest. The "business judgment rule" will exonerate a director if business judgment was exercised in good faith on the information available. If in the course of their duties, directors arrive at a decision within their authority, for which there is a reasonable basis, and they act in good faith, a court will not interfere and substitute its judgment for that of the directors.***

The business judgment rule presupposes good faith on the part of directors; directors cannot invoke it to protect themselves against liability for fraud, gross abuse of discretion, or a complete disregard of the interest of the corporation or the rights of its shareholders. In addition, the business judgment rule will not protect directors who fail to meet the statutory standard of care in performing their duties as provided in B.C.L.§717.

---

*See, Manning, *The Business Judgment Rule and the Director's Duty of Attention: Time for Reality,* 39 Bus. Law. 1477 (1984).
**Auerbach v. Bennett, 47 N.Y.2d 619, 629, 419 N.Y.S.2d 920, 926 (1979).
***Henn, *Laws of Corporations,* 661–2 (3rd ed. 1983). For analysis and comparison of application of business Judgment rule in New York and Delaware, see analysis and discussion in Israels, *Corporate Practice,* 117–9 (3rd ed. 1983). However, this is one area in corporate law that is constantly evolving, and there are proposals currently to amend B.C.L.§717.

3. The Liability of Directors and Officers

Directors and officers may be held liable for violating any duty owed. Liability is most frequently based on a violation of the fiduciary duties owed to the corporation. A director occupies a position of trust and confidence with respect to the corporation, and thus, should not directly or indirectly, derive any personal benefit.

Officers acting on behalf of the corporation are fiduciaries. Similar to directors, officers have a duty to exercise that degree of care that ordinary prudent officers would exercise under the same circumstances. They are liable for any secret profits made in connection with the business of the corporation; they may be liable for willful or reckless acts resulting in damage to the corporation. However, they are not liable for mere errors in judgment committed while execising their discretionary powers, provided they have acted with reasonable prudence and skill.

Officers, in performing their duties, are entitled to rely on information, opinions, reports or statements (including financial statements) prepared or presented by other officers or employees, whom the officer believes to be reliable and competent, or by counsel, accountants or other persons which the officer believes to be within such person's professional or expert competence. See B.C.L.§715(h) for full details. Similarly, a director shall be entitled to rely on information, opinions, reports or statements (including financial statements) prepared or presented by one or more officers or employees, whom the director believes to be reliable and competent, or by counsel, accountants or other persons which the director believes to be within the person's professional or expert competence, or a committee of the Board designated pursuant to the C/I of the by-laws. See B.C.L.§717(1),(2),(3) for details. However, note that in both statutes, in relying on an officer or employee, it must be a person whom the officer or director ". . . believes to be reliable and competent in the matters presented". B.C.L.§715(h)(l) and §717(1); note, also the proviso regarding an outsider ". . . so long as in so relying he shall be acting in good faith and with such degree of care, but he shall not be considered to be acting in good faith if he has knowledge concerning the matter in question that would cause such reliance to be unwarranted". B.C.L.§715(h)(2) and §717(3).

4. Liability for Contracts

If an officer or director enters into contracts on behalf of the corporation, liability for any authorized contract is the liability of the corporation, and not the officer or director. They are insulated from personal liability for the contracts of the corporation. However, if the officer or director exceeds authority, the general rules of agency law govern.

5. Liability for Torts

Officers and directors and others are subject to personal liability for their own intentional wrongdoing or negligent conduct even while engaged in corporate activities, as everyone is responsible for his or her own torts. The liability of corporate officers and directors for tortious conduct is based upon common law rules. A director or officer may also be liable for tort in sanctioning or approving fraudulent conduct. An officer is not personally liable for causing the corporation to terminate an employment contract unless the officer's acts involved individual tortious acts.*

---

*See, Robbins v. Panitz, 61 N.Y.2d 967, 475 N.Y.S.2d 274 (1984).

6. Liability for Crimes*

Directors and officers may be held criminally liable for certain corporate offenses, as several statutes and regulations impose criminal liability upon directors and officers.

In New York, directors may be guilty of a misdemeanor if they pay an illegal dividend, distribute corporate assets to shareholders in violation of statute, issue corporate shares without the corporation receiving full consideration, or if the corporation purchases its own shares without there being sufficient surplus. See Penal Law §190.35 for details.

C. DUTIES AND LIABILITIES IMPOSED BY STATUTES

1. The Securities Laws**

At both the federal and state levels the government is actively involved in regulating the sale of securities. Statutes have been enacted to protect the public and also to impose liability on anyone assisting in the sale of securities in violation of law. These laws are commonly known as blue-sky laws and in N.Y. are referred to as the "Martin Act". See e.g., N.Y. General Business Law §352 et al.; see also Article 16 Security Takeover Disclosure Act, B.C.L.§1600–1613.

A brief overview of some of the liabilities of officers and directors pursuant to violations of the Securities laws will be briefly presented. In a later Chapter dealing with mergers, acquisitions, takeovers, and tender offers, the securities laws will be further explored as to their effect on a merger, consolidation, or takeover. (See Chapter 10.)

The Securities Act of 1933 and the Securities Exchange Act of 1934 expose directors and officers to civil and criminal liability in connection with S.E.C. registration, proxies, and securities offerings.

The responsibility for administering the federal securities law is vested in the S.E.C. To prevent fraudulent sales of securities, the S.E.C. has adopted rules and regulations relating to financial and other information, which must be included in documents filed with the S.E.C. as well as those given to potential investors. It also regulates the various stock exchanges, utility holding companies, investment trusts, and investment advisers.

The Securities Act of 1933 is a disclosure law requiring that securities subject to its provisions be registered and that a prospectus be furnished each investor, the function being to provide the investor with sufficient facts, including financial information about the issuer to enable the prospective buyer to make an intelligent decision.

The Securities Act of 1933 imposes both civil and criminal liability for violation of its provisions. The criminal liability is for fraud in any offer or sale of securities. The civil liability provisions relating to registration statements impose liability on the following persons: every person who signed the registration statement, and every director of the corporation issuing the security; every person who, with his consent, is named in the registration statement as about to become a director; every accountant, engineer, or appraiser who assists in the preparation of the registration statement or its certification; every underwriter. Civil liability is imposed if a registration statement (1) contains untrue statements of material facts, (2) omits material facts required by statute or regulation, and (3) omits information that if not given makes the facts stated misleading.

---

*For exhaustive treatise, see Brickey, *Corporate Criminal Liability* (3 vol. Callahan & Co.).

**See, Hazen, *The Law of Securities Regulation* (1985); Ratner, *Securities Regulation* (3rd ed. 1986); Bloomenthal, *Securities Law Handbook* (1986-7 edition); Knepper, *Liability of Corporate Officers and Directors*, Ch. 10, 11, 12 (3rd ed. 1978 & 1985 Supp.) for background and details of the Securities Laws.

Fraud or manipulation, such as failure to disclose adverse information, in the sale or purchase of securities may give rise to director and officer personal liability for damages and, where deliberate or reckless, criminal penalties. This is pursuant to the Securities and Exchange Act of 1934. In the case of registered securities, a director or officer may incur liability in the solicitation of proxies if there are material misstatements or omissions in proxy communications.

Some of the important provisions of the Securities Exchange Act of 1934 are those relating to insider transactions, particularly relating to short-swing profits. In order to prevent insiders from profiting from the use of information not available to the general public, the law prevents their making short-swing profits.

Pursuant to Section 16(b), any beneficial owner of more than 10% of a registered security must surrender all profits realized on the sale and purchase, where said sale and purchase takes place within 6 months. Thus, if a director or officer realizes profits on the purchase or sale of a security within a six-month period, the profits belong to the company.

The concept of fraud under Section 10b of the S.E.C. encompasses not only untrue statements of material facts but also the omission of material facts necessary to prevent other statements from being misleading. The application of Rule 10b-5 applies to the purchase or sale of any security, which requires those standing in a fiduciary relationship (e.g., director, officer, controlling shareholders) to disclose all material facts before entering into transactions. Rule 10b-5 is violated if the purchaser of a security is not fully informed of any restriction on the resale of the security.

2. Foreign Corrupt Practices Act of 1977*

The Foreign Corrupt Practices Act of 1977 amends section §13(b) of the Securities and Exchange Act of 1934 to require reporting corporations to comply with certain accounting standards. In addition, the Act makes it unlawful for any domestic concern to engage in corrupt practices with foreign officials.

The accounting standards provision applies only to reporting corporations subject to S.E.C. jurisdiction. It requires them to keep books, records, and accounts which, in reasonable detail, accurately and fairly reflect the transactions and dispositions of corporate assets.

The Foreign Corrupt Practices Act of 1977 criminalizes foreign bribery and the lack of specified internal accounting controls; it prohibits officers and directors of certain companies from offering, making, or authorizing payment to foreign officials, political parties or candidates, with the intent to wrongfully influence a foreign government for the purpose of obtaining or retaining business. Any director or officer who willfully violates the Act may incur a fine up to $10,000, which may not be paid directly or indirectly by the company, and a prison sentence of up to five years, or both.

3. R.I.C.O.**

The Racketeering Influenced and Corrupt Organizations Act (R.I.C.O.), part of the Safe Streets Act of 1970, outlaws the use of income from racketeering to acquire or maintain a business. The law outlines 24 federal and eight state crimes, including securities law violations. A person found to have participated in, though not necessarily convicted of, any two of the enumerated

---

*See, Ferrera, *Corporate Board Responsibility Under the Foreign Corrupt Practices Act*, 18 A.B.L.J. 259 (1980); Seidel, *Internal Accounting Control Under the Foreign Corrupt Practices Act*, 18 A.B.L.J. 443 (1981) for background.

**18 U.S.C. §1961–1964. See generally, Knepper, *Liability of Corporate Officers and Directors*, pp. 12–13, 42–44 (1985 Supp). New York State has adopted a form of R.I.C.O. as part of the "Organizd Crime Control Act". See N.Y. Criminal Procedure Law §40.50 et. al., and Penal law §460.20 for criminal sanctions of "enterprise corrruption". See C.P.L.R. §1353–1355 for civil remedies enjoining future activity, upon a conviction under Penal Law §460.20.

crimes within a ten year period is considered to have undertaken a pattern of racketeering. The Act prohibits a racketeer from investing the proceeds of a "pattern of racketeering activity" in any "enterprise" engaged in or affecting interstate commerce. Practically every business entity constitutes an enterprise, and the term encompasses both legitimate and illegitimate enterprises.

Enforcement under R.I.C.O. has been used widely as a basis for prosecution of white collar crimes*; its effect is that a person is prohibited from using income derived from a pattern of racketeering activity to acquire or maintain an interest in an "enterprise"; enterprise is defined to include any individual, partnership, corporation, association, or other legal entity, and also any union or group of individuals associated which may not be a legal entity.

For a federal prosecution under R.I.C.O. the government must prove the enterprise affects interstate commerce. Penalties for violation include fines of up to $25,000 and/or imprisonment of up to 20 years; violations may result in forfeiture of any "interest" in the enterprise whose affairs are in violation of the statute. Although R.I.C.O. was originally enacted to fight organized crime, it has been used increasingly against legitimate business enterprises. In a civil R.I.C.O. action, triple damages may be awarded to the injured party plus attorneys fees; it has become common to include a violation of R.I.C.O. in actions involving business fraud, securities fraud, and also in bank fraud cases.

It has been decided by the U.S. Supreme Court that a criminal conviction is not necessary to the institution of a private civil R.I.C.O. suit.** The court held that R.I.C.O. should be liberally construed.

4. Other Statutes

Directors and officers may incur civil and/or criminal liability for violating various State and Federal statutes. Some of these various additional laws are briefly discussed.

(a) Labor and Employment Discrimination Laws

Specific labor practices are forbidden. In New York, any employer who fails to pay wages due to employees or discriminates on the basis of sex with respect to wages is liable to pay fifty dollars per employee so harmed and court costs. (Labor Law §197). In addition, the knowing failure to pay wages according to state law subjects the employer, officers and their agents to fine and imprisonment, and a similar penalty will be incurred by officers who fail to pay benefits or wage supplements. In addition, any person who directly or indirectly is involved in a wage kickback scheme is guilty of a misdemeanor. See N.Y. Labor Law §198-a,b,c.

It is unlawful for employers to discriminate in the hiring, discharge, compensation, or terms of employment because of race, color, sex, religion or national origin. This is governed by Title VII of The Civil Rights Act of 1964 (the Equal Employment Act),*** which created the Equal Employment Opportunity Commission (E.E.O.C.). The Age Discrimination in Employment Act makes the same prohibition with respect to discrimination based on a person's age. Title VII is applicable to employees engaged in industry affecting commerce having 15 or more employees. If a person claims to be damaged by a discriminatory employment practice, a private cause of action may be maintained under Title VII.

---

*See, e.g., Ginger, *Business' Civil RICO Liability Goes Unchecked,* 24 A.B.L.J. 179 (1986); Brown, *RICO—The New Dimension,* 89 Comm. L.J. 396 (Oct. 1984).
**Sedima, S.P.R.L. v. Imrex Co., 105 S.Ct. 3275 (1985).
***42 U.S.C. §2000e et. seq.

(b) Antitrust Laws*

Violations of federal antitrust laws such as fixing prices, carry with them civil and criminal liability for directors and officers.

(c) Conspiracy; Obstruction of Justice; Mail and Wire Fraud

In connection with the above federal laws, or on an independent basis, a director or officer may be subject to penalties for conspiracy to commit a federal crime or to defraud the government for concealing information from or making false statements to government agencies, in court or before a federal grand jury, for mail fraud, and for wire, radio or television fraud. Fraud is defined to include such conduct as payoffs to public officials and concealment of a conflict of interest.

Violations in obstruction of justice are covered by the Victim and Witness Prosecution Act**, whereby tampering with witnesses, victims and informants is prohibited, and retaliation against such persons is a crime. The law is also aimed as a deterrant to altering or destroying corporate records, and trying to obstruct any judicial (civil/criminal) or administrative proceeding. Penalties are up to a $250,000 fine and 10-year imprisonment.

Mail and wire fraud statutes prohibit use of the mails or interstate electronic communications media to further schemes to defraud.*** Violations may result in a maximum fine of $1,000, or 5 years imprisonment, or both.

(d) State Tax Laws

Violation of state tax laws may lead to civil and criminal charges against directors and officers. Corporate officers and employees who with fraudulent intent fail: to pay state corporate taxes, complete any return or declaration of estimated tax, or supply required information, are each subject to a fine of up to $1,000, if they were under a duty to perform the act in question (Tax Law §1085). Employers are liable for withholding taxes, so that any officer or employee under a duty to effectuate the tax provisions in question who fails to withhold or pay the tax or to supply information is subject to a fine; any willful failure to collect and pay or attempt to evade the tax is penalized by a fine equal to the tax evaded; also, any failure to pay withholding tax, the willful failure to supply an employee with a withholding statement or the furnishing of a fraudulent one, the failure to supply identifying numbers, and the failure to file duplicate copies of wage statements are all subject to penalties. (N.Y. Tax Law §675,685).

Directors and officers may also incur liability for violation of the statutory provisions of the New York Sales and Compensating Use Tax (Tax Law §1145) and other taxes on stock transfer, real estate transfer, and cigarette tax.

(e) Federal Tax Laws

Civil penalties are imposed for failing to file statements of payments, such as interest and dividend disbursements to another person, for failing to deposit taxes as required, for willfully failing to collect and pay over or attempting to evade any tax, or furnishing fraudulent statements to employees as required.

---

*Sherman Act §1,2; Clayton Act §2,3,7,8; Federal Trade Commission Act §5; See Holmes, *1985 Antitrust Law Handbook* for discussion.
**18 U.S.C. §1501.
***18 U.S.C. §1341; 18 U.S.C. §1343.

The Internal Revenue Code* makes it a felony to willfully attempt to evade or defeat any tax. Pursuant to I.R.C. §7201, the crime of tax evasion includes the following elements: tax payment due and owing; willfullness, which includes a voluntary, intentional violation of a known legal duty; and an affirmative act to evade the tax.

Tax evasion and willfully failing to collect and pay over taxes can cost a director or officer up to $10,000 in fines or five years imprisonment or both. Willfully failing to pay a tax, file a return, or supply required information may have the same financial liability, but the criminal penalty is only up to one year of imprisonment. Other criminal acts include willfully providing a fraudulent statement of wages or no statement to an employee; perjury; willfully aiding or assisting in the preparation or filing of materially false documents; concealing property; falsifying or destroying records; willfully given the I.R.S. a fraudulent document and failing to collect and pay over taxes required to be withheld.

(f) Miscellaneous Regulations

Directors and officers should also be aware of the statutes and regulations of government agencies that regulate their specific industries. A director or officer may be subject to personal liability for aiding a corporation in such acts as patent, copyright, or trademark infringements, unfair competition, antitrust violations, violation of the laws relating to discrimination, or violation of the securities laws.

Political contributions by a N.Y. corporation above $5,000 in the aggregate per calender year for any political candidate or party or for any political purpose is unlawful pursuant to §14–116 of the N.Y. Election Law, and unlawful under the Federal Election Campaigns Act (prohibiting any corporate political contribution in federal elections). For the violation of these statutes, directors are responsible.

D. DISSENTING DIRECTORS

Directors in undertaking their duty are required to attend Board meetings and vote on various matters. They should be concerned that they know all the facts and the resulting affect on the corporation before voting.

Pursuant to B.C.L.§719(a), directors who vote for or concur in any crucial matter may be held jointly and severally liable to the corporation for the benefit of its creditors or shareholders to the extent of any injury sustained for the following: declaring any dividend or other distribution contrary to B.C.L.§510(a)(b); purchasing the corporation's own shares by the corporation contrary to B.C.L.§513; distributing assets to shareholders after dissolution of the corporation without paying or adequately providing for corporate creditors; and granting loans to directors contrary to B.C.L.§714.

Even if a director doesn't vote for any of these actions or doesn't attend the meeting, he may still be personally responsible for any resulting damage to the corporation. According to B.C.L.§719(b), a director who attends a meeting where such action is taken shall be presumed to have concurred in the action unless his dissent is entered in the Minutes of the meeting, or unless he submits his written dissent to the secretary before adjournment of the meeting, or delivers in person or by registered mail his dissent to the secretary of the corporation promptly after the meeting. However, if a director voted in favor of a particular action, he cannot later dissent or

---

*See 26 U.S.C. §7201 et. al.

retract his vote to avoid liablity. If a director is absent from the meeting, he is also presumed to have concurred in the vote unless he delivers or sends by registered mail his dissent to the secretary of the corporation or files his dissent with the Minutes of the proceedings of the board or committee within a reasonable time after learning of the action. See B.C.L.§719(b).

Thus a director who does not attend the meeting, who attends and does not vote, who abstains from voting, or who votes against the proposal, is presumed to have voted in favor of such action unless he specifically notes his dissent on the record or submits a written notice to the secretary noting his dissent, and said written notice is attached to the Minutes of the meeting where such action was voted and approved. A director is thus able to protect himself if he is against any actions which are contrary to statute, by noting his dissent on the record, or otherwise complying with B.C.L.§719(b); such director will then not be held personally responsible for any damages sustained.

B.C.L.§719 specifically refers to four (4) enumerated decisions: declaration of an illegal dividend contrary to B.C.L.§510; purchase of the corporation's own shares when there is no Surplus contrary to B.C.L.§513; distribution of assets to shareholders after dissolution without paying creditors; and granting a loan to a director contrary to B.C.L.§714. However, a director can protect himself regarding other decisions also; if he objects he should be sure that his dissent is noted on the record as indicated in B.C.L.§719(b). It is certainly a good procedure to follow for any director if asked to vote upon questionable matters.

E. THE FIDUCIARY DUTY AND CONFLICT OF INTEREST

Directors manage the corporation through officers who are selected by the board; officers are agents of the corporation. Directors and officers are deemed fiduciaries, since their relationship with the corporation and the shareholders is one of trust and confidence.

Cases dealing with breach of fiduciary duty by an officer or director may involve one or more of the following: competing with the corporation; usurping a corporate opportunity; secret profits; self-dealing; having an interest that conflicts with the interests of the corporation; engaging in insider stock trading; authorizing a corporate transaction detrimental to minority shareholders; sale of control of the corporation. Situations may arise, especially with closely held corporations, whereby a director acquires a personal benefit by means of transactions between himself individually and the corporation. In any of these situations, the courts will look very carefully at such transactions for evidence of unfairness to the corporation if a shareholder or other interested party later challenges the transaction.

1. Under Common Law

The duty of loyalty imposed upon directors and officers was derived from the common law fiduciary duty imposed upon agents, partners, trustees, and others in special relationships involving trust and confidence. Combined with the duty of loyalty was the duty to fully disclose all material facts. A person under a fiduciary duty has the duty not to conceal material facts, and also the affirmative duty to fully disclose any material facts.

The failure to fully disclose, which may cause loss to the principal or which derives personal benefit for onself is the equivalent of fraud, which renders the fiduciary liable in damages and accountable for the profits realized from the double dealing. A person is not allowed to serve two masters, and especially not for oneself. The following example illustrates the common law rule:

Example:

> X Corp. is considering the purchase of a building from Y Inc.; Davis is a director of X Corp. and also a majority shareholder of Y Inc.; Davis has a duty to fully disclose his interest in Y Inc. to the other directors of X Corp. before they vote; he also has a duty not to influence the directors of X Corp. He was obliged, in addition to disclosing, not to attend the Board of Directors meeting except to fully disclose his interest; his presence at the meeting could not be counted to constitute a quorum, and he could not vote. If he violated his duty in any way, X Corp. could later rescind the purchase whether the transaction was fair or unfair. If Davis did not disclose his interest in Y Inc. (the seller) or if he violated his duty in any way, X Corp. could later rescind the transaction on the grounds of fraud or misrepresentation.

We will see in a subsequent section that B.C.L.§713 has modified the common law rule regarding conflict of interest.

2. Conflict of Interest

Corporate directors often have many business affiliations; they may even sit on the board of more than one corporation; they are precluded from engaging in or being involved in any business that competes (either directly or indirectly) with the corporation, without full disclosure. The fiduciary duty requires them to make full disclosure of any potential conflict of interest that might arise in any corporate transaction.

In the case of contracts between corporations having interlocking directors (one or more persons who are members of both boards of directors), the courts subject such contracts to the severest scrutiny; such contracts may be set aside and held to be unenforceable unless the transaction was shown to have been fair to the corporation and its shareholders, and entered into in good faith.

3. The Corporate Opportunity

Officers and directors may not take for themselves a business opportunity offered or available to them which is within the scope of the corporation's business. A corporate opportunity is one in which the corporation has a right, property interest, or expectancy. A director or officer may not usurp an opportunity or acquire property which the corporation needs, is seeking, or to which it has a "tangible expectancy." This, however, does not apply where the corporation has refused or is itself incapable of taking advantage of the "deal".

If the director or officer acts upon the "deal" in his or her personal capacity, a conflict of interest arises. To protect against liability arising from this type of transaction, a director or officer should present the proposed deal to the corporation, and only after the corporation decides it is not interested, may the director or officer then act in his or her own personal capacity. If an officer or director learns of a business opportunity through the position in the corporation, and appropriates the deal for his or her own personal benefit, this is a breach of trust, and all the profits received as a result of the transaction belong to the corporation.

4. The Duty Not to Compete

As fiduciaries, directors and officers owe to the corporation the duty of undivided loyalty which does not permit them to compete with the corporation. Although directors and officers may engage in their own business interests, courts will closely scrutinize any interest that competes with the corporation. The fiduciary duty requires constant undivided loyalty to the corporation on the part of directors and officers. A director must account to the corporation for secret profits received in violation of the duty of loyalty as well as secret profits made by using confidential information acquired at a board of directors meeting.

5. The Interested Director under B.C.L.§713

By statute the common law rule regarding interested directors has been greatly and substantially modified. In dealing with modern corporations, strict adherence to common law standards would make it most difficult for two corporations with interlocking directors to enter into binding contracts with each other.

B.C.L.§713 sets standards and rules to be applied regarding the enforceability of such contracts; the mere fact two corporations have common directors does not create a reason to set aside any contractual relations. If a director interested in the transaction is present at the meeting, is counted in the quorum, and even if he votes, this would *not* be grounds to set aside the contract.

Thus, the enactment of B.C.L.§713 substantially reduces the impact of the fiduciary duty upon a director; pursuant to B.C.L.§713, the controlling factors in determining the enforceability of the contract are reduced to the following rules and standards: (1) If the director's interest is disclosed in good faith or known to the board, and approval of the contract or transaction is by a sufficient vote without counting the vote of the interested director (or if the vote of the disinterested directors are insufficient to constitute action of the board pursuant to B.C.L.§708, then by unanimous vote of the disinterested directors) B.C.L.§713(a)(1); or (2) If the director's interest is disclosed in good faith or known to the shareholders entitled to vote, and the transaction is approved by vote of the shareholders B.C.L.§713(a)(2): or (3) If the contract is fair and reasonable to the corporation when adopted, in which case the interested director must affirmatively prove the contract is fair and reasonable. B.C.L.§713(b). If any of these three standards are met, the contract will be enforced, and will not be set aside.

The interested director has the burden of proving the contract is fair and reasonable to the corporation if no full disclosure were made, or if disclosure were made, but there was not a sufficient vote of the disinterested directors to constitute board action. If the contract is fair and reasonable, the contract will stand and may not be avoided by the corporation regardless of whether the interested director had disclosed or whether his vote was necessary to approve the transaction. Only if it is unfair does disclosure and the vote become material.

In addition, The C/I may contain any additional restrictions and provisions for contracts or transactions between a corporation and its directors. B.C.L.§713(d).

Examples:

> (1) Alpha Corp. a corporation, has nine members on its Board of Directors. Johnson, one of its directors, proposes that the corporation purchase a building for expansion purposes. Unknown to the other directors, the building is owned by Johnson's wife. At the Board of Directors meeting, 4 of its members are absent. Including Johnson, there are 5 members present. A minimum quorum is 5; Johnson may be counted in the quorum.

The Board of Directors votes to approve the purchase; Johnson did not disclose his wife's interest in the building. Later, the directors or shareholders discover that Johnson's wife was the seller of the building. The corporation may set aside the transaction unless Johnson is able to affirmatively establish the contract was fair and reasonable to the corporation at the time it was approved.

(2) Same facts as (1) above. Assume Johnson attends the meeting and fully discloses his wife's ownership of the building. The minimum quorum is 5; and Johnson may be counted in the quorum. It is necessary that there be a minimum vote of 3 approving (without counting Johnson's vote). If Johnson votes, there must be a minimum vote of 4 approving.

Assume the vote is 3 in favor, and 2 opposed. The corporation will be able to rescind the transaction unless Johnson is able to affirmatively establish the contract was fair and reasonable to the corporation at the time it was approved.

(3) Same facts as (2) above. Assume the vote is 4 in favor, and 1 opposed; the corporation may enter into the transaction. If the shareholders later complain, there will be no basis for setting aside the transaction under B.C.L.§713 even though Johnson was counted in the quorum, and even though he voted in favor of the action, because there was a sufficient number of disinterested directors voting in favor.

Note that a corporation cannot set aside a transaction merely because a director is "interested". If the material facts of the director's interest are known or fully disclosed to those voting, the transaction is not voidable provided: the board (not counting the interested director's vote) votes to approve; the disinterested directors unanimously approve; or the shareholders vote to approve it. In addition, the interested director may be able to affirmatively prove the transaction was fair and reasonable to the corporation and in which event, the transaction may not be set aside even without disclosure and no matter what the vote was.

6. The Effect of Ratification by the Shareholders

If the board of directors is unable to approve a transaction with a sufficient vote of disinterested directors, it may present the facts of the transaction in question to the shareholders for their ratification or approval at an annual or special meeting. For this purpose, shareholders who may be interested are not disqualified from voting. If a majority of the shareholders ratify the directors' action, it cannot generally later be attacked. However, even a majority of shareholders cannot ratify corporate waste, i.e. the giving away of corporate assets, as the assets belong in part to others who have not consented, namely, the minority shareholders and also the creditors.

Ratification has the effect of transferring the burden of proof on the issue of fairness from the directors involved to the complaining shareholders. There cannot be a valid ratification unless the shareholders have full knowledge of what they are approving.

If the directors are not sure how shareholders will react to certain transactions, they could request that the shareholders ratify the transaction; the directors are thereby absolving themselves of liability, and shifting the risk to the shareholders; as a practical matter, directors often do not submmit questionable transactions to shareholders unless required to, as the shareholders before voting may start asking too many questions.

7. Management Compensation

The board of directors usually determines compensation of officers. In addition, B.C.L.§713(e) expressly authorizes the board of directors to fix the compensation of directors unless there is a contrary provision in the C/I or by-laws.

8. "Insider" Stock Trading*

A special situation involving the question of fiduciary duty arises in situations where directors and officers, possessed with corporate confidential information, use such confidential information for their own personal profit and gain: by buying stock of the corporation or selling their own stock of the corporation (as the case may be) before the confidential information becomes available to the public, thereby causing a rise or fall in the market price of the shares. This has been held to be a breach of fiduciary duty and misappropriation of information for personal use acquired in a fiduciary capacity.

When a director or officer is also a shareholder, insider trading is a potential source of liability. Directors and officers have a fiduciary duty to the corporation with respect to their trading in the corporation's shares, and the corporation may retrieve any profits made from the exploitation of "inside" information. Federal securities laws provide for the forfeiture to the corporation of short swing stock trading profits of persons with inside information. Some of the rules governing securities was covered in prior sections of this Chapter.

F. INDEMNIFICATION OF CORPORATE DIRECTORS AND OFFICERS

Officers and directors of a corporation, by virtue of their position, are exposed to financial liability in performing their duties. Potential liability has increasingly arisen under the federal securities, antitrust and other laws. In addition there have been increasing number of derivative suits brought on behalf of the corporation against the directors and officers; claims of third parties have also been pursued.

Corporate officers and directors may believe they are acting in good faith, and still may find they are being sued by shareholders or other aggrieved parties. The cost of defending these lawsuits and the risks involved have been making it difficult for many corporations to fill the Board of Directors with competent people as these individuals are being discouraged and are refusing to be members of the Board of Directors.

Under common law, law suit expenses in defending a director or officer were borne by them personally; indemnification of expenses was not permitted unless the director or officer was absolved of all liability.

Today, all states have some form of indemnification for officers and directors. Most of the states' statutes distinguish the rules for derivative actions (for the benefit of the Corporation) and for third-party actions.

In 1986, New York amended its indemnification statute. Pursuant to such amendment, the statutory indemnification provisions are not exclusive (as they previously were). Therefore, there can be indemnification provisions in the C/I, the by-laws, or (if so authorized in the C/I or the by-laws) by resolution of the shareholders, or by resolution of the disinterested directors, or by

---

*See, generally, Kempin, *The Use and Misuse of Inside Information By Corporate Managers and other Insiders*, 14 A.B.L.J. 139 (1976).

agreement providing for indemnification. However, there can *not* be any indemnification to a director or officer if a judgment or other final adjudicaton establishes that the acts of the director or officer were committed in bad faith or were the result of active and deliberate dishonesty or that the director gained a financial profit or other advantage. Thus, indemnification could be approved and permitted even where there had been an adjudication by a court that there was damage to the corporation because of the director's negligence. However, indemnificaton could not be permitted if there were active and deliberate dishonesty. See B.C.L.§721 for all details.

Pursuant to B.C.L.§722, there is no longer a distinction for the right to seek indemnification, whether it is a derivative action or a third party action; pursuant to B.C.L.§723, a person who has been successful on the merits or otherwise in the defense of a civil or criminal proceeding shall be entitled to indemnification. It also eliminates the requirement that the party be "wholly" successful and also provides for the advancement of litigation expenses. The corporaton has the power to purchase and maintain insurance for indemnification. B.C.L.§726. See B.C.L.§721–726 as amended for all details.

In July 1986, Delaware amended its indemnification statute. The new Delaware statute permits corporations incorporated in Delaware to limit or eliminate liability of Directors for money damages for injury to the corporation or its shareholders, due to the director's failure to exercise due care. Particularly since the decision of *Smith v. Gorkom*,* Directors have become more concerned regarding being held liable for their decisions. The Delaware Indemnification Statute permits corporations who have obtained shareholder approval to insert in their Incorporation Certificate provisions to relieve Directors of all liability to the corporation or to shareholders for negligence, and limits a Director's potential liability to acts of disloyalty, bad faith, breach of fiduciary duty, willful violation of law, or intentional misconduct.**

The New York Amendment does not require shareholder approval and applies to both Officers and Directors, and also appears to impose a much looser standard whereby indemnification is permitted.

Even though New York State has changed its Indemnification statute in the Summer of 1986, at the time of this writing, there are already proposals for further Amendment.

CASE 18
RAPOPORT v. SCHNEIDER
(Court of Appeals of New York, 29 N.Y.2d 396, 328 N.Y.S.2d 431)(1972)

BREITEL, Judge.

Plaintiffs, in their status both as directors and stockholders, brought this derivative action on behalf of the corporation against other directors to prevent the allegedly improper payment of a duplicate claim for real estate commissions and for an accounting.

• • • •

All plaintiffs and all individual defendants are directors of New York Equities, Inc., a publicly-held corporation. Its real properties were first managed by Strand Management Inc., and later by Helmsley-Spear, Inc. At relevant times, plaintiff Rapoport was the sole owner of Strand; and three

---

*488 A.2d 858 (Del. 1985).
**See analysis of Delaware statute, Veasey, *Delaware Supports Directors with a Three-Legged Stool of Limited Liability, Indemnification and Insurance,* 42 Bus. Law. 399 (1987).

of the defendants, Schneider, Scott, and Winter, were respectively executive vice-president, vice-president, and treasurer of Helmsley.

On September 17, 1970, a special meeting of the board of Equities was convened allegedly without notice to plaintiff Marantz. The stated purpose of the meeting was to consider any defense Equities might have against action by Strand for commissions originally in the amount of $190,000. The directors, by a vote of four to two, adopted a resolution to pay a claim by Helmsley alleged to "duplicate substantially the claims made by Strand". Schneider and Winter, two officers of Helmsley present, voted for the resolution. Plaintiffs Rapoport and Giver voted against it. Plaintiff's argue that defendants Schneider and Winter should have disqualified themselves because of their conflict of interest, and that, if they had, the result would have been different. Payment of the Helmsley claim, it is alleged, "depletes the assets" of Equities by unnecessary disbursement and exposure to a double liability for the same sum.

Plaintiffs have demanded an accounting by the defendant directors, a declaration that the resolution authorizing payment of the Helmsley claim is void, and defendants be enjoined from paying the claim.

Special Term appears to have dismissed the directors' cause of action on the ground that only a stockholders' derivative action was appropriate. This view is erroneous . . . §720[b] of the B.C.L. expressly authorizes directors to sue other directors for misconduct. [See B.C.L.§720].

§720 was derived from sections 60 and 61, and their predecessors, former §90 and §91, of the Gen. Corp. L. The present statute and the predecessor sections embrace common-law and statutory causes of action imposing liability on directors (12 N.Y. Jur., Corporations, §783; see, e.g., Manix v. Fantl, 209 A.D. 756, 205 N.Y.S. 174; People v. Equitable Life Assur. Soc., 124 A.D. 714, 733–735, 109 N.Y.S. 453, 468–470). The statute is broad and covers every form of waste of assets and violation of duty whether as a result of intention, negligence, or predatory acquisition. Since this case involves payment of a duplicated claim and, therefore, a false one, if plaintiff's allegations are true, the cause of action by plaintiffs in their status as directors is within the statute's compass.

Defendants argue, however, that plaintiff directors may not maintain an action under §720 because they too have a conflict of interest. This question of standing, once reserved in passing in Tenney v. Rosenthal, 6 N.Y.2d 204, 210, 189 N.Y.S.2d 158, still need not be decided. True, plaintiff Rapoport has a conflict of interest as a result of his sole ownership of Strand. In searching for a conflict of interest, however, on the part of the other two plaintiffs, the court may look to the complaint and undisputed facts contained in the answer and affidavits. Although defendants' attorney agued orally that plaintiffs Giber and Marantz have a conflict of interest, the record reveals no allegations or evidence of it. It follows, therefore, that at least two plaintiffs are directors without a personal interest in the questioned transaction. Since any benefit derived from this action would accrue to the corporation, the action should not be barred. . . .

As noted above, it is alleged that one director, Marantz, received no notice of the directors' meeting. The lawfulness of the payment or proposed payment of the claim under §720[a][2] and §720[a][3] above depends on the validity of the resolution adopted. If lack of notice renders actions taken at that meeting invalid, then the authorization would be unlawful.

Because this was a special meeting, notice to directors was required. (B.C.L.§711[a]; 12 N.Y. Jur., Corporations, §607). Notice may be waived (see B.C.L.§711[c]), but, absent ratification, failure to notify directors of a special meeting renders actions taken at the meeting invalid (Cirrincione v. Polizzi, 14 A.D.2d 281, 283, 220 N.Y.S.2d 741, 742; 2 Fletcher's Cyclopedia Corporations §406, p. 255. . . . Although it may eventuate upon a trial that notice may have been adequate under the bylaws of Equities (see B.C.L.§711[b]), or, perhaps by the statutory mailing presumption (B.C.L.§108[c]) the unqualified allegation that one director did not receive any notice of the meeting should be sufficient to put the adequacy of notice in issue. Consequently, the first cause of action is sustainable, if for no other reason than on the basis of the alleged lack of notice.

Plaintiff's allege in addition that the resolution is invalid because of participation by interested directors. Defendant directors Schneider and Winter, who voted for the resolution, were, as observed earlier, officers of Helmsley. Plaintiff Rapoport, who voted against the resolution, was the sole owner of Strand, the competing claimant for the commissions. The outside relationships of these three directors were undoubtedly known to all the directors of Equities.

The B.C.L. provides that where "interested" directors, who have disclosed their interest, vote on a resolution, the resolution is nontheless valid if a majority of the disinterested directors vote in its favor (former §713, subd. [a][1], as last amd. by L.1965). A director is "interested" if he is an officer or director of another corporation apparently involved in the questioned transaction. Thus, all three of the directors mentioned are "interested". Not counting the votes of these directors, there remain the votes of two disinterested directors in favor of the resolution, H. Klein and I. Klein, and the vote of one disinterested director, Giber, opposed to the resolution. A quorum of votes cast by disinterested directors is not required. B.C.L.§713[c]. Under the rule of §713, therefore, the resolution is not invalid because of the participation of interested directors.

Despite the validity of the resolution under §713, the interested directors may in any event be liable for having participated in a transaction from which they may derive an indirect personal benefit. It is not necessary, however, to reach this question. To assert liability for waste, it is sufficient to allege that the directors have knowingly authorized payment of a duplicate claim out of corporate funds. It is and has always been general law that a director may be held accountable for the waste of corporate assets whether intentional or negligent without limitation to transactions from which he benefits (e.g., General Rubber Co. v. Benedict, 215 N.Y.18, 21, 109 N.E. 96, 97; Bosworth v. Allen, 168 N.Y. 157, 165–166; Leslie v. Lorillard, 110 N.Y. 519, 536 . . .).

• • • •

The allegations of the "duplication" of the Helmsley claim are adequate to meet the criticism that they are conclusory (cf. Foley v. D'Agostino, 21 A.D.2d 60, 68, 248 N.Y.S.2d 121, 129). The cause of action alleges that Equities had been sued by Strand to recover commissions, that the lawsuit had already been partly settled, and that the Helmsley claim was for substantially the same services as the Strand claim. Although this is a rather skimpy allegation of a duplicated claim, its thrust is plain and unmistakable in establishing, if true, that the claim was a false one. . . .

• • • •

Accordingly, the order of the Appellate Division should be reversed and the motion to dismiss the complaint denied, with costs in all courts. [All judges concur].

CASE 19
ARONOFF v. ALBANESE
(App. Div. 2nd Dep't, 85 A.D.2d 3, 446 N.Y.S.2d 368)(1982)

PER CURIAM.

Plaintiffs, stockholders of defendant Hospital Building Corporation (HBC), commenced this derivative action to recover lost profits of HBC as a result of certain transactions with the individual defendants, who are directors of HBC and also partners of Pelham Bay General Hospital (PBGH) which leases a hospital from HBC. The first transactions involved the rent paid by PBGH to HBC. The rent was $30,000 monthly from 1962 until January, 1975, when it was increased to $36,000 per month. In July, 1976 the monthy rent was reduced to $20,000 due to PBGH's cash flow problems (caused by delay in Medicare reimbursement). In May, 1977 the rent was increased to $30,000 per month. The 10 months of reduced rent caused a loss of $160,000 to HBC. The other transactions which are the subject of objection by the shareholders include the purchase, with HBC funds, of certain permanent equipment for the hospital totaling approximately $600,000, and the installation of an Intensive Care Unit and a central air conditioning system . . . [for] $214,000 . . . [A] 1975 lease modification provided that the landlord would be responsible for major repairs . . . and equipment for a complete hospital. In 1977, a further modification provided that the purchase of additional fixtures and equipment would be accompanied by a corresponding net increase in rent.

To all of this, the individual defendants asserted the defense of ratification on the basis that a majority of HBC stockholders, at a December 15, 1977 meeting, approved the mentioned transactions. . . .

The issue on appeal is whether the questioned transactions can be effectively ratified by the stockholders—that is, whether they are void or merely voidable. The courts have drawn a distinction between transactions which are only voidable at the option of the corporation and transactions which are void. Voidable transactions can be ratified by a majority vote of the stockholders, but a void act is not subject to ratification (Quintal v. Kellner, 264 N.Y. 32; Pollitz v. Wabash R.R. Co., 207 N.Y. 113; . . .). Further, it is settled law that waste or a gift of corporate assets are void acts and cannot be ratified by a majority of stockholders (Meredith v. Camp Hill Estates, 77 A.D.2d 649, 430 N.Y.S.2d 383; see Diamond v. Davis, 38 N.Y.S.2d 103, affd. 265 A.D. 919, 39 N.Y.S.2d 412, affd. 292 N.Y.552; Selman v. Allen, 121 N.Y.S.2d 142; 2 Fletcher, Cyclopedia of Corporations §764). . . .

The essence of a claim of gift is lack of consideration and the essence of waste is the diversion of corporate assets for improper or unnecessary purposes. . . . In Amdur v. Meyer, 15 A.D.2d 425, 430, 224 N.Y.S.2d 440, the court held that certain stock options were not a gift, since "the corporation might reasonably expect benefit to flow to the corporation." . . . a clearly inadequate consideration invokes the same principles as the absence of consideration (see Gottlieb v. McKee, 34 Del. Ch. 537, 107 A.2d 240). In Pollitz v. Wabash R.R. Co., 207 N.Y. 113, the director improperly applied assets to his own use (through issuance of stock without consideration). Other examples of unratifiable acts include the use of corporate funds to discharge personal obligations (Quintal v. Kellner, 264 N.Y. 32), distribution of surplus earnings under guise of additional salaries to directors and officers (Godley v. Crandall & Godley Co., 212 N.Y. 121), transfer of assets without consideration (Meredith v. Camp Hill Estates, 77 A.D.2d 649, 430 N.Y.S.2d 383), use of corporate property given to a foreign corporation without consideration (Boaz v. Sterlingworth Ry. Supply Co., 68 A.D.1, 73 N.Y.S. 1039), payment of a false claim (Continental Securities Co. v. Belmont, 206 N.Y. 7), and payment of excessive investment fees to directors (Saxe v. Brady, 40 Del. Ch. 474, 184 A.2d 602). The directors would be liable for every form of waste of assets regardless of whether it was intentional or negligent (see Rapoport v. Schneider, 29 N.Y.2d 396, 328 N.Y.S.2d 431).

The existence of benefit to the corporation, in turn, is generally committed to the sound business judgment of the directors (See Auerbach v. Bennett, 47 N.Y.2d 619, 419 N.Y.S.2d 920;

Amdur v. Meyer, 15 A.D.2d 425, 224 N.Y.S.2d 440; Cohen v. Ayers, 596 F.2d 733 [7th Cir., applying New York law]). The objecting stockholder must demonstrate that no person of ordinary sound business judgment would say that the corporation received fair benefit. . . . If ordinary businessmen might differ on the sufficiency of consideration received by the corporation, the courts will uphold the transaction (see Saxe v. Brady, supra). The motives or personal benefit to the directors is also a relevant concern. The objecting stockholders must show that the directors must have acted with an intent to serve some outside interest, regardless of the consequence (see Gamble v. Queens County Water Co., 123 N.Y. 91). If there is a great disparity in values between the assets expanded and the benefits received, the courts will infer that the directors are guilty of improper motives, or at least recklessly indifferent to the stockholders' interests (see Alcott v. Hyman, 42 Del. Ch. 233, 208 A.2d 501).

The determination of whether or not there has been a gift of corporate assets is largely a question of fact. . . . The existence of ratification makes the objecting stockholders' burden more difficult since ratification shifts the burden of proof to the opponents of the transactions (see Cohen v. Ayers, 596 F.2d 733 . . .). On the other hand, compliance with §713 of the B.C.L. does not automatically validate any transaction (see Rapoport v. Schneider, supra; Remillard Brick Co. v. Remillard-Dandini Co., 109 Cal.App.2d 405, 241 P.2d 66 [§713 of the B.C.L. is derived from §820 of the Cal. Gen. Corp. L.]).

Turning to the instant case, although plaintiffs never alleged "gift" or "waste" in their complaint, the omission does not bar a consideration of the gift or waste claims. . . . Since the complaint gives sufficient notice of the events out of which plaintiff's grievances arise, it can be construed as relying on a theory of "gift", a transaction which cannot be ratified by a majority of the stockholders. . . .

While the individual defendants may ultimately prevail after trial, it cannot be said, as a matter of law, that a person of ordinary business judgment would say that HBC received fair consideration. On the rent reduction claim, the individual defendants allege that the cash flow problems of PBGH were to blame. In additon, there is a factual issue as to whether the purchase of hospital equipment with HBC funds benefited the corporation and the argument of the individual defendants that the purchases were necessary for the future of the hospital merely makes the question a factual issue for determination at trial. Furthermore, the purchase apparently violated the lease because the lease did not obligate HBC to buy equipment. Once the lease was modified to provide for such purchases, with a corresponding rent increase, the lease apparently was violated again, since no increase in rent was given. In this particular case, the ratification of actions by the majority of stockholders of HBC, together with the then existing financial condition of PBGH, emphasize that any benefit to HBC is a triable issue of fact. . . .

In sum, plaintiffs have demonstrated factual issues with respect to the alleged void acts constituting gift and waste so as to defeat summary judgment.

Judgement of the Supreme Court, Westchester County (MARBACH, J)., entered November 28, 1980, reversed, on the law, with $50 costs and disbursements, and [Defendant's] motion for summary judgment denied.

Discussion Questions:

What types of transactions may the shareholders ratify?

What is the difference between void and voidable transactions? Which may be ratified by the shareholders?

CASE 20
SCHACHTER v. KULIK
(App. Div. 2nd Dept, 96 A.D.2d 1038, 466 N.Y.S.2d 444) (1983)

• • • •

This appeal arises out of three consolidated shareholder derivative actions brought on behalf of the Ketek Electric Corp. (hereinafter Ketek) pursuant to section 626 and 720 of the B.C.L. Schachter and Kulik were social friends who decided to go into business together in 1972 for the purpose of manufacturing and selling an electronic device which would detect letter bombs. On February 2, 1973, a certificate of incorporation was filed in the name of Ketek. Kulik and Schachter, the sole shareholders, each received 100 shares. Schachter was elected president and treasurer and Kulik was elected vice-president and secretary.

The first electronic detector which was manufactured by Ketek was called "Letar-Gard". On September 3, 1974, a design patent for this device was issued in the joint name of Schachter and Kulik. A trademark was issued on August 5, 1975. The parties also developed a device to detect counterfeit bills called "Moni-Gard" and a patent for that device was issued in August, 1976. The assignee of that patent was Ketek.

In 1975, the financial condition of the Ketek corporation became somewhat precarious and the personal relationship between Schachter and Kulik began to deteriorate. At that point, the parties tried to sell the company. In July, 1975, Schachter had asked a Mr. O'Hare to make an offer of $10,000 for the entire business, but Kulik refused to sell. In fact, Kulik claims that he wanted to continue in business even if it meant loaning the corporation money.

On July 25, 1975 Kulik discovered that engineering drawings, sales files, customer lists and the patent file were missing from Ketek's office. Schachter denied knowing the whereabouts of the missing material. When Kulik returned to the office a few days later, he discovered that all the files and drawings and the checkbook were gone. Kulik was later informed that Schachter had taken these items. Schachter claims that he took possession of the items to safeguard them.

On July 20, 1975, Schachter terminated mail service to Ketek, and thereafter Schachter directed that all Ketek mail be placed in his personal box. Schachter also contacted the telephone company and directed that all telephone calls to Ketek be switched to his home number. Thereafter, Schachter received a dispossess notice from the landlord. In late August, Schachter incorporated and became the sole stockholder of another corporation called Hoteltron Systems Inc. He then moved all the Ketek furniture, equipment and inventory to a new office and signed a document on Ketek stationery authorizing Hoteltron to manufacture and sell the products of Ketek. The document also authorized Hoteltron to use any tools, machinery, drawings, furniture or other property of Ketek. In consideration, Hoteltron agreed to pay Ketek a sum equal to five percent of the net sales of the products for one year beginning September 15, 1975 and ending September 14, 1976. Schachter never called a directors' meeting or gave any notice to Kulik that he was doing this.

Kulik's causes of action against Schachter were essentially predicated on the theory that Schachter unlawfully converted Ketek's assets to his own use. Section 717 of the B.C.L. provides that directors and officers of corporations shall discharge their duties diligently and in good faith. Directors and officers, in the performance of their duties, stand in a fiduciary relationship to their corporation. . . .

As such they owe the corporation their undivided loyalty and are not permitted to derive a personal profit at the expense of the corporation (see Foley v. D'Agostino, 21 A.D.2d 60, 248 N.Y.S.2d 121; Limmer v. Medallion Group, 75 A.D.2d 299, 428 N.Y.S.2d 961).

The evidence in the record indicates that Schachter, in complete disregard of his fiduciary duty to the Ketek corporation seized all of the corporate assets of Ketek, entered into a unilateral royalty areement with Hoteltron, a corporation wholly owned by himself, to manufacture and sell the products to which Ketek had patent and trademark rights, and then proceeded to carry on the business for which Ketek was formed under the Hoteltron name. Such conduct cannot be countenanced.

In view of the foregoing, Schachter should be compelled to account for his improper conduct in violation of his fiduciary obligation to the Ketek corporation.

PROBLEMS

60. Frank Corp. had an authorized capital stock of 1,000 shares of $100 par value. On July 1, 1980, its issued and outstanding shares consisted of 500 shares, its assets were $120,000, and its liabilities amounted to $60,000. On that day, its board of directors, consisting of A, B, and C, declared, and thereafter distributed, a stock dividend of 10 per cent.

The Corporation continued to do business and, on July 1, 1981, its assets were $190,000 and its liabilities amounted to $140,000. On that day, July 1, 1981, its board by a vote of A and B for, and C against, declared, and thereafter paid out, a cash dividend of ten cents per share. C's dissent was recorded in the minutes.

On April 1, 1982, Frank Corp. became bankrupt, and thereafter the trustee in bankruptcy brought an action against A, B, and C, contending that both dividends had been improper and illegal and that the creditors had been injured thereby.

(a) Was the stock dividend on July 1, 1980 proper? Explain.

(b) Was the cash dividend on July 1, 1981 proper? Explain.

(c) Are the directors A, B, and C, or any of them responsible for any of these actions? If yes, explain.

(d) Is the trustee in bankruptcy able to maintain this action? (See Chapter 9).

(e) Assume the corporation declared a 10% stock dividend on July 1, 1981 instead of the cash dividend. Would such action be proper? Explain.

61. (a) D was a director of S Corp., S Corp. owns a supermarket chain. A offered to sell D a corner lot which would make a good supermarket site. D bought the lot for $15,000 without telling the other directors about it. 6 months later D sold the lot to S Corp. for $20,000. When an S Corp. shareholder learned the whole story of D's dealings he threatened to sue D on behalf of S Corp. for $5,000—the profit D made upon this transaction. What result?

(b) Suppose D had informed the Board of Directors of S Corp. of the availability of this lot. The Board had voted not to buy it. D had then bought it for $15,000 and had later sold it to Z for $20,000 for use as a furniture store location. An S Corp. shareholder claimed D should pay S Corp. his $5,000 profit. Could this demand be enforced?

62. A Corp. and B Corp. were in completely dissimilar lines of business. X, Y, and Z served as directors of both. Since each corporation had a 5-person board of directors, X, Y, and Z constituted a majority of both boards.

A Corp. made a contract to sell a track of land to B Corp. for a fair price. A's minority directors were against the sale; B's directors were in favor of the purchase. A Corp.'s board approved the sale 3 to 2. B Corp.'s board approved the purchase 5 to 0. A Corp.'s minority directors claimed the contract was unenforceable because X, Y, and Z had the power to approve it for both companies, since they constituted a majority of both boards. Are the minority directors correct?

63. Ace Corp. negotiates with the Jones Construction Co. for the renovation of the Ace Corp. headquarters. Jones, owner of the Jones Construction Co. is also one of the five members of the board of directors of Ace Corp. Jones had previously informed two of the other directors of his interest in the construction company. The contract was approved by Ace's board with a three-to-two vote, with Jones voting with the majority. Discuss whether this contract is binding on the corporation.

64. Litho Corp. was incorporated in New York to operate a printing business. The charter did not give it express powers authorizing the acquisition and holding of real property. The Board of Directors of Litho Corp. consists of five persons, incuding Mrs. X who serves as secretary of the corporation. At a Board of Directors meeting where all directors are present, the Board by a majority vote, votes to purchase a parcel of land at the market price, for the purpose of constructing a building for a new speed press. The owner of the property agrees to take back a mortgage from the corporation for the purchase but insists that the mortgage be signed by the secretary of the corporation. Mrs. X opposes the transaction, and refuses to sign and affix the corporate seal. The Board, by majority vote, immediately removes her as secretary and as director of the corporation and appoints Mr. Z, another director, as the new secreatry. He signs all the documents. None of the directors were aware that Mr. Z is a co-owner of the parcel of land contracted for when he voted for the purchase.

a) Is the Board's removal of Mrs. X as a director valid?

b) Is the Board's removal of Mrs. X as secretary valid?

c) Assuming the Board acted lawfully in removing Mrs. X, does the Board have the power to proceed with the acquisition of the parcel of land?

d) Can the corporation later rescind the contract on the ground of Mr. Z's ownership of the parcel of land? Explain.

65. The Board of Directors of Ace Corp. consists of ten persons, including Carl. At a meeting which was attended by Carl and five other directors, Carl proposed a contract with Ace Corp. for the sale of a printing press owned by Carl which Ace Corp. needs. The price asked by Carl for the press is very high and excessive. Ownership of the press by Carl was disclosed to the other directors. Carl and four of the five directors present at the meeting vote to approve the contract.

The term of office of one of the directors voting to approve the contract had expired but his successor had not yet been elected.

a) The director who voted against the proposal brings suit on behalf of the corporation to avoid the contract on the basis of Carl's financial interest and the fact that he was present and voted at the meeting. What result? Explain.

b) Would the result be different in the above example if the other directors did not know of Carl's ownership of the press? Explain.

c) Assuming the contract is not avoided, are there any grounds upon which the directors who voted to approve the contract and the others who were not at the meeting can be held liable for any damages to the corporation? Explain.

66. The Board of Directors of Starr Corp., a New York corporation, consists of Allen, Buckley and Charles. At a properly called meeting of the Board, with Allen and Buckley present, and Charles absent, Allen and Buckley vote to purchase all the assets of Venture Associates, a partnership which owns and operates movie theatres for $100,000, which is a fair price. Unknown to Allen and Charles, Buckley is a general partner in Venture Associates, which is in desperate financial condition, and Buckley faces personal bankruptcy unless a buyer is found for the assets of Venture Associates.

Can the purchase be set aside or enjoined on the ground that it was not properly authorized by the Board because:

a) Buckley failed to disclose his interest in Venture Associates;

b) The authorization would have been invalid because Buckley was an interested director even if Buckley had disclosed his interest.

c) Even if it was not invalid because Buckley was an interested director, the purchase was still unauthorized because without counting Buckley, there was no quorum at the directors meeting.

Discuss the merits of each of these contentions.

67. Alex Ltd. was a New York corporation whose purpose, as stated in its charter, was "to own farms, to cultivate the farms and sell the produce." The corporaton owned and operated 10 farms in New York state.

At a properly called meeting of the board of directors, the board authorized each of the following:

a) A loan to D, one of the directors;

b) A loan to S, a shareholder of the corporation;

c) The sale of two of the farms to B for reasonable consideration;

d) The creation of an Executive Committee of the board of directors with all the authority of the board; the Certificate of Incorporation and the by-laws made by no mention of committees.

Discuss the legal effect of each of these authorizations.

68. Alpha Corp. owns property which it purchased in 1961 for $100,000 at which figure the property has since been carried on its books. At the present time, the property has a fair market value of $600,000. Last week, the Board of Directors adopted a resolution revaluing the property on the books of the corporation at $250,000, thereby showing a surplus of $75,000 from which a dividend is declared.

In order to raise cash with which to pay the dividend, the corporation borrowed $75,000 from Sara, a shareholder, giving Sara a mortgage on the corporate property as security. The mortgage was approved by a majority of the directors.

(a) Is the dividend legally declared?

(b) Is the corporation permitted to borrow for the purpose of paying a dividend?

(c) Is the corporation permitted to borrow from one of its shareholders?

(d) Is the corporation permitted to mortgage its property?

(e) Assuming that the dividend was declared when the corporation had no surplus, discuss the liability of the approving and dissenting directors, if the corporaton later becomes insolvent?

(f) Was the Board of Directors resolution proper?

(g) Before the Board of Directors adopted the resolution, can you determine whether a Surplus existed, and the amount of such Surplus?

69. The directors of Metals Corp., after surveying existing nationwide facilities for the production of a rare metal and the possible market for such metal, proceeded upon the production of the metal although the venture was very risky. A costly plant was erected. Subsequent events showed that the market for the metal could not be developed on the scale anticipated. The result was a substantial loss to the corporation. Certain shareholders seek to hold the directors liable for the loss. Should they succeed? Explain giving the principle of law involved.

70. On January 10th, at a time when X Corporation's balance sheet showed a surplus of $25,000, the Board of Directors approved a resolution authorizing T, the treasurer, to lend $10,000 to Amy in exchange for her promisory note. The Board of Directors consisted of A, B, and C. B and C voted for the resolution; A dissented and caused his dissent to be noted on the record. The note given by Amy as evidence of a loan was payable on April 10th. At maturity, the note was unpaid. In May the corporation suffered severe losses and was adjudicated a bankrupt. What rights, if any, does the trustee in bankruptcy of X Corporation have against A, B, and C, if it turns out that Amy is:

(a) a director

(b) a shareholder

71. The Board of Directors of Delta Corp. consisted of 6 persons, A, B, C, D, E, and F. At a Board of Directors meeting on June 1, 1980, A, B, C, D, and F attend. E does not attend as he is out of town. The Board votes and approves the corporation granting a $10,000 loan to B. A, B, and C approve; D does not approve and D votes against it. F attends the meeting but does not vote.

The loan is granted to B; B later fails to repay the loan and B is now insolvent.

The new Board of Directors is elected the following year, and in discovering this loan, they feel that A, B, C, D, E, and F are personally repsonsible for granting this loan and should be sued for the $10,000 loss.

E says he is not responsible as he was out of town;

D says he is not responsible as he voted against the loan;

F says he is not responsible as he didn't vote.

(a) Indicate, which, if any, of the Directors (A, B, C, D, E, F) are personally responsible for approving this loan and explain the legal rules involved.

(b) At the same Board of Directors meeting, the Board of Directors approves entering into a contract with Harper & Co., a partnership, to purchase printed stationery at a price of $4,000. The contract was authorized by the Board of Directors, with A, B, and C voting in favor of the contract and D and F voting against it. Unknown to the rest of the directors, C's wife was a partner in Harper & Co.

Assume that the fair price for the printed stationery was approximately $4,000. One of the shareholders complains about this contract, (1) claiming there is a conflict of interest, and also (2) since only 3 out of the 6 Directors approved, there was no majority vote, and therefore this contract does not bind the Corporation. Is the Corporation bound under the contract? Explain and in your answer discuss both of the shareholder's complaints.

72. Clayborn is the president and a director of Marigold Corporation. He currenty owns 1,000 shares of Marigold which he purchased several years ago upon joining the company and assuming the presidency. At that time, he reccived a stock option for 10,000 shares of Marigold at $10 per share. The option is about to expire but Clayborn does not have the money to exercise his option. Credit is very tight at present and most of his assets have already been used to obtain loans. Clayborn spoke to the chairman of Marigold's board about his plight and told the chairman that he is going to borrow $100,000 from Marigold in order to exercise his option. The chairman was responsible for Clayborn's being hired as the president of Marigold and is a close personal friend of Clayborn. Fearing that Clayborn will leave unless he is able to obtain a greater financial interest in Marigold, the chairman told Clayborn: "It is okay with me and you have a green light." Clayborn authorized the issuance of a $100,000 check payable to his order. He then negotiated the check to Marigold in payment for the shares of stock.

What are the legal implications, problems, and issues raisd by the above circumstances? [AICPA-3b-May 1979]

73. Towne is a prominent financier, the owner of 1% of the shares of Toy, Inc., and one of its directors. He is also the chairman of the board of Unlimited Holdings, Inc., an investment company in which he owns 80% of the stock. Toy needs land upon which to build additional warehouse facilities. Toy's president, Arthur, surveyed the land sites feasible for such a purpose. The best location in Arthur's opinion from all standpoints, including location, availability, access to transportation, and price, is an eight-acre tract of land owned by Unlimited. Neither Arthur nor Towne wish to create any legal problems in connection with the possible purchase of the land.

(a) What are the legal parameters within which this transaction may be safely consummated?

(b) What are the legal ramifications if there were to be a $50,000 payment "on the side" to Towne in order that he use his efforts to "smooth the way" for the proposed acquisition? [AICPA-3c-May 1979]

74. The United States Justice Department commenced a criminal action aginst Sky Manufacturing Corporation and its president, Masterson, for conspiring to fix prices on the sale of certain heavy industrial machinery. Both the corporation and Masterson denied the allegations. After a lengthy trial, the jury found that although a conspiracy did exist among certain manufacturers, neither Sky nor Masterson were parties to the illegal conspiracy. The cost to the corporation to defend the action against it was $500,000. Masterson's individual legel fees and expenses amounted to $250,000 of which Sky has paid $50,000 directly. Masterson seeks indemnification for the remaining $200,000.

Heinz, a dissenting shareholder of Sky, advised the board of directors that payment be the corporation of any of Masterson's expenses was improper. In the event no action is taken to recover the $50,000 already advanced, Heinz will commence a shareholder derivative action against Masterson. Fruthermore, unless the board unequivocally promises not to indemnify Masterson for the unpaid balance of his legal expenses, Heinz will seek injunctive relief.

What rights and limitations apply to Sky's payment of Masterson's legal fees and expenses in defending the criminal action brought against him? [AICPA-2c-Nov. 1979].

75. Boswell Realty Corporation, whose sole business is land development, purchased a large tract of land on which it intended to construct a high-rise apartment-house complex. In order to finance the construction, Boswell offered to sell $3,000,000 worth of shares in Boswell Realty to about 1,000 prospective investors located throughout the United States.

(a) Discuss the implications of the Securities Act of 1933 to Boswell's offering to sell shares in the corporation.

(b) The Securities Act of 1933 is considered a disclosure statute. Briefly describe the means provided and the prinipal types of information required to accomplish this objective of disclosure.

(c) If an investor acquires shares of stock in Boswell Realty Corporation, is his interest real or personal property? Explain. [AICPA-5a-Nov. 1975]

76. While examining the financial statements of a corporation, questions may arise regarding the right of a stockholder to share in the earnings of the corporation and the related role, duties, and obligations of the board of directors in declaring and paying dividends.

(a) When does a dividend vest in a stockholder? Discuss.

(b) How large a dividend may a corporation legally declare? Discuss.

(c) What is a director's liability in the event of an illegal dividend? Discuss. [AICPA-4a-Nov. 1972].

77. Cox is a disgruntled shareholder of Hall, Inc. She has owned 6% of the voting stock for several years. Hall is a corporation with 425 shareholders. However, the members of the Hall family own 65% of the corporate stock, dominate the board, and are the principal officers of the corporation. There is one minority board member. Recently, there have been major changes in Hall's board and its officers as the older generation of the family has relinquished the management in favor of the next generation of Halls. It is the action of this new board and management that has caused Cox to contemplate taking drastic action against the current board and officers. Specifically, she objects to the following:

(a) The board has drastically cut the dividend payments on the common stock. The board's explanation is that additional funds for expansion or acquisitions are critical for the growth of the corporation. The earnings have been increasing at a rate of 10% per year during this peroid. Cox claims that the real reason for the dividend cut is to force minority shareholders such as herself to sell. This claim is based on conjecture on her part. Cox is considering an action against the board to compel reinstatement on the prior dividend payout.

(b) The board also decided to sell 5,000 shares of treasury stock at $10 a share to raise additional capital. The stock in question has originally been sold at $16 a share and has a $12 par value. It was reacquired at $13 per share. Cox first alleges that the corporation is prohibited from aquiring its own shares without specific authorization in the articles of incorporation. The articles of incorporation are silent on this matter. Cox also asserts that the corporation is prohibited from selling the shares at a price less than par.

(c) Substantial salaries are paid to the officers of the corporation. Salaries of the newcomers have been increased at an annual rate of 10%, which is far in excess of raises voted by the old board. Cox has evidence to show that the corporation's salary scale has risen from the top 50% to the top 33⅓% of salaries by similar corporations in the industry. Cox asserts that based upon the recipient's ages, experience and contribution to the corporation, they are so grossly overpaid that the payments constitute a waste of corporate assets. Cox demands that the salary increases be repaid.

(d) The board has become factionalized because of hostility within the Hall family. Cox claims that this acrimony has generated useless debate and bickering and is counterproductive to the continued success of Hall, Inc. The majority has threatened to oust the opposition at the next election of the board. Cox claims that all of these actions are seriously impairing the effective management of the corporation and she is contemplating seeking a court ordered dissolution of Hall.

Discuss the merits of each of the above claims and indicate the probable outcome of any court action taken by Cox personally or taken by her for and on behalf of the corporation. [A.I.C.P.A.-#4-May 1983]

**78. [Regarding Wonda Corp.; see problem 19]

During the first year of Wonda's operations certain members of its board of directors were accused of negligence in the performance of their duties. In addition, there were allegations made that these same directors failed to exercise due care by paying cash dividends to shareholders that exceeded the profits and paid in capital. These directors based their decision upon negligently prepared reports issued by the Vice-President of Finance indicating that there were sufficient funds to pay cash dividends to shareholders. These incidents caused Wonda severe liquidity problems and huge losses in the following year of operation. White, a shareholder in Wonda, has properly commenced a suit against these directors.

(a) What are the necessary requirements to properly declare and pay cash dividends?

(b) What defense(s) are available to the directors regarding the charges of negligence in the performance of their duties and the failure to exercise due care in declaring cash dividends? [Adapted from A.I.C.P.A.-#5-November 1984].

CHAPTER 9

Additional Rights, Remedies, and Liabilities of Shareholders

If any of the shareholders are unhappy with decisions made by the Board of Directors, they have the right to try to remedy the situation. The shareholders have four basic means of remedying corporate wrongdoings: (1) they may elect new directors at the next annual shareholders' meetings; (2) they may commence a lawsuit if any of their rights are impaired; (3) they may seek a court order to enjoin the Directors from unlawful or ultra vires activities; and (4) they may bring a derivative suit on behalf of the corporation to enforce the corporation's cause of action.

A. SHAREHOLDERS' RIGHTS AND REMEDIES FOR DAMAGE AND LOSS TO THE SHAREHOLDERS

Action of directors and officers affect not only the corporation, but they may also affect the rights of a shareholder. A shareholder may sue the corporation when deprived of any of its rights, such as if voting rights are denied or in any way impaired, or if the corporation has failed to carry out an agreement to repurchase or redeem the shareholder's shares. A shareholder may also seek court action to direct the corporation or its directors or both to compel declaration of a dividend or to compel payment of a dividend already declared; also, to cancel a subscription agreement obtained by misrepresentation; to enforce the right to inspect corporate records, the right to vote, preemptive rights, or to enforce the right of appraisal. In any of these direct suits, the shareholder is enforcing any claims the shareholder has against the corporation based upon ownership of shares of stock. Any monetary recovery in a direct suit goes to the shareholder directly.

B. LOSSES TO THE CORPORATION

Losses to the corporation's assets, that occur due to breach of the officers and directors duties may result in loss or waste of corporate assets. Such loss is to the corporation, and not to the shareholders, even though the value of their shares may be diminished by the corporate loss.

This type of loss gives rise to any one or more of the following causes of action on behalf of the corporation: (1) To enjoin a proposed illegal or improper transfer of corporate assets; (2) to set aside an unlawful conveyence or transfer of corporate assets; (3) to compel an officer or director to account for the neglect, failure to perform or other violation of duties in the management and disposition of corporate assets; and (4) to compel an officer or director to account for loss or waste of corporate assets due to neglect or failure to perform or violation of duties, or for the acquisition or transfer to others of the corporate assets. See B.C.L.§720(a)(1),(2),(3). The corporation's legal proceeding would be against the corporation's director(s) and officer(s) who participated in and approved the improper transactions, as well as the beneficiaries of the improper or illegal transactions. B.C.L.§720(a).

Since the Board of Directors has the authority to institute and prosecute actions by the corporation, what are the shareholders to do if the Board of Directors refuses to institute and prosecute the action? If the wrongdoers are the Directors themselves, they will be reluctant and refuse to institute such action or proceeding; they are certainly not going to authorize commencing an action against themselves.

Therefore B.C.L.§720(b) provides the legal action or proceeding may be instituted in various ways by different persons. Such legal action may be maintained (1) by the corporation against any one or more of the directors and officers responsible (this would involve a situation where the directors and officers involved are no longer directors and officers of the corporation and the action is authorized by the new board of directors, or the directors involved are in the minority and cannot block the decision of the majority of the board); (2) by a receiver or trustee in bankruptcy of the corporation against the directors and officers involved; (3) by an officer or director of the corporation as agent of the corporation against the directors and officers involved in the misconduct; (4) by a judgment creditor of the corporation against the directors and officers involved; or (5) by a shareholder (or voting trust certificate holder or owner of a beneficial interest in shares) for the benefit of the corporation (to obtain a judgment in favor of the corporation) against the directors and officers involved in the misconduct. This last procedure is commonly known as a shareholders' derivative action. B.C.L.§720(b),§626.

C. THE SHAREHOLDERS' DERIVATIVE SUIT

A shareholder cannot maintain an action in its own right for injuries to the corporation because the corporation is a legal entity, and has a right to bring a lawsuit in its own name. A shareholder cannot bring a lawsuit against the directors or officers of the corporation for negligence, waste, or mismanagement in the conduct of the corporate business. The right to sue for injuries to the corporation rests strictly with the corporation itself, unless otherwise provided by statute.

A shareholder may, however, commence an action known as a shareholders' derivative suit, to enjoin the officers and directors of a corporation from doing anything that would impair the corporate assets; also, the shareholder has a right to bring suit for damages on behalf of the corporation if the officers and directors are permitting waste and loss of corporate assets due to negligent conduct, or are engagng in fraudulent transactions that are injurious to the corporation. B.C.L.§720.

These actions are brought by one or more shareholders on behalf of the corporation (in the nature of a class action); this occurs when the directors who should have authorized commencement of the action by the corporation, refused or failed to do so (most probably because they are the ones who committed the wrongful acts). Therefore, the shareholders have the right to commence the action.

The shareholders' derivative suit is a procedural device whereby a shareholder is permitted to institute and prosecute an action on behalf of the corporation against one or more of its directors and others. When the shareholder commences a derivative suit, it is the same as if the corporation itself had sued; if the corporation did not have a legal claim (a good cause of action), the derivative suit will be dismissed; any defense which the defendant might have against the corporation may also be asserted in the derivative action. It should be noted that shareholders of a foreign corporation doing business in New York also have the right to bring a derivative action. See B.C.L.§1319.

1. Requirements

A shareholder, who is not an agent of the corporation, must show the action was commenced only after efforts were made to get the board of directors to commence the action, or that it appears such efforts would be useless (where the directors who committed the wrongful acts are still in control). B.C.L.§626(c).

The management of a corporation is entrusted to its board of directors, who have the primary responsibility for acting in the name of the corporation and who are in the position to correct abuses without resort to the courts. The requirement that the shareholder(s) make demand upon the board of directors is generally designed to weed out unnecessary or illegitimate shareholder derivative suits.* However, such demand may be excused if it would be an idle gesture.** If the corporation elects to sue in its own right, the derivative suit can not be maintained.***

There is no requirement as to how many shares a shareholder must own, or how many shareholders must act together in order to sue. One shareholder owning as little as one share may commence a "shareholders' derivative action". In such action, the plaintiff must show it was a shareholder at the time of the transaction complained of, and is a shareholder at the time of bringing the action. B.C.L.§626(b). A person would not be allowed to acquire shares of stock for purposes of maintaining a derivative suit.

The corporation must be a party to the action; if the corporation is not the plaintiff, the corporation must be added to the action as a party defendant, not because there is any claim against the corporation, but solely so that the judgment to be entered by the court against the directors and officers involved, will run in favor of the corporation since any recovery belongs to the corporation, and the Judgment will be in favor of the corporation.

2. Special Litigation Committee

Frequently, the Board of Directors will appoint a special litigation committee to investigate and report on its opinion of the litigation; such committee is usually composed of outside directors. The committee generally retains outside counsel, calls witnesses, examines all the evidence, and then issues a report to the board of directors as to its opinion regarding the pending derivative suit; if the special litigation committee concludes the suit is contrary to the best interests of the corporation (because of high costs, disruption of the corporation's business, adverse effect on the public and its employees) and in its opinion, there is no basis to the shareholder complaint, the corporation would then be advised to apply to the court to dismiss the shareholder derivative suit. If a question later arises regarding the special litigation committee's decision, the New York Courts have confined its inquiry to the independence of the special litigation committee and the adequacy of the investigation, and the Courts have held the special litigation committee's decision is beyond judicial inquiry under the business judgment rule.†

---

*See, Barr v. Wackman, 36 N.Y.2d 371, 368 N.Y.S.2d 497 (1975) for discussion of the requirement of a prior demand before commencing a derivative suit.
**See, Norlin Corp. v. Rooney Pace, 724 F.2d 255, 261–262 (2nd Cir. 1984).
***See Silver v. Chase Manhattan Bank, 49 A.D. 2d 851, 374 N.Y.S.2d 8 (1st Dept. 1975).
†See, Auerbach v. Bennett, 47 N.Y.2d 619, 419 N.Y.S.2d 920 (1979); see, also, Parkoff v. Gen. Tel. (case 22).

3. Security for Expenses

B.C.L.§627 provides certain safeguards for the corporation, e.g., the right to demand security for the reasonable expenses (including defendant's attorneys' fees) unless the plaintiff(s) initiating the action owns at least 5% or more of the outstanding shares of any class of stock or whose outstanding shares have a fair value in excess of $50,000. Shareholders may combine so that collectively the plaintiffs initiating the action own at least 5% of the shares of stock in which case they would not be required to post security. B.C.L.§627.

If the security for expenses as directed by the court is not provided, the action cannot proceed to trial, and in effect, the action remains in a state of limbo. If the action is unsuccessful, the plaintiff will be responsible for the defendant's expenses including attorney's fees, payable out of plaintiff's personal assets or out of the security given. The purpose of the security for expenses is to deter shareholders from bringing frivolous lawsuits, and to deter shareholders from deliberately harassing the corporation's officers and directors.

The amount of security as determined by the court may thereafter from time to time be increased or decreased at the discretion of the court. B.C.L.§627.

4. The Recovery

The purpose of the derivative suit is to compensate the corporation for the losses sustained; since the wrongdoing was to the corporation, the cause of action is a corporate asset, and any recovery belongs to the corporation; the judgment is entered in favor of the corporation. Pursuant to B.C.L.§626(d), such derivative action may not be discontinued, compromised, or settled without the approval of the court.

If the action on behalf of the corporation was successful, the court may award plaintiff(s) reasonable expenses including attorney's fees and the plaintiff(s) will be required to account to the corporation for the remainder of any proceeds. B.C.L.§626(e).

A defendant director or officer who successfully defends such an action is entitled to be indemnified by the corporation for expenses incurred, including attorney's fees. Indemnification may be made by the board of directors or by a court. B.C.L.§722, 724, 725; however, if the director or officer has breached his duty to the corporation, no indemnification is allowed. B.C.L.§722(a).

D. OBLIGATIONS TO MINORITY SHAREHOLDERS

Generally, a shareholder is free to vote one's shares in any manner, even though it may conflict with what is best for the corporation. However, majority or controlling shareholders are subject to certain fiduciary duties which prohibit them from committing fraud, oppression or unfairness regarding the minority. Shareholders who own a sufficient number of shares to have effective control over the corporation are referred to as "controlling shareholders". Courts have indicated that controlling shareholders owe a fiduciary duty to the minority shareholders. In closely held corporations, courts have imposed upon the shareholders a fiduciary duty similar to that imposed upon partners; they must discharge their management and shareholder responsibilities in accordance with a good-faith standard and may not act out of self-interest in derogation of their loyalty to other shareholders and/or to the corporation.

The fiduciary duties of dominant shareholders are most frequently brought into question when the dominant shareholders attempt to increase their own power to the detriment of the minority.* For example, the majority might decide to issue and acquire new shares of stock in the corporation (even without violating preemptive rights) thus diluting the voting power of the minority. This may be done by use of treasury shares; the issuance of additional shares solely to "freeze out" the minority may constitute a breach of fiduciary duty.**

As indicated earlier, preemptive rights allow shareholders to maintain their same percentage interest in the corporation. The right may not be viable, however, if, in order to exercise it, a minority shareholder must have a large amount of cash not currently available; if one cannot raise the necessary funds, the shareholder, even though not exercising one's preemptive right, may be able to complain that the majority action is unfair or is acting in bad faith. It should be noted that even if there are no preemptive rights, the majority still has a duty not to fraudulently or unfairly dilute the minority's proportionate interest through issuance of new shares or reacquisition of outstanding shares.

The question may arise in other transactions where the majority seeks to buy out the minority—with the ultimate question being whether the price forced upon the minority is "fair". A majority shareholder is also subject to a fiduciary duty when selling controlling shares to an outside purchaser (thereby transferring control of the corporation).*** The seller must take reasonable care to ensure that the minority shareholders do not become saddled with new ownership whose only intention is to "loot" the corporation by disposing of its assets.

Minority shareholders in New York enjoy several statutory rights, the most significant is that of appraisal, which will be discussed in detail in Chapter 10. Exercise of appraisal rights does not preclude a shareholder from bringing an action against the majority for breach of its fiduciary duty on the ground that the corporate action is fraudulent or unlawful. See B.C.L.§623(k).

Also, a parent corporation, as dominant shareholder of its subsidiary, might decide to vote to merge the subsidiary corporation into itself or into a third corporation and again "freeze out" the minority shareholders of the subsidiary corporation by paying them off in cash. The parent corporation, as a majority shareholder, standing on both sides of the transaction, has the burden of proving the merger was fair and has served some valid business purpose beyond elimination of the minority shareholder(s).

E. EXTRAORDINARY BUSINESS DECISIONS REQUIRING SHAREHOLDER APPROVAL

Certain decisions may have such significance which affect the overall corporate business to such a material degree that directors alone are not authorized to make the decision. Some decisions require the approval of the board of directors, plus the approval of the shareholders. These are mainly decisions which affect the corporation so drastically that the shareholders' investment is now in an entirely different business or those which effectively terminate the business of the corporation.

---

*See Alpert v. 28 Williams St. Corp. 63 N.Y.2d 557, 483 N.Y.S.2d 667 (1984), (case 25). See generally, O'Neal & Thompson, *Oppression of Minority Shareholders* (2nd ed. 1985 & 1986 Supp.)
**See, Schwartz v. Marien, 37 N.Y.2d 487, 373 N.Y.S.2d 122 (1975).
***See, Kaplan, "Fiduciary Responsibility in the Management of the Corporation", 31 Bus. Law. 883, 907 (1976).

In these situations, before such action may legally be taken, the shareholders affected have the right to vote. Some of these situations will be discussed in the sections following.

1. The Right to Vote

The C/I may limit or exclude the right to vote from any class of shares. B.C.L.§613. However, the right to vote cannot be taken away from all shares of stock since full and complete voting rights must be enjoyed by the holders of at least one class of shares. B.C.L.§501.

In any of these special voting situations, the required vote of the shareholders will usually be a majority or two-thirds vote, not of a quorum, but of the holders of all the outstanding shares entitled to vote.

2. Sale, Lease, or Exchange of Substantially all Corporate Assets

A sale, lease, exchange or other disposition of all or substantially all the assets of a corporation, if not made in the usual or regular course of the business actually conducted by the corporation, requires an approving vote of 2/3 of the shareholders entitled to vote. B.C.L.§909. This is discussed in more detail in Chapter 10.

3. Mergers and Consolidations

A merger results when two or more corporations combine into one organization known as the surviving corporation. A consolidation occurs when two or more corporations combine into a newly created corporation known as the consolidated corporation.

To effect a merger or consolidation requires approval of the board of directors of each corporation, and the approval of the holders of 2/3 of the outstanding voting shares of each corporation. Mergers and consolidations are discussed in more detail in Chapter 10.

4. Amendments to the Certificate of Incorporation

A corporation may amend its C/I. The amended certificate must be approved by the board of directors, and approved by a majority vote of all shareholders entitled to vote. See B.C.L.§803 for details, which is covered in Chapter 10.

5. Corporate Guarantees

Guarantees of debts or obligations of other persons or other entities may be categorized as: (1) those in furtherance of the corporate purposes, which can be authorized by the board of directors alone. B.C.L.§202(a)(7); *and* (2) those *not in furtherance* of the corporate purposes, which must be authorized by a two-thirds vote of the holders of all outstanding shares entitled to vote.*
The guarantee may be secured by using corporate property as collateral, if so authorized. See B.C.L.§908.

6. Mortgaging Corporate Property

The board of directors may borrow money for corporate purposes; in addition, it may use corporate property as security for the loan in furtherance of the corporate purposes. B.C.L.§202(a)(7). No shareholder approval is required. However, the C/I may provide that shareholder approval is necessary to authorize obtaining a mortgage of the corporate property. See B.C.L.§911.

---

*See, Collision Plan Unlimited v. Bankers Trust Co., 63 N.Y.2d 827, 482 N.Y.S.2d 252 (1984) for court's interpretation and question of lack of authority.

7. Loans to Directors

A corporation is forbidden to make loans to a director unless authorized by vote of the shareholders. If the director is also a shareholder, any shares owned by the director shall not be voted for such authorization. B.C.L.§714. This was discussed previously in Chapter 8.

8. Dissolution

In order to effectuate a voluntary dissolution of the corporation, a 2/3 vote of the holders of all outstanding shares entitled to vote is needed to approve same (except as otherwise provided in the C/I). B.C.L.§1001. This will be covered in Chapter 11.

9. Abolishment of Abnormal Management Structure

To abolish or amend any abnormal management structure under B.C.L.§620, there must be a 2/3 vote of the holders of all outstanding shares entitled to vote. B.C.L.§620(d).

10. Sale of Assets After Dissolution

After dissolution and payment of all liabilities, the corporation may sell its assets for shares, bonds, other securities, or partly for cash. This must be authorized at a meeting of shareholders by majority vote of the holders of all outstanding shares entitled to vote. See B.C.L§1005(a)(3). If the corporation sells its assets completely for cash, no additional shareholder approval is needed. See Chapter 11 for details.

11. Purchase By the Corporation of Its Own Shares

Pursuant to B.C.L.§513(e), shareholders are required to approve the purchase by the corporation of more than 10% of the corporation's shares for more than fair market value. The approval would be a majority vote of the holders of all outstanding shares; the C/I may require a greater percentage. This provision was included in the B.C.L. in an attempt to thwart corporate takeovers.

12. Approving Other Acts of the Board of Directors

There are many provisions in the B.C.L. which require shareholder vote other than voting for directors, approving by-laws, and voting for extraordinary decisions.

Pursuant to B.C.L.§713(a)(2), shareholders may approve decisions of the Board of Directors where one or more of the directors is interested in the transaction. This was previously discussed in Chapter 8.

In addition, the C/I or by-laws may provide that shareholders vote for certain matters, such as: fixing the consideration for shares without par value (C/I may reserve such right to the shareholders), B.C.L.§504(d); electing officers (if provided in the C/I). B.C.L.§715(b); filling newly-created directorships or vacancies on the board (if C/I or by-laws provides), B.C.L.§705(a). Also, shareholders have the right to vote for removal of directors for cause. B.C.L.§706(a); removal without cause if C/I or by-laws so provide. B.C.L.§706(b), (c); shareholders may also vote to authorize indemnification of officers and directors. B.C.L.§721–726.

F. LIABILITY OF SHAREHOLDERS

Shareholders may under some circumstances assume potential liability. The basic principle is that shareholders are not personally liable for the debts of the corporation. If the corporation loses money and creditors claims are still outstanding, shareholders may lose their investment, but that is generally the limit of their liability. In unusual instances a court may pierce the corporate veil and hold the shareholders individually liable. This was discussed in Chapter 2. Although rare, there are some additional situations in which a shareholder may be personally liable, which will be discussed herein.

1. Stock Subscriptions

A shareholder is responsible for the amounts due pursuant to a stock subscription. Once the subscription agreement is accepted by the corporation, a binding contract is formed. Any refusal to pay the amount agreed in the stock subscription constitutes a breach of contract, resulting in the personal liability of the shareholder. See B.C.L.§503(c),(d),§628(a).

2. Watered Stock

(a) Corporation Has Not Received the Full Consideration

When the corporation issues and delivers shares of stock, the shareholder is liable for the agreed price. If the corporation has issued shares of stock without receiving the full consideration in violation of B.C.L.§504(a) or (b), the shareholder has received "watered" stock, and the shareholder is responsible to pay the full consideration. See also B.C.L.§628(a).

(b) Corporation Has Issued Par Value Shares for Less Than Par Value

When a corporation issues par value shares for less than its par value, the shares of stock issued are "watered" stock. See B.C.L.§504(c).

Each shareholder must pay, in the form of money, property, or services actually performed, at least the par value of the shares issued. B.C.L.§504.

For par value shares sold, the corporation must receive at least the par value; for any no par value shares, the corporation must receive the value of the shares as determined by the board. When shares are issued by the corporation for less, the shares are "watered", and the shareholder who receives "watered" stock must pay the difference to the corporation.

3. Illegal Dividends

By statute, dividends are to be distributed only from Surplus and in compliance with B.C.L.§510. If dividends are improperly paid without there being sufficient surplus, or if the corporation is insolvent, or if payment of the dividend causes the corporation to become insolvent, the dividends are unlawful. B.C.L.§510.

The obligation of a shareholder to repay illegally declared dividends generally depends upon the knowledge of the shareholder receiving the unlawful dividend. A shareholder who receives unlawful dividends either as a result of one's own fraudulent act or with knowledge they are unlawful, is under a duty to refund them to the corporation. If the corporation is insolvent, a dividend may not be retained by the shareholder even though it was received in good faith and without knowledge of the insolvency. The assets of an insolvent corporation are regarded as a trust fund for its creditors, and therefore a shareholder must pay back the unlawful dividend.

In all cases of unlawful and improper dividends, the board of directors may be held personally liable for the amount of the payment. B.C.L.§719. If the directors can show a shareholder knew the dividend was unlawful when it was received, the directors, after being sued by or on behalf of the corporation, are entitled to subrogation rights against the shareholder.

The general rule is that an unlawful dividend received in good faith can be recovered from shareholders if the corporation was insolvent, but there is no right of recovery if the corporation was solvent. However, there have been no New York reported cases indicating this distinction.

4. Defective Incorporation

As a general rule the liability of a shareholder is limited to his or her investment. If a purported corporation is defectively formed, shareholders who actively participated may be personally liable for the obligations incurred. See discussion of de facto corporations in Chapter 3.

5. Disregard of the Corporate Entity—Piercing the Corporate Veil

Where justice requires, courts may "pierce the corporate veil" and impose personal liability upon shareholders which may occur in extreme cases of fraud. See discussion in Chapter 2 for details.

6. Wages and Salaries to Employees

Pursuant to B.C.L.§630, the 10 largest shareholders of a corporation, whose shares are not listed on a national exchange, may be personally liable for unpaid wages and salary claims. See B.C.L.§630 and discussion in Chapter 2 for details.

CASE 21
LEWIS v. S. L. & E. INC. et al
(U.S. Court of Appeals, 2nd Cir. 629 F. 2d 764) (1980)

[In a shareholder' derivative suit which arose out of an intra-family dispute over the management of two closely-held affiliated corporations, the United States District Court entered judgement in favor of defendant directors, awarded attorneys' fees to them and to plaintiff's corporation, granted the other corporation specific performance of plaintiff's agreement to sell his stock, and plaintiff appealed.]

KEARSE, Circuit Judge:

This case arises out of an intra-family dispute over the management of two closely-held affiliated corporations. Plaintiff Donald E. Lewis ("Donald"), a shareholder of S.L. & E., Inc. ("SLE"), appeals from judgments entered against him in the U.S. District Court after a bench trial of his derivative claim against directors of SLE, and of a claim asserted against him by the other corporation, Lewis General Tires, Inc. ("LGT"), which intervened in the suit. The defendants Alan E. Lewis ("Alan"), Leon E. Lewis, Jr. ("Leon, Jr."), and Richard E. Lewis ("Richard"), are the brothers of Donald; they were, at pertinent times herein, directors of SLE and officers, directors and shareholders of LGT. Donald charged that his brothers had wasted the assets of SLE by causing SLE to lease business premises to LGT from 1966 to 1972 at an unreasonably low rental. LGT was permitted to intervene in the action, and filed a complaint seeking specific performance of an agreement by Donald to sell his SLE stock to LGT in 1972. The district court held that Donald had failed to prove waste by the defendant directors, and entered judgment in their favor. The court also awarded attorneys' fees to the defendant directors and to SLE, and granted LGT specific performance of Donald's agreement to sell his SLE stock.

On appeal, Donald argues that the district court improperly allocated to him the burden of proving his claims of waste, and that since defendants failed to prove that the transactions in question were fair and reasonable, he was entitled to judgment. Donald also argues that the awards of attorneys' fees were improper. We agree with each of these contentions, and therefore reverse and remand.

For many years Leon Lewis, Sr., the father of Donald and the defendant directors, was the principal shareholder of SLE and LGT. LGT, formed in 1933, operated a tire dealership in Rochester, New York. SLE, formed in 1943, owned the land and complex of buildings at 260 East Avenue in Rochester. This property was SLE's only significant asset. Prior to 1956 LGT occupied SLE's premises without benefit of a lease; the rent paid was initially $200 per month, and had increased over the years to $800 per month by 1956, when additional parcels were added. On February 28, 1956, SLE granted LGT a 10-year-lease on the newly expanded property ("the Property"), for a rent of $1,200 per month, or $14,400 per year. Under the terms of the lease, SLE was responsible for payment of real estate taxes on the Proeprty, while all other current expenses were to be borne by the tenant, LGT.

In 1962, Leon Lewis, Sr., tranferred his SLE stock, 90 shares in all, to his six children (defendants Richard, Alan and Leon, Jr., plaintiff Donald, and two daughters, Margaret and Carol), giving 15 shares to each. At that time Richard, Alan and Leon, Jr., were already shareholders, officers and directors of LGT. Contemporaneously with their receipt of SLE stock, all six of the children entered into a "shareholders' agreement" with LGT, under which each child who was not a shareholder of LGT on June 1, 1972 would be required to sell his or her SLE shares to LGT, within 30 days of that date, at a price equal to the book value of the SLE stock as of June 1, 1972.

LGT's lease on the SLE property expired on February 28, 1966. At that time the directors of SLE were Richard, Alan, Leon, Jr., Leon, Sr., and Henry Etsberger; these five were also the directors of LGT. In 1966 Alan owned 44% of LGT, Richard owned 30%, Leon, Jr., owned 19%, and Leon, Sr. owned 7%. From 1967 to 1972 Richard owned 61% of LGT and Leon, Jr. owned the remaining 39%. When the lease expired in 1966, no new lease was entered into. LGT nonetheless continued to occupy the property and to pay SLE at the old rate, $14,400 per year. According to the defendants' testimony at trial, there was never any thought or discussion among the SLE directors of entering into a new lease or of increasing the rent. Richard testified: "We never gave consideration to a new lease." From all that appears, the defendant directors viewed SLE as existing purely for the benefit of LGT. Richard testified, for example, that although real estate taxes rose sharply during the period 1966–1971, from approximately $7,800 to more than $11,000, to be paid by SLE out of its constant $14,400 rental income, raising the rent was never mentioned. He testified that SLE was "only a shell to protect the operating company [LGT]." When this suit was commenced there had not been a formal meeting of either the shareholders or the directors of SLE since 1962. Richard, Alan and Leon, Jr., had largely ignored SLE's separate corporate existence and disregarded the fact that SLE had shareholders who were not shareholders of LGT and who therefore could not profit from actions that used SLE solely for the benefit of LGT.

Neither Donald nor his sisters ever owned LGT stock. As the June 1972 date approached for the required sale of their SLE stock to LGT, Donald apparently came to believe that SLE's book value was lower than it should have been. He sought SLE financial information from Richard, who had been president of SLE since 1967. Richard refused to provide information. Donald therefore refused to sell his SLE shares in 1972, and commenced this shareholders' derivative action in the district court in August 1973, basing jurisdiction on diversity of citizenship. The sole claim raised in the complaint was that the defendant directors had wasted the assets of SLE by "grossly undercharging" LGT for the latter's occupancy and use of the Property. . . . LGT intervened and demanded specific performance of Donald's agreement to sell his SLE stock. Donald did not contest his ultimate obligation to sell, but took the position that since the book value of the shares would be increased if he prevailed on his derivative claim, specific performance should be granted only after adjudication of that claim.

There ensued an eight-day bench trial, at which plaintiff sought to prove, by the testimony of several expert witnesses, that the fair rental value of the Property was greater than the $14,400 per year that SLE had been paid by LGT. Defendants sought to show that the rental paid was reasonable, by offering evidence concerning the financial straits of LGT, the cost to LGT of operating the Property, the general economic decline of the East Avenue neighborhood, and rentals paid on two other properties in that neighborhood. LGT presented expert testimony that the value of plaintiff's stock as of June 1972, assuming a successful defense of the derivative claims, was $15,650

Turning first to the question of burden of proof, we conclude that the district court erred in placing upon plaintiff the burden of proving waste. Because the directors of SLE were also officers, directors and/or shareholders of LGT, the burden was on the defendant directors to demonstrate that the transactions between SLE and LGT were fair and reasonable. B.C.L.§713(b); see Cohen v. Ayers, 596 F.2d 733, 739–40 (7th Cir. 1979).

Under normal circumstances the directors of a corporation may determine, in the exercise of their business judgment, what contracts the corporation will enter into and what consideration is adequate, without review of the merits of their decisions by the courts. The business judgment rule places a heavy burden on shareholders who would attack corporate transactions. Galef v. Alexander, 615 F.2d 51, 57; 58 (2d Cir. 1980); Auerbach v. Bennett, 47 N.Y.2d 619, 629, 419 N.Y.2d 920, 926 (1979); . . . . But the business judgment rule presupposes that the directors have no conflict of interest. When a shareholder attacks a transaction in which the directors have an interest other than as directors of the corporation, the directors may not escape review of the merits of the transaction. At common law such a transaction was voidable unless shown by its proponent to be fair, and reasonable to the corporation. B.C.L.§713, in both its current and its prior versions, carries forward this common law principle, and provides special rules for scrutiny of a transaction between the corporation and an entity in which its directors are directors or officers or have a substantial financial interest.

The current version of §713, which became effective on September 1, 1971, and governs at least so much of the dealing between SLE and LGT as occurred after that date, expressly provides that a contract between a corporation and an entity in which its directors are interested may be set aside unless the proponent of the contract "shall establish affirmatively that the contract or transaction was fair and reasonable as to the corporation at the time it was approved by the Board . . ." §713(b). Thus when the transaction is challenged in a derivative action against the interested directors, they have the burden of proving that the transaction was fair and reasonable to the corporation. Cohen v. Ayers, supra.

The same was true under the predecessor §713(b), former §713(a)(3), which was in effect prior to September 1, 1971. §713(a)(3) was not explicit as to the burden of proof, but simply stated that a transaction with interested directors would not be voidable "If the contract or transaction is fair and reasonable as to the corporation at the time it is approved by the board. . . ." The consensus among the commentators was that Section 713(a)(3) carried forward the common law rule, which placed the burden of proof as to fairness on the interested directors. . . . We agree with this construction. . . .

During the entire period 1966–1972, Richard, Alan and Leon, Jr., were directors of both SLE and LGT; there were no SLE directors who were not also directors of LGT. Richard, Alan and Leon, Jr., were all shareholders of LGT in 1966; and from 1967 to 1972 Richard and Leon, Jr., were the sole shareholders of LGT. Under B.C.L.§713, therefore, Richard, Alan and Leon, Jr., had the burden of proving that $14,400 was a fair and reasonable annual rent for the SLE property for the period February 28, 1966 through June 1, 1972.

• • • •

Quite clearly Richard, Alan and Leon, Jr., had made no effort to determine contemporaneously what rental would be fair during the years 1966–1972. Their view was that the rent should simply cover expenses and that SLE existed for the benefit of LGT. During this period no appraisals were made; no attempts were made to sell or rent the Property; no thought whatever was given to whether $14,400 was a fair and reasonable rent even when real estate taxes had risen to consume nearly all of that amount.

• • • •

The defendants argued, however, that LGT could not have afforded to pay SLE rent higher than $14,400. They produced evidence designed to show that LGT had made little profit; that this low profitability was due to the expenses of maintenance and upkeep of the 260 East Avenue property; and that LGT therefore would not have been able to pay a higher rent to SLE. The district court credited this evidence, finding that LGT had "experienced a number of years of very severe losses," that during the period from 1962–1973, LGT's overall profit was only $53,876, and that payment of rent at the rate of $39,099 per year during this period could have led to the "demise" of LGT.

• • • •

Moreover, the propostion that LGT could not afford to pay as rent more than what its own books showed as profits ignores the fact that LGT was owned and managed by members of the Lewis family, some of whom were also employees of that corporation. It is entirely possible that these family members granted to themselves unusually high salaries or other perquisites, thus reducing LGT's paper profits. For example, in 1966 Richard's salary was approximately $21,000; Leon, Jr.'s compensation was $3,000 salary plus commissions. In 1967, LGT acquired all of Alan's LGT stock; and Richard and Leon, Jr., acquired all of the LGT stock of their father, agreeing to pay the purchase price over a ten-year period. Richard and Leon, Jr., thus became LGT's only shareholders, and their LGT salaries were immediately increased by a total of $23,000 per year (Richard's salary went from $21,000 to $36,000; Leon, Jr.'s went from $3,000 to $11,000), to cover the cost of the LGT stock they had just acquired. . . . Even given the general downward trend of the East Avenue neighborhood, it is entirely possible that at least during the early years of the 1966–1972 period, such a tenant might have been secured. No effort was made during that period to rent to anyone other than LGT.

We conclude, therefore, that defendants failed to prove that the rental paid by LGT to SLE for the years 1966–1972 was fair and reasonable. Thus, Donald is not required to sell his SLE shares to LGT without such upward adjustment in the June 1, 1972 book value of SLE as may be necessary to reflect the amount by which the fair rental value of the Property exceeded $14,400 in any of the years 1966–1972.

• • • •

We remand to the district court (a) for the entry of judgment in favor of SLE against Richard, Alan and Leon, Jr., jointly and severally, in such amount as the district court shall determine to be equal to the amounts by which the annual fair rental value of the Property exceeded $14,400 in the period February 28, 1966–June 1, 1972, (b) for an accounting as to the value of Donald's SLE shares as of June 1, 1972, in light of such judgment, (c) for an order, following such accounting, of specific performance of the shareholders' agreement, and (d) for such other proceedings as are not inconsistent with this opinion.

Note: For additional cases involving derivative suits, see e.g., COHEN v. AYERS, 596 F.2d 733 (7th Cir. 1979), applying N.Y. Law; AUERBACH v. BENNETT, 47 N.Y.2d 619, 419 N.Y.S.2d 920 (1979).

CASE 22
PARKOFF v. GENERAL TELEPHONE & ELECTRONICS CORP. et al
(App. Div. 1st Dep't., 74 A.D.2d 762, 425 N.Y.S.2d 599) (1980)

• • • •

This action is one of a number of stockholder's derivative suits for alleged waste of corporate assets and breach of fiduciary duties commenced following GTE's disclosure of questionable payments made abroad to public officials or political parties and the report of a resulting S.E.C. investigation. In consequence of the commencement of these actions, GTE formed a Special Litigation Committee of three outside directors who were not directors at the time of the events in issue. This committee was to review an investigative report of GTE's Audit Committee and recommend a course of action with respect to the stockholder's suits. One Blauvelt was chairman of the Special Litigation Committee. Ultimately it recommended that it would not be in the corporation's best interest for this and the other stockholder's actions to proceed.

In denying GTE's motion to dismiss, Special Term held, inter alia, that a determination of the good faith and independence of GTE's Special Litigation Committee should await completion of discovery by the plaintiff. In another of the stockholder's derivative actions against GTE, (Auerbach v. Bennett), the Appellate Division, Second Department made a simliar ruling, but the Court of Appeals reversed and granted summary judgment dismissing the complaint. . . , holding upon the proof submitted there that there was no "triable issue of fact as to the independence and distinterested status of these three directors [of the Special Litigation Committee]." The appellants contend that this court should dismiss, just as Auerbach was dismissed, based upon the business judgment of the Special Litigation Committee.

The business judgment rule (see B.C.L.§717) bars judicial inquiry into actions of corporate directors taken in good faith and in the exercise of honest judgment in the lawful furtherance of corporate purposes (Blaustein v. Pan American Petroleum & Transport Co. 293 N.Y. 281, 303). The claim here asserted is corporate property and, as with questions of policy and management, the decision, whether, or to what extent, to prosecute such claims lies within the judgment of the corporation's board of directors (Auerbach v. Bennett, 47 N.Y.2d 619, 631, 419 N.Y.S.2d 920, 927). Therefore, absent evidence of bad faith or fraud the court must respect the decision of the Special Litigation Committee. . . .

Special Term's decision to await completion of discovery was influenced by plaintiff's allegation that the committee, Blauvelt in particular, was not independent, but the only evidence plaintiff could muster was that Blauvelt had attended a board of directors meeting when the board was informed that a questionable payment arrangement in the Philippines was being terminated. No showing was made how this would compromise Blauvelt's independence, and what information he could have gained from the meeting would have been available to him in the Audit Committee report that he was assigned to review. (This information about Blauvelt was before the Court of Appeals in Auerbach and that court was not persuaded that it was of sufficient import to defer dismissal of the complaint until after discovery.)

Since a court may also inquire "as to the adequacy and appropriateness of the committee's investigative procedures and methodologies" (Auerbach v. Bennett, supra, . . .), plaintiff assails the Special Litigation Committee's procedures, claiming as evidence that they were found defective in Cramer v. General Telephone & Electronics Corp., 582 F.2d 259 (3rd Circ.). This assertion has no merit; the Cramer court never addressed the methodology of the Special Litigation Committee. (In Auerbach, the Court of Appeals did address the committee's method and on the evidence there found nothing that would raise an issue of fact).

In view of the necessity to reverse and grant summary judgment dismissing the complaint because of the bar of the business judgment rule, there is no need to address the other points raised on appeal.

Note: This decision was affirmed by the Court of Appeals, 53 N.Y.2d 412, 442 N.Y.S.2d 432 (1981).

CASE 23
MEREDITH V. CAMP HILL ESTATES, INC.
(App. Div. 2nd Dept. 77 A.D. 2d 649, 430 N.Y.S.2d 383) (1980)

In a shareholder's derivative action alleging waste of corporate assets and seeking money damages and to set aside a conveyance of real property, plaintiff appeals from a judgment of the Supreme Court . . . which, dismissed the complaint. . . . Plaintiff Meredith, owner of a 28-acre parcel of land in Pomona, Rockland County, sold such parcel to the defendant Camp Hill Estates, Inc. (Camp Hill) in 1973. Camp Hill was formed that year to make the necessary purchase. Plaintiff retained an interest in the subject parcel by becoming a 20% shareholder of Camp Hill, and as part of the purchase price, plaintiff took back a purchase money mortgage of $124,170. The mortgage provided for release of 25% of the land purchased without further consideration. Thereafter, on or about June 4, 1976, plaintiff, as mortgagee, released from the mortgage lien approximately 7-acres of the 28-acre parcel. At a shareholders' meeting on June 17, 1976, defendants-respondents Occhipiniti, ("O"), Landa ("L") and Stern ("S") each of whom was a director, and owned or controlled 20% of the shares of Camp Hill, voted to convey the 7-acre portion to the defendant-respondent Cherdine Realty Corp. (Cherdine) without consideration. Plaintiff objected to the transfer, and defendant-respondent Klingher, ("K"), the remaining 20% shareholder, did not object to it. . . .

The record also reveals that up to June 17, 1976, the date of the conveyance to Cherine, all payments were made under the terms of the purchase money mortgage held by plaintiff. . . .

At the trial defendant "O" (one of the 20% shareholders) testified that Camp Hill's difficulties began in 1976 when "K" (another 20% shareholder) refused to continue paying money into the corporation to be used for payment of interest and taxes on the mortgaged propery. "O" sought from Meredith a moratorium on payments "since it was during a recession time of real estate; that at a later date we could merchandise this property for a profit." After the attempt to negotiate a moratorium failed and it became clear that Meredith would insist on fulfillment of Camp Hill's obligations under the mortgage, the transfer without consideration to Cherdine was effected on June 17, 1976. Thereafter no further payments of principal, interest or taxes were made on the mortgage.

"K" testified that his prime involvement with Camp Hill Estates, aside from his involvement in the corporation's formation, was as an investor and that the corporation had "no day-to-day operations, really. It was just a question of getting the bills and paying the taxes, what would happen is every so often I would get a note saying send X dollars for interest and X dollars for taxes and I would do it." . . .

. . . [T]he record convincingly demonstrates that the prime motivation for the transfer to Cherdine was to accommodate the personal investment decision of Mr. "K", and not to confer a benefit upon the corporation. In particular, the record suggests an investment decision on the part of the majority shareholders, after the moratorium proposal collapsed, to default on the mortgage payments to Meredith and to minimize their personal losses by insulating the 7-acre parcel (via the transfer to Cherdine) from a possible deficiency judgment in Meredith's favor after the foreclosure on the mortgaged 21-acre parcel.

Plaintiff has succeeded in establishing that the transfer without consideration of the 7-acre parcel of real property owned by Camp Hill Estates to the defendant Cherdine was "so far opposed to the true interests" of Camp Hill "as to lead to the clear inference that no one thus acting could have been influenced by any honest desire to secure such interests." . . . The transfer constituted a waste of corporate assets which may not be ratified by a majority of the shareholders. . . .

Respondents attempt to reply to the contention of corporate waste by emphasizing appellant Meredith's status as Camp Hill's creditor. Meredith qua shareholder, they argue, does not really seek to benefit the corporation, becuase his obvious motivation in the derivative action is to return the 7-acre parcel to Camp Hill for the benefit of Meredith qua creditor and to the detriment of the shareholders. Such argument is specious. Plaintiff correctly observes that a derivative action lies whenever there is a clear legal right to maintain the action, regardless of the plaintiff shareholder's individual motive for bringing the suit. . . . When the 7-acre parcel is returned to Camp Hill Estates, it will undoubtedly reap a benefit, one incidental aspect of which will be an improved ability to meet outstanding debts. Assuming the Camp Hill shareholders suffer a loss after the debts are paid, such happenstance would occur because the value of their stock declined in the normal course of events and not because of any illicit motive underlying the bringing of appellant's derivative action.

However, although we believe plaintiff should prevail in his action for corporate waste, at this juncture of the action we are unable to ascertain what relief should be granted him. Therefore the matter is remitted to the trial court for a further hearing and a determination as to plaintiff's appropriate remedy and of his resonable expenses, including attorney's fees. (see B.C.L.§626[e]).

PROBLEMS

79. The Certificate of Incorporation of K Corp. authorizes the issuance of 100,000 shares of common stock, all of which have been outstanding for more than five years. Paul owns 4,000 shares, whish he purchased four months ago. Last month, when the fair market value was $10 per share. Paul commmenced a derivative action on behalf of K Corp. against X, Y, and Z who constitute the entire Board of Directors of K Corp.

Paul's complaint alleges that six months ago, X, Y, and Z authorized the purchase of machinery by K Corp. from Singer at an unreasonably high price in exchange for a bribe that was paid by Singer to X, Y, and Z.

(a) May Paul be required to post security before he can proceed with the action? Explain.
(b) Who should Paul list as defendants in the law suit? Explain.
(c) Will the defendants succeed in a proceeding to dismiss the complaint? Explain.
(d) Does Paul have the right to examine K Corp.'s records to determine the names and addressess of, and the number of shares held by the other shareholders of K Corp.? Explain.

80. Able Corp's assets in the sum of $50,000 were lost as the result of negligent and fraudulent mismanagement of its directors. The corporation has 100 shares outstanding. Amy, a shareholder, who owns one share of stock in the corporation states this has diminished the book value of her shares by $500 and that the directors are liable to her for $500.

(a) Is Amy correct? Explain fully.
(b) Is there any legal remedy whereby Amy can compel the directors to account for the $50,000 loss to the corporation? Explain.
(c) Explain fully the procedures involved, including who will be the plaintffs, who will be listed as defendants, any requirements, etc.

**81. William Harrelson is president of the Billings Corporation, a medium-size manufacturer of yogurt. While serving as president, Harrelson learns of an interesting new yogurt product loaded with vitamin additives and with a potentially huge market. He immediately forms another corporation, the Wexler Corporation, to produce and market the new product. In his zeal, however, Harrelson overextends his personal credit and utilizes Billing's credit, along with its plant and employees, as needed, to produce the new product. The new product becomes a big success. As a result, Harrelson's Wexler stock is presently worth millions of dollars.

Billing's shareholders contend that Harrelson's actions are improper and seek a remedy against him. Will they succeed and what remedies are available to them? [A.I.C.P.A.—#3a—November 1982].

**82. Grandiose secured an option to purchase a tract of land for $100,000. He then organized the Dunbar Corporation and subscribed to 51% of the shares of stock of the corporation for $100,000, which was issued to him in exchange for his three-month promissory note for $100,000. Controlling the board of directors through his share ownership, he had the corporation authorize the purchase of the land from him for $200,000. He made no disclosure to the board or to other shareholders that he was making a $100,000 profit. He promptly paid the corporation for his shares and redeemed his promissory note. A disgruntled shareholder subsequently learned the full details of the transaction and brought suit against Grandiose on the corporation's behalf.

Discuss the shareholders position. Explain and discuss all legal implications. [Adapted from A.I.C.P.A.—13—May 1980].

CHAPTER **10**

Amendments, Mergers, Consolidations, Acquisitions, and Sale of the Corporate Assets

A. AMENDMENTS TO THE CERTIFICATE OF INCORPORATION

A Certificate of Incorporation (C/I) may be amended in any manner, so long as the amendments could have lawfully been included in the original C/I. The Certificate of Amendment may amend any one or more of the following: the corporate name; the purposes, by changing, adding, or limiting them; the location of the office of the corporation; the mailing address to which the Secretary of State shall mail process; the duration of the corporation (which can be extended if not perpetual, or its existence can be revived if the duration expired, but the duration cannot be reduced); the increase or decrease of the number of authorized shares by creating a new class or extinguishing an old class of shares; changing shares from par value to no par value, or vice versa; reducing or increasing the par value; designating rights, preferences or limitations of any class of shares of stock; the designation, change or revocation of a registered agent; the addition of, striking out, or changing any authorized management provision. B.C.L.§801, §802. The Amendment may amend any one or all of the above items.

1. Authorization Required

Amendments to change the location of the office of the corporation, the address to which the Secretary of State shall mail a copy of any process served against the corporation, or to make, revoke or change the designation of a registered agent may be authorized by the board of directors alone. B.C.L.§803(b). This can be accomplished by a Certificate of Change. B.C.L.§805-A.

Any other amendments must be authorized by the board, followed by vote of the holders of a majority of all outstanding shares entitled to vote. B.C.L.§803(a). There are some amendments which require a vote higher than a majority, such as to amend management structure as per B.C.L.§620(b), which requires a 2/3 vote. In order to adopt a supermajority voting requirement for shareholders or directors meetings (which must be in the C/I to be enforceable), same may be adopted by the holders of a majority of the outstanding shares entitled to vote; however to change or strike out such provisions requires a 2/3 vote. See B.C.L.§616(b) and §709(lb).

Any class of shareholders affected by an amendment which excludes or limits their right to vote, changes their shares or otherwise adversely affects their class, or subordinates the class to a new class shall have the right to vote on the amendment even if they do not otherwise have voting rights. A majority of the outstanding shares of each class affected must approve. B.C.L.§804.

2. Amendments Regarding Stated Capital

If any of the amendments amend the authorized shares, additional considerations must be had as to their affect on Stated Capital. If the par value is increased or reduced, Stated Capital shall reflect the change. B.C.L.§806. If existing par value shares are changed to no par value, Stated Capital remains the same. If there is a reduction in the number of shares, Stated Capital is reduced pro rata. If the change produces shares with and without par value, Stated Capital shall be the par value of the resulting par value shares, and the excess is Stated Capital as to the no par value shares. Any changes in par value shall comply with the definition of Stated Capital, as contained in B.C.L.§102(a) (12). Shareholders whose rights may be affected by the amendment may have a right of appraisal which will be discussed later in this Chapter. B.C.L.§806(b) (6).

3. Filing with the Secretary of State

The Amendment is accomplished by filing a Certificate of Amendment to the C/I which sets forth the name of the corporation, the date its C/I was filed, the full text of each amendment, and the manner in which it was authorized. The Certificate of Amendment together with the filing fee is filed with the Secretary of State. B.C.L.§805. See also B.C.L.805-A (Certificate of Change). After filing and approval by the Secretary of State, the C/I is deemed amended.

B. MERGERS

A merger occurs when two or more corporations combine into one single corporation, with one corporation surviving and the other corporation(s) being eliminated; the surviving corporation continues its existence and absorbs the other; the other corporation then ceases to have an independent existence. The surviving corporation ends up with the combined assets of both corporations. All debts and liabilities of the constituent corporations are assumed by the surviving corporation. The shareholders of the constituent corporations receive stock or other securities issued by the surviving corporation, as provided in the plan of merger.

A merger may be represented symbolically as $A + B = A$. After the merger, A is recognized as a single corporation, possessing all the rights, privileges, purposes, and powers of A and B; A automatically acquires all of B's property and assets without the necessity of any further act or deed; A becomes liable for all of B's liabilities, obligations and penalties; A's C/I is deemed amended to include any changes that are in the Certificate of Merger. By the same token, the merger could also have symbolically been represented as $A + B = B$, where B would be the surviving corporation.

1. Authorization Required

The board of directors of each corporation planning to take part in the merger adopts the plan for merger which sets forth: the name of each constituent corporation; the name of the surviving corporation; a specification of the kind and number of shares of each class of each constituent corporation, specifying the class or series entitled to vote; the terms of the merger, including the manner and basis of converting the shares of the corporation to be eliminated into shares of the surviving corporation, and the terms or conditions of any other consideration for the shares to be paid or delivered in exchange; and a statement of any amendments or changes in the C/I of the surviving corporation necessary to be effected by the merger. See B.C.L.§902.

The board of directors of each corporation approves the plan, and then submits a copy of the plan to all the shareholders of each constituent corporation (whether or not entitled to vote), together with notice of the proposed shareholders' meeting. The plan must be adopted by vote of the holders of two-thirds of the outstanding shares entitled to vote of each corporation. B.C.L.§903.

The holders of shares of a class or series shall be entitled to vote as a class if the plan of merger contains any provision which if contained in an amendment to the C/I would entitle the holders of shares of such class or series to vote as a class thereon, even though there may be no voting rights in said class of shares. In such case the Merger shall be authorized in addition by vote of the holders of two-thirds of all outstanding shares of each such class or series. B.C.L.§903(a)(2).

2. Filing with the Secretary of State

The Merger is accomplished by filing a Certificate of Merger, setting forth the plan, the effective date (which may be up to 30 days after filing), the provisions for the new C/I, and the manner of authorization with respect to each constituent corporation. See B.C.L. §904. The Merger is effective after filing with the Secretary of State and payment of the filing fees. B.C.L.§906. The surviving corporation is required to file a certified copy of the certificate in the County Clerk's Office in each county in which an office of the constituent corporation is located and in each county where any real property of a constituent corporation is located. B.C.L.§904(b).

3. Effect of the Merger

The surviving corporation shall have all the rights, privileges, powers and purposes of the constituent corporations. All assets of the constituent corporations including real property, personal property, stock subscriptions, causes of action, and all other assets vest in the surviving corporation, without the necessity of any further transfer.

The surviving corporation shall assume and be liable for all the liabilities, obligations, and penalties of each of the constituent corporations. All liabilities of shareholders, directors, or officers remain unaffected. B.C.L.§906(b) (3).

The C/I shall automatically be amended to the extent of any changes in the plan of merger; such changes are automatically part of the new C/I for the surviving corporation.

The shareholders of the surviving corporation are still shareholders; the shareholders of the constituent corporation(s) become shareholders of the surviving corporation, pursuant to the plan of merger.

4. The Subsidiary Merger

Where a corporation (parent) owns at least 90% of the outstanding shares of each class of shares of a subsidiary corporation, the subsidiary may be merged into the parent corporation by vote of the board of directors of the parent corporation alone without necessity of any shareholder approval. B.C.L.§905. After the board of directors of the parent corporation approves the plan, the plan or an outline of the plan is submitted to each minority shareholder of each subsidiary corporation; the plan indicates the method of exchanging one's shares. If less than 90% of the shares are owned, the merger must proceed under the provisions of B.C.L.§903, requiring approval of the shareholders.

5. Merger of Domestic and Foreign Corporation

One or more foreign corporations and one or more domestic corporations may be merged into a domestic corporation or into a foreign corporation. See B.C.L.§907 for details.

C. CONSOLIDATIONS   C+D=E

A consolidation is the combining of two or more corporations, whereby a new corporation is created and the constituent corporations are eliminated. If corporation C and corporation D consolidate, the consolidated corporation would be corporation E; corporations C and D are then eliminated.

A symbolic representation of consolidation is C + D = E, whereby E is recognized as a new corporation, a single entity; C and D cease to exist. E accedes to all the rights, privileges, and powers previously held by C and D. Title to any property and assets owned by C and D pass to E without formal transfer. E assumes liability for all debts and obligations owed by C and D. The Certificate of Consolidation takes the place of C's and D's original C/I. Shareholders of each of the constituent corporations will receive shares of stock or other securities (not necessarily of the same class) issued to them by the new corporation pursuant to the plan of consolidation, in exchange for their shares of stock in the constituent corporations.

1. Authorization Required

The board of directors of each corporation planning to take part in the consolidation adopts a plan for consolidation which sets forth: the name of each constituent corporation and of the consolidated corporation; specification of the kind and number of shares of each class of each constituent specifying the class or series entitled to vote; the terms of the consolidation, including the manner and basis of converting the shares of each of the constituent corporations into shares of the consolidated corporation, and the terms or conditions of any other consideration for the shares to be paid or delivered in exchange. See B.C.L.§902.

The board of directors of each corporation approves the plan, and then submits a copy of the plan to all the shareholders of each constituent corporation (whether or not entitled to vote), together with notice of the proposed shareholders' meeting. The plan must be adopted by a vote of the holders of two-thirds of the outstanding shares entitled to vote of each corporation. B.C.L.§903.

The holders of shares of a class or series shall be entitled to vote as a class if the plan of consolidation contains any provision which if contained in an amendment to the C/I would entitle the holders of shares of such class or series to vote as a class thereon, even though such class had no voting rights thereon. In such case, the Consolidation shall be authorized by vote of the holders of two-thirds of the outstanding shares of each such class or series. B.C.L.§903(a)(2).

2. Filing with the Secretary of State

The Consolidation is accomplished by filing a Certificate of Consolidation, setting forth the plan, the effective date (which may be up to 30 days after filing), the provisions for the new C/I and the manner of authorization with respect to each constituent corporation. See B.C.L.§904. The Consolidation is effective after filing with the Secretary of State and payment of the filing fees. B.C.L.§906. The consolidated corporation is required to file a certified copy of the certificate in the County Clerk's Office in each county in which an office of each constituent corporation is located and in each county where any real property of a constituent corporation is located. B.C.L.§904(b).

3. Effect of the Consolidation

In a consolidation, the shareholders of the constituent corporations become shareholders of the new corporation by surrendering their old shares in return for new ones at a predetermined exchange.

The consolidated corporation has all the rights, privileges, powers and purposes of the constituent corporations. All assets of the constituent corporations including real property, personal property, stock subscriptions, causes of action, and all other assets vest in the consolidated corporation, without the necessity of any further transfer.

The consolidated corporation shall assume and be liable for all the liabilities, obligations, and penalties of each of the constituent corporations; all liabilities of shareholders, directors, or officers remain unaffected. B.C.L.§906(b) (3). The shareholders of the constituent corporations are now shareholders of the consolidated corporation.

4. Consolidation of Domestic and Foreign Corporation

One or more foreign corporations and one or more domestic corporations may be consolidated into a domestic corporation or into a foreign corporation. See B.C.L.§907 for details.

D. ACQUISITIONS

A Consolidation or Merger should be distinguished from an acquisition. An acquisition occurs when one corporation buys all or most of the stock or assets of another.

An acquisition may be of different types—it may be an acquisition of stock whereby Corp. J acquires all or a large majority of the shares of Corp. K's stock; or it may be an acquisition of assets whereby Corp. G acquires all or substantially all of the assets of Corp. H. Each of these situations takes on different legal considerations as to the legal effect and status of the corporations and the shareholders.

E. ACQUISITION OF SHARES OF STOCK

When one corporation acquires all or a controlling number of shares of another corporation, there is no change in the legal existence of either corporation. A parent corporation and subsidiary corporation relationship exists and each corporation maintains its separate corporate identity. The acquiring corporation acts through its board of directors in the purchase; the corporation which becomes a subsidiary does not act, as the sale of shares of stock is by its shareholders. The capital structure of the subsidiary corporation remains unchanged, and that of the parent corporation is usually not altered. Such acquisition of corporate shares enables the acquiring corporation to control the acquired or (target) corporation.

It should be noted the result is the purchase of shares of stock, and the resulting effect is that they are separate corporate entities, each with its own assets, liabilities, and its own shareholders.

Example:

> Assume Corp. J acquires all or substantially all of Corp. K's stock; Corp. J would then be the sole or principal shareholder of Corp. K; Corp K is a subsidiary of Corp. J; each has its own assets and liabilities. However, the value of K's shares of stock owned by J would be an asset of J.

There is no requirement for shareholder approval. There would be no filing required with the Secretary of State; each corporation would continue to have its own C/I, its own assets, liabilities, and its own shareholders; one corporation would act as the subsidiary of the other. Very often after such an acquisition of shares, the acquired (subsidiary) corporation might be dissolved, or might be merged into the parent corporation.

1. Tender Offers

With public companies having a large number of shareholders, it is usually difficult or impossible to acquire a large controlling block of shares in the corporation since there are so many shareholders involved. However, this might be accomplished by means of a tender offer.

The acquiring person or corporation would make an offer to all shareholders of the corporation to be acquired (the target corporation) to purchase their shares of stock at a certain price by a certain date. This is called a tender offer (an offer that is publicly advertised and addressed to all shareholders of the target company). The price of the stock in the tender offer is generally higher than the market price of the stock prior to the announcement. The higher price may induce shareholders to tender their shares. The tender offer may be conditioned upon the receipt of a specified number of outstanding shares by a specified date. The offering corporation may make a tender offer in which it offers target shareholders its own securities in exchange for their target stock. In a cash tender offer, the offeror offers the target shareholders cash.

The person making the tender offer is the offeror; the shareholder is the offeree; if the offeree accepts the tender offer, he (or she) must comply with the terms of the tender offer and if the terms are complied with by a certain date (e.g., the acquiring of a certain total number of shares by the acquirer), the shareholder sells its shares to the acquirer, and the acquirer thus can become a controlling shareholder in the target company (the company being acquired).

Federal securities laws strictly control the terms, duration, and circumstances, under which most tender offers are made. Tender offers are governed by the Williams Act*; the tender offer bidder must file a statement with the S.E.C. and satisfy certain publication requirements within 5 business days of the public announcement of intention to make an offer. In addition, see B.C.L.§1600 et. al. for New York rules applying.

In the past few years we have seen many hostile tender offers, many of which have involved substantial litigation. Many states have enacted anti-takeover statutes; New York enacted such a statute in December 1985;** pursuant to the N.Y. statute, a corporation can not engage in any business combination with any interested shareholder (defined as one who owns 20% or more of the outstanding voting stock) for a period of five years following such interested shareholder's acquisition unless the acquisition is approved by the corporation's Board of Directors prior to the acquisition date. B.C.L.§912(b). The statute contains many definitions and also provides that the corporation can elect not to be governed by the statute, by a provision in its C/I or by-law adopted prior to March 31, 1986. B.C.L.§1612 provides Requirements for Takeover Bids, and pertains to situations where the takeover bid is not subject to the Williams Act. A registration statement is required to be filed with the N.Y.S. Attorney General. B.C.L.§1602. Pursuant to B.C.L.§1612(f), the Attorney General can schedule public hearings and conduct investigations, and may issue an

---

*Sections 14(e) and 14(f) of the Securities Act of 1934 (15 U.S.C.§78m and §78n); see Note, *State Regulation of Tender Offers;* 54 Fordham L. Rev. 885 (1986).

**See B.C.L.§912, amendment to §513, and amendment to Article 16 of the B.C.L. - Security Takeover Disclosure Act (Revised).

order, staying the offeror from purchasing or paying for the shares tendered. In addition, pursuant to B.C.L.§1613, there is a right of private action for an injunction, damages, and reasonable attorneys fees by anyone who has been injured by a violation of Article 16 of the B.C.L.

F. ACQUISITION OF CORPORATE ASSETS

Another form of acquisition is the acquiring of the corporation's assets. When a corporation acquires all or substantially all the assets of another corporation by direct purchase, the purchasing corporation simply owns and controls more physical assets, and no change is effected in the legal personality of either corporation; the acquiring corporation is thus not required to obtain shareholder approval for the purchase.

The corporation that is selling its assets is substantially changing its business and most probably substantially altering its ability to carry out its corporate purposes. Therefore, the corporation whose assets are being acquired must obtain approval of both the board of directors and the shareholders. If such sale of all or substantially all of its assets is in the usual course of business of the selling corporation, approval by its board of directors would be sufficient; *shareholder approval is necessary only if such sale is not in the ordinary course of business.*

A sale, lease, exchange or other disposition of all or substantially all the assets of a corporation, if not made in the usual or regular course of the business actually conducted by the corporation, requires a vote of the holders of 2/3 of all outstanding shares entitled to vote. B.C.L.§909. Usually such transaction would be a sale of the business as a going concern complete with all or most of its assets, or sale of a substantial unit in the business (e.g. the sale of a major department or branch), or sale of the sole income producing asset, so that the sale is not part of the usual or regular course of business.

1. Authorization Required

B.C.L.§909 provides for the following procedure: the board of directors would authorize the proposed transaction, and then submit the proposal to the vote of the shareholders; notice of the meeting must be given to all shareholders; the shareholders (by vote of the holders of two-thirds of all outstanding shares entitled to vote) must approve the transaction and may fix terms and conditions, or authorize the board to fix them, and may specify the consideration that may be accepted by the corporation: all or partly in cash, other property, or shares in the purchasing corporation. There is no requirement for any filing with the Secretary of State; if one of the corporations sells substantially all its assets including the corporate name to a new corporation formed under the same name, compliance must be had with the requirements of B.C.L.§909(d), (e). If the corporation fails to follow the prescribed procedure, the proposed transaction may be set aside by the shareholders. See B.C.L.§909.

2. Effect of the Sale

After the sale, each corporation as a separate entity still exists, each with its own liabilities and its own shareholders; however, the composition of the assets of each corporation may be different after the sale.

3. The Rights of Creditors

In dealing with the sale or transfer of corporate assets, the purchasing corporation does *not* by operation of law assume the liabilities, obligations, and penalties of the selling corporation; by comparison, in a merger or consolidation, the surviving or consolidated corporation "shall assume and be liable for all the liabilities, obligations and penalties of each of the constituent corporations." B.C.L.§906(b)(3).

Therefore, creditors of the selling corporation do *not* become creditors of the corporation that now owns all the assets, unless there is a specific assumption agreement. When one is a creditor, care should be taken to distinguish between each of these different transactions. Of course, it should be noted that the purchasing corporation should comply with the Bulk Sales Law—See Article 6 of the U.C.C.

Example:

(1) Assume Corp. G sells all of its assets to Corp. H; after the sale, both corporations still exist. H now has all the assets of H and G.

However, H does not assume any of the liabilities or obligations of Corp. G, except under an assumption agreement.

The shareholders of Corp. H are still shareholders of H; the shareholders of Corp. G are shareholders of G.

Corp.G has substitute assets, the consideration it received for the sale of G's assets, which may be cash, other property, or shares of stock or bonds of H Corp. or of another corporation. Corp. G retains its own liabilities, obligations and creditors, and still has its same shareholders.

(2) Assume Creditor X is a creditor of Corp. G. After the sale of G's assets to H, X is still a creditor of G; X is not a creditor of H, unless H has specifically agreed to assume G's liabilities.

If there is no assumption agreement, X can enforce its claim only against G (whether or not G has any assets left); X can not enforce its claims against H.

G. MERGERS, CONSOLIDATIONS, ACQUISITIONS, AND THE U.S. GOVERNMENT*

The Securities Act of 1933 applies to mergers, consolidations and acquisitions of corporations whose stock is registered. The S.E.C. has ruled that the typical merger or consolidation is a "sale" of securities; hence, registration with the S.E.C. is required. In addition, the Securities Exchange Act of 1934 applies in any of these situations, so as to protect investors against manipulation of stock prices.

Large corporations which control a significant portion of the market for a product should also be concerned with the possibility of antitrust problems. Horizontal and vertical mergers may come under attack by the Federal Trade Commission and the Justice Department if competition in the industry in question is adversely affected. In a horizontal merger a manufacturer merges with another manufacturer of the same product, thus ending competition between them. In a vertical merger, a manufacturer merges with either its supplier or retail outlets or both, thus excluding a competitor from either a substantial source of supply or principal market for the goods. If the merger, consolidation, or acquisition, whatever its form, makes even a small impact on industry-wide competition, there is the possibility the merger, consolidation, or acquisition may be set aside by the federal government.

---

*See, Henn, *Laws of Corporation,* pp. 851–859 (1983). In addition, see section in Chapter 8 regarding the Securities Law.

H. THE RIGHTS OF A SHAREHOLDER WHO OBJECTS

Certain extraordinary business decisions require shareholder approval. If the required approval is obtained, the corporation's action becomes binding upon the corporation and all the shareholders, whether or not they consent, and whether or not they were entitled to vote. As a general rule, dissenting minority shareholders are bound by the decision and have no recourse except to continue as shareholders or sell their stock on the market. With respect to some of these unusual proceedings, dissenting shareholders may have an additional right—to require the corporation to buy back their shares of stock; this is known as a shareholder's right of appraisal and is covered by B.C.L.§623 and §910.

If a shareholder disapproves of a merger or consolidation (or other extraordinary decision), but is outvoted by the other shareholders, the law recognizes a dissenting shareholder should not be forced to become an unwilling shareholder in a corporation that is new or different from the one in which the shareholder originally invested. The shareholder has the right to dissent and may be entitled to be paid the fair value of the shares held.

The appraisal right is provided for by B.C.L.§623, which may be lost if the elaborate statutory procedures are not precisely followed.

1. Circumstances Giving Rise to the Right

The proceedings in which such right may exist are as follows:

(a) Sale, lease, exchange or other disposition of all or substantially all the corporation's assets not in the ordinary course of business other than a transaction wholly for cash. B.C.L.§910(a)(1)(B). Where a proposed sale is wholly for cash, the corporation is to be dissolved as part of the sale, and the assets are to be distributed in one year, there is no right other than to participate in the liquidation. In all other circumstances the appraisal right exists. For example, if the sale is not for cash, but for stock in the purchasing corporation, or if the selling corporation is to acquire new property in exchange, the dissenting shareholders have the right of appraisal. See B.L.C. §910(a)(1)(B),§909.

(b) Amendments to the Certificate of Incorporation affecting classification of shares. If the amendment adversely affects the shares by altering preferential rights, redemption rights, preemptive rights, or abolishing or limiting voting rights except by giving voting rights to newly created shares of an existing class or to a new class, the holders of the shares adversely affected have the right of appraisal. Note that the right does not exist for shareholders with voting rights when the corporation issues additional shares as the shareholder can protect one's voting rights by exercising the preemptive right to buy up part of the new shares. See B.C.L.§804, §806(b).

(c) Consolidation: Dissenting shareholders of both constituent corporations have the right of appraisal.B.C.L.§910(a)(1)(A).

(d) Merger: The shareholders of the eliminated corporation have the appraisal right; shareholders of the surviving corporation may also have the right if such merger adversely affects the shareholder's rights as in the amendment situation, specified in B.C.L.§806(b)(6). See B.C.L. §910(a)(1)(A).

(e) Subsidiary Merger: The 10% or less minority shareholders of the subsidiary corporation have the right of appraisal. The shareholders of the parent corporation have no such right. See B.C.L.§905, §910(a)(1)(A)(i).

2. How the Right Is Exercised

Prior to the adoption of B.C.L.§623, a dissenting shareholder did not have a right of appraisal and could not require that the corporation buy back his shares of stock and pay him the fair value of the shares. Now, however, a dissenting shareholder does have this right under certain circumstances, but the shareholder must proceed with the detailed procedure for enforcement of this right as set forth in B.C.L.§623.

The objecting shareholder should file written objection to the proposed action before the shareholder vote is actually taken. B.C.L.§623(a). The shareholder must state in the objection that he intends to demand payment for his shares if the specified action is taken, and must file with the corporation a written notice of election to dissent covering all shares beneficially owned by the shareholder and submit the shares to the corporation for notation on the face of the shares that such election was made. The corporation is then given an opportunity to agree on a price to pay to the objecting shareholder for his shares.

The corporation subsequently is required to make a uniform written offer to all dissenting shareholders to pay the specified price for their shares which the corporation considers to be their actual value. This offer must be accompanied by the latest available balance sheet and a corporate profit and loss statement for the 12-month period ended on the balance sheet date. In the event the corporation fails to make an offer or there is no agreement on the price, the shareholder or the corporation may institute a judicial proceeding to fix the value of the shares. The court thereupon determines the fair value of the shares and interest may be awarded or withheld; costs and expenses including the fees and expenses of counsel and expert witnesses may be allocated between the corporation and the dissenting shareholder in the court's discretion. The detailed procedure for this shareholder's right of appraisal is contained in B.C.L.§623.

B.C.L.§623(g) also provides that a corporation's offer to purchase a dissenting shareholder's shares must be accompanied by a statement setting forth the aggregate number of shares with respect to which notice of election to dissent has been received and the aggregate number of holders of such shares. If the corporate action has been consummated, such offer must be accompanied by (1) advance payment, to each shareholder who has submitted the certificates representing his shares to the corporation as provided in B.C.L.§623, of an amount equal to 80% of the amount of such offer or (2) as to each such shareholder who has not yet submitted his certificates a statement that advance payment to him of an amount equal to 80% of the amount of such offer will be made by the corporation promptly upon submission of his certificates. Every such advance payment to the shareholder will be accompanied by a statement to the effect that acceptance of such payment does not constitute a waiver of such dissenting shareholder's rights.

The court determines the fair value without a jury and without referral to an appraiser or referee, and each party to such proceeding is to bear its own costs and expenses.

If the corporation is insolvent or payment will make it insolvent, the corporation is not permitted to make the payment. B.C.L.§623(j). In such case, the dissenting shareholder may at his option withdraw his notice of election or retain his status as a claimant against the corporation. See B.C.L.§623(j)(1)(2)(3) for details.

The enforcement by a shareholder of his right to receive payment for his shares under B.C.L.§623 shall exclude the enforcement by such shareholder of any other right to which he might otherwise be entitled by virtue of share ownership, except as provided in B.C.L.§623(e).

However, the shareholder will still have the right to bring or maintain an appropriate action to obtain relief on the ground that such corporate action will be or is unlawful or fraudulent as to him.B.C.L.§623(k).

Upon consummation of the corporate action, the shareholder ceases to have any rights of a shareholder other than the right to be paid the fair value of his shares. B.C.L.§623(e).

Shares reacquired by the corporation in this way become treasury shares unless cancelled. See B.C.L.§623(i).

I. TAKEOVERS AND THE FIDUCIARY DUTY*

When the corporation is faced with a merger, consolidation, acquisition or other type of takeover, members of the Board of Directors should be concerned that they are fulfilling their fiduciary duty to the corporation and to the minority shareholders.

1. The Closely Held Corporation—"Freeze outs"

In the closely held corporation, a common device is a two-stage merger, thus freezing out the minority shareholder(s); the shareholder may then seek the right of appraisal. If fraud or illegality is alleged, the right of appraisal is not the exclusive remedy; pursuant to B.C.L. §623(k) (in such instance) an action for equitable relief may be had. Courts have held that a "freeze out" merger can be justified if related to the advancement of the corporation's interest and there exists an independent corporate purpose for the merger.** If justification can be shown, the appraisal procedure would be the exclusive remedy for any injury sustained by the minority shareholder(s), and if a shareholder fails to avail itself of the appraisal rights afforded in B.C.L. §623, this bars an action for an accounting and damages.***

2. Public Corporations—Defensive Measures

In recent years, many takeovers have been accomplished by use of greenmail, junk bonds, golden parachutes, proxy fights and other devices.† Corporations and their Boards of Directors have attempted to include various defensive measures such as the counter tender offer, the Poison pill, charter amendments, supermajority voting provisions, "White Squire" arrangements, cash or stock acquisitions by the target company, and others.

In any of these situations, the members of the Board of Directors of the target company have a great duty of care and obligation of good faith in making the decision to adopt defensive measures and in determining what to adopt or recommend to the shareholders.‡ As an element of due

---

*See Booth, *Management Buyouts, Shareholder Welfare, and the Limits of Fiduciary Duty*, 60 N.Y.U.L. Rev. 630 (1985). See, generally, O'Neal & Thompson, *Oppression of Minority Shareholders* (2nd ed. 1985 & 1986 Supp.) (2 vol.).
**See, e.g., Alpert v. 28 Williams St. Corp. (Case 25).
***See, Walter J. Schloss Ass. v. Arwin Ind., 61 N.Y. 2d 700, 472 N.Y.S.2d 605 (1984), based upon dissenting opinion in 90 A.D.2d 149, 153–162, 455 N.Y.S.2d 844, 847–52.
†There has evolved a whole new terminology to identify these various devices. For discussion and explanation of several defensive measures, see, Lipton & Brownstein, *Takeover Responses and Directors' Responsibilities*—An Update, 40 Bus. Law. 1403 (1985); Dawson, *Poison Pill Defensive Measures*, 42 Bus. Law. 423 (1987); Note, *Internal Transfers of Control Under Poison Pill Preferred Issuances to Preferred Shareholders*, 60 St. John's L. Rev. 94 (1985); Note, *Love Me Tender? Judicial Treatment of Takeover Defensive Tactics*, 30 Corp. J. 75 (1986).
‡See, *Guidelines for Directors: Planning for and Responding to Unsolicited Tender Offers*, 41 BUS. LAW. 209 (1985).

care, directors should consider seeking outside professional assistance such as investment bankers and legal counsel.

The directors have a duty to review each proposal to evaluate the business rationale of each regarding the corporation, and not their own personal motives. The defensive tactics employed will vary widely with the particular circumstances of the offer and the target corporation's situation. In a case based upon N.Y. law, the court held that defensive measures affecting the corporation's capital (whereby voting control was vested in the board of directors) as a response to a threatened takeover bid were invalid.* The court in that case held that a member of the board has the duty of loyalty and the duty of care; as to the duty of care, the court adheres to the business judgment rule; the duty of loyalty is derived from the fiduciary duty of prohibiting self-dealing, and once there is a prima facie showing the director has a self-interest in the transaction, the burden shifts for the directors to demonstrate that the transaction is fair and serves the best interests of the corporation and its shareholders.

In a Delaware case (*Smith* v. *Van Gorkom*) the court imposed personal liability on the directors (including outside directors) of Trans Union Corp. because the court felt they had not been careful enough and had not made inquiry before approving and recommending to the shareholders a cashout merger at a price that was less than the "intrinsic value" of the shares.** The Delaware Court found the directors action did not fall within the protection of the business judgment rule, and the directors were held personaly liable for damages suffered by the shareholders. The court held the board did not reach an informed business decision; they did not adequately inquire into the offer and price, and were uninformed as to the value of the company; the court found the directors were grossly negligent in approving the merger, after only two hours of consideration at a meeting, with no prior notice. There were no merger documents before them, no written summary of the terms, and no documents to support the adequacy of the price; the directors merely relied on the oral statements of Van Gorkom (Trans Union's Chairman and Chief executive officer) of the substance of an agreement that he had never read. The Court stated the directors were under a duty to make reasonable inquiry of Mr. Van Gorkom, and if they did, . . . "the inadequacy of that upon which they now claim to have relied would have been apparent."

After this court decision, Delaware, New York and other states have amended their indemnification statutes. (See Chapter 8, section F).

---

*See, Norlin Corp. v. Rooney Pace Inc., 744 F.2d 255 (2nd Cir. 1984), applying both the law of N.Y. and the law of Panama. In this case, the board of directors approved the issuance of Norlin's shares to a subsidiary and to a second subsidiary's Employees' Stock Option Plan, thus vesting the board of directors with voting control of the Corporation. This was a shareholders' derivative suit. The court determined the purpose of the stock transaction was not to benefit the employees, but to solidify management's control of the corporation to resist the threatened takeover; thus the transaction was the result of self-interest on the board's part.

**Smith v. Van Gorkom, 488 A.2d 858 (Del. 1985); see Analysis of Case in Manning, *Reflections and Practical Tips on Life In the Boardroom After Van Gorkom,* 41 BUS. LAW. 1 (1985); *Smith v. Van Gorkom: The State of the Business Judgment Rule In the State of Delaware,* 30 Corp. J. 123 (1986).

Case 24
BILLY v. CONSOLIDATED MACHINE TOOL CORP. et al
(Court of Appeals of New York, 51 N.Y.2d 152, 432 N.Y.S.2d 879) (1980)

GABRIELLI, Judge.

As a general rule, when an employee is injured in the course of his employment, his sole remedy against his employer lies in his entitlement to a recovery under the Workers' Compensation Law (§11). . . . We have not previously been called upon to consider, however, a situation in which the employer's liability, if any, is alleged to have arisen solely from its independent assumption, by contract or operation of law, of the obligations and liabilities of a third-party tortfeasor. . . .

Plaintiff's decedent, an employee of defendant USM Corporation, was killed when a 4,600-pound "ram" from a vertical boring mill broke loose and struck him. There was no doubt that the October 21, 1976 accident occurred "in the course of" the decedent's employment. . . . Although the decedent's widow applied for and received workers' compensation benefits, she subsequently commenced a common-law tort action against USM Corporation seeking recompense for the decedent's personal injuries and wrongful death. Also named as party defendants were Emhart Corporation, the parent of USM, and Consolidated Machine Tool Corporation, Farrel-Birmingham Company and Farrel Corporation, all of which had been absorbed by USM through corporate mergers prior to the accident. In her complaint, plaintiff alleged that the accident had been caused by certain defects in the manufacture and design of the vertical boring mill . . . and a 4,600-pound "ram."

After preliminary discovery had taken place, each of the five corporate defendants moved for summary judgment. USM Corporation, the decedent's employer, based its summary judgment motion primarily upon §11 of the Worker's Compensation Law. . . .

It is undisputed that the vertical boring mill which allegedly caused decedent's injuries was designed several decades ago and manufactured during the early 1950's by Consolidated Machine Tool Corporation and Farrel-Birmingham Company. It was also established through discovery that Consolidated Machine Tool Corporation had played a significant role in the design of the 4,600-pound "ram" that eventually broke loose from the machine and killed the decedent. Farrel-Birmingham Company was apparently responsible for the 1955 installation of the vertical boring mill in the plant now operated by USM.

Through a series of consolidations and mergers that took place during the 1950's and 1960's, Consolidated Machine Tool Corp. and Farrel-Birmingham Co. were ultimately absorbed into USM Corp. In 1954, Farrel-Birmingham, which had acquired a controlling interest in Consolidated three years earlier, dissolved that corporation and, concededly, assumed its assets and liabilities. In 1963, the name of the resulting corporate entity was changed from Farrel-Birmingham Company to Farrel Corporation. Farrel Corporation was finally merged into USM Corporation, the decedent's employer, in 1968, eight years before the accident in question occurred. It is not seriously disputed that this merger resulted in the assumption by USM, a N.J. corporation, of the liabilities and obligations of Farrel, a Conn. corporation, including those liabilities that Farrel had inherited from Consolidated. . . .

• • • •

In the present case, had the corporate identities of Consolidated Machine Tool Corp. and Farrel-Birmingham Company been preserved, plaintiff would have had a right to maintain an action against those corporations on the theory that they exposed her deceased husband to the risk of injury by designing and manufacturing a defective vertical boring mill and "ram". It is only because these corporations were consolidated and then merged with USM Corp. that plaintiff is now without the means to hold them directly accountable as third-party tort-feasors.

As previously noted, USM has not seriously disputed that it had succeeded to the liabilities and obligations of Consolidated and Farrel-Birmingham as a result of the 1968 merger (see B.C.L.§906[b][3]). In effect, USM stands in the shoes of these two defunct corporations and, in the ordinary course of events, would be fully answerable to plaintiff for their tortious conduct. Under the circumstances of this case, we cannot accept USM's contention that the obligations it inherited through corporate merger may be avoided simply because of the fortuity that the injured party was an employee covered by the . . . Workers' Compensation Law. . . .

• • • •

Conceptually, the deceased employee's executrix is suing not the decedent's former employer, but rather the successor to the liabilities of the two alleged tort-feasors. That USM also happens to have been the injured party's employer is not of controlling significance, since the obligation upon which it is being sued arose not out of the employment relation, but rather out of an independent business transaction between USM and Farrel. . . . The tort, if any, was committed by third parties, which, as it appears on the present record, never had an employer-employee relationship with the injured party. . . .

Through its merger with Consolidated and Farrel, USM voluntarily assumed any obligations that those corporations may have had to individuals who might suffer injury as a result of a defect in their product. It would be grossly inequitable to permit USM to avoid its assumed obligations solely because the injured party was coincidentally an employee and the injuries in question arose in the course of his employment. . . . Inasmuch as plaintiff's action represents essentially an attempt to recover from third-party manufacturers through a suit against their corporate successor, plaintiff should be permitted to maintain the action, notwithstanding that the successor corporation is also an employer which would otherwise be immune from suit. . . . Accordingly, we hold that it was error for the courts below to dismiss plaintiff's causes of action against USM on the basis of its status as employer.

We note that plaintiff had also named Emhart Corporation, USM's parent, as a party defendant in the action. It was plaintiff's position that Emhart should be answerable for the obligations of USM because its involvement in its subsidiary's management was so extensive as to render the subsidiary a mere "alter ego" of the parent. . . .

As a general rule, the law treats corporations as having an existence separate and distinct from that of their shareholders and consequently, will not impose liability upon shareholders for the acts of the corporation. . . . Indeed, the avoidance of personal liability for obligations incurred by a business enterprise is one of the fundamental purposes of doing business in the corporate form. . . . It is true that, on occasion, the courts will disregard the separate legal personality of the corporation and assign liability to its owners where necessary "to prevent fraud or to achieve equity" (International Aircraft Trading v. Manufacturers Trust Co., 297 N.Y. 285). But, such liability can never be predicated solely upon the fact of a parent corporation's ownershp of a controlling interest in the shares of its subsidiary. At the very least, there must be direct intervention by the parent in the management of the subsidiary to such an extent that "the subsidiary's paraphernalia of incorporation, directors and officers" are completely ignored (Lowendahl v. Baltimore & Ohio R.R. Co., 247 A.D. 144, 155, 287 N.Y.S. 62, affd. 272 N.Y. 360).

Here, there has been no showing whatsoever that Emhart disregarded the separate identity of USM and involved itself directly in the affairs of that corporation. In response to Emhart's moving papers, which assert that Emhart is merely a holding company with no employees involved in the management of USM, plaintiff has stated only that her claim against Emhart is "based on the fact that the defendant USM Corp. is [a] wholly-owned subsidiary [of Emhart]". Of course, this fact alone would not be sufficient to support the imposition of liability upon Emhart for the acts of its subsidiary.

• • • •

Consequently, Emhart is entitled to summary judgment on its motion.

Finally, we hold that the dismissal of the complaint as it pertained to defendants Consolidated Machine Tool Corporation, Farrel-Birmingham Company and Farrel Corporation was entirely proper. Those corporations had long since ceased to exist at the time the instant action was commenced, and there is no indication that there remain any assets or insurance coverage which would provide a source of recovery. Inasmuch as these corporations have been completely absorbed by USM, plaintiff's sole remedy for any injuries resulting from their tortious conduct lies in an action against that corporate entity.

Accordingly, the order of the Appellate Division should be modified, with costs to plaintiff against USM Corp., by reinstating plaintiff's causes of action against USM Corp. in accordance with the opinion herein and, as so modified, affirmed, with costs to the remaining defendants against plaintiff.

Dissenting opinion by J. Meyer.

Discussion Questions

1. Was plaintiff able to maintain an action against the surviving corporation for the torts committed by the constituent corporations?

2. Was plaintiff attempting to pierce the corporate veil? of which orporation?

3. Did plaintiff succeed on that ground?

CASE 25
ALPERT v. 28 WILLIAMS ST. CORP.
(Court of Appeals, 63 N.Y.2d 557, 483 N.Y.S.2d 667) (1984)

COOKE, Chief Judge.

The subject of contention in this litigation is a valuable 17-story office building, located at 79 Madison Avenue in Manhattan. In dispute is the propriety of a complex series of transactions that had the net effect of permitting defendants, who were outside investors. to gain ownership of the property and to eliminate the ownership interests of plaintiffs, who were minority shareholders of the corporation that formerly owned the building. This was achieved through what is commonly known as a "two-step" merger: (1) an outside investor purchases control of the majority shares of the target corporation by tender offer or through private negotiations; (2) this newly acquired control is used to arrange for the target and a second corporation controlled by the outside investor to merge with one condition being the "freeze-out" of the minority shareholders of the target corporation by the forced cancellation of their shares, generally through a cash purchase. This accomplishes the investor's original goal of complete ownership of the target corporation.

Since 1955, the office building was owned by 79 Realty Corp. (Realty Corp.), which had no other substantial assets. About two thirds of Realty Corp.'s outstanding shares were held by two couples, the Kimmelmans and the Zauderers, who were also the company's sole directors and officers. Plaintiffs owned 26% of the outstanding shares. The remaining shares were owned by persons who are not parties to this litigation.

Defendants, a consortium of investors, formed a limited partnership, known as Madison 28 Associates (Madison Associates), for the purpose of purchasing the building. In March 1980, Madison Associates began negotiations with the Kimmelmans and the Zauderers to purchase the latter's controlling block of stock at a price equal to its proportion of the building's value, agreed in June 1980 to be $6,500,000. In addition, Madison Associates promised that it would also offer to purchase plaintiff's stock under the same terms within four months of the closing of the stock purchase agreement in September 1980.

Madison Associates formed a separate, wholly owned company, 28 Williams Street Corp. (Williams St.), to act as the nominal purchaser and owner of the Kimmelman and Zauderer interests. The stock purchase agreement was actually signed by Williams St. and its principal asset was the newly acquired shares of Realty Corp. Upon selling their shares, the Kimmelmans and the Zauderers resigned their positions with Realty Corp. and were replaced by four partners of Madison Associates. Now acting as the controlling directors of Realty Corp. on October 17, 1980, the partners of Madison Associates approved a plan to merge Realty Corp. with Williams St., Realty Corp. being the surviving corporation. Together with a notice for a shareholders meeting to vote on the proposed merger, a statement of intent was sent to all shareholders of Realty Corp., explaining the procedural and financial aspects of the merger, as well as defendants' conflict of interest and the intended exclusion of the minority shareholders from the newly constituted Realty Corp. through a cash buy-out. Defendants also disclosed that they planned to dissolve Realty Corp. after the merger and thereafter to operate the business as a partnership. The merger plan did not require approval by any of the minority shareholders.

The merger proposed by the directors was approved at the shareholders meeting, held on November 7, 1980. As a result, the office building was owned by the "new" Realty Corp. which, in turn, was wholly owned by Madison Associates. In accordance with the merger plan, Realty Corp. was dissolved within a month of the merger and its principal asset, title to the building, devolved to Madison Associates.

••••

The plaintiffs instituted this action on October 31, 1980, initially seeking to enjoin the shareholders meeting called to approve the merger. Failing to temporarily enjoin the Realty Corp.'s merger with Williams St., plaintiffs later amended their complaint to include a request for equitable relief in the form of rescission of the merger.

••••

On this appeal, the principal task facing this court is to prescribe a standard for evaluating the validity of a corporate transaction that forcibly eliminates minority shareholders by means of a two-step merger. It is concluded that the analysis employed by the courts below was correct: the majority shareholders' exclusion of minority interests through a two-step merger does not violate the former's fiduciary obligations so long as the transaction viewed as a whole is fair to the minority shareholders and is justified by an independent corporate business purpose. . . .

In New York, two or more domestic corporations are authorized to "merge into a single corporation which shall be one of the constituent corporations", known as the "surviving corporation" (see B.C.L.§901). The statute does not delineate substantive justifications for mergers, but only requires compliance with certain procedures: [See B.C.L.§902, 903].

Generally, the remedy of a shareholder dissenting from a merger and the offered "cash-out" price is to obtain the fair value of his or her stock through an appraisal proceeding (see B.C.L.§623). This protects the minority shareholder from being forced to sell at unfair values imposed by those dominating the corporation while allowing the majority to proceed with its desired merger (Endicott Johnson Corp. v. Bade, 37 N.Y. 2d 585, 590, 376 N.Y.S.2d 103; Klurfeld v. Equity Enterprises, 79 A.D.2d 124, 134, 436 N.Y.S.2d 303; . . .). The pursuit of an appraisal proceeding generally constitutes the dissenting stockholder's exclusive remedy (B.C.L.§623[1]; Breed v. Barton, 54 N.Y.2d 82, 85, 444 N.Y.S.2d 609). An exception exists, however, when the merger is unlawful or fraudulent as to that shareholder, in which event an action for equitable relief is authorized. (B.C.L.§623[k]; Willcox v. Stern, 18 N.Y.2d 195, 204, 273 N.Y.S.2d 38).

Because the power to manage the affairs of a corporation is vested in the directors and majority shareholders, they are cast in the fiduciary role of "guardians of the corporate welfare" (Leibert v. Clapp, 13 N.Y.2d 313, 317, 247 N.Y.S.2d 102). . . . In this position of trust, they have an obligation to all shareholders to adhere to fiduciary standards of conduct and to exercise their responsibilities in good faith when undertaking any corporate action, including a merger (Pepper v. Litton, 308 U.S. 295; Leibert v. Clapp, . . .). . . .

The fiduciary must treat all shareholders, majority and minority, fairly (Schwartz v. Marien, 37 N.Y.2d 487, 491, 373 N.Y.S.2d 122; Katowitz v. Sidler, 24 N.Y.2d 512, 518, 301 N.Y.S.2d 470 . . .). Moreover, all corporate responsibilities must be discharged in good faith and with "conscientious fairness, morality and honesty in purpose". . . . Also imposed are the obligations of candor . . . and of good and prudent management of the corporation. . . . When a breach of fiduciary duty occurs, that action will be considered unlawful and the aggrieved shareholder may be entitled to equitable relief. . . .

While noting the existence of fiduciary duties is an uncomplicated task, the same may not be said of defining precisely what is proper conduct in the context of a particular corporate transaction. In reviewing a freeze-out merger, the essence of the judicial inquiry is to determine whether the transaction, viewed as a whole, was "fair" as to all concerned. This concept has two principal components: the majority shareholders must have followed a course of fair dealing toward minority holders . . . and they must also have offered a fair price for the minority's stock. . . .

. . . When the directors and majority shareholders of each corporation are independent and negotiate at arm's length, it is more likely that the negotiations will reflect the full exertion of each party's bargaining power and the final terms of the transaction will be the best attainable. When, however, there is a common directorship or majority ownership, the inherent conflict of interest and the potential for self-dealing requires careful scrutiny of the transaction. . . .

Generally, the plaintiff has the burden of proving that the merger violated the duty of fairness, but when there is an inherent conflict of interest, the burden shifts to the interested directors or shareholders to prove good faith and the entire fairness of the merger. . . .

Fair dealing is also concerned with the procedural fairness of the transaction, such as its timing, initiation, structure, financing, development, disclosure to the independent directors and shareholders, and how the necessary approvals were obtained. . . .

The fairness of the transaction cannot be determined without considering the component of the financial remuneration offered the dissenting shareholders. When the merger seeks to cancel the minority's shares in exchange for cash, the fiduciaries must ensure that the compensation is equitable. This duty may be satisfied when the cash-out price is reasonably related to the value that might be set by an appraisal proceeding. . . .

In determining whether there was a fair price, the court need not ascertain the precise "fair value" of the shares as it would be determined in an appraisal proceeding. It should be noted, however, that the factors used in an appraisal proceeding are relevant here (B.C.L.§623; Klurfeld v. Equity Enterprises, supra). This would include but would not be limited to net asset value, book value, earnings, market value, and investment value. . . . Elements of future value arising from the accomplishment or expectation of the merger which are known or susceptable of proof as of the date of the merger and not the product of speculation may also be considered (B.C.L. §623[h][4]; Weinberger v. UOP, Inc., 457 A.2d 701, 713 (Del.); Note, Reappraising Minority Shareholder Protection in Freezeout Mergers, 58 St. John's L.Rev. 144, 158–161). Evidence that an independent investment firm was retained to render a fairness opinion on the price offered to the minority may be a good means of demonstrating the price which would have been set by arm's length negotiations. . . .

Fair dealing and fair price alone will not render the merger acceptable. As mentioned, there exists a fiduciary duty to treat all shareholders equally. . . . This duty arises as a concomitant to the power reposed in the majority over corporate governance. . . . The fact remains, however, that in a freeze-out merger the minority shareholders are being treated in a different manner: the majority is permitted continued participation in the equity of the surviving corporation while the minority has no choice but to surrender their shares for cash. On its face, the majority's conduct would appear to breach this fiduciary obligation.

Majority shareholders, however, have an overriding duty to provide good and prudent management, which demands that decisions be made for the welfare, advantage, and best interests of the corporation and the shareholders as a whole. . . . But, it has long been recognized in this State that, under certain circumstances, "the particular interest of the few must give way to the general interest of the many". . . Thus, "[d]eparture from precisely uniform treatment of stockholders may be justified, of course, where a bona fide business purpose indicates that the best interests of the corporation would be served by such departure". . . .

In the context of a freeze-out merger, variant treatment of the minority shareholders,—i.e., causing their removal—will be justified when related to the advancement of a general corporate interest. The benefit need not be great, but it must be for the corporation. For example, if the sole purpose of the merger is reduction of the number of profit shares—in contrast to increasing the corporation's capital or profits, or improving its management structure—there will exist no "independent corporate interest". . . . All of these purposes ultimately seek to increase the individual wealth of the remaining shareholders. What distinguishes a proper corporate purpose from an improper one is that, with the former, removal of the minority shareholders furthers the objective of conferring some general gain upon the corporation. Only then will the fiduciary duty of good and prudent management of the corporation serve to override the concurrent duty to treat all shareholders fairly. . . . We further note that a finding that there was an independent corporate purpose for the action taken by the majority will not be defeated merely by the fact that the corporate objective could have been accomplished in another way, or by the fact that the action chosen was not the best way to achieve the bona fide business objective.

In sum, in entertaining an equitable action to review a freeze-out merger, a court should view the transaction as a whole to determine whether it was tainted with fraud, illegality, or self-dealing, whether the minority shareholders were dealt with fairly, and whether there exists any independent corporate purpose for the merger.

As noted, the courts below applied the correct legal standard in concluding that the merger here was proper. . . .

Noting that defendants had not employed any neutral committees in negotiating the merger, Supreme Court conducted its own objective review of the transaction. There is evidence in the record to support its conclusion that, viewed as a whole, the transaction was fair. Full disclosure of material information was made in the statement of intent mailed to plaintiffs who also had access to Realty Corp's books. The stock price was tied to the fair market value of the office building, the corporation's only substantial asset, which was determined in arm's length negotiations.

Without passing on all of the business purposes cited by Supreme Court as underlying the merger, it is sufficient to note that at least one justified the exclusion of plaintiff's interests: attracting additional capital to effect needed repairs of the building. There is proof that there was a good-faith belief that additional, outside capital was required. Moreover, this record supports the conclusion that this capital would not have been available through the merger had not plaintiff's interest in the corporation been eliminated. Thus, the approval of the merger, which would extinguish plaintiffs' stock, was supported by a bona fide business purpose to advance this general corporate interest of obtaining increased capital.

Accordingly, the order of the Appellate Division should be affirmed. [All concur].

CASE 26
BUFFALO FORGE CO. v. OGDEN CORP.
(U.S. Court of Appeals, 717 F. 2d 757, 2nd Cir.) (1983)

This appeal presents us with questions concerning the legality of management's attempts to thwart a corporate takeover where the bidder has made a financially unsatisfactory tender offer. The facts are set forth in detail in the district court's opinion reported in 555 F. Supp. at 892 and require only brief summarization herein.

In response to a tender offer of $25 per share made on January 2, 1981 by plaintiff, Ampco-Pittsburgh Corp., the individual defendants (the Board of Directors of Buffalo Forge) began a search for more favorable offers. After some negotiations, they approved a merger proposal from defendant, Ogden Corp., calling for an even exchange of Ogden stock, then trading at $32.75, for shares of Buffalo Forge. As part of the "Agreement and Plan of Reorganization" between the parties, the directors agreed to sell Ogden 425,000 shares of Buffalo Forge treasury stock at $32.75 per share, to be paid for by a ten-year, nine percent note in the face amount of $13,918,750, and gave Ogden a one-year option to purchase an additional 143,400 treasury shares on similar terms. A bidding war between Ampco and Ogden ensued, which Ampco won with a bid of $37.50 per share.

After completing the takeover through its wholly-owned subsidiary, (Ampco-Pittsburgh Securities II Corp.), Ampco refused to recognize the Ogden agreement, contending that it resulted from a breach of the directors' fiduciary duties and constituted a manipulative device in violation of section 14(e) of the Williams Act, 15 U.S.C. §78n(e). Ampco refused the tender of Ogden's 425,000 shares, refused to pay dividends on the stock held by Ogden, and denied Ogden the right to exercise its option for the purchase of additional shares. Ampco sued for rescission of the transaction and sought damages from the individual defendants in the event rescission was denied.

After a bench trial in the U.S. District Court . . . [the Court] dismissed Ampco's claims, . . . [and] held that the Buffalo Forge directors did not violate their fiduciary obligations in selling the treasury stock to Ogden and that the sale was not a manipulative device prohibited by the Williams Act . . . that Ogden was entitled to $37.50 for each of the treasury shares it owned or had attempted to buy on option and that it was entitled to the declared but unpaid dividend. . . . Judgment was entered denying plaintiffs all relief and awarding Ogden judgment against plaintiffs in the amount of $24,598,272. We affirm.

In view of the district court's findings, all of which have substantial support in the evidence, appellants' contentions concerning alleged breaches of fiduciary duty by the defendant directors merit little more comment than is contained in the district court's opinion. The district court found:

(1) None of the directors was "motivated to oppose Ampco's tender offer and accept Ogden's offer due to self-interest" and the directors "voted for the Ogden $32.75 offer because it was the best offer available."

(2) The directors were not guilty of fraud or bad faith,

(3) There were no improprieties in the relationships between the directors and the company's financial and legal advisors or in the directors' reliance upon the counsel which the advisors gave,

(4) The negotiations with Ogden were at arm's length, and the price received for the treasury stock, based on the discounted value of Ogden's note, exceeded the cost of the stock, its book value and its normal trading price.

Under the circumstances, it would have been a mistake for the district court to substitute its judgment for the business judgment of the directors, the exercise of which brought about an increase in Ampco's tender offer from $25 a share to $37.50 a share. See Auerbach v. Bennett, 47 N.Y.2d 619, 630–31, 419 N.Y.S.2d 920, (1979); Treadway Cos. v. Care Corp., 638 F.2d 357, 382–83 (2d Cir. 1980); Crouse-Hinds Co. v. Internorth, Inc., 634 F.2d 690, 701–04 (2d Cir. 1980); N.Y.B.C.L.§§504(e), 717.

It also would have been a mistake for the district court to adopt Ampco's argument that the sale of the treasury stock violated section 14(e) of the Williams Act, 15 U.S.C. §78n(e), which proscribes "fraudulent, deceptive, or manipulative acts or practices, in connection with any tender offer." In advancing this argument, Ampco relied on the case of Mobil Corp. v. Marathon Oil Corp., 669 F.2d 366 (6th Cir. 1981). In that case, Marathon, in an attempt to avoid a takeover by Mobil, gave U.S. Steel Corp., a competing bidder, an option to purchase a large number of Marathon's treasury shares and an option to purchase a valuable oil field. The court held that the options, individually and in combination, circumvented the natural forces of market demand and, therefore, were manipulative acts under the statute. . . . It concluded that Mobil was entitled to injunctive relief.

We believe that Marathon was an unwarranted extension of the Williams Act. "The purpose of the Williams Act is to insure that public shareholders who are confronted by a cash tender offer for their stock will not be required to respond without adequate information regarding the qualifications and intentions of the offering party." Rondeau v. Mosinee Paper Corp., 422 U.S. 49, 58, (1975). The Act "was designed solely to get needed information to the investor." Piper v. Chris-Craft Indus., Inc., 430 U.S. 1, 31, (1977). An essential ingredient of a section 14(e) cause of action, therefore, is misrepresentation, i.e., the omission or misstatement of material facts. . . .

• • • •

Congress felt that it was for fully-informed investors to decide whether takeover offers were fair and equitable and that the investors should "be free to make their own decisions." Congress's ban on "manipulative acts and practices" was directed only at rigged transactions that might mislead investors in the making of these decisions. . . .

There were no misleading, manipulative acts in the instant case. In short, we agree with the district court that . . . the defendants herein did not violate section 14(e). . . .

• • • •

The judgment of the district court is affirmed.

PROBLEMS

83. In March, 1980, Alpha Corp., a corporation organized to operate a trucking business, bought all the outstanding shares of stock of Baker Inc., a corporation also organized to operate a trucking business.

In April, Baker Inc. entered into a contract with Smith Department Store, whereby, Baker Inc. undertook to provide for one year, commencing in June, the trucking services for Smith.

In May, the directors of Alpha Corp. filed a certificate with the Secretary of State, merging Baker Inc. with it. After the merger, Smith demanded that Alpha Corp. perform the contract, but Alpha Corp. refused.

(a) Was the purchase of Baker Inc.'s stock valid?

(b) Was the decision of the directors of Alpha Corp. to merge invalid because the shareholders of Alpha Corp. were not consulted?

(c) Was the corporate life of Baker Inc. terminated by the filing of the certificate of merger?

(d) Would the performance of Baker Inc.'s contract by Alpha Corp. be required on the part of Alpha Corp.?

(e) Would Smith have the option to terminate the contract, if Alpha Corp. were willing to perform?

84. Paula owns 100 shares of the preferred stock and 100 shares of the common stock of Acme Corp. When Paula acquired her shares, the authorized capital of Acme Corp., all of which was issued and outstanding, consisted of 10,000 shares of preferred and 10,000 shares of common stock. The preferred shares were preferred as to dividends and assets, but carried no right to vote in the election of directors.

Subsequently, the certificate of incorporation of Acme Corp. was duly amended to increase the number of preferred shares to 20,000 and the number of common shares to 50,000.

Paula filed with the secretary of Acme Corp. a timely dissent in writing to the proposed increases:
  (a) As a preferred shareholder
    (1) may she compel the corporation to buy her preferred shares?
    (2) does she have the right to subscribe to the additional preferred shares?
  (b) As a common shareholder
    (1) may Paula compel the corporation to buy her common shares?
    (2) does she have the right to subscribe to the additional common shares?

85. Russ Corp. owns 9,100 of the 10,000 shares of the outstanding common stock of Sony Inc., which has no other class of stock. The Board of Directors of Russ Corp. unanimously favors merging Sony Inc. into Russ Corp.
  (a) Explain how such merger would be brought about, and who, if anyone, would have to consent.
  (b) Assume that the merger was effectuated, and that Robert, a shareholder of Russ Corp., and Sam, a shareholder of Sony Inc., object to the plan of merger. What are the rights, if any, of:
    (1) Robert? Explain.
    (2) Sam? Explain.

86. Ann owns 10,000 shares of Bara Corp. Her shares represent a 10 percent ownership in Bara; Tom Corp. is interested in aquiring Bara Corp. by merger; the board of directors of each corporation has approved the merger. The shareholders of Tom Corp. have already approved the merger. Bara Corp. has called a shareholders' meeting to approve the merger. Ann disapproves of the merger and does not want to accept Tom Corp. shares for the Bara Corp. shares she owns. Pursuant to the merger, she will receive one share of Tom Corp. for each share of Bara Corp. stock that she owns.
  Discuss Ann's rights in this matter.

**87. Rex Corporation, one of your clients, has engaged you to examine its financial statements in connection with a prospective merger or a consolidation with King Corporation. Both methods of acquisition are being considered under applicable corporate statutory law. Rex is the larger of the two corporations and is in reality acquiring King Corporation.
  (a) Discuss the meaning of the terms merger and consolidation as used in corporate law with particular emphasis on the legal differences between the two.
  (b) What are the major legal procedures which must be met in order to accomplish either a merger or consolidation?[AICPA–4c–Nov. 1976]

**88. Duval is the chairman of the board and president of Monolith Industries, Inc. He is also the largest individual shareholder, owning 40 percent of the shares outstanding. The corporation is publicly held, and there is a dissenting minority. In addition to his position with Monolith, Duval owns 85 percent of Variance Enterprises, a corporation created under the laws of the Bahamas. During 1977 Carlton, the president of Apex Industries, Inc., approached Duval and suggested that a tax-free merger of Monolith and Apex made good sense to him and that he was prepared to recommend such a course of action to the Apex board and to the shareholders. Duval studied the proposal and decided that Apex was a most desirable candidate for acquisition. Duval informed the president of Variance about the overture, told him it was a real bargain, and suggested that Variance pick it up for cash and notes. Not hearing from Duval or Monolith, Carlton accepted an offer from Variance and the business was sold to Variance. Several dissenting shareholders of Monolith learned the facts surrounding the Variance acquisition and engaged counsel to represent them. The Variance acquisition of Apcx proved to be highly profitable.

Discuss the rights of the dissenting Monolith shareholders and the probable outcome of a legal action by them. [AICPA–4b–May 1978].

**89. Parker Pastry, Inc., is a closely held corporation. Curtis and Smith, two of Parker's directors, together own 55% of the corporation's outstanding stock. Devlin, an elderly retired executive, owns 25% of Parker's outstanding stock. The remaining 20% of the outstanding stock is held by five other unrelated persons. There have been no ownership changes in recent years. Parker's stock has no-par value and a present book value of $50 per share.

Baxter Bakeries Corp. is a large, publicly held corporation whose stock is traded on a national securities exchange. The Baxter stock has a par value of $75 per share and is presently being traded at about $100 per share.

Baxter is seeking control of Parker. For tax reasons, Baxter must acquire 80% of Parker's stock to make the acquisition economically feasible. It is not interested at this time in acquiring more than this 80%. Baxter's president proposes to Curtis and Smith that Baxter exchange one share of its stock for one share of Parker stock provided that no less than 80% nor more than 85% of Parker's stock is thus acquired by Baxter.

Without revealing Baxter's offer, Curtis and Smith purchase the Parker stock owned by Devlin at book value. Thereafter, Smith and Curtis deliver their now 80% of Parker's outstanding stock to Baxter in exchange for Baxter stock.

In order for Baxter to acquire the Parker stock, Baxter was required to deliver 30,000 of its shares in exchange for the Parker stock. Baxter had 12,000 shares in its treasury and was currently authorized by its charter to issue 100,000 additional shares. The Baxter directors formally authorized the delivery of the 12,000 treasury shares and the issuance of 18,000 additional shares to acquire the Parker stock. As the auditor of Baxter's financial statements, you are concerned about the contingency that Baxter might incur a liability from stockholder's objections to this Board action. Baxter stockholders might argue that the exchange was unfair, considering the fact that the Parker stock had a book value of $50 per share and was being exchanged for Baxter stock on a share-for-share basis.

(a) Was the action of Baxter's directors proper?

(b) Could any Baxter stockholder successfully assert a preemptive right to acquire any of the shares to be delivered by Baxter? Explain. [AICPA–4b–May 1973].

**90. Several years after acquiring 80% of the stock of Parker, Baxter decided to merge Parker into itself. Under applicable state law, the merger required approval of only two-thirds of the Parker shares. Baxter voted its 80% of Parker's stock in favor of the merger which provided that each minority stockholder of Parker receive one share of Baxter stock in exchange for three shares of Parker stock. In connection with your examination of Baxter's financial statements, you have discovered that some of the minority stockholders voted against the merger. You are concerned that Baxter properly disclose in its financial statements the liability, if any, to the minority stockholders voting against the merger.

(a) What are the rights of Parker stockholders who oppose the merger?

(b) What steps must a stockholder ordinarily take to protect his rights in these circumstances? [AICPA–4d–May 1973].

CHAPTER 11
Dissolution of the Corporation

Dissolution of a corporation may occur in different ways: (1) by the corporation's voluntarily filing a Certificate of Dissolution; (2) by a court entering judgment of Dissolution after a hearing; or (3) by proclamation of the Secretary of State or Attorney General. After dissolution, the corporation can no longer engage in its authorized buisness but must devote its further existence to "winding up," to wit: liquidating its assets, extinguishing its liabilities to creditors, and distributing the remaining assets or funds to the shareholders.

Although the words "termination", "dissolution", and "liquidation" are often used as if interchangeable, termination occurs only after various stages have been completed, to wit: cease operating the corporation's business ("dissolution"); conclude the corporation's predissolution business and reduce corporate assets to liquid form ("winding up"); and distribute the assets to the corporation's creditors, other claimants, and the shareholders ("liquidation"). After dissolution and before termination, the corporation still exists, but only for purposes of "winding up" and liquidation; during the "winding up" and liquidation stage, the corporation has the authority to sue and be sued. B.C.L.§1006(a)(4).

A. VOLUNTARY DISSOLUTION

1. Which Circumstances

Pursuant to B.C.L.§1001, a corporation may be dissolved by a two-thirds vote of its shareholders. In addition, the corporation's Certificate of Incorporation (C/I) may provide for dissolution under various situations: upon vote of the shareholders, or upon the occurrence of a contingency. B.C.L.§1002(a).

2. Filing with the Secretary of State

The completed Certificate of Dissolution must be delivered to the New York Department of State for filing; the consent of the New York State Tax Commission must also be obtained and submitted to be sure the corporation does not owe any franchise or other state taxes; consent to the filing will be withheld until the corporation pays all such taxes in full. After the Tax Commission has given its consent, the Department of State will then file the Certificate of Dissolution provided it complies with B.C.L.§1003. The corporation is dissolved when the Certificate of Dissolution is filed. B.C.L.§1004.

B. DISSOLUTION BY COURT DECREE

The New York State Supreme Court may order dissolution of the corporation upon receiving a petition to do so under certain specified grounds; all parties involved must receive notice of the proceeding. The petition may be filed with the court under various circumstances by the New York Attorney General, by resolution of the board of directors, or by a specified percentage of the shareholders, as provided by statute.

In addition, if the corporation has failed to file its annual franchise tax reports and pay such taxes for two consecutive years, the Secretary of State may dissolve the corporation by proclamation. (See Tax Law §203-a).

I. Who May File the Petition?

(a) The Attorney General

B.C.L.§1101 provides the Attorney General may petition the Supreme Court to dissolve a corporation upon one or more of the following grounds: The corporation was formed by fraudulent misrepresentation or concealment of a material fact; has exceeded its authority by ultra vires acts; has carried on, conducted or transacted business in a persistently fraudulent or illegal manner; has violated provisions of the law whereby it has forfeited its charter, or by abuse of its powers contrary to public policy. See B.C.L.§1101 for details.

(b) The Board of Directors

The corporation may petition the court for dissolution upon resolution of a majority of the board of directors which finds the corporate assets are insufficient to discharge its liabilities, or that a dissolution will be beneficial to the shareholders. See B.C.L.§1102.

(c) The Shareholders—Special Meeting

B.C.L.§1103 provides that holders of a majority of the outstanding voting shares of a corporation may adopt a resolution to dissolve the corporation, on the grounds that (1) the corporation's assets are not sufficient to discharge its liabilities, or (2) they believe a dissolution to be beneficial to the shareholders. B.C.L.§1103(a). A shareholders' meeting to consider such resolution may be called by the holders of 10 percent of all outstanding voting shares (the C/I may provide the holders of a lesser proportion to call the meeting). A meeting for this purpose may not be called more often than once a year. B.C.L.§1103(b).

(d) The Shareholders On Grounds of Deadlock

The shareholders owning one-half of the outstanding shares entitled to vote may petition the court for dissolution if management is equally divided so as to create a deadlock and thus corporate action cannot be taken. The deadlock must be in one or more of the following respects: (1) division among the directors regarding management of the corporate affairs so that board action is impossible; (2) division among shareholders so that directors cannot be elected; (3) internal dissension and two or more factions of shareholders are so divided that dissolution would be beneficial to the shareholders. B.C.L.§1104(a).

If the C/I provides for a higher proportion of votes for board action or for shareholder election of directors, then holders of more than one third of the outstanding shares entitled to vote may commence the deadlock proceeding. B.C.L.§1104(b).

In addition, any shareholder entitled to vote for directors may petition the court on the ground that the shareholders are so divided that they have failed for at least two annual meetings to elect successors to directors whose terms would otherwise have expired. B.C.L.§1104(c).

The court in its discretion must determine that the deadlock pertains to matters which are material and essential to the existence of the corporation, and renders the corporation unable to function. The fact that the corporation has or has not been operating at a profit is not a determining factor. B.C.L.§1111(b)(3).

(e) 20% of the Shareholders

Holders of 20% or more of the outstanding voting shares of a corporation (not listed on a national exchange) may petition the Supreme Court for dissolution on one or more of the following grounds: (1) the directors or those in control of the corporation have committed illegal, fraudulent or oppressive actions toward the complaining shareholders; (2) the property or assets of the corporation are being looted, wasted or diverted for non-corporate purposes by its directors, officers or those in control. B.C.L.§1104-a.

In such proceeding the court will consider whether dissolution and liquidation is the only feasible way for the complaining shareholders to reasonably expect a fair return on their investment, and is reasonably necessary to protect the rights and interests of a substantial number of the shareholders.

Within 90 days of filing the petition, the corporation or any other shareholders of the corporation may elect to purchase the shares owned by the petitioners by paying the fair market value for the shares on terms and conditions as may be approved by the court. The corporation or the shareholders who elect to purchase the shares may request the court to stay the dissolution proceeding pending the determination of the fair market value of the shares. See B.C.L.§1118(b).

The impact of B.C.L.§1104-a is to give dissenting shareholders who hold at least 20% of the shares a powerful tool—the threat of dissolution. It would be strongly advisable that a shareholder agreement adequately provide a means of evaluating the shares in case of such attempted dissolution proceeding.

Several cases have come before the courts in New York since the enactment of B.C.L. §1104-a. In such proceedings, the courts have searched and held hearings so as to determine what is "oppressive conduct".

In any valuation proceeding to determine "fair value", courts have held that the "fair value" determination in an appraisal proceeding (pursuant to B.C.L.§623) does not control the fair value in a proceeding for a buy-out (pursuant to B.C.L.§1104-a and §1118).*

(f) What If Shareholders Own Less Than 20%?

If the shareholders allege fraudulent or oppressive conduct of the directors, but the shareholders own less than 20% of the shares, what are they to do? The shareholders can *not* seek relief pursuant to B.C.L.§1104-a; However, the shareholders may seek other dissolution relief. Courts have held there is a common law right to dissolution available to the minority shareholders where the officers or directors are engaged in conduct in violation of their fiduciary duty to the shareholders.**

---

*See cases of Blake v. Blake Agency, 107 A.D.2d 139, 486 N.Y.S.2d 341 (A.D.2nd Dept. 1985) and Matter of Gift Pax, 107 A.D.2d 97, 486 N.Y.S.2d 272 (A.D.2nd Dept. 1985) for court's discussion of method of valuation of "fair value".

**See, Leibert v. Clapp, 13 N.Y.2d 313, 247 N.Y.S.2d 102 (1922) (common law); this was applied in Lewis v. Jones, 107 A.D.2d 931, 483 N.Y.S.2d 868 (3rd Dept. 1985), a 19% shareholder.

2. Procedure in Court

A copy of the Petition and papers must be served upon the State Tax Commission, upon the corporation, and upon each shareholder, creditor or claimant. B.C.L.§1106(c). In addition, it is to be published in newspapers of general circulation as the court directs. The court, with notice to all interested parties, orders a hearing to ascertain the facts, and consider all the conflicting interests. The court may order the corporation, its officers and directors, to provide any information the court requests, including statements of the corporation's assets and liabilities, and the name and address of each claimant. B.C.L.§1106(a).

At any stage of the action or proceeding, the court may grant an injunction, restraining the corporation and its directors and officers from transacting unauthorized business and from collecting or receiving any debt or property of the corporation and from paying out or otherwise transferring any of the corporate property, except by permission of the court; the court may also restrain creditors from proceeding except by permission of the court. See B.C.L.§1115.

During and pending the proceeding for Judicial dissolution, any sale, mortgage, conveyance or other transfer of the property of the corporation without prior court approval, in payment of or as security for an existing or prior debt shall be void as against such person.*

If, in the court's discretion, the corporation should be dissolved, the court makes a judgment or final order accordingly. B.C.L.§1111(a). A copy of the court order of dissolution is filed with the Department of State, and the corporation is then dissolved. B.C.L.§1111(d). In addition, a certified copy of the Judgment or final order of dissolution is filed in the County Clerk's Office in the county where the corporation's office is located.

C. "WINDING UP" AND LIQUIDATION OF THE CORPORATION

When the corporation has been dissolved, whether voluntarily or involuntarily, it cannot carry on any business except for the purpose of "winding up" its affairs. B.C.L.§1005(a)(1). The corporation should fulfill or discharge its contracts, collect its assets, sell its assets for cash (at a public or private sale), discharge or pay its liabilities, and do all other acts appropriate to liquidate the business. B.C.L.§1005(a)(2). A dissolved corporation may continue to function, but only for purposes of "winding up" the affairs of the corporation; It may continue to function in the same manner as if dissolution had not taken place, but only for the purpose of "winding up". See B.C.L.§1006. A dissolved corporation's power to wind up its affairs include the power to take care of the corporation's property until winding up is complete, including the power to keep the property adequately insured against fire and other hazards.** In fact, a corporation has the continuing obligation to respond to subpoenas regarding pre-dissolution activities and is amenable to sanctions should it ignore the subpoena.***

The corporation continues to exist during "winding up" and is a legal entity for purposes of actions and proceedings, by or against it. Upon petition of any interested party, a court may supervise the winding up. B.C.L.§1008. In an involuntary dissolution, the corporation's "winding up" will be under the supervision of the Supreme Court. B.C.L.§1113.

---

*See, Matter of Rappaport, 110 A.D.2d 639, 487 N.Y.S.2d 376 (1985), where issuance of one share of stock by owner of 50% interest in corporation to brother-in-law subsequent to commencement of dissolution proceeding was null and void.
**See case of Igbara Realty Corp. v. New York Property Ins. Underwriting Assn, 94 A.D.2d 79, 463 N.Y.S.2d 211 (1983), aff'd and modified, 63 N.Y. 2d 201, 481 N.Y.S.2d 60, on remand, 104 A.D.2d 258, 482 N.Y.S.2d 741 (1984).
***See, In Re Grand Jury Subpoenas Issued to Thirteen Corporations, 775 F. 2d 43 (2nd Cir. 1985).

1. Filing of Claims by Creditors

An important task in "winding up" a dissolved corporation is the identification of creditors of the corporation. The procedure in both voluntary and involuntary dissolution is provided for in B.C.L.§1007. After dissolution, the corporation publishes a "legal notice" once a week for two weeks in a local newspaper of general circulation requiring all creditors and claimants (including those with unliquidated or contingent claims and any with whom the corporation has unfulfilled contracts) to present in writing their claims by a date at least six months after the notice first appears. The corporation must also mail copies of this notice to each person it knows to be a creditor or claimant. B.C.L.§1007(a). Any claim filed within the six-month period which the corporation disputes (in whole or in part) may be submitted to the Supreme Court for review under B.C.L.§1008. Any claim which is not filed within the six-month period and any claim which is filed but disallowed by the Supreme Court under B.C.L.§1008, is forever barred against the corporation. The Court may, however, allow a late claim to be filed against remaining corporate assets if the creditor can provide a satisfactory explanation for its lateness. B.C.L.§1007(b).

2. Distribution—Priority of Creditors

Once a corporation has been dissolved and the "winding up" process is complete—i.e., the corporate assets have been reduced to liquid form and the creditors and claimants have been identified, all that remains to be done is the distribution of the net assets to creditors, and then to the shareholders of the corporation.

The I.R.S. and the N.Y.S. Tax Commission have priority on corporate assets for most tax claims. B.C.L.§1007(c). Wage claims and unfunded pension liabilities are preferred claims. B.C.L.§1007(d). Of course, if corporate assets are not sufficient to pay wage claims, the ten largest shareholders of a closely-held corporation will be personally responsible for payment of the wage claim. B.C.L.§630(a).

Secured creditors are ranked according to the priority of their respective liens. In general, unsecured creditors are then entitled to share in the distribution of the assets.

3. Distribution to Shareholders

After providing for all creditors, the remaining assets may be sold; with the consent of a majority of the voting shareholders, the assets may be sold for shares, bonds, or other securities, or partly for cash and partly for shares of another corporation. If the consideration is other than cash, a dissenting shareholder has the right of appraisal to receive payment for his shares in cash. B.C.L.§1005, §623.

Any remaining assets are distributed among the shareholders according to their respective rights as set forth in the corporation's C/I. B.C.L.§1005(a)(3).

Generally, preferred shareholders are entitled on liquidation to the full par value of their shares before the common shareholders receive anything. Preferred shareholders may also have the right to be paid any dividends which have not been paid to them while the corporation was actively in operation; this will depend upon their rights as indicated in the C/I. Preferred shareholders may have liquidation preference, in addition to the par value.

If distribution of assets are made to shareholders without adequately providing for payment of claims due to the creditors of the corporation, the shareholders who receive such distribution, hold same as trustee for the benefit of the creditors of the corporation. In addition, the directors who approved such payment without adequately providing for the payments of amounts due to creditors, incur personal liability. See B.C.L.§719(a)(3).

4. Court Supervision of Liquidation

At any stage in the liquidation, a court may be requested, by the corporation or by any interested party to continue the liquidation under court supervision; in this connection the court may make determination regarding the following: determination of the validity of a voluntary dissolution; the adequacy of notice to creditors; the validity and amount of claims; the disallowance of claims and barring creditors who have not timely filed; the validity and enforcement of liability against directors or officers for mismanagement; liability of shareholders and subscribers for shares; payment, satisfaction, or compromise of claims; disposition of corporate records; issuance of injunctions against transfer of corporate assets without permission of the court, or against creditors from taking or continuing separate court action.

At any stage in the proceeding, where it is necessary to protect the interests of claimants, a court may take liquidation out of the hands of the officers and directors, and appoint a Receiver, for the purpose of carrying out the necessary steps of liquidation and distribution. See B.C.L.§1008 for jurisdiction of court.

D. RECEIVERSHIP

1. Which Circumstances

The best interests of all concerned shall determine whether a receiver is to be appointed by the court or is necessary. A receiver of a New York corporation's assets may be appointed in any one of the following actions or proceedings: (1) for voluntary or involuntary dissolution of the corporation; (2) by a judgment creditor for sequestration of the corporation's assets under B.C.L.§1201; and (3) by the New York Attorney General or by a shareholder to preserve the assets of the corporation if the corporation has no officer within this state qualified to administer them. B.C.L.§1202.

2. Procedure

A Receiver may be appointed by the court, and at all times is subject to court supervision; the court may appoint a Temporary Receiver or a Permanent Receiver. The Receiver may be an outsider, or a director, officer, or shareholder; the Receiver is vested with ownership of the corporate assets, and may sue and initiate proceedings to recover corporate property, sell corporate assets, examine persons under oath, and settle claims. B.C.L.§1207–§1209. The Receiver makes distribution of the corporate assets as provided by B.C.L.§1210–§1212. The Receiver is required to keep true accounts of all moneys received and expended and to present verified statements of the same to the court. (B.C.L.§1207(a)(3)), and is entitled to commissions for services rendered to be paid out of the corporate assets, B.C.L.§1216, §1217.

Once creditors and claimants have been identified, and all corporate assets collected or otherwise accounted for are reduced to cash, the receiver must settle the accounts and pay all outstanding claims against the corporation in the order of priority as established by B.C.L.§1210, §1211. After final distribution of creditors, the Receiver shall distribute any balance among the shareholders in accordance with their respective rights, after deducting the charges and expenses of the Receiver. B.C.L.§1212.

CASE 27
INDEPENDENT INVESTOR PROTECTIVE LEAGUE v. TIME, INC.
(Court of Appeals of New York, 50 N.Y.2d 259, 428 N.Y.S. 2d 671) (1980)

COOKE, Chief Judge.

It is determined here that a shareholder derivative action may be maintained even though commenced after the subject corporation has effected a dissolution and distributed its assets.

This derivative suit, brought in the name and on behalf of Sterling Communications, Inc., was commenced by plaintiffs against defendants, Time, Inc., and the officers and directors of Sterling. The thrust of the litigation is directed at the relationship of Time and Sterling. Beginning in 1965, Time made investments in Sterling and by 1973 Time played a dominant role in the corporation, owning approximately 80% of the stock and controlling Sterling's management. A majority of Sterling's directors are alleged to have been officers of Time.

On September 7, 1973, Sterling shareholders approved the sale of all corporate assets to Time, and authorized the dissolution of Sterling and distribution of its assets. These actions were accomplished almost immediately and the present action was commenced approximately six months later. According to the complaint, the officers and directors of Sterling, at the behest of Time, engaged in a course of deliberate mismanagement between 1970 and 1973 which depressed the value of Sterling stock, enabling Time to acquire Sterling at a price below its true value. The relief sought, on behalf of Sterling, is the difference between the 1970 value and the 1973 depressed value, approximately $15,000,000 as measured by the decline in the price of stock.

Time moved for summary judgment on the ground that plaintiffs lacked standing to sue. The motion was granted, with a finding that plaintiffs were not shareholders of Sterling at the time the suit was brought, and thus a derivative action would not lie under B.C.L.§626(b). A unanimous Appellate Division agreed, and stated "since Sterling had been dissolved prior to commencement of the action, plaintiffs lack necessary standing to proceed by or in the right of the corporation. . . . [A]t the time suit was instituted, the corporate entity did not exist". The order of the Appellate Division should be reversed.

• • • •

[The N.Y. rule] . . . is now codified in the B.C.L., which permits a dissolved corporation to "sue or be sued in all courts and participate in actions and proceedings". B.C.L.§1006[a][4]. . . . Thus a corporation continues to exist as a legal entity after dissolution in New York, at least for the purposes of actions and proceedings. Moving a step further, the question now arises as to whether a shareholder has standing to maintain an action on behalf of such a corporation.

B.C.L.§626(b) imposes upon the plaintiff in a derivative action a dual requirement as to the ownership of stock: "it shall be made to appear that the plaintiff is . . . [a shareholder] at the time of bringing the action and . . . at the time of the transaction of which he complains." Ownership at the time of the alleged wrong, . . . was adopted by State courts and Legislatures "to prevent litigious persons from buying stock for the purpose of bringing suit as to alleged past mismanagement.". . .

The requirement that ownership continue until commencement of the derivative action, on the other hand, is rooted in practical considerations. Although in a theoretical sense a derivative action is brought for the benefit of the corporation, "In a very real sense . . . the standing of the shareholder is based on the fact that . . . he is defending his own interests as well as those of the corporation" (Tenney v. Rosenthal, 6 N.Y.2d 204, 211, 189 N.Y.S.2d 158, 163, 160, . . .). Where the plaintiff voluntarily disposes of the stock, his rights as a shareholder cease, and his interest in the litigation is terminated. . . . Being a stranger to the corporation, the former stockowner lacks standing to institute or continue the suit.

But when the corporation has dissolved, the shareholder's interest does not abruptly end. At a minimum, the stockholder possesses a substantial interest in the distribution of corporate assets. And, even if dissolution and distribution of assets are accomplished contemporaneously, the shareholder's stake in any cause of action existing in favor of the corporation remains quite real. From a purely analytical standpoint, then, a shareholder of a dissolved corporation has sufficient interest in a derivative action to satisfy the spirit of the rule requiring ownership at the commencement of the action.

This analysis is confirmed by B.C.L.§1006, which provides that "The dissolution of a corporation shall not affect any remedy available to . . . [its] shareholders for any right or claim existing . . . before such dissolution". Under this statute, the rights and remedies of the shareholders existing prior to dissolution are viewed as if the dissolution never occurred. It follows that the corporate dissolution in itself cannot preclude a qualified plaintiff from being deemed a shareholder "at the time of bringing the [derivative] action" (B.C.L.§626[b]).

The only obstacle raised by defendant to the maintenance of this derivative action was the alleged lack of standing of the plaintiff shareholders after dissolution. Since the dissolution, without more, did not deprive the shareholders of their derivative remedy, the action was improperly dismissed except as to those shareholders who availed themselves of their appraisal rights under B.C.L.§623(e)

[All Judges concur].

Discussion Questions

After dissolution, does the corporation have the right to maintain a law suit?

After dissolution, should a shareholders' derivative suit be permitted?

CASE 28
LORISA CAPITAL CORP. v. GALLO et. al.
(App. Div. 2nd Dep't., 506 N.Y.S.2d 662) (1986).

GIBBONS, Justice Presiding.

At issue on this appeal is (1) . . . and (2) whether plaintiff Lorisa Capital Corp., a corporation dissolved by proclamation of the Secretary of State for nonpayment of franchise taxes in 1978, had capacity to bring this action to enforce obligations arising out of prohibited new business conducted five years after dissolution. We conclude that the . . . plaintiff lacked the capacity to institute this action.

• • • •

Lorisa's proposed supplemental complaint falsely alleged that it was a duly organized and *existing* corporation under the laws of New York State.

• • • •

. . . Regarding its own corporate status, Lorisa asserted that the transactions supporting the foreclosure action were conducted in the course of winding up its corporate affairs, and thus, it had capacity to sue pursuant to B.C.L. §1006(a)(4). In the alternative, Lorisa offered to pay the outstanding back taxes and revive the corporate entity, if necessary.

• • • •

Upon dissolution, a corporation's legal existence terminates (Lattin, Corporations, 183, p. 642 2d ed). This rule is qualified by statute to provide that a corporation retains a limited de jure existence for the purpose of winding up (B.C.L. §1005(a)(1), 1006). Lorisa acknowledges that it was dissolved in September 1978 pursuant to Tax Law §203-a by proclamation of the Secretary of State for nonpayment of franchise taxes. Its complaint alleged that in 1983 it first acquired rights to the mortgages in suit, four years and five months after its statutory dissolution. . . . Accordingly, we consider whether a corporation, dissolved pursuant to Tax Law §203-a, has capacity to bring suit on a claim arising out of the conduct of prohibited new business (see, B.C.L. §1005(a)(1)).

Statutory dissolution by proclamation of the Secretary of State pursuant to Tax Law §203-a is intended to encourage voluntary* payment of franchise taxes (see, Bowditch v. 57 Laight St. Corp., 111 Misc.2d 255, 443 N.Y.S.2d 785). After dissolution, a delinquent corporation retains a limited de jure existence solely for the purpose of winding up its affairs, and retains capacity to bring suit for that purpose (see, Tax Law §203-a(10); B.C.L. §1009, 1006). All new business is prohibited (B.C.L. §1005(a)(1)). Accordingly, a corporation is encouraged to pay franchise taxes, as delinquency for a period of two years in either filing a franchise tax report or paying the taxes due will result in dissolution and forfeiture of the corporate charter (see, Tax Law §203-a(1), (2), (3)). The statutory scheme is further designed to encourage voluntary compliance by providing that a delinquent corporation may be reinstated nunc pro tunc upon the filing of a certificate of the tax commission stating that all franchise taxes, penalties and interest charges have been paid (Tax Law §203-a(7)). Payment of such preproclamation indebtedness by a corporation which has failed to cease its business activities may not be avoided by an attempt to reincorporate (D & W Cen. Sta. Alarm Co. v. Copymasters, Inc., 122 Misc. 2d 453, 471 N.Y.S.2d 464). It is apparent from the statutory scheme that the Legislature did not intend a delinquent corporation which has not sought reinstatement to enjoy the privileges of corporate existence, which include the right to acquire a mortgage interest and the right to bring suit in the courts of this State (see, . . . Note: Dissolution and Suspension as Remedies for Corporate Franchise Tax Delinquency: . . . 41 N.Y.U. L. Rev. 602, 612, 617). Lorisa advances several theories to avoid that result and dismissal of its case, including the doctrine of de facto corporations, estoppel theory, and the unavailability under B.C.L. §203 of the ultra vires defense. We find none of Lorisa's arguments persuasive.

First, a delinquent corporation may not avail itself of the de facto doctrine to preclude third parties from challenging its capacity to sue. De facto recognition requires both a good faith exercise of corporate powers and colorable compliance with the enabling statute (see, Lattin, Corporations, 57, p. 184 (2d ed); Corporate Tax Delinquency, 41 NYU L. Rev. 602, 613, Garzo v. Maid of Mist Steamboat Co., 303 N.Y. 516, 104 N.E.2d 882 (de facto status recognized where good faith exercise of corporate powers, including the payment of dividends and taxes, followed inadvertent failure to timely file certificate extending corporate life under enabling statute)). A

---

*The large number of corporations that become delinquent each year renders a system dependent upon state-initiated collection methods administratively and economically unworkable. As of 1986, between 9,000 and 13,000 corporations were dissolved in New York each year. . . .

delinquent corporation lacks both prerequisites. There is neither a good faith exercise of corporate duties, nor compliance with statutes requiring the payment of franchise taxes for the privilege of conducting business in the corporate form (Tax Law §209). Moreover, a corporation's de jure existence is removed for the very purpose of securing compliance with the tax statute. Recognition of de facto status would directly subvert the effectiveness of the sanctions for franchise tax delinquency, removing all incentive for a dissolved corporation to seek reinstatement. . . . As it has been previously stated:

"A corporation dissolved under Section 203-a of the tax law is legally dead and can no longer sue . . . except in the limited respects specifically permitted by the statute. Its existence has been terminated and it is not even a de facto corporation" (Brady v. State Tax Commission, 176 Misc. 1053, 29 N.Y.S.2d 88, affd 263 App. Div. 955, 33 N.Y.S.2d 384; see, also, Delpad Realty Corp. v. Rappaport, 119 NYS2d 675).

We agree. . . .

• • • •

We note that should Lorisa pay its back taxes as it offered to do in its papers . . . and, thus, be reinstated to de jure status nunc pro tunc, its contracts entered into during the period of delinquency would be retroactively validated. By statute, the corporate powers, rights, duties and obligations are reinstated nunc pro tunc, as if "such proclamation of dissolution had not been made or published" (Tax Law §203-a(7)(8)). Moreover, once the delinquent corporation has paid its taxes and penalties, "it serves no revenue purpose to permit avoidance of corporate contracts executed during delinquency". (see Corporate Tax Delinquency, 41 NYU L.Rev. 603 608). "A majority of states that have considered this problem have ruled that such contracts are retroactively validated"; see, Bowditch v. 57 Laight St. Corp., 111 Misc.2d 255, 259, 443 N.Y.S.2d 785, . . . As noted, the fact that Lorisa may be reinstated to viable corporate status, and thereby secure retroactive validation of its contracts, will not resolve the issues in this foreclosure action, but merely initiate consideration of the multifaceted problems that appear from the record to constitute a deficiency in its interest in the property.

We now turn our attention to the third theory offered to sustain Lorisa's capacity. One commentator has relied upon B.C.L. 203 to advance the view that a claim arising out of the conduct of prohibited new business by a delinquent corporation should be enforceable, as the delinquent corporation enjoys a de facto status, and under B.C.L.§203, the defense of ultra vires conduct is available only in specifically enumerated circumstances to shareholders and the Attorney General (see, 4 White, New York Corporations, §1006.08). First, the defense of ultra vires conduct goes to the validity of an action taken by a de jure corporation which is beyond the powers granted in its corporate charter (see, Jemison v. Citizens, Savings Bank of Jefferson, 122 N.Y. 135, 140, 25 N.E. 264). . . . Moreover, a delinquent corporation has forfeited its charter, and is prohibited from conducting any new business. To what extent B.C.L. §203 is impliedly applicable to de facto corporations under Garzo v. Maid of Mist Steamboat Co., . . . need not concern us here, for as we have already stated, a delinquent corporation does not enjoy de facto status. . . .

Finding each of Lorisa's arguments unpersuasive, we hold that it lacks capacity to use the courts of this State to enforce obligations arising out of the conduct of prohibited new business during the period of delinquency until it has secured retroactive de jure status by payment of delinquent franchise taxes.

In recognition that Lorisa may wish to avail itself of retroactive reinstatement, and in order to conserve judicial resources by eliminating the need to reinstate this suit, should Lorisa wish to do so, the foreclosure action should be dismissed unless within 45 days after service upon it of the order to be made herein, with notice of entry, Lorisa has paid its preproclamation franchise taxes, penalties and interest, and has secured reinstatement. Should this period of time prove insufficient to complete the necessary procedures with the Tax Commission and Secretary of State, Lorisa may seek an extension from this court upon proof of payment.

• • • •

Discussion Questions

What is Winding Up?

Does a corporation have a right to maintain an action after it has been dissolved?

CASE 29
IN THE MATTER OF KEMP & BEATLEY, INC.
(Court of Appeals of New York, 64 N.Y.2d 63, 484 N.Y.S.2d 799) (1984).

COOKE, Chief Judge.

When the majority shareholders of a close corporation award *de facto* dividends to all shareholders except a class of minority shareholders, such a policy may constitute "oppressive actions" and serve as a basis for an order made pursuant to section 1104-a of the B.C.L. dissolving the corporation.

The business concern of Kemp & Beatley, incorporated under the laws of New York, designs and manufactures table linens and sundry tabletop items. The company's stock consists of 1,500 outstanding shares held by eight shareholders. Petitioner Dissin had been employed by the company for 42 years when, in June 1979, he resigned. Prior to resignation, Dissin served as vice-president and a director of Kemp & Beatley. Over the course of his employment, Dissin had acquired stock in the company and currently owns 200 shares.

Petitioner Gardstein, like Dissin, had been a long-time employee of the company. Hired in 1944, Gardstein was for the next 35 years involved in various aspects of the business including material procurement, product design, and plant management. His employment was terminated by the company in December 1980. He currently owns 105 shares of Kemp & Beatley stock.

Apparent unhappiness surrounded petitioners' leaving the employ of the company. Of particular concern was that they no longer received any distribution of the company's earnings. Petitioners considered themselves to be "frozen out" of the company; whereas it had been their experience when with the company to receive a distribution of the company's earnings according to their stockholdings, in the form of either dividends or extra compensation; that distribution was no longer forthcoming.

Gardstein and Dissin, together holding 20.33% of the company's outstanding stock, commenced the instant proceeding in June 1981, seeking dissolution of Kemp & Beatley pursuant to section 1104-a of the B.C.L. Their petition alleged "fraudulent and oppressive" conduct by the company's board of directors such as to render petitioners' stock "a virtually worthless asset". . . .

The involuntary-dissolution statute (B.C.L.§1104-a) permits dissolution when a corporation's controlling faction is found guilty of "oppressive action" toward the complaining shareholders.

The referee considered oppression to arise when "those in control" of the corporation "have acted in such a manner as to defeat those expectations of the minority stockholders which formed the basis of [their] participation in the venture". The expectations of petitioners that they would not be arbitrarily excluded from gaining a return on their investment and that their stock would be purchased by the corporation upon termination of employment, were deemed defeated by prevailing corporate policies. Dissolution was recommended in the referee's report, subject to giving respondent corporation an opportunity to purchase petitioners' stock.

Supreme Court confirmed the referee's report. . . . The Appellate Division affirmed, without opinion.

At issue in this appeal is the scope of section 1104-a of the B.C.L. Specifically, this court must determine whether the provision for involuntary dissolution when the "directors or those in control of the corporation have been guilty of. . . "oppressive actions toward the complaining shareholders" was properly applied in the circumstances of this case. We hold this it was, and therefore affirm. . . . Statutes permitting judicial dissolution of corporation either limited the types of corporations under their purview or restricted the parties who could petition for dissolution to the Attorney-General, or the directors, trustees, or majority shareholders of the corporation (see generally, §§1101–1104).

Minority shareholders were granted standing in the absence of statutory authority to seek dissolution of corporations when controlling shareholders engaged in certain egregious conduct (see Leibert v. Clapp 13 N.Y.2d 313, 247 N.Y.S.2d 102, . . .). Predicated on the majority shareholders' fiduciary obligation to treat all shareholders fairly and equally, to preserve corporate assets, and to fulfill their responsibilities of corporate management with "scrupulous good faith", the courts' equitable power can be invoked when "it appears that the directors and majority shareholders 'have so palpably breached the fiduciary duty they owe to the minority shareholders that they are disqualified from exercising the exclusive discretion and dissolution power given to them by statute' ". (Leibert v. Clapp, 13 N.Y.2d at 317, 247 N.Y.S.2d 102 supra quoting Hoffman, New Horizons For The Close Corporation, 28 Brooklyn L. Rev. 1, 14). True to the ancient principle that equity juridiction will not lie when there exists a remedy at law, the courts have not entertained a minority's petition in equity when their rights and interests could be adequately protected in a legal action, such as by a shareholder's derivative suit (see Matter of Nelkin v. H.J.R. Realty Corp., 25 N.Y.2d 543, 550, 307 N.Y.S.2d 454 . . .).

Supplementing this principle of judicially ordered equitable dissolution of a corporation, the Legislature has shown a special solicitude toward the rights of minority shareholders of closely held corporations by enacting section 1104-a of the B.C.L. That statute provides a mechanism for the holders of at least 20% of the outstanding shares of a corporation whose stock is not traded on a securities market to petition for its dissolution "under special circumstance" (see B.C.L. §1104-a[a]). The circumstances that give rise to dissolution fall into two general classifications: mistreatment of complaining shareholders ([a][1]), or misappropriation of corporate assets ([a][2]) by controlling shareholders, directors of officers.

Section 1104-a([a][1]) describes three types of proscribed activity: "illegal", "fraudulent", and "oppressive" conduct. The first two terms are familiar words that are commonly understood at law. The last, however, does not enjoy the same certainty gained through long usage. As no definition is provided by the statute, it falls upon the courts to provide guidance. . . .

The statutory concept of "oppressive actions" can, perhaps, best be understood by examining the characteristics of close corporations and the Legislature's general purpose in creating this involuntary-dissolution statute. It is widely understood that, in addition to supplying capital to contemplated or ongoing enterprise and expecting a fair and equal return, parties comprising the ownership of a close corporation may expect to be actively involved in its management and operation (O'Neal, Close Corporations 2d ed. §§1.07–1.09; Davidian. Corporate Dissolution in New York, 56 St. John's L.Rev. 24, 26; Note, Involuntary Dissolution of Close Corporation for Mistreatment of Minority Shareholder, 60 Wash. U.L.Q. 1119, 1139–1143; Ann., 56 A.L.R.3rd 358, 363–367; . . .).

As a leading commentator in the field has observed; "Unlike the typical shareholder in a publicly held corporation who may be simply an investor or a speculator and cares nothing for the responsibilities of management, the shareholder in a close corporation is a co-owner of the business and wants the privileges and powers that go with ownership. His participation in that particular corporation is often his principal or sole source of income. As a matter of fact, providing employment for himself may have been the principal reason why he participated in organizing the corporation. He may or may not anticipate an ultimate profit from the sale of his interest, but he normally draws very little from the corporation as dividends. In his capacity as an officer or employee of the corporation, he looks to his salary for the principal return on his capital investment because earnings of a close corporation, as is well known, are distributed in major part in salaries, bonuses and retirement benefits". (O'Neal, Close Corporations 2d ed. §1.07, at pp. 21–22).

Shareholders enjoy flexibility in memorializing these expectations through agreements setting forth each party's rights and obligations in corporate governance (see, generally, Kessler, Shareholder-Managed Close Corporation, 43 Fordham L. Rev. 197 . . .). In the absence of such an agreement, however, ultimate decision-making power respecting corporate policy will be reposed in the holders of a majority interest in the corporation. . . .

As the stock of closely held corporations generally is not readily salable, a minority shareholder at odds with management policies may be without either a voice in protecting his or her interests or any reasonable means of withdrawing his or her investment. This predicament may fairly be considered the legislative concern underlying the provision at issue in this case; inclusion of the criteria that the corporation's stock not be traded on securities markets and that the complaining shareholder be subject to oppressive actions supports this conclusion.

Defining oppressive conduct as distinct from illegality in the present context has been considered in other forums. The question has been resolved by considering oppressive actions to refer to conduct that substantially defeats the "reasonable expectations" held by minority shareholders in committing their capital to the particular enterprise (see, e.g., Mardikos v. Arger, 116 Misc.2d 1028, 457 N.Y.S.2d 371; Matter of Barry One Hour Photo Process, 111 Misc.2d 559, 444 N.Y.S.2d 540, Matter of Topper v. Park Sheraton Pharmacy, 107 Misc.2d 25, 433 N.Y.S.2d 359, Capitol Toyota v. Gervin, 381 So.2d 1038 (Miss.); Exadaktilos v. Cinnaminson Realty Co., 167 N.J.Super 141, 153–156 400 A.2d 554, affd. 173 N.J. Super. 559, 414 A.2d 994; . . . O'Neal Oppression of Minority Shareholders §3.01–3.11; O'Neal, Close Corporations: Existing Legislation and Recommended Reform, 33 Bus. Law. 873. . . .) . . . A shareholder who reasonably expected that ownership in the corporation would entitle him or her to a job, a share of corporate earnings, a place in corporate management, or some other form of security, would be oppressed in a very real sense when others in the corporation seek to defeat those expectations and there exists no effective means of salvaging the investment.

Given the nature of close corporations and the remedial purpose of the statute, this court holds that utilizing a complaining shareholder's "reasonable expectations" as a means of identifying and measuring conduct alleged to be oppressive is appropriate. A court considering a petition alleging oppressive conduct must investigate what the majority shareholders knew, or should have known, to be the petitioner's expectations in entering the particular enterprise. . . .

* * * *

The appropriateness of an order of dissolution is in every case vested in the sound discretion of the court considering the application (see B.C.L.§1111 [a]). Under the terms of this statute, courts are instructed to consider both whether "liquidation of the corporation is the only feasible means" to protect the complaining shareholder's expectation of a fair return on his or her investment and whether dissolution "is reasonably necessary" to protect "the rights or interests of any substantial number of shareholders" not limited to those complaining (B.C.L.§ 1104-a [b][1],[2]). Implicit in this direction is that once oppressive conduct is found, consideration must be given to the totality of circumstances surrounding the current state of corporate affairs and relations to determine whether some remedy short of or other than dissolution constitutes a feasible means of satisfying both the petitioner's expectations and the rights and interest of any other substantial group of shareholders. . . .

By invoking the statute, a petitioner has manifested his or her belief that dissolution may be the only appropriate remedy. Assuming the petitioner has set forth a prima facie case of oppressive conduct, it should be incumbent upon the parties seeking to forestall dissolution to demonstrate to the court the existence of an adequate, alternative remedy. A court has broad latitude in fashioning alternative relief, but when fulfillment of the oppressed petitioner's expectations by these means is doubtful such as when there has been a complete deterioration of relations between the parties, a court should not hesitate to order dissolution. Every order of dissolution, however, must be conditioned upon permitting any shareholder of the corporation to elect to purchase the complaining shareholder's stock at fair value (see B.C.L.§1118).

One further observation is in order. The purpose of this involuntary dissolution statute is to provide protection to the minority shareholder whose reasonable expectations in undertaking the venture have been frustrated and who has no adequate means of recovering his or her investment. It would be contrary to this remedial purpose to permit its use by minority shareholders as merely a coercive tool. . . .

There was sufficient evidence presented at the hearing to support the conclusion that Kemp & Beatley had a long-standing policy of awarding de facto dividends based on stock ownership in the form of "extra compensation bonuses". Petitioners, both of whom had extensive experience in the management of the company, testified to this effect. Moreover, both related that receipt of this compensation, whether as true dividends or disguised as "extra compension", was a known incident to ownership of the company's stock understood by all of the company's principals. Finally, there was uncontroverted proof that this policy was changed either shortly before or shortly after petitioners' employment ended. Extra compensation was still awarded by the company. The only difference was that stock ownership was no longer a basis for the payments; it was asserted that the basis became services rendered to the corporation. It was not unreasonable for the fact finder to have determined that this change in policy amounted to nothing less than an attempt to exclude petitioners from gaining any return on their investment through the mere recharacterization of distributions of corporate income. Under the circumstances of this case, there was no error in determining that this conduct constituted oppressive action within the meaning of section 1104-a of the B.C.L.

. . . After the referee had found that the controlling faction of the company was, in effect, attempting to "squeeze-out" petitioners by offering them no return on their investment and increasing other executive compensation, respondents, in opposing the report's confirmation, attempted only to controvert the factual basis of the report. They suggested no feasible, alternative remedy to the forced dissolution. In light of an apparent deterioration in relations between petitioners and the governing shareholders of Kemp & Beatley, it was not unreasonable for the court to have determined that a forced buy-out of petitioners' shares or liquidation of the corporation's assets was the only means by which petitioners could be guaranteed a fair return on their investments.

• • • •

PROBLEMS

91. Arthur Gerth owned 53 percent of the XYZ Corporation's common stock and half of its preferred stock. His brother, Harry, owned 1 percent of its common stock, and Kruger owned the remainder of its common and preferred stock. The XYZ Corporation was in the retail lumber business. Of the three shareholders, Gerth was the only employee of the corporation. As its president, he paid himself a combined salary and bonus of approximately $10,000 annually. This left less than $2,000 in profits to be distributed as dividends. Kruger brought suit to have XYZ Corporation dissolved on the ground that Gerth was drawing an excessive salary and bonus and was thus wasting corporate assets and leaving an insufficient amount available for dividends. Under Gerth's leadership, the XYZ Corporation had become quite successful, and Gerth claimed that he deserved the salary and bonus because of his efforts. Should XYZ be dissolved?

92. Alpha Corp. was dissolved; its obligations were all discharged; and its assets distributed among its shareholders.

Subsequently, an additional asset was discovered in the form of an account receivable due to the corporation, which had been overlooked at the time of dissolution. An action is now instituted by Alpha Corp. against Jones for the $800 amount due. Jones defends on the ground that Alpha Corp. is no longer in existence, and therefore has no capacity to sue.

May the corporation maintain this action even though it is dissolved? Discuss.

93. X Corp. has three directors. One of the three directors is out of town and refuses to attend meetings. Thereafter the remaining two directors deadlock in voting on any action by the corporation.

(a) Could either of these two directors commence an action to dissolve the corporation? Explain and discuss.

(b) Can the shareholders bring an action to dissolve the corporation? Explain and discuss.

94. Gladys sold and delivered goods to X Corp. in the sum of $1,000. Thereafter Gladys went to China on an extended business trip. Upon her return to New York she learned that X Corp. had been dissolved pursuant to §1001 of the B.C.L. and all its assets were distributed among the preferred shareholders in the sum of $10,000; no distribution was made to common shareholders because the assets were insufficient to do so. Gladys has not been paid. May Gladys proceed to enforce the payment of her claim against any of the following:
   (a) A director?
   (b) A preferred shareholder?
   (c) A common shareholder?
Discuss and explain.

95. Jayne is a shareholder in the Nova Corporation. Jayne owns 22% of the shares of stock. She has been a shareholder and officer in this corporation since 1970 and has invested her life savings in the corporation. In 1982 arguments started developing between Jayne and Michael and Esther, who are majority shareholders; Michael and Esther together own 70% of the outstanding shares, and control the Board of Directors. At a meeting of the Board of Directors on December 1, 1982, Jayne was discharged from the corporation. Jayne is no longer an officer of the corporation and has not received any salary from the corporation since that date. No dividends have been paid by the corporation. Jayne comes to you and seeks legal advice regarding the following court proceedings she would like to institute:
   (a) To direct the Directors to pay dividends.
   (b) To be reinstated as an officer.
   (c) To require the corporation to buy back her shares of stock.
   (d) To dissolve the corporation.
The majority shareholders refuse all of her requests. Indicate which proceedings, if any, could be brought on Jayne's behalf regarding each of her requests, and indicate the details of the proceedings.
   (e) Assume that Jayne only owned 19.5% of the outstanding shares of stock in Nova Corporation. Indicate if any of your decisions and reasons in (a), (b), (c) and (d) above would be any different; and indicate any of the different procedures.

96. Nicholas is a 25% shareholder in the Ingot Corporation. The other shareholders are various cousins who own a total of 75% of the outstanding shares. The majority shareholders are pretty sure that Nicholas had been stealing funds from the corporation, which total in excess of $100,000. They do not wish to bring criminal proceedings against Nicholas because of the family relationship; however, three years ago they threw him out of the corporation and refused to allow him to visit the premises. He is not receiving any salary and is not receiving any dividends. Nicholas seeks legal advice as to what he should do regarding his 25% ownership of the outstanding shares. What advice can you offer to Nicholas?

APPENDIX **1**

N.Y. Business Corporation Law (B.C.L.)

[Note: Because of space limitations, some of the sections or subsections of the Statute have been deleted; any deletions have been so indicated].

§ 101. Short title.

This chapter shall be known as the "Business Corporation Law".

§ 102. Definitions.

(a) As used in this chapter, unless the context otherwise requires, the term:

(1) "Bonds" includes secured and unsecured bonds, debentures, and notes.

(2) "Capital surplus" means the surplus other than earned surplus.

(3) "Certificate of incorporation" includes (A) the original certificate of incorporation or any other instrument filed or issued under any statute to form a domestic or foreign corporation, as amended, supplemented or restated by certificates of amendment, merger or consolidation or other certificates or instruments filed or issued under any statue; or (B) a special act or charter creating a domestic or foreign corporation, as amended, supplemented or restated.

(4) "Corporation" or "domestic corporation" means a corporation for profit formed under this chapter, or existing on its effective date and theretofore formed under any other general statute or by any special act of this state for a purpose or purposes for which a corporation may be formed under this chapter, other than a corporation which may be formed under the cooperative corporations law.

(5) "Director" means any member of the governing board of a corporation, whether designated as director, trustee, manager, governor, or by any other title. The term "board" means "board of directors".

(6) "Earned surplus" means the portion of the surplus that represents the net earnings, gains or profits, after deduction of all losses, that have not been distributed to the shareholders as dividends, or transferred to stated capital or capital surplus, or applied to other purposes permitted by law. Unrealized appreciation of assets is not included in earned surplus.

(7) "Foreign corporation" means a corporation for profit formed under laws other than the statutes of this state, which has as its purpose or among its purposes a purpose for which a corporation may be formed under this chapter, other than a corporation which, if it were to be formed

currently under the laws of this state, could not be formed under this chapter. "Authorized", when used with respect to a foreign corporation, means having authority under article 13 (Foreign corporations) to do business in this state.

(7–a) "Infant" mean a person who has not attained the age of eighteen years.

(8) "Insolvent" means being unable to pay debts as they become due in the usual course of the debtor's business.

(9) "Net assets" means the amount by which the total assets exceed the total liabilities. Stated capital and surplus are not liabilities.

(10) "Office of a corporation" means the office the location of which is stated in the certificate of incorporation of a domestic corporation, or in the application for authority of a foreign corporation or an amendment thereof. Such office need not be a place where business activities are conducted by such corporation.

(11) "Process" means judicial process and all orders, demands, notices or other papers required or permitted by law to be personally served on a domestic or foreign corporation, for the purpose of acquiring jurisdiction of such corporation in any action or proceeding, civil or criminal, whether judicial, administrative, arbitrative or otherwise, in this state or in the federal courts sitting in or for this state.

(12) "Stated capital" means the sum of (A) the par value of all shares with par value that have been issued, (B) the amount of the consideration received for all shares without par value that have been issued, except such part of the consideration therefore as may have been allocated to surplus in a manner permitted by law, and (C) such amounts not included in clauses (A) and (B) as have been transferred to stated capital, whether upon the distribution of shares or otherwise, minus all reductions from such sums as have been effected in a manner permitted by law.

(13) "Surplus" means the excess of net assets over stated capital.

(14) "Treasury shares" means shares which have been issued, have been subsequently acquired, and are retained uncancelled by the corporation. Treasury shares are issued shares, but not outstanding shares, and are not assets.

§ 103. Application.

(a) This chapter applies to every domestic corporation and to every foreign corporation which is authorized or does business in this state. This chapter also applies to any other domestic corporation or foreign corporation of any type or kind to the extent, if any, provided under this chapter or any law governing such corporation and, if no such provision for application is made, to the extent, if any, that the stock corporation law applied to such corporation immediately prior to the effective date of this chapter.

This chapter also applies to a corporation of any type or kind, formed for profit under any other chapter of the laws of this state except a chapter of the consolidated laws, to the extent that provisions of this chapter do not conflict with the provisions of such unconsolidated law. If an applicable provision of such unconsolidated law relates to a matter embraced in this chapter but is not in conflict therewith, both provisions shall apply. Any corporation to which this chapter is made applicable by this paragraph shall be treated as a "corporation" or "domestic corporation" as such terms are used in this chapter, except that the purposes of any such corporation formed or formable under such unconsolidated law shall not thereby be extended. For the purpose of this paragraph, the effective date of this chapter as to corporations to which this chapter is made applicable by this paragraph shall be June one, nineteen hundred seventy-three.

This chapter shall not apply to a domestic corporation of any type or kind heretofore or hereafter formed under the banking law, insurance law, railroad law, transportation corporations law or cooperative corporations law, or under any other statute or special act for a purpose or purposes for which a corporation may be formed under any of such laws except to the extent, if any, provided under such law. It shall not apply, except to the extent, if any, provided under the banking law, insurance law, railroad law, transportation corporations law or cooperative corporations law, to a foreign corporation of any type or kind heretofore or hereafter formed which (1) has as its purpose or among its purposes a purpose for which a corporation may be formed only under the insurance law, banking law, railroad law, transportation corporations law or cooperative corporations law, and (2) is either an authorized insurer as defined in the insurance law or does in this state only the kind of business which can be done lawfully by a corporation formed under the banking law, railroad law, transportation corporations law or cooperative corporations law, as the case may be. . . .

§ 104. Certificates, requirements, signing, filing, effectiveness.

(a) Every certificate or other instrument relating to a domestic or foreign corporation which is delivered to the department of state for filing under this chapter, other than a certificate of existence under section 1304 (Application for authority; contents), shall be in the English language, except that the corporate name may be in another language if written in English characters or letters.

(b) Whenever such instrument is required to set forth an address, it shall include the street and number, or other particular description instead of a street and number. This requirement does not apply where a post office address is specified to be set forth.

(c) Whenever such instrument is required to set forth the date when a certificate of incorporation was filed by the department of state, the original certificate of incorporation is meant. This requirement shall be satisfied, in the case of a corporation created by special act, by setting forth the chapter number and year of passage of such act.

(d) Every such certificate required under this chapter to be signed and delivered to the department of state shall, except as otherwise specified in the section providing for such certificate, be signed either (1) by the holders of all outstanding shares entitled to vote thereon, or (2) by the chairman of the board, the president or a vice president and by the secretary or an assistant secretary, or (3) if there are no such officers by a majority of the directors or such directors as are designated by a majority of the directors in office, or (4) if also there are no directors, by the holders, or such of them as are designated by the holders, of record of a majority of all outstanding shares entitled to vote thereon, or (5) if also there is no shareholder of record, by a subscriber for shares whose subscription has been accepted or his successor in interest or (6) if also no subscription for shares has been accepted, by an incorporator or anyone acting in his stead under paragraph (c) of section 615 (Written consent of shareholders, subscribers or incorporators without a meeting). His name and the capacity in which any person signs such certificate shall be stated beneath or opposite his signature. The person signing such certificate or, if more than one person signs it, one of such persons shall verify or acknowledge the certificate if required by the section providing for such certificate. In lieu of being signed and verified or acknowledged, the certificate may be subscribed by such person and affirmed by him as true under the penalties of perjury.

• • • •

(g) The department shall make, certify and transmit a copy of each such instrument to the clerk of the county in which the office of the domestic or foreign corporation is and is to be located. The county clerk shall file and index such copy.

§ 104–A. Fees.

* * * *

§ 105. Certificates; corrections.

Any certificate or other instrument relating to a domestic or foreign corporation filed by the department of state under this chapter may be corrected with respect to any informality or error apparent on the face or defect in the execution thereof including the deletion of any matter not permitted to be stated therein. A certificate, entitled "Certificate of correction of . . . . (correct title of certificate and name of corporation)" shall be signed, verified or acknowledged as provided in this chapter with respect to the certificate being corrected and delivered to the department of state. It shall set forth the name of the corporation, the date the certificate to be corrected was filed by the department of state, the provision in the certificate as corrected or eliminated and if the execution was defective, the proper execution. The filing of the certificate by the department of state shall not alter the effective time of the instrument being corrected, which shall remain as its original effective time, and shall not affect any right or liability accrued or incurred before such filing. A corporate name may not be changed or corrected under this section.

§ 106. Certificates as evidence.

(a) Any certificate or other instrument filed by the department of state relating to a domestic or foreign corporation and containing statements of fact required or permitted by law to be contained therein, shall be received in all courts, public offices and official bodies as prima facie evidence of such facts and of the execution of such instrument.

(b) Whenever by the laws of any jurisdiction other than this state, any certificate by any officer in such jurisdiction or a copy of any instruments certified or exemplified by any such officer, may be received as prima facie evidence of the incorporation, existence or capacity of any foreign corporation incorporated in such jurisdiction, or claiming so to be, such certificate when exemplified, or such copy of such instrument when exemplified shall be received in all courts, public offices and official bodies of this state, as prima facie evidence with the same force as in such jurisdiction. Such certificate or certified copy of such instrument shall be so received, without being exemplified, if it is certified by the secretary of state, or official performing the equivalent function as to corporate records, of such jurisdiction.

§ 107. Corporate seal as evidence.

The presence of the corporate seal on a written instrument purporting to be executed by authority of a domestic or foreign corporation shall be prima facie evidence that the instrument was so executed.

§ 108. **When notice or lapse of time unnecessary; notices dispensed with when delivery is prohibited.**

* * * *

§ 109. Actions or special proceedings by attorney-general.

(a) The attorney-general may maintain an action or special proceeding:

(1) To annul the corporate existence or dissolve a corporation that has acted beyond its capacity or power or to restrain it from the doing of unauthorized business;

(2) To annul the corporate existence or dissolve any corporation that has not been duly formed;

(3) To restrain any person or persons from acting as a domestic or foreign corporation within this state without being duly incorporated or from exercising in this state any corporate rights, privileges or franchises not granted to them by the law of the state;

(4) To procure a judgment removing a director of a corporation for cause under section 706 (Removal of directors);

(5) To dissolve a corporation under article 11 (Judicial dissolution);

(6) To restrain a foreign corporation or to annul its authority to do business in this state under section 1303 (Violations).

(7) Upon written application, ex parte, for an order to the supreme court at a special term held within the judicial district where the office of the corporation is located, and if the court so orders, to inspect the books and records of the corporation to the extent that such inspection is available to shareholders and directors under the law of this state. Such application shall contain a statement that the inspection is necessary to protect the interests of the people of this state. This paragraph applies to every corporation, no shares of which are listed on a national securities exchange or regularly quoted in an over-the-counter market by one or more members of a national or an affiliated securities association. This paragraph does not apply to a corporation all shares of which are owned either directly or through a wholly owned subsidiary by a corporation or corporations to which this paragraph does not apply.

(b) In an action or special proceeding brought by the attorney-general under any of the provisions of this chapter:

(1) If an action, it is triable by jury as a matter of right.

(2) The court may confer immunity in accordance with the provisions of section 50.20 of the criminal procedure law.

(3) A temporary restraining order to restrain the commission or continuance of the unlawful acts which form the basis of the action or special proceeding may be granted upon proof, by affidavit, that the defendant or defendants have committed or are about to commit such acts. Application for such restraining order may be made ex parte or upon such notice as the court may direct.

(4) If the action or special proceeding is against a foreign corporation, the attorney-general may apply to the court at any stage thereof for the appointment of a temporary receiver of the assets in this state of such foreign corporation, whenever it has assets or property of any kind whatsoever, tangible or intangible, within this state.

(5) When final judgment in such action or special proceeding is rendered against the defendant or defendants, the court may direct the costs to be collected by execution against any or all of the defendants or by order of attachment or other process against the person of any director or officer of a corporate defendant.

(6) In connection with any such proposed action or special proceeding, the attorney-general may take proof and issue subpoenas in accordance with the civil practice law and rules.

(c) In any such action or special proceeding against a foreign corporation which has not designated the secretary of state as its agent for service of process under section 304 (Statutory designation of secretary of state as agent for service of process), any of the following acts in this state by such foreign corporation shall constitute the appointment by it of the secretary of state as its agent upon whom process against such foreign corporation may be served:

(1) As used in this paragraph the term "resident" shall include individuals, domestic corporations and foreign corporations authorized to do business in the state.

(2) Any act done, or representation made as part of a course of the solicitation of orders, or the issuance, or the delivery, of contracts for, or the sale of, property, or the performance of services to residents which involves or promotes a plan or scheme to defraud residents in violation of the laws or the public policy of the state.

(3) Any act done as part of a course of conduct of business in the solicitation of orders from residents for property, goods or services, to be delivered or rendered within this state to, or on their behalf, where the orders or contracts are executed by such residents within this state and where such orders or contracts are accompanied or followed by an earnest money deposit or other down payment or any installment payment thereon or any other form of payment, which payment is either delivered in or transmitted from the state.

(4) Any act done as part of the conduct of a course of business with residents which defrauds such residents or otherwise involves or promotes an attempt by such foreign corporation to circumvent the laws of this state.

(d) Paragraphs (b), (c), (d) and (e) of section 307 (Service of process on unauthorized foreign corporation) shall apply to process served under paragraph (c).

§ 110. Reservation of power.

The legislature reserves the right, at pleasure, to alter, amend, suspend or repeal in whole or in part this chapter, or any certificate of incorporation or any authority to do business in this state, of any domestic or foreign corporation, whether or not existing or authorized on the effective date of this chapter.

§ 111. Effect of invalidity of part of chapter; severability.

If any provision of this chapter or application thereof to any person or circumstances is held invalid, such invalidity shall not affect other provisions or applications of this chapter which can be given effect without the invalid provision or application, and to this end the provisions of this chapter are declared severable.

§ 201. Purposes.

(a) A corporation may be formed under this chapter for any lawful business purpose or purposes except to do in this state any business for which formation is permitted under any other statute of this state unless such statute permits formation under this chapter. If, immediately prior to the effective date of this chapter, a statute of this state permitted the formation of a corporation under the stock corporation law for a purpose or purposes specified in such other statute, such statute shall be deemed and construed to permit formation of such corporation under this chapter and any conditions, limitations or restrictions in such other statute upon the formation of such corporation under the stock corporation law shall apply to the formation thereof under this chapter.

(b) The approval of the industrial board of appeals is required for the filing with the department of state of any certificate of incorporation, certificate of merger or consolidation or application of a foreign corporation for authority to do business in this state which states as the purpose or one of the purposes of the corporation the formation of an organization of groups of working men or women or wage earners, or the performance, rendition or sale of services as labor consultant or as advisor on labor-management relations or as arbitrator or negotiator in labor-management disputes.

(c) In time of war or other national emergency, a corporation may do any lawful business in aid thereof, notwithstanding the purpose or purposes set forth in its certificate of incorporation, at the request or direction of any competent governmental authority.

(d) A corporation may not include as its purpose or among its purposes the establishment or operation of a day care center for children, unless its certificate of incorporation shall so state and such certificate shall have annexed thereto the approval of the commissioner of social services.

(e) A corporation may not include as its purpose or among its purposes the establishment or maintenance of a hospital or facility providing health related services, as those terms are defined in article twenty-eight of the public health law unless its certificate of incorporation shall so state and such certificate shall have annexed thereto the approval of the public health council.

§ 202. General powers.

(a) Each corporation, subject to any limitations provided in this chapter or any other statute of this state or its certificate of incorporation, shall have power in furtherance of its corporate purposes.

(1) To have perpetual duration.

(2) To sue and be sued in all courts and to participate in actions and proceedings, whether judicial, administrative, arbitrative or otherwise, in like cases as natural persons.

(3) To have a corporate seal, and to alter such seal at pleasure, and to use it by causing it or a facsimile to be affixed or impressed or reproduced in any other manner.

(4) To purchase, receive, take by grant, gift, devise, bequest or otherwise, lease, or otherwise acquire, own, hold, improve, employ, use and otherwise deal in and with, real or personal property, or any interest therein, wherever situated.

(5) To sell, convey, lease, exchange, transfer or otherwise dispose of, or mortgage or pledge, or create a security interest in, all or any of its property, or any interest therein, wherever situated.

(6) To purchase, take, receive, subscribe for, or otherwise acquire, own, hold, vote, employ, sell, lend, lease, exchange, transfer, or otherwise dispose of, mortgage, pledge, use and otherwise deal in and with, bonds and other obligations, shares, or other securities or interests issued by others, whether engaged in similar or different business, governmental, or other activities.

(7) To make contracts, give guarantees and incur liabilities, borrow money at such rates of interest as the corporation may determine, issue its notes, bonds and other obligations, and secure any of its obligations by mortgage or pledge of all or any of its property or any interest therein, wherever situated.

(8) To lend money, invest and reinvest its funds, and take and hold real and personal property as security for the payment of funds so loaned or invested.

(9) To do business, carry on its operations, and have offices and exercise the powers granted by this chapter in any jurisdiction within or without the United States.

(10) To elect or appoint officers, employees and other agents of the corporation, define their duties, fix their compensation and the compensation of the directors, and to indemnify corporate personnel.

(11) To adopt, amend or repeal by-laws, including emergency by-laws made pursuant to subdivision seventeen of section twelve of the state defense emergency act, relating to the business of the corporation, the conduct of its affairs, its rights or powers or the rights or powers of its shareholders, directors or officers.

(12) To make donations, irrespective of corporate benefit, for the public welfare or for community fund, hospital, charitable, educational, scientific, civic or similar purposes, and in time of war or other national emergency in aid thereof.

(13) To pay pensions, establish and carry out pension, profit-sharing, share bonus, share purchase, share option, savings, thrift and other retirement, incentive and benefit plans, trusts and provisions for any or all of its directors, officers and employees.

(14) To purchase, receive, take, or otherwise acquire, own, hold, sell, lend, exchange, transfer or otherwise dispose of, pledge, use and otherwise deal in and with its own shares.

(15) To be a promoter, partner, member, associate or manager of other business enterprises or ventures, or to the extent permitted in any other jurisdiction to be an incorporator of other corporations of any type or kind.

(16) To have and exercise all powers necessary or convenient to effect any or all of the purposes for which the corporation is formed.

(b) No corporation shall do business in New York state under any name, other than that appearing in its certificate of incorporation, without compliance with the filing provisions of section one hundred thirty of the general business law governing the conduct of business under an assumed name.

§ 203. Defense of ultra vires.

(a) No act of a corporation and no transfer of real or personal property to or by a corporation, otherwise lawful, shall be invalid by reason of the fact that the corporation was without capacity or power to do such act or to make or receive such transfer, but such lack of capacity or power may be asserted:

(1) In an action by a shareholder against the corporation to enjoin the doing of any act or the transfer of real or personal property by or to the corporation. If the unauthorized act or transfer sought to be enjoined is being, or is to be, performed or made under any contract to which the corporation is a party, the court may, if all of the parties to the contract are parties to the action and if it deems the same to be equitable, set aside and enjoin the performance of such contract, and in so doing may allow to the corporation or to the other parties to the contract, as the case may be, such compensation as may be equitable for the loss or damage sustained by any of them from the action of the court in setting aside and enjoining the performance of such contract; provided that anticipated profits to be derived from the performance of the contract shall not be awarded by the court as a loss or damage sustained.

(2) In an action by or in the right of the corporation to procure a judgment in its favor against an incumbent or former officer or director of the corporation for loss or damage due to his unauthorized act.

(3) In an action or special proceeding by the attorney-general to annul or dissolve the corporation or to enjoin it from the doing of unauthorized business.

§ 301. Corporate name; general.

(a) Except as otherwise provided in this chapter, the name of a domestic or foreign corporation:

(1) Shall contain the word "corporation", "incorporated" or "limited", or an abbreviation of one of such words; or, in the case of a foreign corporation, it shall, for use in this state, add at the end of its name one of such words or an abbreviation thereof.

(2) Shall not be the same as the name of a corporation of any type or kind, or a fictitious name of an authorized foreign corporation filed pursuant to article thirteen of this chapter, as such name appears on the index of names of existing domestic and authorized foreign corporations of any type or kind, including fictitious names of authorized foreign corporations filed pursuant to article thirteen of this chapter, in the department of state, division of corporations, or a name the right to which is reserved, or a name so similar to any such name as to tend to confuse or deceive.

(3) Shall not contain any word or phrase, or any abbreviation or derivative thereof, the use of which is prohibited or restricted by any other statute of this state, unless in the latter case the restrictions have been complied with.

(4) Shall not contain any word or phrase, or any abbreviation or derivative thereof, in a context which indicates or implies that the corporation, if domestic, is formed or, if foreign, is authorized for any purpose or is possessed in this state of any power other than a purpose for which, or a power with which, the domestic corporation may be and is formed or the foreign corporation is authorized.

(5)(A) Shall not contain any of the following phrases, or any abbreviation or derivative thereof:

board of trade	state police	urban development
chamber of commerce	state trooper	urban relocation
community renewal	tenant relocation	

(B) Shall not contain any of the following words, or any abbreviation or derivative thereof:

acceptance	endowment	loan
annuity	fidelity	mortgage
assurance	finance	savings
bank	guaranty	surety
benefit	indemnity	title
bond	insurance	trust
casualty	investment	underwriter
doctor	lawyer	

unless the approval of the superintendent of banks or the superintendent of insurance, as appropriate, is attached to the certificate of incorporation, or application for authority or amendment thereof; or that the word "doctor" or "lawyer" or an abbreviation or derivation thereof is used in the name of a professional service corporation formed pursuant to article fifteen of this chapter, or a foreign professional service corporation authorized to do business in this state pursuant to article fifteen–A of this chapter, the shareholders of which are composed exclusively of doctors or lawyers, respectively, or are used in a context which clearly denotes a purpose other than the practice of law or medicine.

(6) Shall not, unless the approval of the state board of standards and appeals is attached to the certificate of incorporation, or application for authority or amendment thereof, contain any of the following words or phrases, or any abbreviation or derivative thereof: union, labor, council, industrial organization, in a context which indicates or implies that the domestic corporation is

formed or the foreign corporation authorized as an organization of working men or women or wage earners or for the performance, rendition or sale of services as labor or management consultant, adviser or specialist, or as negotiator or arbitrator in labor-management disputes.

(7) Shall not, unless the approval of the state department of social services is attached to the certificate of incorporation, or application for authority or amendment thereof, contain the word "blind" or "handicapped". Such approval shall be granted by the state department of social services, if in its opinion the word "blind" or "handicapped" as used in the corporate name proposed will not tend to mislead or confuse the public into believing that the corporation is organized for charitable or non-profit purposes related to the blind or the handicapped.

(8) Shall not contain any words or phrases, or any abbreviations or derivation thereof in a context which will tend to mislead the public into believing that the corporation is an agency or instrumentality of the United States or the state of New York or a subdivision thereof or is a public corporation.

(9) Shall not contain any word or phrase, or any abbreviation or derivation thereof, which, separately or in context, shall be indecent or obscene, or shall ridicule or degrade any person, group, belief, business or agency of government, or indicate or imply any unlawful activity.

(10) Shall not, unless the approval of the attorney general is attached to the certificate of incorporation, or application for authority or amendment thereof, contain the word "exchange" or any abbreviation or derivative thereof. Such approval shall not be granted by the attorney general, if in his opinion the use of the word "exchange" in the proposed corporate name would falsely imply that the corporation conducts its business at a place where trade is carried on in securities or commodities by brokers, dealers, or merchants.

§ 302. Corporate name; exceptions.

(a) Any reference to a corporation in this section except as otherwise provided herein shall include both domestic and foreign corporations.

(b) The provisions of section 301 (Corporate name; general):

(1) Shall not require any corporation, existing or authorized under any statute on the effective date of this chapter, to add to, modify or otherwise change its corporate name; provided, however, that any corporation organized or qualified to do business in this state under this chapter which contains in its name any of the following words or phrases or any abbreviation or derivation thereof, "community renewal", "tenant relocation", "urban development" or "urban relocation", shall plainly and legibly state immediately following its name in any writing issued or authorized to be issued by it upon which its name appears, including, but not limited to, advertising material letterheads, business cards and building directories and signs, the phrase "not a governmental agency".

(2) Shall not prevent a corporation with which another corporation is merged, or which is formed by the reorganization or consolidation of one or more other corporations or upon a sale, lease, exchange or other disposition to a domestic corporation of all or substantially all the assets of another domestic corporation, including its name, as provided in paragraph (b) of section 909 (Sale, lease, exchange or other disposition of assets), from having the same name as any of such corporations if at the time such other corporation was authorized or existing under any statute of this state.

(3) Shall not prevent a foreign corporation from being authorized under a name which is similar to the name of a corporation of any type or kind existing or authorized under any statute, if the department of state finds, upon proof by affidavit or otherwise as it may determine, that a

difference between such names exists in the terms or abbreviations indicating corporate character or otherwise, that the applicant has engaged in business as a corporation under its said name for not less than ten consecutive years immediately prior to the date of its application that the business to be conducted in this state is not the same as or similar to the business conducted by the corporation with whose name it may conflict and that the public is not likely to be confused or deceived, and if the applicant shall agree in its application for authority to use with its corporate name, in this state, to be placed immediately under or following such name, the words "a . . . . (name of jurisdiction of incorporation) corporation".

(4) Shall not prevent a "small business investment corporation" as defined in an act of congress entitled "Small Business Investment Act of 1958" from including the word "investment" as part of its name if such word is coupled with the words "small business".

(5) Shall not prevent an "investment company" as defined in an act of congress entitled "Investment Company Act of 1940" from including the word "finance" or "bond" as part of its name, if the approval of the superintendent of banks is attached to the certificate of incorporation, application for authority, or amendment thereof.

(6) Shall not prevent a broker or dealer in securities, as defined in an act of congress entitled "Securities Exchange Act of 1934", from including the word "investment" as part of its name if such word is coupled with the words "broker" or "brokers" and if such broker or dealer is registered with the securities and exchange commission under the provisions of section fifteen of the securities exchange act of nineteen hundred thirty-four and is also registered with the attorney general under the provisions of section three hundred fifty-nine-e of the general business law.

(7) Shall not prevent an association of banks or trust companies organized as a non-profit membership corporation for the promotion of the interests of member banks from including the word "bankers" as part of the corporate name.

(8) Shall not prevent a bank holding company, as long as it is required to be registered under article III-A of the banking law or under the federal Bank Holding Company Act as each may be amended from time to time, from using the words "bank", "banker" or "trusts" or any abbreviation, derivative or combination thereof as part of its corporate name, if the approval of the superintendent of banks is attached to the certificate of incorporation, application for authority, or amendment thereof.

§ 303. Reservation of name.

(a) A corporate name may be reserved by:

(1) Any person intending to form a domestic corporation.

(2) Any domestic corporation intending to change its name.

(3) Any foreign corporation intending to apply for authority to do business in this state.

(4) Any authorized foreign corporation intending to change its name.

(5) Any person intending to incorporate a foreign corporation and to have it apply for authority to do business in this state.

(b) A fictitious name for use pursuant to section 1301 of this chapter, may be reserved by:

(1) Any foreign corporation intending to apply for authority to do business in this state, pursuant to paragraph (d) of section 1301 of this chapter.

(2) Any authorized foreign corporation intending to change its fictitious name under which it does business in this state.

(3) Any authorized foreign corporation which has changed its corporate name in its jurisdiction, such new corporate name not being available in this state.

(c) Application to reserve a corporate name shall be delivered to the department of state. It shall set forth the name and address of the applicant, the name to be reserved and a statement of the basis under paragraph (a) or (b) for the application. The secretary of state may require that there be included in the application a statement as to the nature of the business to be conducted by the corporation. If the name is available for corporate use, the department of state shall reserve the name for the use of the applicant for a period of sixty days and issue a certificate of reservation. The restrictions and qualifications set forth in subparagraphs (a) (3), (4), (5), (6) and (7) of section 301 (Corporate name; general) are not waived by the issuance of a certificate of reservation. The certificate of reservation shall include the name of the applicant, the name reserved and the date of the reservation. The certificate of reservation (or in lieu thereof an affidavit by the applicant or by his agent or attorney that the certificate of reservation has been lost or destroyed) shall accompany the certificate of incorporation or the application for authority when either is delivered to the department of state.

(d) The secretary of state may extend the reservation for additional periods of not more than sixty days each, upon the written request of the applicant, his attorney or agent delivered to the department of state, to be filed before the expiration of the reservation period then in effect. Such request shall have attached to it the certificate of reservation of name. Not more than two such extensions shall be granted.

(e) Upon the request of the applicant, delivered to the department of state before the expiration of the reserved period, the department shall cancel the reservation.

(f) Any application or request under this section shall be signed by the applicant, his attorney or agent.

§ 304. Statutory designation of secretary of state as agent for service of process.

(a) The secretary of state shall be the agent of every domestic corporation and every authorized foreign corporation upon whom process against the corporation may be served.

(b) No domestic or foreign corporation may be formed or authorized to do business in this state under this chapter unless in its certificate of incorporation or application for authority it designates the secretary of state as such agent.

(c) Any designation by a domestic or a foreign corporation of the secretary of state as such agent, which designation is in effect on the effective date of this chapter, shall continue. Every domestic or foreign corporation, existing or authorized on the effective date of this chapter, which has not designated the secretary of state as such agent, shall be deemed to have done so. Any designation prior to the effective date of this chapter by a foreign corporation of an agent other than the secretary of state shall terminate on the effective date of this chapter.

(d) Any designated post office address to which the secretary of state shall mail a copy of process served upon him as agent of a domestic corporation or a foreign corporation, shall continue until the filing of a certificate under this chapter directing the mailing to a different post office address.

§ 305. Registered agent for service of process.

(a) In addition to such designation of the secretary of state, every domestic corporation or authorized foreign corporation may designate a registered agent in this state upon whom process against such corporation may be served. The agent shall be a natural person who is a resident of or has a business address in this state or a domestic corporation or foreign corporation of any type or kind formed, or authorized to do business in this state, under this chapter or under any other statute of this state.

(b) Any such designation of a registered agent may be made, revoked or changed as provided in this chapter.

(c) A registered agent may resign as such agent. A certificate, entitled "Certificate of resignation or registered agent of . . . . (name of designating corporation) under section 305 of the Business Corporation Law", shall be signed, verified by him and delivered to the department of state. It shall set forth:

(1) That he resigns as registered agent for the designating corporation.

(2) The date the certificate of incorporation or the application for authority of the designating corporation was filed by the department of state.

(3) That he has sent a copy of the certificate of resignation by registered mail to the designating corporation at the post office address on file in the department of state specified for the mailing of process or if such address is the address of the registered agent, then to the office of the designating corporation in the jurisdiction of its formation or incorporation.

(d) The designation of a registered agent shall terminate thirty days after the filing by the department of state of a certificate of resignation or a certificate containing a revocation or change of the designation, whichever is filed earlier. A certificate designating a new registered agent may be delivered to the department of state by the corporation within the thirty days or thereafter.

§ 306. Service of process.

(a) Service of process on a registered agent may be made in the manner provided by law for the service of a summons, as if the registered agent was a defendant.

(b) Service of process on the secretary of state as agent of a domestic or authorized foreign corporation shall be made by personally delivering to and leaving with him or his deputy, or with any person authorized by the secretary of state to receive such service, at the office of the department of state in the city of Albany, duplicate copies of such process together with the statutory fee, which fee shall be a taxable disbursement. Service of process on such corporation shall be complete when the secretary of state is so served. The secretary of state shall promptly send one of such copies by certified mail, return receipt requested, to such corporation, at the post office address, on file in the department of state, specified for the purpose. If a domestic or authorized foreign corporation has no such address on file in the department of state, the secretary of state shall so mail such copy, in the case of a domestic corporation, in care of any director named in its certificate of incorporation at his address stated therein or, in the case of an authorized foreign corporation, to such corporation at the address of its office within this state on file in the department.

(c) If an action or special proceeding is instituted in a court of limited jurisdiction, service of process may be made in the manner provided in this section if the office of the domestic or foreign corporation is within the territorial jurisdiction of the court.

(d) Nothing in this section shall affect the right to serve process in any other manner permitted by law.

§ 307. Service of process on unauthorized foreign corporation.

(a) In any case in which a non-domiciliary would be subject to the personal or other jurisdiction of the courts of this state under article three of the civil practice law and rules, a foreign corporation not authorized to do business in this state is subject to a like jurisdiction. In any such case, process against such foreign corporation may be served upon the secretary of state as its agent. Such process may issue in any court in this state having jurisdiction of the subject matter.

(b) Service of such process upon the secretary of state shall be made by personally delivering to and leaving with him or his deputy, or with any person authorized by the secretary of state to receive such service, at the office of the department of state in the city of Albany, a copy of such process together with the statutory fee, which fee shall be a taxable disbursement. Such service shall be sufficient if notice thereof and a copy of the process are:

(1) Delivered personally without this state to such foreign corporation by a person and in the manner authorized to serve process by law of the jurisdiction in which services is made, or

(2) Sent by or on behalf of the plaintiff to such foreign corporation by registered mail with return receipt requested, at the post office address specified for the purpose of mailing process, on file in the department of state, or with any official or body performing the equivalent function, in the jurisdiction of its incorporation, or if no such address is there specified, to its registered or other office there specified, or if no such office is there specified, to the last address of such foreign corporation known to the plaintiff.

(c) 1. Where service of a copy of process was effected by personal service, proof of service shall be by affidavit of compliance with this section filed, together with the process, within thirty days after such service, with the clerk of the court in which the action or special proceeding is pending. Service of process shall be complete ten days after such papers are filed with the clerk of the court.

2. Where service of a copy of process was effected by mailing in accordance with this section, proof of service shall be by affidavit of compliance with this section filed, together with the process, within thirty days after receipt of the return receipt signed by the foreign corporation, or other official proof of delivery or of the original envelope mailed. If a copy of the process is mailed in accordance with this section, there shall be filed with the affidavit of compliance either the return receipt signed by such foreign corporation or other official proof of delivery or, if acceptance was refused by it, the original envelope with a notation by the postal authorities that acceptance was refused. If acceptance was refused, a copy of the notice and process together with notice of the mailing by registered mail and refusal to accept shall be promptly sent to such foreign corporation at the same address by ordinary mail and the affidavit of compliance shall so state. Service of process shall be complete ten days after such papers are filed with the clerk of the court. The refusal to accept delivery of the registered mail or to sign the return receipt shall not affect the validity of the service and such foreign corporation refusing to accept such registered mail shall be charged with knowledge of the contents thereof.

(d) Service made as provided in this section shall have the same force as personal service made within this state.

(e) Nothing in this section shall affect the right to serve process in any other manner permitted by law.

§ 308. Records and certificates of department of state.

The department of state shall keep a record of each process served upon the secretary of state under this chapter, including the date of service. It shall, upon request made within ten years of such service, issue a certificate under its seal certifying as to the receipt of the process by an authorized person, the date and place of such service and the receipt of the statutory fee. Process served upon the secretary of state under this chapter shall be destroyed by him after a period of ten years from such service.

§ 401. Incorporators.

One or more natural persons of the age of eighteen years or over may act as incorporators of a corporation to be formed under this chapter.

§ 402. Certificate of incorporation; contents.

(a) A certificate, entitled "Certificate of incorporation of . . . . (name of corporation) under section 402 of the Business Corporation Law", shall be signed by each incorporator, with his name and address stated beneath or opposite his signature, acknowledged and delivered to the department of state. It shall set forth:

(1) The name of the corporation.

(2) The purpose or purposes for which it is formed, it being sufficient to state, either alone or with other purposes, that the purpose of the corporation is to engage in any lawful act or activity for which corporations may be organized under this chapter, provided that it also state that it is not formed to engage in any act or activity requiring the consent or approval of any state official, department, board, agency or other body without such consent or approval first being obtained. By such statement all lawful acts and activities shall be within the purposes of the corporation, except for express limitations therein or in this chapter, if any.

(3) The county within this state in which the office of the corporation is to be located.

(4) The aggregate number of shares which the corporation shall have the authority to issue, if such shares are to consist of one class only, the par value of the shares or a statement that the shares are without par value; or, if the shares are to be divided into classes, the number of shares of each class and the par value of the shares having par value and a statement as to which shares, if any, are without par value.

(5) If the shares are to be divided into classes, the designation of each class and a statement of the relative rights, preferences and limitations of the shares of each class.

(6) If the shares of any preferred class are to be issued in series, the designation of each series and a statement of the variations in the relative rights, preferences and limitations as between series insofar as the same are to be fixed in the certificate of incorporation, and a statement of any authority to be vested in the board to establish and designate series and to fix the variations in the relative rights, preferences and limitations as between series.

(7) A designation of the secretary of state as agent of the corporation upon whom process against it may be served and the post office address within or without this state to which the secretary of state shall mail a copy of any process against it served upon him.

(8) If the corporation is to have a registered agent, his name and address within this state and a statement that the registered agent is to be the agent of the corporation upon whom process against it may be served.

(9) The duration of the corporation if other than perpetual.

(b) The certificate of incorporation may set forth any provision, not inconsistent with this chapter or any other statute of this state, relating to the business of the corporation, its affairs, its rights or powers, or the rights or powers of its shareholders, directors or officers including any provision relating to matters which under this chapter are required or permitted to be set forth in the by-laws. It is not necessary to set forth in the certificate of incorporation any of the powers enumerated in this chapter.

§ 403. Certificate of incorporation; effect, authority of attorney-general.

Upon the filing of the certificate of incorporation by the department of state, the corporate existence shall begin, and such certificate shall be conclusive evidence that all conditions precedent have been fulfilled and that the corporation has been formed under this chapter, except in an action or special proceeding brought by the attorney-general. Notwithstanding the above, a certificate of incorporation may set forth a date subsequent to filing, not to exceed ninety days after filing, upon which date corporate existence shall begin.

§ 404. Organization meeting.

(a) After the corporate existence has begun, an organization meeting of the incorporator or incorporators shall be held within or without this state, for the purpose of adopting by-laws, electing directors to hold office until the first annual meeting of shareholders, except as authorized under section 704 (Classification of directors), and the transaction of such other business as may come before the meeting. If there are two or more incorporators, the meeting may be held at the call of any incorporator, who shall give at least five days' notice thereof by mail to each other incorporator, which notice shall set forth the time and place of the meeting. Notice need not be given to any incorporator who attends the meeting or submits a signed waiver of notice before or after the meeting. If there are more than two incorporators, a majority shall constitute a quorum and the act of the majority of the incorporators present at a meeting at which a quorum is present shall be the act of the incorporators. An incorporator may act in person or by proxy signed by the incorporator or his attorney-in-fact.

(b) Any action permitted to be taken at the organization meeting may be taken without a meeting if each incorporator or his attorney-in-fact signs an instrument setting forth the action so taken.

(c) If an incorporator dies or is for any reason unable to act, action may be taken as provided in such event in paragraph (c) of section 615 (Written consent of shareholders, subscribers or incorporators without a meeting).

§ 405. Day care center for children; approval of certificate.

Every certificate of incorporation which includes among its corporate purposes the establishment or operation of a day care center for children shall have endorsed thereon or annexed thereto the approval of the state department of social services.

§ 406. Filing of a certificate of incorporation; facility for alcoholism or alcohol abuse.

Every certificate of incorporation which includes among its corporate purposes the establishment or operation of a program of services for alcoholism or alcohol abuse shall have endorsed thereon or annexed thereto the approval of the director of the state division of alcoholism and alcohol abuse.

§ 407. Substance abuse program; consent to certificate.

Every certificate of incorporation which includes among the purposes of the corporation, the establishment or operation of a substance abuse program shall have endorsed thereon or annexed thereto the consent of the director of the division of substance abuse services to its filing by the department of state.

§ 501. Authorized shares.

(a) Every corporation shall have power to create and issue the number of shares stated in its certificate of incorporation. Such shares may be all of one class or may be divided into two or more classes. Each class shall consist of either shares with par value or shares without par value, having such designation and such relative voting, dividend, liquidation and other rights, preferences and limitations, consistent with this chapter, as shall be stated in the certificate of incorporation. The certificate of incorporation may deny, limit or otherwise define the voting rights and may limit or otherwise define the dividend or liquidation rights of shares of any class, but no such denial, limitation or definition of voting rights shall be effective unless at the time one or more classes of outstanding shares or bonds, singly or in the aggregate, are entitled to full voting rights, and no such limitation or definition of dividend or liquidation rights shall be effective unless at the time one or more classes of outstanding shares, singly or in the aggregate, are entitled to unlimited dividend and liquidation rights.

(b) If the shares are divided into two or more classes, the shares of each class shall be designated to distinguish them from the shares of all other classes. Shares which are entitled to preference in the distribution of dividends or assets shall not be designated as common shares. Shares which are not entitled to preference in the distribution of dividends or assets shall be common shares, even if identified by a class or other designation, and shall not be designated as preferred shares.

(c) Subject to the designations, relative rights, preferences and limitations applicable to separate series, each share shall be equal to every other share of the same class. With respect to corporations owning or leasing residential premises and operating the same on a cooperative basis, however, provided that maintenance charges, general assessments pursuant to a proprietary lease, and voting, liquidation or other distribution rights are substantially equal per share, shares of the same class shall not be considered unequal because of variations in fees or charges payable to the corporation upon sale or transfer of shares and appurtenant proprietary leases that are provided for in proprietary leases, occupancy agreements or offering plans or properly approved amendments to the foregoing instruments.

§ 502. Issue of any class of preferred shares in series.

(a) If the certificate of incorporation so provides, a corporation may issue any class of preferred shares in series. Shares of each such series when issued, shall be designated to distinguish them from shares of all other series.

(b) The number of shares included in any or all series of any classes of preferred shares and any or all of the designations, relative rights, preferences and limitations of any or all such series may be fixed in the certificate of incorporation, subject to the limitation that, if the stated dividends and amounts payable on liquidation are not paid in full, the shares of all series of the same class shall share ratably in the payment of dividends including accumulations, if any, in accordance with the sums which would be payable on such shares if all dividends were declared and paid in full, and in any distribution of assets other than by way of dividends in accordance with the sums which would be payable on such distribution if all sums payable were discharged in full.

(c) If any such number of shares or any such designation, relative right, preference or limitation of the shares of any series is not fixed in the certificate of incorporation, it may be fixed by the board, to the extent authorized by the certificate of incorporation.

(d) Before the issue of any shares of a series established by the board, a certificate of amendment under section 805 (Certificate of amendment; contents) shall be delivered to the department of state. Such certificate shall set forth:

(1) The name of the corporation, and, if it has been changed, the name under which it was formed.

(2) The date the certificate of incorporation was filed by the department of state.

(3) That the certificate of incorporation is thereby amended by the addition of a provision stating the number, designation, relative rights, preferences, and limitations of the shares of the series as fixed by the board, setting forth in full the text of such provision.

§ 503. Subscription for shares; time of payment, forfeiture for default.

(a) Unless otherwise provided by the terms of the subscription, a subscription for shares of a corporation to be formed shall be irrevocable, except with the consent of all other subscribers or the corporation, for a period of three months from its date.

(b) A subscription whether made before or after the formation of a corporation, shall not be enforceable unless in writing and signed by the subscriber.

(c) Unless otherwise provided by the terms of the subscription, subscriptions for shares, whether made before or after the formation of a corporation, shall be paid in full at such time, or in such installments and at such times, as shall be determined by the board. Any call made by the board for payment on subscriptions shall be uniform as to all shares of the same class or of the same series. If a receiver of the corporation has been appointed, all unpaid subscriptions shall be paid at such times and in such installments as such receiver or the court may direct.

(d) In the event of default in the payment of any installment or call when due, the corporation may proceed to collect the amount due in the same manner as any debt due the corporation or the board may declare a forfeiture of the subscriptions. The subscription agreement may prescribe other penalties, not amounting to forfeiture, for failure to pay installments or calls that may become due. No forfeiture of the subscription shall be declared as against any subscriber unless the amount due thereon shall remain unpaid for a period of thirty days after written demand has been made therefor. If mailed, such written demand shall be deemed to be made when deposited in the United States mail in a sealed envelope addressed to the subscriber at his last post office address known to the corporation, with postage thereon prepaid. Upon forfeiture of the subscription, if at least fifty percent of the subscription price has been paid, the shares subscribed for shall be offered for sale for cash at a price at least sufficient to pay the full balance owed by the delinquent subscriber plus the expenses incidental to such sale, and any excess of net proceeds realized over the amount owed on such shares shall be paid to the delinquent subscriber or to his legal representative. If no prospective purchaser offers a cash price sufficient to pay the full balance owed by the delinquent subscriber plus the expenses incidental to such sale, or if less than fifty percent of the subscription price has been paid, the shares subscribed for shall be cancelled and restored to the status of authorized but unissued shares and all previous payments thereon shall be forfeited to the corporation and transferred to capital surplus.

§ 504. Consideration and payment for shares.

(a) Consideration for the issue of shares shall consist of money or other property, tangible or intangible, or labor or services actually received by or performed for the corporation or for its benefit or in its formation or reorganization, or a combination thereof. In the absence of fraud in the transaction, the judgment of the board or shareholders, as the case may be, as to the value of the consideration received for shares shall be conclusive.

(b) Neither obligations of the subscriber for future payments nor future services shall constitute payment or part payment for shares of a corporation.

(c) Shares with par value may be issued for such consideration, not less than the par value thereof, as is fixed from time to time by the board.

(d) Shares without par value may be issued for such consideration as is fixed from time to time by the board unless the certificate of incorporation reserves to the shareholders the right to fix the consideration. If such right is reserved as to any shares, a vote of the shareholders shall either fix the consideration to be received for the shares or authorize the board to fix such consideration.

(e) Treasury shares may be disposed of by a corporation on such terms and conditions as are fixed from time to time by the board.

(f) Upon distribution of authorized but unissued shares to shareholders, that part of the surplus of a corporation which is concurrently transferred to stated capital shall be the consideration for the issue of such shares.

(g) In the event of a conversion of bonds or shares into shares, or in the event of an exchange of bonds or shares for shares; with or without par value, the consideration for the shares so issued in exchange or conversion shall be the sum of (1) either the principal sum of, and accrued interest on, the bonds so exchanged or converted, or the stated capital then represented by the shares so exchanged or converted, plus (2) any additional consideration paid to the corporation for the new shares, plus (3) any stated capital not theretofore allocated to any designated class or series which is thereupon allocated to the new shares, plus (4) any surplus thereupon transferred to stated capital and allocated to the new shares.

(h) Certificates for shares may not be issued until the full amount of the consideration therefor has been paid, except as provided in paragraphs (e) and (f) of section 505 (Rights and options to purchase shares; issue of rights and options to directors, officers and employees).

(i) When the consideration for shares has been paid in full, the subscriber shall be entitled to all the rights and privileges of a holder of such shares and to a certificate representing his shares, and such shares shall be fully paid and nonassessable.

§ 505. Rights and options to purchase shares; issue of rights and options to directors, officers and employees.

(a) Except as otherwise provided in this section or in the certificate of incorporation, a corporation may create and issue, whether or not in connection with the issue and sale of any of its shares or bonds, rights or options entitling the holders thereof to purchase from the corporation, upon such consideration, terms and conditions as may be fixed by the board, shares of any class or series, whether authorized but unissued shares, treasury shares or shares to be purchased or acquired.

(b) The consideration for shares to be purchased under any such right or option shall comply with the requirements of section 504 (Consideration and payment for shares).

(c) The terms and conditions of such rights or options, including the time or times at or within which and the price or prices at which they may be exercised and any limitations upon transferability, shall be set forth or incorporated by reference in the instrument or instruments evidencing such rights or options.

(d) The issue of such rights or options to one or more directors, officers or employees of the corporation or a subsidiary or affiliate thereof, as an incentive to service or continued service with the corporation, a subsidiary or affiliate thereof, or to a trustee on behalf of such directors, officers or employees, shall be authorized at a meeting of shareholders by the vote of the holders of a majority of all outstanding shares entitled to vote thereon, or authorized by and consistent with a plan adopted by such vote of shareholders. If, under the certificate of incorporation, there are preemptive rights to any of the shares to be thus subject to rights or options to purchase, either such issue or such plan, if any shall also be approved by the vote or written consent of the holders of a majority of the shares entitled to exercise preemptive rights with respect to such shares and such vote or written consent shall operate to release the preemptive rights with respect thereto of the holders of all the shares that were entitled to exercise such preemptive rights.

In the absence of preemptive rights, nothing in this paragraph shall require shareholder approval for the issuance of rights or options to purchase shares of the corporation in substitution for or upon the assumption of, rights or options issued by another corporation, if such substitution or assumption is in connection with such other corporation's merger or consolidation with, or the acquisition of its shares or all or part of its assets by, the corporation or its subsidiary.

(e) A plan adopted by the shareholders for the issue of rights or options to directors, officers or employees shall include the material terms and conditions upon which such rights or options are to be issued, such as, but without limitation thereof, any restrictions on the number of shares that eligible individuals may have the right or option to purchase, the method of administering the plan, the terms and conditions of payment for shares in full or in installments, the issue of certificates for shares to be paid for in installments, any limitations upon the transferability of such shares and the voting and dividend rights to which the holders of such shares may be entitled, though the full amount of the consideration therefor has not been paid; provided that under this section no certificate for shares shall be delivered to a shareholder, prior to full payment therefor, unless the fact that the shares are partly paid is noted conspicuously on the face or back of such certificate.

(f) If there is shareholder approval for the issue of rights or options to individual directors, officers or employees, but not under an approved plan under paragraph (e), the terms and conditions of issue set forth in paragraph (e) shall be permissible except that the grantees of such rights or options shall not be granted voting or dividend rights until the consideration for the shares to which they are entitled under such rights or options has been fully paid.

(g) If there is shareholder approval for the issue of rights and options, such approval may provide that the board is authorized by certificate of amendment under section 805 (Certificate of amendment; contents) to increase the authorized shares of any class or series to such number as will be sufficient, when added to the previously authorized but unissued shares of such class or series, to satisfy any such rights or options entitling the holders thereof to purchase from the corporation authorized but unissued shares of such class or series.

(h) In the absence of fraud in the transaction, the judgment of the board shall be conclusive as to the adequacy of the consideration, tangible or intangible, received or to be received by the corporation for the issue of rights or options for the purchase from the corporation of its shares.

(i) The provisions of this section are inapplicable to the rights of the holders of convertible shares or bonds to acquire shares upon the exercise of conversion privileges under section 519 (Convertible shares and bonds).

§ 506. Determination of stated capital.

(a) Upon issue by a corporation of shares with a par value, the consideration received therefor shall constitute stated capital to the extent of the par value of such shares.

(b) Upon issue by a corporation of shares without par value, the entire consideration received therefor shall constitute state capital unless the board within a period of sixty days after issue allocates to surplus a portion, but not all, of the consideration received for such shares. No such allocation shall be made of any portion of the consideration received for shares without par value having a preference in the assets of the corporation upon involuntary liquidation except all or part of the amount, if any, of such consideration in excess of such preference, nor shall such allocation be made of any portion of the consideration for the issue of shares without par value which is fixed by the shareholders pursuant to a right reserved in the certificate of incorporation, unless such allocation is authorized by vote of the shareholders.

(c) The stated capital of a corporation may be increased from time to time by resolution of the board transferring all or part of the surplus of the corporation to stated capital. The board may direct that the amount so transferred shall be stated capital in respect of any designated class or series of shares.

§ 507. Compensation for formation, reorganization and financing.

The reasonable charges and expenses of formation or reorganization of a corporation, and the reasonable expenses of and compensation for the sale or underwriting of its shares may be paid or allowed by the corporation out of the consideration received by it in payment for its shares without thereby impairing the fully paid and nonassessable status of such shares.

§ 508. Certificates representing shares.

(a) The shares of a corporation shall be represented by certificates or shall be uncertificated shares. Certificates shall be signed by the chairman or a vice-chairman of the board or the president or a vice-president and the secretary or an assistant secretary or the treasurer or an assistant treasurer of the corporation, and may be sealed with the seal of the corporation or a facsimile thereof. The signatures of the officers upon a certificate may be fascimiles if: (1) the certificate is countersigned by a transfer agent, or registered by a registrar other than the corporation itself or its employee, or (2) the shares are listed on a registered national security exchange. In case any officer who has signed or whose facsimile signature has been placed upon a certificate shall have ceased to be such officer before such certificate is issued, it may be issued by the corporation with the same effect as if he were such officer at the date of issue.

(b) Each certificate representing shares issued by a corporation which is authorized to issue shares of more than one class shall set forth upon the face or back of the certificate, or shall state that the corporation will furnish to any shareholder upon request and without charge, a full statement of the designation, relative rights, preferences and limitations of the shares of each class authorized to be issued and, if the corporation is authorized to issue any class of preferred shares in series, the designation, relative rights, preferences and limitations of each such series so far as the same have been fixed and the authority of the board to designate and fix the relative rights, preferences and limitations of other series.

(c) Each certificate representing shares shall state upon the face thereof:

(1) That the corporation is formed under the laws of this state.

(2) The name of the person or persons to whom issued.

(3) The number and class of shares, and the designation of the series, if any, which such certificate represents.

(d) Shares shall be transferable in the manner provided by law and in the by-laws.

(e) The corporation may issue a new certificate for shares in place of any certificate theretofore issued by it, alleged to have been lost or destroyed, and the board may require the owner of the lost or destroyed certificate, or his legal representative, to give the corporation a bond sufficient to idemnify the corporation against any claim that may be made against it on account of the alleged loss or destruction of any such certificate or the issuance of any such new certificate.

(f) Unless otherwise provided by the articles of incorporation or bylaws, the board of directors of a corporation may provide by resolution that some or all of any or all classes and series of its shares shall be uncertificated shares, provided that such resolution shall not apply to shares represented by a certificate until such certificate is surrendered to the corporation. Within a reasonable time after the issuance or transfer of uncertificated shares, the corporation shall send to the registered owner thereof a written notice containing the information required to be set forth or stated on certificates pursuant to paragraphs (b) and (c) of this section. Except as otherwise expressly provided by law, the rights and obligations of the holders of uncertificated shares and the rights and obligations of the holders of certificates representing shares of the same class and series shall be identical.

§ 509. Fractions of a share or scrip authorized.

(a) A corporation may, but shall not be obliged to, issue fractions of a share either represented by a certificate or uncertificated where necessary to effect share transfers, share distributions or reclassifications, mergers, consolidations or reorganizations, which shall entitle the holder, in proportion to his fractional holdings, to exercise voting rights, receive dividends and participate in liquidating distributions.

(b) As an alternative, a corporation may pay in cash the fair value of fractions of a share as of the time when those entitled to receive such fractions are determined.

(c) As an alternative, a corporation may issue scrip in registered or bearer form over the manual or facsimile signature of an officer of the corporation or of its agent, exchangeable as therein provided for full shares, but such scrip shall not entitle the holder to any rights of a shareholder except as therein provided. Such scrip may be issued subject to the condition that it shall become void if not exchanged for certificates representing full shares or uncertificated full shares before a specified date, or subject to the condition that the shares for which such scrip is exchangeable may be sold by the corporation and the proceeds thereof distributed to the holders of such scrip, or subject to any other conditions which the board may determine.

(d) A corporation may provide reasonable opportunity for persons entitled to fractions of a share or scrip to sell such fractions of a share or scrip or to purchase such additional fractions of a share or scrip as may be needed to acquire a full share.

§ 510. Dividends or other distributions in cash or property.

(a) A corporation may declare and pay dividends or make other distributions in cash or its bonds or its property, including the shares or bonds of other corporations, on its outstanding shares, except when currently the corporation is insolvent or would thereby be made insolvent, or when the declaration, payment or distribution would be contrary to any restrictions contained in the certificate of incorporation.

(b) Dividends may be declared or paid and other distributions may be made out of surplus only, so that the net assets of the corporation remaining after such declaration, payment or distribution shall at least equal the amount of its stated capital; except that a corporation engaged in the exploitation of natural resources or other wasting assets, including patents, or formed primarily for the liquidation of specific assets, may declare and pay dividends or make other distributions in excess of its surplus, computed after taking due account of depletion and amortization, to the extent that the cost of the wasting or specific assets has been recovered by depletion reserved, amortization or sale, if the net assets remaining after such dividends or distributions are sufficient to cover the liquidation preferences of shares having such preferences in involuntary liquidation.

(c) When any dividend is paid or any other distribution is made, in whole or in part, from sources other than earned surplus, it shall be accompanied by a written notice (1) disclosing the amounts by which such dividend or distribution affects stated capital, capital surplus and earned surplus, or (2) if such amounts are not determinable at the time of such notice, disclosing the approximate effect of such dividend or distribution upon stated capital, capital surplus and earned surplus and stating that such amounts are not yet determinable.

§ 511. Share distributions and changes.

(a) A corporation may make pro rata distributions of its authorized but unissued shares to holders of any class or series of its outstanding shares, subject to the following conditions:

(1) If a distribution of shares having a par value is made, such shares shall be issued at not less than the par value thereof and there shall be transferred to stated capital at the time of such distribution an amount of surplus equal to the aggregate par value of such shares.

(2) If a distribution of shares without par value is made, the amount of stated capital to be represented by each such share shall be fixed by the board, unless the certificate of incorporation reserves to the shareholders the right to fix the consideration for the issue of such shares, and there shall be transferred to stated capital at the time of such distribution an amount of surplus equal to the aggregate stated capital represented by such shares.

(3) A distribution of shares of any class or series may be made only to holders of the same class or series of shares unless the certificate of incorporation permits distribution subject to the preemptive rights of holders of any outstanding shares, to holders of another class or series, or unless such distribution is approved, when there are no outstanding preemptive rights, by the affirmative vote or the written consent of the holders of a majority of the outstanding shares of the class or series to be distributed.

(b) A corporation making a pro rata distribution of authorized but unissued shares to the holders of any class or series of outstanding shares may at its option make an equivalent distribution upon treasury shares of the same class or series and any shares so distributed shall be treasury shares.

(c) A change of issued shares of any class which increases the stated capital represented by those shares may be made if the surplus of the corporation is sufficient to permit the transfer, and a transfer is concurrently made, from surplus to stated capital, of an amount equal to such increase.

(d) No transfer from surplus to stated capital need be made by a corporation making a distribution of its treasury shares to holders of any class of outstanding shares; nor upon a split up or division of issued shares of any class into a greater number of shares of the same class, or a combination of issued shares of any class into a lesser number of shares of the same class, if there is no increase in the aggregate stated capital represented by them.

(e) Nothing in this section shall prevent a corporation from making other transfers from earned surplus to stated capital or capital surplus in connection with share distributions or otherwise.

(f) Every distribution to shareholders of certificates representing a share distribution or a change of shares which affects stated capital, capital surplus or earned surplus shall be accompanied by a written notice (1) disclosing the amounts by which such distribution or change affects stated capital, capital surplus and earned surplus, or (2) if such amounts are not determinable at the time of such notice, disclosing the approximate effect of such distribution or change upon stated capital, capital surplus and earned surplus and stating that such amounts are not yet determinable.

(g) When issued shares are changed in any manner which affects stated capital, capital surplus or earned surplus, and no distribution to shareholders of certificates representing any shares resulting from such change is made, disclosure of the effect of such change upon the stated capital,

capital surplus and earned surplus shall be made in the next financial statement covering the period in which such change is made that is furnished by the corporation to holders of shares of the class or series so changed or, if practicable, in the first notice of dividend or share distribution or change that is furnished to such shareholders between the date of the change of shares and the next such financial statement, and in any event within six months of the date of such change.

§ 512. Redeemable shares.

(a) A corporation may provide in its certificate of incorporation for one or more classes or series of shares which are redeemable, in whole or in part, at the option of the corporation or, except as provided in paragraph (b) of this section, at the option of the holder, at such price or prices, within such period or periods and under such conditions as are stated in the certificate of incorporation.

(b) A corporation shall not issue common shares which purport by their terms to grant to any holder thereof the right to compel the corporation to redeem such shares except that an open-end investment company, as defined in an act of congress entitled "Investment Company Act of 1940", may, if its certificate of incorporation so provides and upon compliance with that act, issue shares which are redeemable at the option of the holder at a price approximately equal to the share's proportionate interest in the net assets of the corporation, and a shareholder may compel redemption of such shares in accordance with their terms.

(c) No redeemable common shares, other than such shares of an investment company or of a member corporation of a national securities exchange registered under a statute of the United States such as the Securities Exchange Act of 1934, shall be issued or redeemed unless the corporation at the time has outstanding a class of common shares that is not subject to redemption.

(d) Nothing in this section shall prevent a corporation from creating sinking funds for the redemption or purchase of its shares to the extent permitted by section 513 (Purchase or redemption by a corporation of its own shares).

§ 513. Purchase or redemption by a corporation of its own shares.

(a) A corporation, subject to any restrictions contained in its certificate of incorporation, may purchase its own shares, or redeem its redeemable shares, out of surplus except when currently the corporation is insolvent or would thereby be made insolvent.

(b) A corporation may purchase its own shares out of stated capital except when currently the corporation is insolvent or would thereby be made insolvent, if the purchase is made for the purpose of:

(1) Eliminating fractions of shares;
(2) Collecting or compromising indebtedness to the corporation; or
(3) Paying shareholders entitled to receive payment for their shares under section 623 (Procedure to enforce shareholder's right to receive payment for shares).

(c) A corporation, subject to any restrictions contained in its certificate of incorporation, may redeem or purchase its redeemable shares out of stated capital except when currently the corporation is insolvent or would thereby be made insolvent and except when such redemption or purchase would reduce net assets below the stated capital remaining after giving effect to the cancellation of such redeemable shares.

(d) When its redeemable shares are purchased by a corporation within the period of redeemability, the purchase price thereof shall not exceed the applicable redemption price stated in the certificate of incorporation. Upon a call for redemption, the amount payable by the corporation for shares having a cumulative preference on dividends may include the stated redemption price plus accrued dividends to the next dividend date following the date of redemption of such shares.

(e) No resident domestic corporation which is subject to the provisions of section nine hundred twelve of this chapter shall purchase or agree to purchase more than ten percent of the stock of the resident domestic corporation from a shareholder for more than the market value thereof unless such purchase or agreement to purchase is approved by the affirmative vote of the board of directors followed by the affirmative vote of the holders of a majority of all outstanding shares entitled to vote thereon at a meeting of shareholders unless the certificate of incorporation requires a greater percentage of the outstanding shares to approve.

The provisions of this paragraph shall not apply when the resident domestic corporation offers to purchase shares from all holders of stock or for stock which the holder has been the beneficial owner of for more than two years.

The terms "resident domestic corporation", "stock", "beneficial owner", and "market value" shall be as defined in section nine hundred twelve of this chapter.

§ 514. Agreements for purchase by a corporation of its own shares.

(a) An agreement for the purchase by a corporation of its own shares shall be enforceable by the shareholder and the corporation to the extent such purchase is permitted at the time of purchase by section 513 (Purchase or redemption by a corporation of its own shares).

(b) The possibility that a corporation may not be able to purchase its shares under section 513 shall not be a ground for denying to either party specific performance or an agreement for the purchase by a corporation of its own shares, if at the time for performance the corporation can purchase all or part of such shares under section 513.

§ 515. Reacquired shares.

(a) Shares that have been issued and have been purchased, redeemed or otherwise reacquired by a corporation shall be cancelled if they are reacquired out of stated capital, or if they are converted shares, or if the certificate of incorporation requires that such shares be cancelled upon reacquisition.

(b) Any shares reacquired by the corporation and not required to be cancelled may be either retained as treasury shares or cancelled by the board at the time of reacquisition or at any time thereafter.

(c) Neither the retention of reacquired shares as treasury shares, nor their subsequent distribution to shareholders or disposition for a consideration shall change the stated capital. When treasury shares are disposed of for a consideration, the capital surplus shall be increased by the full amount of the consideration received unless the corporation exercises the option granted in subparagraph (a) (5) of section 517 (Special provisions relative to surplus and reserves).

(d) When reacquired shares other than converted shares are cancelled, the stated capital of the corporation is thereby reduced by the amount of stated capital then represented by such shares plus any stated capital not theretofore allocated to any designated class or series which is thereupon allocated to the shares cancelled. The amount by which stated capital has been reduced by cancellation of reacquired shares during a stated period of time shall be disclosed in the next financial statement covering such period that is furnished by the corporation to all its shareholders or, if practicable, in the first notice of dividend or share distribution that is furnished to the holders of each class or series of its shares between the end of the period and the next such financial statement, and in any event to all its shareholders within six months of the date of the reduction of capital.

(e) Shares cancelled under this section are restored to the status of authorized but unissued shares. However, if the certificate of incorporation prohibits the reissue of any shares required or permitted to be cancelled under this section, the board of certificate of amendment under section 805 (Certificate of amendment; contents) shall reduce the number of authorized shares accordingly.

§516. Reduction of stated capital in certain cases.

(a) Except as otherwise provided in the certificate of incorporation, the board may at any time reduce the stated capital of a corporation by eliminating from stated capital amounts previously transferred by the board from surplus to stated capital and not allocated to any designated class or series of shares, or by eliminating any amount of stated capital represented by issued shares having a par value which exceeds the aggregate par value of such shares, or by reducing the amount of stated capital represented by issued shares without par value. However, if the consideration for the issue of shares without par value was fixed by the shareholders under section 504 (Consideration and payment for shares), the board shall not reduce the stated capital represented by such shares except to the extent, if any, that the board was authorized by the shareholders to allocate any portion of such consideration to surplus.

(b) No reduction of stated capital shall be made under this section unless after such reduction the stated capital exceeds the aggregate preferential amounts payable upon involuntary liquidation upon all issued shares having preferential rights in the assets plus the par value of all other issued shares with par value.

(c) When a reduction of stated capital has been effected under this section, the amount of such reduction shall be disclosed in the next financial statement covering the period in which such reduction is made that is furnished by the corporation to all its shareholders or, if practicable, in the first notice of dividend or share distribution that is furnished to the holders of each class or series of its shares between the date of such reduction and the next such financial statement, and in any event to all its shareholders within six months of the date of such reduction.

§ 517. Special provisions relative to surplus and reserves.

(a) Whenever under this chapter it is necessary for a corporation to determine the amount or availability of its earned surplus, the following rules shall apply:

(1) The amount of the earned surplus of a corporation may be computed either from the date of formation or from the latest date when a deficit was eliminated as permitted in this section by an application of the corporation's capital surplus provided that:

(A) The board of any corporation formed before the effective date of this chapter may determine the amount of the corporation's earned surplus before the declaration of the first dividend after the effective date of this chapter, and such determination if made in good faith shall be conclusive; and

(B) After merger, consolidation or combination of two or more corporations by purchase or otherwise, the amount of the earned surplus of the surviving, consolidated or purchasing corporation shall not exceed the aggregate net earned surplus of the component corporations as it existed immediately prior to such merger, consolidation or combination, reduced by such distributions to shareholders and transfers of earned surplus to stated capital or capital surplus as were made in connection with the issue of shares or otherwise at the time of merger, consolidation or combination.

(2) All or part of the earned-surplus of a corporation may be transferred by the board at any time to capital surplus or to stated capital.

(3) Any surplus resulting from reduction of stated capital shall be capital surplus.

(4) A corporation may apply any part or all of its capital surplus to the elimination of any deficit in the earned surplus account, upon approval by vote of the shareholders. The application of capital surplus to the elimination of a deficit in the earned surplus account shall be disclosed in the next financial statement covering the period in which such elimination is made that is furnished by the corporation to all its shareholders or, if practicable, in the first notice of dividend or share distribution that is furnished to holders of each class or series of its shares between the date of such elimination and the next such financial statement, and in any event to all its shareholders within six months of the date of such action.

(5) When a corporation has applied its earned surplus to the acquisition of treasury shares and such shares are subsequently disposed of for a consideration, the corporation may, at its option, restore to earned surplus, out of the consideration received and on an appropriate basis per share, all or part of the amount by which earned surplus was reduced at the time of acquisition of such shares. If the consideration received exceeds the amount by which earned surplus was reduced with respect to such shares, the excess shall be capital surplus.

(b) Nothing in this section shall prevent a corporation from creating reserves from its earned surplus or capital surplus for any proper purpose or purposes, or from increasing, decreasing or abolishing any such reserve.

§518. Corporate bonds.

(a) No corporation shall issue bonds except for money or other property, tangible or intangible, or labor or services actually received by or performed for the corporation or for its benefit or in its formation or reorganization, or a combination thereof. In the absence of fraud in the transaction, the judgment of the board as to the value of the consideration received shall be conclusive.

(b) If a distribution of its own bonds is made by a corporation to holders of any class or series of its outstanding shares, there shall be concurrently transferred to the liabilities of the corporation in respect of such bonds an amount of surplus equal to the principal amount of, and any accrued interest on, such bonds. The amount of the surplus so transferred shall be the consideration for the issue of such bonds.

(c) A corporation may, in its certificate of incorporation, confer upon the holders of any bonds issued or to be issued by the corporation, rights to inspect the corporate books and records and to vote in the election of directors and on any other matters on which shareholders of the corporation may vote.

§ 519. Convertible shares and bonds.

(a) When so provided in the certificate of incorporation, and subject to the restrictions in paragraph (d), a corporation may issue shares convertible,

(1) at the option of the holder only, into shares of any class or into shares of any series of any class, except into a class of shares having rights or preferences as to dividends or distribution of assets upon liquidation which are prior or superior in rank to those of the shares being converted, and

(2) if a member corporation of a national securities exchange registered under a statute of the United States such as the Securities Exchange Act of 1934, at the option of the corporation or upon the happening of a specified event, into shares of any class or into shares of any series of

any class or into any other security of the corporation. Authorized shares, whether issued or unissued, may be made so convertible within such period and upon such terms and conditions as are stated in the certificate of incorporation.

(b) Unless otherwise provided in the certificate of incorporation, and subject to the restrictions of paragraph (d), a corporation may issue its bonds convertible into other bonds or into shares of the corporation within such period and upon such terms and conditions as are fixed by the board.

(c) If there is shareholder approval for the issue of bonds or shares convertible into shares of the corporation, such approval may provide that the board is authorized by certificate of amendment under section 805 (Certificate of amendment; contents) to increase the authorized shares of any class or series to such number as will be sufficient, when added to the previously authorized but unissued shares of such class or series, to satisfy the conversion privileges of any such bonds or shares convertible into shares of such class or series.

(d) No issue of bonds or shares convertible into shares of the corporation shall be made unless:

(1) A sufficient number of authorized but unissued shares of the appropriate class or series are reserved by the board to be issued only in satisfaction of the conversion privileges of such convertible bonds or shares when issued; or

(2) The aggregate conversion privileges of such convertible bonds or shares when issued do not exceed the aggregate of any shares reserved under subparagraph (1) and any additional shares which may be authorized by the board under paragraph (c).

(e) No conversion of shares shall result in a reduction of stated capital. No privilege of conversion may be conferred upon, or altered in respect to, any shares or bonds that would result in the receipt by the corporation of less than the minimum consideration required to be received upon the issue of new shares. The consideration for shares issued upon the exercise of a conversion privilege shall be that provided in paragraph (g) of section 504 (Consideration and payment for shares).

(f) When shares have been converted, they shall be cancelled and disclosure of the conversion of shares during a stated period of time and its effect, if any, upon stated capital shall be made in the next financial statement covering such period that is furnished by the corporation to all its shareholders or, if practicable, in the first notice of dividend or share distribution that is furnished to the holders of each class or series of its shares between the end of such period and the next such financial statement, and in any event to all its shareholders within six months of the date of the conversion of shares. When bonds have been converted, they shall be cancelled and not reissued except upon compliance with the provisions governing the issue of convertible bonds.

§ 520. Liability for failure to disclose required information.

Failure of the corporation to comply in good faith with the notice or disclosure provisions of paragraph (c) of section 510 (Dividends or other distributions in cash or property), or paragraphs (f) and (g) of section 511 (Share distributions and changes), or paragraph (d) of section 515 (Reacquired shares), or paragraph (c) of section 516 (Reduction of stated capital in certain cases), or subparagraph (a) (4) of section 517 (Special provisions relative to surplus and reserves), or paragraph (f) of section 519 (Convertible shares and bonds), shall make the corporation liable for any damage sustained by any shareholder in consequence thereof.

§601. By-laws.

(a) The initial by-laws of a corporation shall be adopted by its incorporator or incorporators at the organization meeting. Thereafter, subject to section 613 (Limitations on right to vote), by-laws may be adopted, amended or repealed by vote of the holders of the shares at the time entitled to vote in the election of any directors. When so provided in the certificate of incorporation or a by-law adopted by the shareholders, by-laws may also be adopted, amended or repealed by the board by such vote as may be therein specified, which may be greater than the vote otherwise prescribed by this chapter, but any by-law adopted by the board may be amended or repealed by the shareholders entitled to vote thereon as herein provided. Any reference in this chapter to a "by-law adopted by the shareholders" shall include a by-law adopted by the incorporator or incorporators.

(b) If any by-law regulating an impending election of directors is adopted, amended or repealed by the board, there shall be set forth in the notice of the next meeting of shareholders for the election of directors the by-law so adopted, amended or repealed, together with a concise statement of the changes made.

(c) The by-laws may contain any provision relating to the business of the corporation, the conduct of its affairs, its rights or powers or the rights or powers of its shareholders, directors or officers, not inconsistent with this chapter or any other statute of this state or the certificate of incorporation.

§ 602. Meetings of shareholders.

(a) Meetings of shareholders may be held at such place, within or without this state, as may be fixed by or under the by-laws, or if not so fixed, at the office of the corporation in this state.

(b) A meeting of shareholders shall be held annually for the election of directors and the transaction of other business on a date fixed by or under the by-laws. A failure to hold the annual meeting on the date so fixed or to elect a sufficient number of directors to conduct the business of the corporation shall not work a forfeiture or give cause of dissolution of the corporation, except as provided in paragraph (c) of section 1104 (Petition in case of deadlock among directors or shareholders).

(c) Special meetings of the shareholders may be called by the board and by such person or persons as may be so authorized by the certificate of incorporation or the by-laws. At any such special meeting only such business may be transacted which is related to the purpose or purposes set forth in the notice required by section 605 (Notice of meetings of shareholders).

§ 603. Special meeting for election of directors.

(a) If, for a period of one month after the date fixed by or under the by-laws for the annual meeting of shareholders, or if no date has been so fixed, for a period of thirteen months after the formation of the corporation or the last annual meeting, there is a failure to elect a sufficient number of directors to conduct the business of the corporation, the board shall call a special meeting for the election of directors. If such special meeting is not called by the board within two weeks after the expiration of such period or if it is so called but there is a failure to elect such directors for a period of two months after the expiration of such period, holders of ten percent of the shares entitled to vote in an election of directors may, in writing, demand the call of a special meeting for the election of directors specifying the date and month thereof, which shall not be less than sixty nor more than ninety days from the date of such written demand. The secretary of the corporation upon receiving the written demand shall promptly give notice of such meeting, of if he fails to do so within five business days thereafter, any shareholder signing such demand may give such notice. The meeting shall be held at the place fixed in the by-laws or, if not so fixed, at the office of the corporation.

(b) At any such special meeting called on demand of shareholders, notwithstanding section 608 (Quorum of shareholders), the shareholders attending, in person or by proxy, and entitled to vote in an election of directors shall constitute a quorum for the purpose of electing directors, but not for the transaction of any other business.

§ 604. Fixing record date.

(a) For the purpose of determining the shareholders entitled to notice of or to vote at any meeting of shareholders or any adjournment thereof, or to express consent to or dissent from any proposal without a meeting, or for the purpose of determining shareholders entitled to receive payment of any dividend or the allotment of any rights, or for the purpose of any other action, the by-laws may provide for fixing or, in the absence of such provision, the board may fix, in advance, a date as the record date for any such determination of shareholders. Such date shall not be more than fifty nor less than ten days before the date of such meeting, nor more than fifty days prior to any other action.

(b) If no record date is fixed:

(1) The record date for the determination of shareholders entitled to notice of or to vote at a meeting of shareholders shall be at the close of business on the day next preceding the day on which notice is given, or, if no notice is given, the day on which the meeting is held.

(2) The record date for determining shareholders for any purpose other than that specified in subparagraph (1) shall be at the close of business on the day on which the resolution of the board relating thereto is adopted.

(c) When a determination of shareholders of record entitled to notice of or to vote at any meeting of shareholders has been made as provided in this section, such determination shall apply to any adjournment thereof, unless the board fixes a new record date under this section for the adjourned meeting.

§ 605. Notice of meetings of shareholders.

(a) Whenever under the provisions of this chapter shareholders are required or permitted to take any action at a meeting, written notice shall be given stating the place, date and hour of the meeting and, unless it is the annual meeting, indicating that it is being issued by or at the direction of the person or persons calling the meeting. Notice of a special meeting shall also state the purpose or purposes for which the meeting is called. If, at any meeting, action is proposed to be taken which would, if taken, entitle shareholders fulfilling the requirements of section 623 (Procedure to enforce shareholder's right to receive payment for shares) to receive payment for their shares, the notice of such meeting shall include a statement of that purpose and to that effect and shall be accompanied by a copy of section 623 or an outline of its material terms. A copy of the notice of any meeting shall be given, personally or by first class mail, not fewer than ten nor more than fifty days before the date of the meeting, provided, however, that a copy of such notice may be given by third class mail not fewer than twenty-four nor more than fifty days before the date of the meeting, to each shareholder entitled to vote at such meeting. If mailed, such notice is given when deposited in the United States mail, with postage thereon prepaid, directed to the shareholders at his address as it appears on the record of shareholders, or, if he shall have filed with the secretary of the corporation a written request that notices to him be mailed to some other address, then directed to him at such other address. An affidavit of the secretary or other person giving the notice or of a transfer agent of the corporation that the notice required by this section has been given shall, in the absence of fraud, be prima facie evidence of the facts therein stated.

(b) When a meeting is adjourned to another time or place, it shall not be necessary, unless the by-laws require otherwise, to give any notice of the adjourned meeting if the time and place to which the meeting is adjourned are announced at the meeting at which the adjournment is taken, and at the adjourned meeting any business may be transacted that might have been transacted on the original date of the meeting. However, if after the adjournment the board fixes a new record date for the adjourned meeting, a notice of the adjourned meeting shall be given to each shareholder of record on the new record date entitled to notice under paragraph (a).

§ 606. **Waivers of notice.**

Notice of meeting need not be given to any shareholder who submits a signed waiver of notice, in person or by proxy, whether before or after the meeting. The attendance of any shareholder at a meeting, in person or by proxy, without protesting prior to the conclusion of the meeting the lack of notice of such meeting, shall constitute a waiver of notice by him.

§ 607. **List of shareholders at meetings.**

A list of shareholders as of the record date, certified by the corporate officer responsible for its preparation or by a transfer agent, shall be produced at any meeting of shareholders upon the request thereat or prior thereto of any shareholder. If the right to vote at any meeting is challenged, the inspectors of election, or person presiding thereat, shall require such list of shareholders to be produced as evidence of the right of the persons challenged to vote at such meeting, and all persons who appear from such list to be shareholders entitled to vote thereat may vote at such meeting.

§ 608. **Quorum of shareholders.**

(a) The holders of a majority of the shares entitled to vote thereat shall constitute a quorum at a meeting of shareholders for the transaction of any business, provided that when a specified item of business is required to be voted on by a class or series, voting as a class, the holders of a majority of the shares of such class or series shall constitute a quorum for the transaction of such specified item of business.

(b) The certificate of incorporation or by-laws may provide for any lesser quorum not less than one-third of the shares entitled to vote, and the certificate of incorporation may, under section 616 (Greater requirement as to quorum and vote of shareholders), provide for a greater quorum.

(c) When a quorum is once present to organize a meeting, it is not broken by the subsequent withdrawal of any shareholders.

(d) The shareholders present may adjourn the meeting despite the absence of a quorum.

§ 609. **Proxies.**

(a) Every shareholder entitled to vote at a meeting of shareholders or to excess consent or dissent without a meeting may authorize another person or persons to act for him by proxy.

(b) Every proxy must be signed by the shareholder or his attorney-in-fact. No proxy shall be valid after the expiration of eleven months from the date thereof unless otherwise provided in the proxy. Every proxy shall be revocable at the pleasure of the shareholder executing it, except as otherwise provided in this section.

(c) The authority of the holder of a proxy to act shall not be revoked by the incompetence or death of the shareholder who executed the proxy unless, before the authority is exercised, written notice of an adjudication of such incompetence or of such death is received by the corporate officer responsible for maintaining the list of shareholders.

(d) Except when other provision shall have been made by written agreement between the parties, the record holder of shares which he holds as pledgee or otherwise as security or which belong to another, shall issue to the pledgor or to such owner of such shares, upon demand therefor and payment of necessary expenses thereof, a proxy to vote or take other action thereon.

(e) A shareholder shall not sell his vote or issue a proxy to vote to any person for any sum of money or anything of value, except as authorized in this section and section 620 (Agreements as to voting; provision in certificate of incorporation as to control of directors).

(f) A proxy which is entitled "irrevocable proxy" and which states that it is irrevocable, is irrevocable when it is held by any of the following or a nominee of any of the following:

(1) A pledgee;

(2) A person who has purchased or agreed to purchase the shares;

(3) A creditor or creditors of the corporation who extend or continue credit to the corporation in consideration of the proxy if the proxy states that it was given in consideration of such extension or continuation of credit, the amount thereof, and the name of the person extending or continuing credit;

(4) A person who has contracted to perform services as an officer of the corporation, if a proxy is required by the contract of employment, if the proxy states that it was given in consideration of such contract of employment, the name of the employee and the period of employment contracted for;

(5) A person designated by or under an agreement under paragraph (a) of section 620.

(g) Notwithstanding a provision in a proxy, stating that it is irrevocable, the proxy becomes revocable after the pledge is redeemed, or the debt of the corporation is paid, or the period of employment provided for in the contract of employment has terminated, or the agreement under paragraph (a) of section 620 has terminated; and, in a case provided for in subparagraphs (f) (3) or (4), becomes revocable three years after the date of the proxy or at the end of the period, if any, specified therein, whichever period is less, unless the period of irrevocability is renewed from time to time by the execution of a new irrevocable proxy as provided in this section. This pararaph does not affect the duration of a proxy under paragraph (b).

(h) A proxy may be revoked, notwithstanding a provision making it irrevocable, by a purchaser of shares without knowledge of the existence of the provision unless the existence of the proxy and its irrevocability is noted conspicuously on the face or back of the certificate representing such shares.

§ 610. Selection of inspectors at shareholders' meetings.

If the by-laws require inspectors at any shareholders' meeting, such requirement is waived unless compliance therewith is requested by a shareholder present in person or by proxy and entitled to vote at such meeting. Unless otherwise provided in the by-laws, the board, in advance of any shareholders' meeting, may appoint one or more inspectors to act at the meeting or any adjournment thereof. If inspectors are not so appointed, the person presiding at a shareholders' meeting may, and on the request of any shareholder entitled to vote thereat shall appoint one or more inspectors. In case any person appointed fails to appear or act, the vacancy may be filled by appointment made by the board in advance of the meeting or at the meeting by the person presiding thereat. Each inspector, before entering upon the discharge of his duties, shall take and sign an oath faithfully to execute the duties of inspector at such meeting with strict impartiality and according to the best of his ability.

§ 611. Duties of inspectors at shareholders' meetings.

The inspectors shall determine the number of shares outstanding and the voting power of each, the shares represented at the meeting, the existence of a quorum, the validity and effect of proxies, and shall receive votes, ballots or consents, hear and determine all challenges and questions arising in connection with the right to vote, count and tabulate all votes, ballots or consents, determine the result, and do such acts as are proper to conduct the election or vote with fairness to all shareholders. On request of the person presiding at the meeting or any shareholder entitled to vote thereat, the inspectors shall make a report in writing of any challenge, question or matter determined by them and execute a certificate of any fact found by them. Any report or certificate made by them shall be prima facie evidence of the facts stated and of the vote as certified by them.

§ 612. Qualification of voters.

(a) Every shareholder of record shall be entitled at every meeting of shareholders to one vote for every share standing in his name on the record of shareholders, unless otherwise provided in the certificate of incorporation.

(b) Treasury shares and shares held by another domestic or foreign corporation of any type or kind, if a majority of the shares entitled to vote in the election of directors of such other corporation is held by the corporation, shall not be shares entitled to vote or to be counted in determining the total number of outstanding shares.

(c) Shares held by an administrator, executor, guardian, conservator, committee, or other fiduciary, except a trustee, may be voted by him, either in person or by proxy, without transfer of such shares into his name. Shares held by a trustee may be voted by him, either in person or by proxy, only after the shares have been transferred into his name as trustee or into the name of his nominee.

(d) Shares held by or under the control of a receiver may be voted by him without the transfer thereof into his name if authority so to do is contained in an order of the court by which such receiver was appointed.

(e) A shareholder whose shares are pledged shall be entitled to vote such shares until the shares have been transferred into the name of the pledgee, or a nominee of the pledgee.

(f) Redeemable shares which have been called for redemption shall not be deemed to be outstanding shares for the purpose of voting or determining the total number of shares entitled to vote on any matter on and after the date on which written notice of redemption has been sent to holders thereof and a sum sufficient to redeem such shares has been deposited with a bank or trust company with irrevocable instruction and authority to pay the redemption price to the holders of the shares upon surrender of certificates therefor.

(g) Shares standing in the name of another domestic or foreign corporation of any type or kind may be voted by such officer, agent or proxy as the by-laws of such corporation may provide, or, in the absence of such provision, as the board of such corporation may determine.

(h) If shares are registered on the record of shareholders of a corporation in the name of two or more persons, whether fiduciaries, members of a partnership, joint tenants, tenants in common, tenants by the entirety or otherwise, or if two or more persons have the same fiduciary relationship respecting the same shares, unless the secretary of the corporation is given written notice to the contrary and is furnished with a copy of the instrument or order appointing them or creating the relationship wherein it is so provided, their acts with respect to voting shall have the following effect:

(1) If only one votes, the vote shall be accepted by the corporation as the vote of all;

(2) If more than one vote, the act of the majority so voting shall be accepted by the corporation as the vote of all;

(3) If more than one vote, but the vote is equally divided on any particular matter, the vote shall be accepted by the corporation as a proportionate of the shares; unless the corporation has evidence, on the record of shareholders or otherwise, that the shares are held in a fiduciary capacity. Nothing in this paragraph shall alter any requirement that the exercise of fiduciary powers be by act of a majority, contained in any law applicable to such exercise of powers (including section 10–10.7 of the estates, powers and trusts law);

(4) When shares as to which the vote is equally divided are registered on the record of shareholders of a corporation in the name of, or have passed by operation of law or by virute of any deed of trust or other instrument to two or more fiduciaries, any court having jurisdiction of their accounts, upon peitition by any of such fiduciaries or by any party in interest, may direct the voting of such shares for the best interest of the beneficiaries. This subparagraph shall not apply in any case where the instrument or order of the court appointing fiduciaries shall otherwise direct how such shares shall be voted; and

(5) If the instrument or order furnished to the secretary of a corporation shows that a tenancy is held in unequal interests, a majority or equal division for the purposes of this paragraph shall be a majority or equal division in interest.

(i) Notwithstanding the foregoing paragraphs, a corporation shall be protected in treating the persons in whose names shares stand on the record of shareholders as the owners thereof for all purposes.

§ 613. Limitations on right to vote.

The certificate of incorporation may provide, except as limited by section 501 (Authorized shares), either absolutely or conditionally, that the holders of any designated class or series of shares shall not be entitled to vote, or it may otherwise limit or define the respective voting powers of the several classes of series of shares, and, except as otherwise provided in this chapter, such provisions of such certificate shall prevail, according to their tenor, in all elections and in all proceedings, over the provisions of this chapter which authorizes any action by the shareholders.

§ 614. Vote of shareholders.

(a) Directors shall, except as otherwise required by this chapter or by the certificate of incorporation as permitted by this chapter, be elected by a plurality of the votes cast at a meeting of shareholders by the holders of shares entitled to vote in the election.

(b) Whenever any corporate action, other than the election of directors, is to be taken under this chapter by vote of the shareholders, it shall, except as otherwise required by this chapter or by the certificate of incorporation as permitted by this chapter, be authorized by a majority of the votes cast at a meeting of shareholders by the holders of shares entitled to vote thereon.

§ 615. Written consent of shareholders, subscribers or incorporators without a meeting.

(a) Whenever under this chapter shareholders are required or permitted to take any action by vote, such action may be taken without a meeting on written consent, setting forth the action so taken, signed by the holders of all outstanding shares entitled to vote thereon. This paragraph shall not be construed to alter or modify the provisions of any section or any provision in a certificate of incorporation not inconsistent with this chapter under which the written consent of the holders of less than all outstanding shares is sufficient for corporate action.

(b) Written consent thus given by the holders of all outstanding shares entitled to vote shall have the same effect as a unanimous vote of shareholders and any certificate with respect to the authorization or taking of any such action which is to be delivered to the department of state shall recite that the authorization was by unanimous written consent.

(c) When there are no shareholders of record, such action may be taken on the written consent signed by a majority in interest of the subscribers for shares whose subscriptions have been accepted or their successors in interest or, if no subscription has been accepted, on the written consent signed by the incorporator or a majority of the incorporators. When there are two or more incorporators, if any dies or is for any reason unable to act, the other or others may act. If there is no incorporator able to act, any person for whom an incorporator was acting as agent may act in his stead, or if such other person also dies or is for any reason unable to act, his legal representative may act.

§ 616. Greater requirement as to quorum and vote of shareholders.

(a) The certificate of incorporation may contain provisions specifying either or both of the following:

(1) That the proportion of shares, or the proportion of shares of any class or series thereof, the holders of which shall be present in person or by proxy at any meeting of shareholders, including a special meeting for election of directors under section 603 (Special meeting for election of directors), in order to constitute a quorum for the transaction of any business or of any specified item of business, including amendments to the certificate of incorporation, shall be greater than the proportion prescribed by this chapter in the absence of such provision.

(2) That the proportion of votes of the holders of shares, or of the holders of shares of any class or series thereof, that shall be necessary at any meeting of shareholders for the transaction of any business or of any specified item of business, including amendments to the certificate of incorporation, shall be greater than the proportion prescribed by this chapter in the absence of such provision.

(b) An amendment of the certificate of incorporation which changes or strikes out a provision permitted by this section, shall be authorized at a meeting of shareholders by vote of the holders of two-thirds of all outstanding shares entitled to vote thereon, or of such greater proportion of shares, or class or series of shares, as may be provided specifically in the certificate of incorporation for changing or striking out a provision permitted by this section.

(c) If the certificate of incorporation of any corporation contains a provision authorized by this section, the existence of such provision shall be noted conspicuously on the face or back of every certificate for shares issued by such corporation, except that this requirement shall not apply to any corporation having any class of any equity security registered pursuant to Section twelve of the Securities Exchange Act of 1934, as amended.

§ 617. Voting by class or classes of shares.

(a) The certificate of incorporation may contain provisions specifying that any class or classes of shares or of any series thereof shall vote as a class in connection with the transaction of any business or of any specified item of business at a meeting of shareholders, including amendments to the certificate of incorporation.

(b) Where voting as a class is provided in the certificate of incorporation, it shall be by the proportionate vote so provided or, if no proportionate vote is provided, in the election of directors, by a plurality of the votes cast at such meeting by the holders of shares of such class entitled to vote in the election, or for any other corporate action, by a majority of the votes cast at such meeting by the holders of shares of such class entitled to vote thereon.

(c) Such voting by class shall be in addition to any other vote, including vote by class, required by this chapter and by the certificate of incorporation as permitted by this chapter.

§ 618. Cumulative voting.

The certificate of incorporation of any corporation may provide that in all elections of directors of such corporations each shareholder shall be entitled to as many votes as shall equal the number of votes which, except for such provisions as to cumulative voting, he would be entitled to cast for the election of directors with respect to his shares multiplied by the number of directors to be elected, and that he may cast all of such votes for a single director or may distribute them among the number to be voted for, or any two or more of them, as he may see fit, which right, when exercised, shall be termed cumulative voting.

§ 619. Powers of supreme court respecting elections.

Upon the petition of any shareholder aggrieved by an election, and upon notice to the persons declared elected thereat, the corporation and such other persons as the court may direct, the supreme court at a special term held within the judicial district where the office of the corporation is located shall forthwith hear the proofs and allegations of the parties, and confirm the election, order a new election, or take such other action as justice may require.

§ 620. Agreements as to voting; provision in certificate of incorporation as to control of directors.

(a) An agreement between two or more shareholders, if in writing and signed by the parties thereto, may provide that in exercising any voting rights, the shares held by them shall be voted as therein provided, or as they may agree, or as determined in accordance with a procedure agreed upon by them.

(b) A provision in the certificate of incorporation otherwise prohibited by law because it improperly restricts the board in its management of the business of the corporation, or improperly transfers to one or more shareholders or to one or more persons or corporations to be selected by him or them, all or any part of such management otherwise within the authority of the board under this chapter, shall nevertheless be valid:

(1) If all the incorporators or holders of record of all outstanding shares, whether or not having voting power, have authorized such provision in the certificate of incorporation or an amendment thereof; and

(2) If, subsequent to the adoption of such provision, shares are transferred or issued only to persons who had knowledge or notice thereof or consented in writing to such provision.

(c) A provision authorized by paragraph (b) shall be valid only so long as no shares of the corporation are listed on a national securities exchange or regularly quoted in an over-the-counter market by one or more members of a national or affiliated securities association.

(d) Except as provided in paragraph (e), an amendment to strike out a provision authorized by paragraph (b) shall be authorized at a meeting of shareholders by vote of the holders of two-thirds of all outstanding shares entitled to vote thereon or by the holders of such greater proportion of shares as may be required by the certificate of incorporation for that purpose.

(e) Alternatively, if a provision authorized by paragraph (b) shall have ceased to be valid under this section, the board may authorize a certificate of amendment under section 805 (Certificate of amendment; contents) striking out such provision. Such certificate shall set forth the event by reason of which the provision ceased to be valid.

(f) The effect of any such provision authorized by paragraph (b) shall be to relieve the directors and impose upon the shareholders authorizing the same or consenting thereto the liability for managerial acts or omissions that is imposed on directors by this chapter to the extent that and so long as the discretion or powers of the board in its management of corporate affairs is controlled by any such provision.

(g) If the certificate of incorporation of any corporation contains a provision authorized by paragraph (b), the existence of such provision shall be noted conspicuously on the face or back of every certificate for shares issued by such corporation.

§ 621. Voting trust agreements.

(a) Any shareholder or shareholders, under an agreement in writing, may transfer his or their shares to a voting trustee or trustees for the purpose of conferring the right to vote thereon for a period not exceeding ten years upon the terms and conditions therein stated. The certificates for shares so transferred shall be surrendered and cancelled and new certificates therefor issued to such trustee or trustees stating that they are issued under such agreement, and in the entry of such ownership in the record of the corporation that fact shall also be noted, and such trustee or trustees may vote the shares so transferred during the term of such agreement.

(b) The trustee or trustees shall keep available for inspection by holders of voting trust certificates at his or their office or at a place designated in such agreement or of which the holders of voting trust certificates have been notified in writing, correct and complete books and records of account relating to the trust, and a record containing the names and addresses of all persons who are holders of voting trust certificates and the number and class of shares represented by the certificates held by them and the dates when they became the owners thereof. The record may be in written form or any other form capable of being converted into written form within a reasonable time.

(c) A duplicate of every such agreement shall be filed in the office of the corporation and it and the record of voting trust certificate holders shall be subject to the same right of inspection by a shareholder of record or a holder of a voting trust certificate, in person or by agent or attorney, as are the records of the corporation under section 624 (Books and records; right of inspection, prima facie evidence). The shareholder or holder of a voting trust certificate shall be entitled to the remedies provided in that section.

(d) At any time within six months before the expiration of such voting trust agreement as originally fixed or as extended one or more times under this paragraph, one or more holders of voting trust certificates may, by agreement in writing, extend the duration of such voting trust agreement, nominating the same or substitute trustee or trustees, for an additional period not exceeding ten years. Such extension agreement shall not affect the rights or obligations of persons not parties thereto and shall in every respect comply with and be subject to all the provisions of this section applicable to the original voting trust agreement.

§ 622. Preemptive rights.

(a) As used in this section, the term:

(1) "Unlimited dividend rights" means the right without limitation as to amount either to all or to a share of the balance of current or liquidating dividends after the payment of dividends on any shares entitled to a preference.

(2) "Equity shares" means shares of any class, whether or not preferred as to dividends or assets, which have unlimited dividend rights.

(3) "Voting rights" means the right to vote for the election of one or more directors, excluding a right so to vote which is dependent on the happening of an event specified in the certificate of incorporation which would change the voting rights of any class of shares.

(4) "Voting shares" means shares of any class which have voting rights, but does not include bonds on which voting rights are conferred under section 518 (Corporate bonds).

(5) "Preemptive right" means the right to purchase shares or other securities to be issued or subjected to rights or options to purchase, as such right is defined in this section.

(b) Except as otherwise provided in the certificate of incorporation, and except as provided in this section, the holders of equity shares of any class, in case of the proposed issuance by the corporation of, or the proposed granting by the corporation of rights or options to purchase, its equity shares of any class or any shares or other securities convertible into or carrying rights or options to purchase its equity shares of any class, shall, if the issuance of the equity shares proposed to be issued or issuable upon exercise of such rights or options or upon conversion of such other securities, would adversely affect the unlimited dividend rights of such holders, have the right during a reasonable time and on reasonable conditions, both to be fixed by the board, to purchase such shares or other securities in such proportions as shall be determined as provided in this section.

(c) Except as otherwise provided in the certificate of incorporation, and except as provided in this section, the holders of voting shares of any class, in case of the proposed issuance by the corporation of, or the proposed granting by the corporation of rights or options to purchase, its voting shares of any class or any shares or other securities convertible into or carrying rights or options to purchase its voting shares of any class, shall, if the issuance of the voting shares proposed to be issued or issuable upon exercise of such rights or options or upon conversion of such other securities, would adversely affect the voting rights of such holders, have the right during a reasonable time and on reasonable conditions, both to be fixed by the board, to purchase such shares or other securities in such proportions as shall be determined as provided in this section.

(d) The preemptive right provided for in paragraphs (b) and (c) shall entitle shareholders having such rights to purchase the shares or other securities to be offered or optioned for sale as nearly as practicable in such proportions as would, if such preemptive right were exercised, preserve the relative unlimited dividend rights and voting rights of such holders and at a price or prices not less favorable than the price or prices at which such shares or other securities are proposed to be offered for sale to others, without deduction of such reasonable expenses of and compensation for the sale, underwriting or purchase of such shares or other securities by underwriters or dealers as may lawfully be paid by the corporation. In case each of the shares entitling the holders thereof to preemptive rights does not confer the same unlimited dividend right or voting right, the board shall apportion the shares or other securities to be offered or optioned for sale among the shareholders having preemptive rights to purchase them in such proportions as in the opinion of the board shall preserve as far as practicable the relative unlimited dividend rights and voting rights of the holders at the time of such offering. The apportionment made by the board shall, in the absence of fraud or bad faith, be binding upon all shareholders.

(e) Unless otherwise provided in the certificate of incorporation, shares or other securities offered for sale or subjected to rights or options to purchase shall not be subject to preemptive rights if they:

(1) Are to be issued by the board to effect a merger or consolidation or offered or subjected to rights or options for consideration other than cash;

(2) Are to be issued or subjected to rights or options under paragraph (d) of section 505 (Rights and options to purchase shares; issue of rights and options to directors, officers and employees);

(3) Are to be issued to satisfy conversion or option rights theretofore granted by the corporation;

(4) Are treasury shares;

(5) Are part of the shares or other securities of the corporation authorized in its original certificate of incorporation and are issued, sold or optioned within two years from the date of filing such certificate; or

(6) Are to be issued under a plan of reorganization approved in a proceeding under any applicable act of congress relating to reorganization of corporations.

(f) Shareholders of record entitled to preemptive rights on the record date fixed by the board under section 604 (Fixing record date), or, if no record date is fixed, then on the record date determined under section 604, and no others shall be entitled to the right defined in this section.

(g) The board shall cause to be given to each shareholder entitled to purchase shares or other securities in accordance with this section, a notice directed to him in the manner provided in section 605 (Notice of meetings of shareholders) setting forth the time within which and the terms and conditions upon which the shareholder may purchase such shares or other securities and also the apportionment made of the right to purchase among the shareholders entitled to preemptive rights. Such notice shall be given personally or by mail at least fifteen days prior to the expiration of the period during which the shareholder shall have the right to purchase. All shareholders entitled to preemptive rights to whom notice shall have been given as aforesaid shall be deemed conclusively to have had a reasonable time in which to exercise their preemptive rights.

(h) Shares of other securities which have been offered to shareholders having preemptive rights to purchase and which have not been purchased by them within the time fixed by the board may thereafter, for a period of not exceeding one year following the expiration of the time during which shareholders might have exercised such preemptive rights, be issued, sold or subjected to rights or options to any other person or persons at a price, without deduction of such reasonale expenses of and compensation for the sale, underwriting or purchase of such shares by underwriters or dealers as may lawfully be paid by the corporation, not less than that at which they were offered to such shareholders. Any such shares or other securities not so issued, sold or subjected to rights or options to others during such one year period shall thereafter again be subject to the preemptive rights of shareholders.

(i) Except as otherwise provided in the certificate of incorporation and except as provided in this section, no holder of any shares of any class shall as such holder have any preemptive right to purchase any other shares or securities of any class which at any time may be sold or offered for sale by the corporation. Unless otherwise provided in the certificate of incorporation, holders of bonds on which voting rights are conferred under section 518 shall have no preemptive rights.

§ 623. Procedure to enforce shareholder's right to receive payment for shares.

(a) A shareholder intending to enforce his right under a section of this chapter to receive payment for his shares if the proposed corporate action referred to therein is taken shall file with the corporation, before the meeting of shareholders at which the action is submitted to a vote, or at such meeting but before the vote, written objection to the action. The objection shall include a notice of his election to dissent, his name and residence address, the number and classes of shares as to which he dissents and a demand for payment of the fair value of his shares if the action is taken. Such objection is not required from any shareholder to whom the corporation did not give notice of such meeting in accordance with this chapter or where the proposed action is authorized by written consent of shareholders without a meeting.

(b) Within ten days after the shareholders' authorization date, which term as used in this section means the date on which the shareholders' vote authorizing such action was taken, or the date on which such consent without a meeting was obtained from the requisite shareholders, the corporation shall give written notice of such authorization or consent by registered mail to each shareholder who filed written objection or from whom written objection was not required, excepting any shareholder who voted for or consented in writing to the proposed action and who thereby is deemed to have elected him not to enforce his right to receive payment for his shares.

(c) Within twenty days after the giving of notice to him, any shareholder from whom written objection was not required and who elects to dissent shall file with the corporation a written notice of such election, stating his name and residence address, the number and classes of shares as to which he dissents and a demand for payment of the fair value of his shares. Any shareholder who elects to dissent from a merger under section 905 (Merger of subsidiary corporation) or paragraph (c) of section 907 (Merger or consolidation of domestic and foreign corporations) or from a share exchange under paragraph (g) of section 913 (Share exchanges) shall file a written notice of such election to dissent within twenty days after the giving to him of a copy of the plan of merger or an outline of the material features thereof under section 905 or 913.

(d) A shareholder may not dissent as to less than all of the shares, as to which he has a right to dissent, held by him of record, that he owns beneficially. A nominee or fiduciary may not dissent on behalf of any beneficial owner as to less than all of the shares of such owner, as to which such nominee or fiduciary has a right to dissent, held of record by such nominee or fiduciary.

(e) Upon consummation of the corporate action, the shareholder shall cease to have any of the rights of a shareholder except the right to be paid the fair value of his shares and any other rights under this section. A notice of election may be withdrawn by the shareholder at any time prior to his acceptance in writing of an offer made by the corporation, as provided in paragraph (g), but in no case later than sixty days from the date of consummation of the corporate action except that if the corporation fails to make a timely offer, as provided in paragraph (g), the time for withdrawing a notice of election shall be extended until sixty days from the date an offer is made. Upon expiration of such time, withdrawal of a notice of election shall require the written consent of the corporation. In order to be effective, withdrawal of a notice of election must be accompanied by the return to the corporation of any advance payment made to the shareholder as provided in paragraph (g). If a notice of election is withdrawn, or the corporate action is rescinded, or a court shall determine that the shareholder is not entitled to receive payment for his shares, or the shareholder shall otherwise lose his dissenter's rights, he shall not have the right to receive payment for his shares and he shall be reinstated to all his rights as a shareholder as of the consummation of the corporate action, including any intervening preemptive rights and the right to payment of any intervening dividend or other disribution or, if any such rights have expired or any such dividend or distribution other than in cash has been completed, in lieu thereof, at the election of the corporation, the fair value thereof in cash as determined by the board as of the time of such expiration or completion, but without prejudice otherwise to any corporate proceedings that may have been taken in the interim.

(f) At the time of filing the notice of election to dissent or within one month thereafter the shareholder of shares represented by certificates shall submit the certificates representing his shares to the corporation, or to its transfer agent, which shall forthwith note conspicuously thereon that a notice of election has been filed and shall return the certificates to the shareholder or other person who submitted them on his behalf. Any shareholder of shares represented by certificates who fails to submit his certificates for such notation as herein specified shall, at the option of the corporation exercised by written notice to him within forty-five days from the date of filing of such notice of election to dissent, lose his dissenter's rights unless a court, for good cause shown, shall otherwise direct. Upon transfer of a certificate bearing such notation, each new certificate issued therefor shall bear a similar notation together with the name of the original dissenting holder of the shares and a transferee shall acquire no rights in the corporation except those which the original dissenting shareholder had at the time of transfer.

(g) Within fifteen days after the expiration of the period within which shareholders may file their notices of election to dissent, or within fifteen days after the proposed corporate action is consummated, whichever is later (but in no case later than ninety days from the shareholders' authorization date), the corporation or, in the case of a merger or consolidation, the surviving or new corporation, shall make a written offer by registered mail to each shareholder who has filed such notice of election to pay for his shares at a specified price which the corporation considers to be their fair value. Such offer shall be accompanied by a statement setting forth the aggregate number of shares with respect to which notices of election to dissent have been received and the aggregate number of holders of such shares. If the corporate action has been consummated: such offer shall also be accompanied by (1) advance payment to each such shareholder who has submitted the certificates representing his shares to the corporation, as provided in paragraph (f), of an amount equal to eighty percent of the amount of such offer, or (2) as to each shareholder who has not yet submitted his certificates a statement that advance payment to him of an amount equal to eighty percent of the amount of such offer will be made by the corporation promptly upon submission of his certificates. If the corporate action has not been consummated at the time of the making of the offer, such advance payment or statement as to advance payment shall be sent to each shareholder entitled thereto forthwith upon consummation of the corporate action. Every advance payment or statement as to advance payment shall include advice to the shareholder to the effect that acceptance of such payment does not constitute a waiver of any dissenters' rights. If the corporate action has not been consummated upon the expiration of the ninety day period after the shareholders' authorization date, the offer may be conditioned upon the consummation of such action. Such offer shall be made at the same price per share to all dissenting shareholders of the same class, or if divided into series, of the same series and shall be accompanied by a balance sheet of the corporation whose shares the dissenting shareholder holds as of the latest available date, which shall not be earlier than twelve months before the making of such offer, and a profit and loss statement or statements for not less than a twelve month period ended on the date of such balance sheet or, if the corporation was not in existence throughout such twelve month period, for the portion thereof during which it was in existence. Notwithstanding the foregoing, the corporation shall not be required to furnish a balance sheet or profit and loss statement or statements to any shareholder to whom such balance sheet or profit and loss statement or statements were previously furnished, nor if in connection with obtaining the shareholders' authorization for or consent to the proposed corporate action the shareholders were furnished with a proxy or information statement, which included financial statements, pursuant to Regulation 14A or Regulation 14C of the United States Securities and Exchange Commission. If within thirty days after the making of such offer, the corporation making the offer and any shareholder agree upon the price to be paid for his shares, payment therefor shall be made within sixty days after the making of such offer or the consummation of the proposed corporate action, whichever is later, upon the surrender of the certificates for any such shares represented by certificates.

(h) The following procedure shall apply if the corporation fails to make such offer within such period of fifteen days, or if it makes the offer and any dissenting shareholder or shareholders fail to agree with it within the period of thirty days thereafter upon the price to be paid for their shares:

(1) The corporation shall, within twenty days after the expiration of whichever is applicable of the two periods last mentioned, institute a special proceeding in the supreme court in the judicial district in which the office of the corporation is located to determine the rights of dissenting shareholders and to fix the fair value of their shares. If, in the case of merger or consolidation, the survivor or new corporation is a foreign corporation without an office in this state, such proceeding shall be brought in the county where the office of the domestic corporation, whose shares are to be valued, was located.

(2) If the corporation fails to institute such proceeding within such period of twenty days, any dissenting shareholder may institute such proceeding for the same purpose not later than thirty days after the expiration of such twenty day period. If such proceeding is not instituted within such thirty day period, all dissenter's rights shall be lost unless the supreme court, for good cause shown, shall otherwise direct.

(3) All dissenting shareholders, excepting those who, as provided in paragraph (g), have agreed with the corporation upon the price to be paid for their shares, shall be made parties to such proceeding, which shall have the effect of an action quasi in rem against their shares. The corporation shall serve a copy of the petition in such proceeding upon each dissenting shareholder who is a resident of this state in the manner provided by law for the service of a summons, and upon each nonresident dissenting shareholder either by registered mail and publication, or in such other manner as is permitted by law. The jurisdiction of the court shall be plenary and exclusive.

(4) The court shall determine whether each dissenting shareholder, as to whom the corporation requests the court to make such determination, is entitled to receive payment for his shares. If the corporation does not request any such determination or if the court finds that any dissenting shareholder is so entitled, it shall proceed to fix the value of the shares, which, for the purposes of this section, shall be the fair value as of the close of business on the day prior to the shareholders' authorization date. In fixing the fair value of the shares, the court shall consider the nature of the transaction giving rise to the shareholder's right to receive payment for shares and its effects on the corporation and its shareholders, the concepts and methods then customary in the relevant securities and financial markets for determining fair value of shares of a corporation engaging in a similar transaction under comparable circumstances and all other relevant factors. The court shall determine the fair value of the shares without a jury and without referral to an appraiser or referee. Upon application by the corporation or by any shareholder who is a party to the proceeding, the court may, in its discretion, permit pretrial disclosure, including, but not limited to, disclosure of any expert's reports relating to the fair value of the shares whether or not intended for use at the trial in the proceeding and notwithstanding subdivision (d) of section 3101 of the civil practice law and rules.

(5) The final order in the proceeding shall be entered against the corporation in favor of each dissenting shareholder who is a party to the proceeding and is entitled thereto for the value of his shares so determined.

(6) The final order shall include an allowance for interest at such rate as the court finds to be equitable, from the date the corporate action was consummated to the date of payment. In determining the rate of interest, the court shall consider all relevant factors, including the rate of interest which the corporation would have had to pay to borrow money during the pendency of the proceeding. If the court finds that the refusal of any shareholder to accept the corporate offer of payment for his shares was arbitrary, vexatious or otherwise not in good faith, no interest shall be allowed to him.

(7) Each party to such proceeding shall bear its own costs and expenses, including the fees and expenses of its counsel and of any experts employed by it. Notwithstanding the foregoing, the court may, in its discretion, apportion and assess all or any part of the costs, expenses and fees incurred by the corporation against any or all of the dissenting shareholders who are parties to the proceeding, including any who have withdrawn their notices of election as provided in paragraph (e), if the court finds that their refusal to accept the corporate offer was arbitrary, vexatious or otherwise not in good faith. The court may, in its discretion, apportion and assess all or any part of the costs, expenses and fees incurred by any or all of the dissenting shareholders who are parties to the proceeding against the corporation if the court finds any of the following: (A) that the fair value of the shares as determined materially exceeds the amount which the corporation offered to pay; (B) that no offer or required advance payment was made by the corporation; (C) that the corporation failed to institute the special proceeding within the period specified therefor; or (D) that the action of the corporation in complying with its obligations as provided in this section was arbitrary, vexatious or otherwise not in good faith. In making any determination as provided in clause (A), the court may consider the dollar amount or the percentage, or both, by which the fair value of the shares as determined exceeds the corporate offer.

(8) Within sixty days after final determination of the proceeding, the corporation shall pay to each dissenting shareholder the amount found to be due him, upon surrender of the certificates for any such shares represented by certificates.

(i) Shares acquired by the corporation upon the payment of the agreed value therefor or of the amount due under the final order, as provided in this section, shall become treasury shares or be cancelled as provided in section 515 (Reacquired shares), except that, in the case of a merger or consolidation, they may be held and disposed of as the plan of merger or consolidation may otherwise provide.

(j) No payment shall be made to a dissenting shareholder under this section at a time when the corporation is insolvent or when such payment would make it insolvent. In such event, the dissenting shareholder shall, at his option:

(1) Withdraw his notice of election, which shall in such event be deemed withdrawn with the written consent of the corporation; or

(2) Retain his status as a claimant against the corporation and, if it is liquidated, be subordinated to the rights of creditors of the corporation, but have rights superior to the non-dissenting shareholders, and if it is not liquidated, retain his right to be paid for his shares, which right the corporation shall be obliged to satisfy when the restrictions of this paragraph do not apply.

(3) The dissenting shareholder shall exercise such option under subparagraph (1) or (2) by written notice filed with the corporation within thirty days after the corporation has given him written notice that payment for his shares cannot be made because of the restrictions of this paragraph. If the dissenting shareholder fails to exercise such option as provided, the corporation shall exercise the option by written notice given to him within twenty days after the expiration of such period of thirty days.

(k) The enforcement by a shareholder of his right to receive payment for his shares in the manner provided herein shall exclude the enforcement by such shareholder of any other right to which he might otherwise be entitled by virtue of share ownership, except as provided in paragraph (e), and except that this section shall not exclude the right of such shareholder to bring or maintain an appropriate action to obtain relief on the ground that such corporate action will be or is unlawful or fraudulent as to him.

(l) Except as otherwise expressly provided in this section, any notice to be given by a corporation to a shareholder under this section shall be given in the manner provided in section 605 (Notice of meetings of shareholders).

(m) This section shall not apply to foreign corporations except as provided in subparagraph (e) (2) of section 907 (Merger or consolidation of domestic and foreign corporations).

§ 624. Books and records; right of inspection, prima facie evidence.

(a) Each corporation shall keep correct and complete books and records of account and shall keep minutes of the proceedings of its shareholders, board and executive committee, if any, and shall keep at the office of the corporation in this state or at the office of its transfer agent or registrar in this state, a record containing the names and addressses of all shareholders, the number and class of shares held by each and the dates when they respectively became the owners of record thereof. Any of the foregoing books, minutes or records may be in written form or in any other form capable of being converted into written form within a reasonable time.

(b) Any person who shall have been a shareholder of record of a corporation for at least six months immediately preceding his demand, or any person holding, or thereunto authorized in writing by the holders of, at least five percent of any class of the outstanding shares, upon at least five days' written demand shall have the right to examine in person or by agent or attorney, during usual business hours, its minutes of the proceedings of its shareholders and record of shareholders and to make extracts therefrom. Holders of voting trust certificates representing shares of the corporation shall be regarded as shareholders for the purpose of this section. If the corporation has failed to pay wages as defined in paragraph (b) of section 630 (Liability of shareholders for wages due to laborers, servants or employees), any person to whom a shareholder may be liable thereunder upon at least five days' written demand shall have the right to examine in person or by agent or attorney during usual business hours, the record of shareholders and to make extracts therefrom.

(c) An inspection authorized by paragraph (b) may be denied to such shareholder or other person upon his refusal to furnish to the corporation, its transfer agent or registrar an affidavit that such inspection is not desired for a purpose which is in the interest of a business or object other than the business of the corporation and that he has not within five years sold or offered for sale any list of shareholders of any corporation of any type or kind, whether or not formed under the laws of this state, or aided or abetted any person in procuring any such record of shareholders for any such purpose. The enforcement of liability under section 630 shall not be an object other than the business of the corporation.

(d) Upon refusal by the corporation or by an officer or agent of the corporation to permit an inspection of the minutes of the proceedings of its shareholders or of the record of shareholders as herein provided, the person making the demand for inspection may apply to the supreme court in the judicial district where the office of the corporation is located, upon such notice as the court may direct, for an order directing the corporation, its officer or agent to show cause why an order should not be granted permitting such inspection by the applicant. Upon the return day of the order to show cause, the court shall hear the parties summarily, by affidavit or otherwise, and if it appears that the applicant is qualified and entitled to such inspection, the court shall grant an order compelling such inspection and awarding such further relief as to the court may seem just and proper.

(e) Upon the written request of any person who shall have been a shareholder of record for at least six months immediately preceding his request, or of any person holding, or thereunto authorized in writing by the holders of, at least five percent of any class of the outstanding shares, the corporation shall give or mail to such shareholder an annual balance sheet and profit and loss statement for the preceding fiscal year, and, if any interim balance sheet or profit and loss statement has been distributed to its shareholders or otherwise made available to the public, the most recent such interim balance sheet or profit and loss statement. The corporation shall be allowed a reasonable time to prepare such annual balance sheet and profit and loss statement.

(f) Nothing herein contained shall impair the power of courts to compel the production for examination of the books and records of a corporation.

(g) The books and records specified in paragraph (a) shall be prima facie evidence of the facts therein stated in favor of the plaintiff in any action or special proceeding against such corporation or any of its officers, directors or shareholders.

§ 625. Infant shareholders and bondholders.

(a) A corporation may treat an infant who holds shares or bonds of such corporation as having capacity to receive and to empower others to receive dividends, interest, principal and other payments and distributions to, vote or express consent or dissent, in person or by proxy, and to make elections and exercise rights relating to such shares or bonds, unless, in the case of shares, the corporate officer responsible for maintaining the list of shareholders or the transfer agent of the corporation or, in the case of bonds, the treasurer or paying officer or agent has received written notice that such holder is an infant.

(b) An infant holder of shares or bonds of a corporation who has received or empowered others to receive payments or distributions, voted or expressed consent or dissent, or made an election or exercised a right relating thereto, shall have no right thereafter to disaffirm or avoid, as against the corporation, any such act on his part, unless prior to such receipt, vote, consent, dissent, election or exercise, as to shares, the corporate officer responsible for maintaining the list of shareholders or its transfer agent or, in the case of bonds, the treasurer or paying officer had received written notice that such holder was an infant.

(c) This section does not limit any other statute which authorizes any corporation to deal with an infant or limits the right of an infant to disaffirm his acts.

§ 626. Shareholders' derivative action brought in the right of the corporation to procure a judgment in its favor.

(a) An action may be brought in the right of a domestic or foreign corporation to procure a judgment in its favor, by a holder of shares or of voting trust certificates of the corporation or of a beneficial interest in such shares or certificates.

(b) In any such action, it shall be made to appear that the plaintiff is such a holder at the time of bringing the action and that he was such a holder at the time of the transaction of which he complains, or that his shares or his interest therein devolved upon him by operation of law.

(c) In any such action, the complaint shall set forth with particularity the efforts of the plaintiff to secure the initiation of such action by the board or the reasons for not making such effort.

(d) Such action shall not be discontinued, compromised or settled, without the approval of the court having jurisdiction of the action. If the court shall determine that the interests of the shareholders or any class or classes thereof will be substantially affected by such discontinuance, compromise, or settlement, the court, in its discretion, may direct that notice, by publication or otherwise, shall be given to the shareholders or classes thereof whose interests it determines will be so affected; if notice is so directed to be given, the court may determine which one or more of the parties to the action shall bear the expense of giving the same, in such amount as the court shall determine and find to be reasonable in the circumstances, and the amount of such expense shall be awarded as special costs of the action and recoverable in the same manner as statutory taxable costs.

(e) If the action on behalf of the corporation was successful, in whole or in part, or if anything was received by the plaintiff or plaintiffs or a claimant or claimants as the result of a judgment, compromise or settlement of an action or claim, the court may award the plaintiff or plaintiffs, claimant or claimants, reasonable expenses, including reasonable attorney's fees, and shall direct him or them to account to the corporation for the remainder of the proceeds so received by him or them. This paragraph shall not apply to any judgment rendered for the benefit of injured shareholders only and limited to a recovery of the loss or damage sustained by them.

§ 627. Security for expenses in shareholders' derivative action brought in the right of the corporation to procure a judgment in its favor.

In any action specified in section 626 (Shareholders' derivative action brought in the right of the corporation to procure a judgment in its favor), unless the plaintiff or plaintiffs hold five percent or more of any class of the outstanding shares or hold voting trust certificates or a beneficial interest in shares representing five percent or more of any class of such shares, or the shares, voting trust certificates and beneficial interest of such plaintiff or plaintiffs have a fair value in excess of fifty thousand dollars, the corporation in whose right such action is brought shall be entitled at any stage of the proceedings before final judgment to require the plaintiff or plaintiffs to give security for the reasonable expenses, including attorney's fees, which may be incurred by it in connection with such action and by the other parties defendant in connection therewith for which the corporation may become liable under this chapter, under any contract or otherwise under law, to which the corporation shall have recourse in such amount as the court having jurisdiction of such action shall determine upon the termination of such action. The amount of such security may thereafter from time to time be increased or decreased in the discretion of the court having jurisdiction of such action upon showing that the security provided has or may become inadequate or excessive.

§ 628. Liability of subscribers and shareholders.

(a) A holder of or subscriber for shares of a corporation shall be under no obligation to the corporation for payment for such shares other than the obligation to pay the unpaid portion of his subscription which in no event shall be less than the amount of the consideration for which such shares could be issued lawfully.

(b) Any person becoming an assignee or transferee of shares or of a subscription for shares in good faith and without knowledge or notice that the full consideration therefor has not been paid shall not be personally liable for any unpaid portion of such consideration, but the transferor shall remain liable therefor.

(c) No person holding shares in any corporation as collateral security shall be personally liable as a shareholder but the person pledging such shares shall be considered the holder thereof and shall be so liable. No executor, administrator, guardian, trustee or other fiduciary shall be personally liable as a shareholder, but the estate and funds in the hands of such executor, administrator, guardian, trustee or other fiduciary shall be liable.

§ 629. Certain transfers or assignments by shareholders or subscribers; effect.

Any transfer or assignment by a shareholder of his shares, or by a subscriber for shares of his interest in the corporation, shall not relieve him of any liability as a shareholder or subscriber if at the time of such transfer or assignment the aggregate of the corporation's property, exclusive of any property which it may have conveyed, transferred, concealed, removed, or permitted to be concealed or removed, with intent to defraud, hinder or delay its creditors, is not at a fair valuation sufficient in amount to pay its debts, or if such condition is imminent.

§ 630. Liability of shareholders for wages due to laborers, servants or employees.

(a) The ten largest shareholders, as determined by the fair value of their beneficial interest as of the beginning of the period during which the unpaid services referred to in this section are performed, of every corporation (other than an investment company registered as such under an act of congress entitled "Investment Company Act of 1940"), no shares of which are listed on a national securities exchange or regularly quoted in an over-the-counter market by one or more members of a national or an affiliated securities association, shall jointly and severally be personally liable for all debts, wages or salaries due and owing to any of its laborers, servants or employees other than contractors, for services performed by them for such corporation. Before such laborer, servant or employee shall charge such shareholder for such services, he shall give notice in writing to such shareholder that he intends to hold him liable under this section. Such notice shall be given within one hundred and eighty days after termination of such services, except that if, within such period, the laborer, servant or employee demands an examination of the record of shareholders under paragraph (b) of section 624 (Books and records; right of inspection, prima facie evidence), such notice may be given within sixty days after he has been given the opportunity to examine the record of shareholders. An action to enforce such liability shall be commenced within ninety days after the rerun of an execution unsatisfied against the corporation upon a judgment recovered against it for such services.

(b) For the purposes of this section, wages or salaries shall mean all compensation and benefits payable by an employer to or for the account of the employee for personal services rendered by such employee. These shall specifically include but not be limited to salaries, overtime, vacation, holiday and serverance pay; employer contributions to or payments of insurance or welfare benefits; employer contributions to pension or annuity funds; and any other moneys properly due or payable for services rendered by such employee.

(c) A shareholder who has paid more than his pro rata share under this section shall be entitled to contribution pro rata from the other shareholders liable under this section with respect to the excess so paid, over and above his pro rata share, and may sue them jointly or severally or any number of them to recover the amount due from them. Such recovery may be had in a separate action. As used in this paragraph "pro rata" means in proportion to beneficial share interest. Before a shareholder may claim contribution from other shareholders under this paragraph, he shall, unless they have been given notice by a laborer, servant or employee under paragraph (a), give them notice in writing that he intends to hold them so liable to him. Such notice shall be given by him within twenty days after the date that notice was given to him by a laborer, servant or employee under paragraph (a).

§ 701. Board of directors.

Subject to any provision in the certificate of incorporation authorized by paragraph (b) of section 620 (Agreements as to voting; provision in certificate of incorporation as to control of directors) or by paragraph (b) of section 715 (Officers), the business of a corporation shall be managed under the direction of its board of directors, each of whom shall be at least eighteen years of age. The certificate of incorporation or the by-laws may prescribe other qualifications for directors.

§ 702. Number of directors.

(a) The number of directors constituting the entire board shall not be less than three, except that where all the shares of a corporation are owned beneficially and of record by less than three shareholders, the number of directors may be less than three but not less than the number of shareholders. Subject to such limitation, such number may be fixed by the by-laws, or by action of the shareholders or of the board under the specific provisions of a by-law adopted by the shareholders. If not otherwise fixed under this paragraph, the number shall be three. As used in this article, "entire board" means the total number of directors which the corporation would have if there were no vacancies.

(b) The number of directors may be increased or decreased by amendment of the by-laws, or by action of the shareholders or of the board under the specific provisions of a by-law adopted by the shareholders, subject to the following limitations:

(1) If the board is authorized by the by-laws to change the number of directors, whether by amending the by-laws or by taking action under the specific provisions of a by-law adopted by the shareholders, such amendment or action shall require the vote of a majority of the entire board.

(2) No decrease shall shorten the term of any incumbent director.

§ 703. Election and term of directors.

(a) At each annual meeting of shareholders, directors shall be elected to hold office until the next annual meeting except as authorized by section 704 (Classification of directors). The certificate of incorporation may provide for the election of one or more directors by the holders of the shares of any class or series, or by the holders of bonds entitled to vote in the election of directors pursuant to section 518 (Corporate bonds), voting as a class.

(b) Each director shall hold office until the expiration of the term for which he is elected, and until his successor has been elected and qualified.

§ 704. Classification of directors.

(a) The certificate of incorporation or the specific provisions of a by-law adopted by the shareholders may provide that the directors be divided into either two, three or four classes. All classes shall be as nearly equal in number as possible, and no class shall include less than three directors.

The terms of office of the directors initially classified shall be as follows: that of the first class shall expire at the next annual meeting of shareholders, the second class at the second succeeding annual meeting, the third class, if any, at the third succeeding annual meeting, and the fourth class, if any, at the fourth succeeding annual meeting.

(b) At each annual meeting after such initial classification, directors to replace those whose terms expire at such annual meeting shall be elected to hold office until the second succeeding annual meeting if there are two classes, the third succeeding annual meeting if there are three classes, or the fourth succeeding annual meeting if there are four classes.

(c) If directors are classified and the number of directors is thereafter changed:

(1) Any newly created directorships or any decrease in directorships shall be so apportioned among the classes as to make all classes as nearly equal in number as possible.

(2) When the number of directors is increased by the board and any newly created directorships are filled by the board, there shall be no classification of the additional directors until the next annual meeting of shareholders.

§ 705. Newly created directorships and vacancies.

(a) Newly created directorships resulting from an increase in the number of directors and vacancies occurring in the board for any reason except the removal of directors without cause may be filled by vote of the board. If the number of the directors then in office is less than a quorum, such newly created directorships and vacancies may be filled by vote of a majority of the directors then in office. Nothing in this paragraph shall affect any provision of the certificate of incorporation or the by-laws which provides that such newly created directorships or vacancies shall be filled by vote of the shareholders, or any provision of the certificate of incorporation specifying greater requirements as permitted under section 709 (Greater requirements as to quorum and vote of directors).

(b) Unless the certificate of incorporation or the specific provisions of a by-law adopted by the shareholders provide that the board may fill vacancies occurring in the board by reason of the removal of directors without cause, such vacancies may be filled only by vote of the shareholders.

(c) A director elected to fill a vacancy, unless elected by the shareholders, shall hold office until the next meeting of shareholders at which the election of directors is in the regular order of business, and until his successor has been elected and qualified.

§ 706. Removal of directors.

(a) Any or all of the directors may be removed for cause by vote of the shareholders. The certificate of incorporation or the specific provisions of a by-law adopted by the shareholders may provide for such removal by action of the board, except in the case of any director elected by cumulative voting, or by the holders of the shares of any class or series, or holders of bonds, voting as a class, when so entitled by the provisions of the certificate of incorporation.

(b) If the certificate of incorporation or the by-laws so provide, any or all of the directors may be removed without cause by vote of the shareholders.

(c) The removal of directors, with or without cause, as provided in paragraphs (a) and (b) is subject to the following:

(1) In the case of a corporation having cumulative voting, no director may be removed when the votes cast against his removal would be sufficient to elect him if voted cumulatively at an election at which the same total number of votes were cast and the entire board, or the entire class of directors of which he is a member, were then being elected; and

(2) When by the provisions of the certificate of incorporation the holders of the shares of any class or series, or holders of bonds, voting as a class, are entitled to elect one or more directors, any director so elected may be removed only by the applicable vote of the holders of the shares of that class or series, or the holders of such bonds, voting as a class.

(d) An action to procure a judgment removing a director for cause may be brought by the attorney-general or by the holders of ten percent of the outstanding shares, whether or not entitled to vote. The court may bar from re-election any director so removed for a period fixed by the court.

§ 707. Quorum of directors.

Unless a greater proportion is required by the certificate of incorporation, a majority of the entire board shall constitute a quorum for the transaction of business or of any specified item of business, except that the certificate of incorporation or the by-laws may fix the quorum at less than a majority of the entire board but not less than one-third thereof.

§ 708. Action by the board.

(a) Except as otherwise provided in this chapter, any reference in this chapter to corporate action to be taken by the board shall mean such action at a meeting of the board.

(b) Unless otherwise restricted by the certificate of incorporation or the by-laws, any action required or permitted to be taken by the board or any committee thereof may be taken without a meeting if all members of the board or the committee consent in writing to the adoption of a resolution authorizing the action. The resolution and the written consents thereto by the members of the board or committee shall be filed with the minutes of the proceedings of the board or committee.

(c) When authorized by the certificate of incorporation or the by-laws, any one or more members of the board or any committee thereof may participate in a meeting of such board or committee by means of a conference telephone or similar communications equipment allowing all persons participating in the meeting to hear each other at the same time. Participation by such means shall constitute presence in person at a meeting.

(d) Except as otherwise provided in this chapter, the vote of a majority of the directors present at the time of the vote, if a quorum is present at such time, shall be the act of the board.

§ 709. Greater requirement as to quorum and vote of directors.

(a) The certificate of incorporation may contain provisions specifying either or both of the following:

(1) That the proportion of directors that shall constitute a quorum for the transaction of business or of any specified item of business shall be greater than the proportion prescribed by this chapter in the absence of such provision.

(2) That the proportion of votes of directors that shall be necessary for the transaction of business or of any specified item of business shall be greater than the proportion prescribed by this chapter in the absence of such provision.

(b) An amendment of the certificate of incorporation which changes or strikes out a provision permitted by this section shall be authorized at a meeting of shareholders by vote of the holders of two-thirds of all outstanding shares entitled to vote thereon, or of such greater proportion of shares or class or series of shares, as may be provided specifically in the certificate of incorporation for changing or striking out a provision permitted by this section.

(c) If the certificate of incorporation of any corporation contains a provision authorized by this section, the existence of such provision shall be noted conspicuously on the face or back of every certificate for shares issued by such corporation, except that this requirement shall not apply to any corporation having any class of any equity security registered pursuant to section twelve of the Securities Exchange Act of 1934, as amended.

§ 710. Place and time of meetings of the board.

Meetings of the board, regular or special, may be held at any place within or without this state, unless otherwise provided by the certificate of incorporation or the by-laws. The time and place for holding meetings of the board may be fixed by or under the by-laws, or, if not so fixed, by the board.

§ 711. Notice of meetings of the board.

(a) Unless otherwise provided by the by-laws, regular meetings of the board may be held without notice if the time and place of such meetings are fixed by the by-laws or the board. Special meetings of the board shall be held upon notice to the directors.

(b) The by-laws may prescribe what shall constitute notice of meeting of the board. A notice, or waiver of notice, need not specify the purpose of any regular or special meeting of the board, unless required by the by-laws.

(c) Notice of a meeting need not be given to any director who submits a signed waiver of notice whether before or after the meeting, or who attends the meeting without protesting, prior thereto or at its commencement, the lack of notice to him.

(d) A majority of the directors present, whether or not a quorum is present, may adjourn any meeting to another time and place. If the by-laws so provide, notice of any adjournment of a meeting of the board to another time or place shall be given to the directors who were not present at the time of the adjournment and, unless such time and place are announced at the meeting, to the other directors.

§ 712. Executive committee and other committees.

(a) If the certificate of incorporation or the by-laws so provide, the board, by resolution adopted by a majority of the entire board, may designate from among its members an executive committee and other committees, each consisting of three or more directors, and each of which, to the extent provided in the resolution or in the certificate of incorporation or by-laws, shall have all the authority of the board, except that no such committee shall have authority as to the following matters:

(1) The submission to shareholders of any action that needs shareholders' approval under this chapter.

(2) The filling of vacancies in the board of directors or in any committee.

(3) The fixing of compensation of the directors for serving on the board or on any committee.

(4) The amendment or repeal of the by-laws, or the adoption of new by-laws.

(5) The amendment or repeal of any resolution of the board which by its terms shall not be so amendable or repealable.

(b) The board may designate one or more directors as alternate members of any such committee, who may replace any absent member or members at any meeting of such committee.

(c) Each such committee shall serve at the pleasure of the board. The designation of any such committee, the delegation thereto of authority, or action by any such committee pursuant to such authority shall not alone constitute performance by any member of the board who is not a member of the committee in question, of his duty to the corporation under section 717 (Duty of directors).

§ 713. Interested directors.

(a) No contract or other transaction between a corporation and one or more of its directors, or between a corporation and any other corporation, firm, association or other entity in which one or more of its directors are directors or officers, or have a substantial financial interest, shall be either void or voidable for this reason alone or by reason alone that such director or directors are present at the meeting of the board, or of a committee thereof, which approves such contract or transaction, or that his or their votes are counted for such purpose:

(1) If the material facts as to such director's interest in such contract or transaction and as to any such common directorship, officership or financial interest are disclosed in good faith or known to the board or committee, and the board or committee approves such contract or transaction by a vote sufficient for such purpose without counting the vote of such interested director or, if the votes of the disinterested directors are insufficient to constitute an act of the board as defined in this section 708 (Action by the board), by unanimous vote of the disinterested directors; or

(2) If the material facts as to such director's interest in such contract or transaction and as to any such common directorship, officership or financial interest are disclosed in good faith or known to the shareholders entitled to vote thereon, and such contract or transaction is approved by vote of such shareholders.

(b) If such good faith disclosure of the material facts as to the director's interest in the contract or transaction and as to any such common directorship, officership or financial interest is made to the directors or shareholders, or known to the board or committee or shareholder approving such contract or transaction, as provided in paragraph (a), the contract or transaction may not be avoided by the corporation for the reasons set forth in the paragraph (a). If there was no such disclosure or knowledge, or if the vote of such interested director was necessary for the approval of such contract or transaction at a meeting of the board or committee at which it was approved, the corporation may avoid the contract or transaction unless the party or parties thereto shall establish affirmatively that the contract or transaction was fair and reasonable as to the corporation at the time it was approved by the board, a committee or the shareholders.

(c) Common or interested directors may be counted in determining the presence of a quorum at a meeting of the board or of a committee which approves such contract or transaction.

(d) The certificate of incorporation may contain additional restrictions on contracts or transactions between a corporation and its directors and may provide that contracts or transactions in violation of such restrictions shall be void or voidable by the corporation.

(e) Unless otherwise provided in the certificate of incorporation or the by-laws, the board shall have authority to fix the compensation of directors for services in any capacity.

§ 714. Loans to directors.

A loan shall not be made by a corporation to any director unless it is authorized by vote of the shareholders. For this purpose, the shares of the director who would be the borrower shall not be shares entitled to vote. A loan made in violation of this section shall be a violation of the duty to the corporation of the directors approving it, but the obligation of the borrower with respect to the loan shall not be affected thereby.

§ 715. Officers.

(a) The board may elect or appoint a president, one or more vice-presidents, a secretary and a treasurer, and such other officers as it may determine, or as may be provided in the by-laws.

(b) The certificate of incorporation may provide that all officers or that specified officers shall be elected by the shareholders instead of by the board.

(c) Unless otherwise provided in the certificate of incorporation or the by-laws, all officers shall be elected or appointed to hold office until the meeting of the board following the next annual meeting of shareholders or, in the case of officers elected by the shareholders, until the next annual meeting of shareholders.

(d) Each officer shall hold office for the term for which he is elected or appointed, and until his successor has been elected or appointed and qualified.

(e) Any two or more offices may be held by the same person, except the offices of president and secretary. When all of the issued and outstanding stock of the corporation is owned by one person, such person may hold all or any combination of offices.

(f) The board may require any officer to give security for the faithful performance of his duties.

(g) All officers as between themselves and the corporation shall have such authority and perform such duties in the management of the corporation as may be provided in the by-laws or, to the extent not so provided, by the board.

(h) An officer shall perform his duties as an officer in good faith and with that degree of care which an ordinarily prudent person in a like position would use under similar circumstances. In performing his duties, an officer shall be entitled to rely on information, opinions, reports or statements including financial statements and other financial data, in each case prepared or presented by:

(1) one or more other officers or employees of the corporation or of any other corporation of which at least fifty percentum of the outstanding shares of stock entitling the holders thereof to vote for the election of directors is owned directly or indirectly by the corporation, whom the officer believes to be reliable and competent in the matters presented, or

(2) counsel, public accountants or other persons as to matters which the officer believes to be within such person's professional or expert competence, so long as in so relying he shall be acting in good faith and with such degree of care, but he shall not be considered to be acting in good faith if he has knowledge concerning the matter in question that would cause such reliance to be unwarranted. A person who so performs his duties shall have no liability by reason of being or having been an officer of the corporation.

§ 716. Removal of officers.

(a) Any officer elected or appointed by the board may be removed by the board with or without cause. An officer elected by the shareholders may be removed, with or without cause, only by vote of the shareholders, but his authority to act as an officer may be suspended by the board for cause.

(b) The removal of an officer without cause shall be without prejudice to his contract rights, if any. The election or appointment of an officer shall not of itself create contract rights.

(c) An action to procure a judgment removing an officer for cause may be brought by the attorney-general or by the holders of ten percent of the outstanding shares, whether or not entitled to vote. The court may bar from re-election or reappointment any officer so removed for a period fixed by the court.

§ 717. Duty of directors.

A director shall perform his duties as a director, including his duties as a member of any committee of the board upon which he may serve, in good faith and with that degree of care which an ordinarily prudent person in a like position would use under similar circumstances. In performing his duties, a director shall be entitled to rely on information, opinions, reports or statements including financial statements and other financial data, in each case prepared or presented by:

(1) one or more officers or employees of the corporation or of any other corporation of which at least fifty percentum of the outstanding shares of stock entitling the holders thereof to vote for the election of directors is owned directly or indirectly by the corporation, whom the director believes to be reliable and competent in the matters presented,

(2) counsel, public accountants or other persons as to matters which the director believes to be within such person's professional or expert competence, or

(3) a committee of the board upon which he does not serve, duly designated in accordance with a provision of the certificate of incorporation or the by-laws, as to matters within its designated authority, which committee the director believes to merit confidence, so long as in so relying he shall be acting in good faith and with such degree of care, but he shall not be considered to be acting in good faith if he has knowledge concerning the matter in question that would cause such reliance to be unwarranted. A person who so performs his duties shall have no liability by reason of being or having been a director of the corporation.

§ 718. List of directors and officers.

(a) If a shareholder or creditor of a corporation, in person or by his attorney or agent, or a representative of the district attorney or of the secretary of state, the attorney general, or other state official makes a written demand on a corporation to inspect a current list of its directors and officers and their residence addresses, the corporation shall, within two business days after receipt of the demand and for a period of one week thereafter, make the list available for such inspection at its office during usual business hours.

(b) Upon refusal by the corporation to make a current list of its directors and officers and their residence addresses available, as provided in paragraph (a), the person making a demand for such list may apply, ex parte, to the supreme court at a special term held within the judicial district where the office of the corporation is located for an order directing the corporation to make such list available. The court may grant such order or take such other action as it may deem just and proper.

§ 719. Liability of directors in certain cases.

(a) Directors of a corporation who vote for or concur in any of the following corporate actions shall be jointly and severally liable to the corporation for the benefit of its creditors or shareholders, to the extent of any injury suffered by such persons, respectively, as a result of such action:

(1) The declaration of any dividend or other distribution to the extent that it is contrary to the provisions of paragraphs (a) and (b) of section 510 (Dividends or other distributions in cash or property).

(2) The purchase of the shares of the corporation to the extent that it is contrary to the provisions of section 513 (Purchase or redemption by a corporation of its own shares).

(3) The distribution of assets to shareholders after dissolution of the corporation without paying or adequately providing for all known liabilities of the corporation, excluding any claims not filed by creditors within the time limits set in a notice given to creditors under articles 10 (Non-judicial dissolution) or 11 (Judicial dissolution).

(4) The making of any loan contrary to section 714 (Loans to directors).

(b) A director who is present at a meeting of the board, or any committee thereof, when action specified in paragraph (a) is taken shall be presumed to have concurred in the action unless his dissent thereto shall be entered in the minutes of the meeting, or unless he shall submit his written dissent to the person acting as the secretary of the meeting before the adjournment thereof, or shall deliver or send by registered mail such dissent to the secretary of the corporation promptly after the adjournment of the meeting. Such right to dissent shall not apply to a director who voted in favor of such action. A director who is absent from a meeting of the board, or any committee thereof, when such action is taken shall be presumed to have concurred in the action unless he shall deliver or send by registered mail his dissent thereto to the secretary of the corporation or shall cause such dissent to be filed with the minutes of the proceedings of the board or committee within a reasonable time after learning of such action.

(c) Any director against whom a claim is successfully asserted under this section shall be entitled to contribution from the other directors who voted for or concurred in the action upon which the claim is asserted.

(d) Directors against whom a claim is successfully asserted under this section shall be entitled, to the extent of the amounts paid by them to the corporation as a result of such claims:

(1) Upon payment to the corporation of any amount of an improper dividend or distribution, to be subrogated to the rights of the corporation against shareholders who received such dividend or distribution with knowledge of facts indicating that it was not authorized by section 510, in proportion to the amounts received by them respectively.

(2) Upon payment to the corporation of any amount of the purchase price of an improper purchase of shares, to have the corporation rescind such purchase of shares and recover for their benefit, but at their expense, the amount of such purchase price from any seller, who sold such shares with knowledge of facts indicating that such purchase of shares by the corporation was not authorized by section 513.

(3) Upon payment to the corporation of the claim of any creditor by reason of a violation of subparagraph (a) (3), to be subrogated to the rights of the corporation against shareholders who received an improper distribution of assets.

(4) Upon payment to the corporation of the amount of any loan made contrary to section 714, to be subrogated to the rights of the corporation against a director who received the improper loan.

(e) A director shall not be liable under this section if, in the circumstances, he performed his duty to the corporation under section 717.

(f) This section shall not affect any liability otherwise imposed by law upon the director.

§ 720. Action against directors and officers for misconduct.

(a) An action may be brought against one or more directors or officers of a corporation to procure a judgment for the following relief:

(1) To compel the defendant to account for his official conduct in the following cases:

(A) The neglect of, or failure to perform, or other violation of his duties in the management and disposition of corporate assets committed to his charge.

(B) The acquisition by himself, transfer to others, loss or waste of corporate assets due to any neglect of, or failure to perform, or other violation of his duties.

(2) To set aside an unlawful conveyance, assignment or transfer of corporate assets, where the transferee knew of its unlawfulness.

(3) To enjoin a proposed unlawful conveyance, assignment or transfer of corporate assets, where there is sufficient evidence that it will be made.

(b) An action may be brought for the relief provided in this section, and in paragraph (a) of section 719 (Liability of directors in certain cases) by a corporation, or a receiver, trustee in bankruptcy, officer, director or judgment creditor thereof, or, under section 626 (Shareholders's derivative action brought in the right of the corporation to procure a judgment in its favor), by a shareholder, voting trust certificate holder, or the owner of a beneficial interest in shares thereof.

(c) This section shall not affect any liability otherwise imposed by law upon any director or officer.

§ 721. Nonexclusivity of statutory provisions for indemnification of directors and officers.

The indemnification and advancement of expenses granted pursuant to, or provided by, this article shall not be deemed exclusive of any other rights to which a director or officer seeking indemnification or advancement of expenses may be entitled, whether contained in the certificate of incorporation or the by-laws or, when authorized by such certificate of incorporation or by-laws, (i) a resolution of shareholders, (ii) a resolution of directors, or (iii) an agreement providing for such indemnification, provided that no indemnification may be made to or on behalf of any director or officer if a judgment or other final adjudication adverse to the director or officer establishes that his acts were committed in bad faith or were the result of active and deliberate dishonesty and were material to the cause of action so adjudicated, or that he personally gained in fact a financial profit or other advantage to which he was not legally entitled. Nothing contained in this article shall affect any rights to indemnification to which corporate personnel other than directors and officers may be entitled by contract or otherwise under law.

§ 722. Authorization for indemnification of directors and officers.

(a) A corporation may indemnify any person made, or threatened to be made, a party to an action or proceeding (other than one by or in the right of the corporation to procure a judgment in its favor), whether civil or criminal, including an action by or in the right of any other corporation of any type or kind, domestic or foreign, or any partnership, joint venture, trust, employee benefit plan or other enterprise, which any director or officer of the corporation served in any capacity at the request of the corporation, by reason of the fact that he, his testator or intestate, was a director or officer of the corporation, or served such other corporation, partnership, joint venture, trust, employee benefit plan or other enterprise in any capacity, against judgments, fines, amounts paid in settlement and reasonable expenses, including attorneys' fees actually and necessarily incurred as a result of such action or proceeding, or any appeal therein, if such director or officer acted, in good faith, for a purpose which he reasonably believed to be in, or, in the case of service for any other corporation or any partnership, joint venture, trust, employee benefit plan or other enterprise, not opposed to, the best interests of the corporation and, in criminal actions or proceedings, in addition, had no reasonable cause to believe that his conduct was unlawful.

(b) The termination of any such civil or criminal action or proceeding by judgment, settlement, conviction or upon a plea of nolo contendere, or its equivalent, shall not in itself create a presumption that any such director or officer did not act, in good faith, for a purpose which he reasonably believed to be in, or, in the case of service for any other corporation or any partnership, joint venture, trust, employee benefit plan or other enterprise, not opposed to, the best interests of the corporation or that he had reasonable cause to believe that his conduct was unlawful.

(c) A corporation may indemnify any person made, or threatened to be made, a party to an action by or in the right of the corporation to procure a judgment in its favor by reason of the fact that he, his testator or intestate, is or was a director or officer of the corporation, or is or was serving at the request of the corporation as a director or officer of any other corporation of any type or kind, domestic or foreign, of any partnership, joint venture, trust, employee benefit plan or other enterprise, against amounts paid in settlement and reasonable expenses, including attorneys' fees, actually and necessarily incurred by him in connection with the defense or settlement of such action, or in connection with an appeal therein, if such director or officer acted, in good faith, for a purpose which he reasonably believed to be in, or, in the case of service for any other corporation or any partnership, joint venture, trust, employee benefit plan or other enterprise, not opposed to, the best interests of the corporation, except that no indemnification under this paragraph shall be made in respect of (1) a threatened action, or a pending action which is settled or otherwise disposed of, or (2) any claim, issue or matter as to which such person shall have been adjudged to be liable to the corporation, unless and only to the extent that the court in which the action was brought, or, if no action was brought, any court of competent jurisdiction, determines upon application that, in view of all the circumstances of the case, the person is fairly and reasonably entitled to indemnity for such portion of the settlement amount and expenses as the court deems proper.

(d) For the purpose of this section, a corporation shall be deemed to have requested a person to serve an employee benefit plan where the performance by such person of his duties to the corporation also imposes duties on, or otherwise involves services by, such person to the plan or participants or beneficiaries of the plan; excise taxes assessed on a person with respect to an employee benefit plan pursuant to applicable law shall be considered fines; and action taken or omitted by a person with respect to an employee benefit plan in the performance of such person's duties for a purpose reasonably believed by such person to be in the interest of the participants and beneficiaries of the plan shall be deemed to be for a purpose which is not opposed to the best interests of the corporation.

§ 723. Payment of indemnification other than by court award.

(a) A person who has been successful, on the merits or otherwise, in the defense of a civil or criminal action or proceeding of the character described in section 722 shall be entitled to indemnification as authorized in such section.

(b) Except as provided in paragraph (a), any indemnification under section 722 or otherwise permitted by section 721, unless ordered by a court under section 724 (Indemnification of directors and officers by a court), shall be made by the corporation, only if authorized in the specific case:

(1) By the board acting by a quorum consisting of directors who are not parties to such action or proceeding upon a finding that the director or officer has met the standard of conduct set forth in section 722 or established pursuant to section 721, as the case may be, or,

(2) If a quorum under subparagraph (1) is not obtainable or, even if obtainable, a quorum of disinterested directors so directs;

(A) By the board upon the opinion in writing of independent legal counsel that indemnification is proper in the circumstances because the applicable standard of conduct set forth in such sections has been met by such director or officer, or

(B) By the shareholders upon a finding that the director or officer has met the applicable standard of conduct set forth in such sections.

(c) Expenses incurred in defending a civil or criminal action or proceeding may be paid by the corporation in advance of the final disposition of such action or proceeding upon receipt of an undertaking by or on behalf of such director or officer to repay such amount as, and to the extent, required by paragraph (a) of section 725.

§ 724. Indemnification of directors and officers by a court.

(a) Notwithstanding the failure of a corporation to provide indemnification, and despite any contrary resolution of the board or of the shareholders in the specific case under section 723 (Payment of indemnification other than by court award), indemnification shall be awarded by a court to the extent authorized under section 722 (Authorization for indemnification of directors and officers), and paragraph (a) of section 723. Application therefor may be made, in every case, either:

(1) In the civil action or proceeding in which the expenses were incurred or other amounts were paid, or

(2) To the supreme court in a separate proceeding, in which case the application shall set forth the disposition of any previous application made to any court for the same or similar relief and also reasonable cause for the failure to make application for such relief in the action or proceeding in which the expenses were incurred or other amounts were paid.

(b) The application shall be made in such manner and form as may be required by the applicable rules of court or, in the absence thereof, by direction of a court to which it is made. Such application shall be upon notice to the corporation. The court may also direct that notice be given at the expense of the corporation to the shareholders and such other persons as it may designate in such manner as it may require.

(c) Where indemnification is sought by judicial action, the court may allow a person such reasonable expenses, including attorneys' fees, during the pendency of the litigation as are necessary in connection with his defense therein, if the court shall find that the defendant has by his pleadings or during the course of the litigation raised genuine issues of fact or law.

§ 725. Other provisions affecting indemnification of directors and officers.

(a) All expenses incurred in defending a civil or criminal action or proceeding which are advanced by the corporation under paragraph (c) of section 723 (Payment of indemnification other than by court award) or allowed by a court under paragraph (c) of section 724 (Indemnification of directors and officers by a court) shall be repaid in case the person receiving such advancement or allowance is ultimately found, under the procedure set forth in this article, not to be entitled to indemnification or, where indemnification is granted, to the extent the expenses so advanced by the corporation or allowed by the court exceed the indemnification to which he is entitled.

(b) No indemnification, advancement or allowance shall be made under this article in any circumstance where it appears:

(1) That the indemnification would be inconsistent with the law of the jurisdiction of incorporation of a foreign corporation which prohibits or otherwise limits such indemnification;

(2) That the indemnification would be inconsistent with a provision of the certificate of incorporation, a by-law, a resolution of the board or of the shareholders, an agreement or other proper corporate action, in effect at the time of the accrual of the alleged cause of action asserted in the threatened or pending action or proceeding in which the expenses were incurred or other amounts were paid, which prohibits or otherwise limits indemnification; or

(3) If there has been a settlement approved by the court, that the indemnification would be inconsistent with any condition with respect to indemnification expressly imposed by the court in approving the settlement.

(c) If any expenses or other amounts are paid by way of indemnification, otherwise than by court order or action by the shareholders, the corporation shall, not later than the next annual meeting of shareholders unless such meeting is held within three months from the date of such payment, and, in any event, within fifteen months from the date of such payment, mail to its shareholders of record at the time entitled to vote for the election of directors a statement specifying the persons paid, the amounts paid, and the nature and status at the time of such payment of the litigation or threatened litigation.

(d) If any action with respect to indemnification of directors and officers is taken by way of amendment of the by-laws, resolution of directors, or by agreement, then the corporation shall, not later than the next annual meeting of shareholders, unless such meeting is held within three months from the date of such action, and, in any event, within fifteen months from the date of such action, mail to its shareholders of record at the time entitled to vote for the election of directors a statement specifying the action taken.

(e) The provisions of this article relating to indemnification of directors and officers and insurance therefor shall apply to domestic corporations and foreign corporations doing business in this state, except as provided in section 1320 (Exemption from certain provisions).

§ 726. Insurance for indemnification of directors and officers.

(a) Subject to paragraph (b), a corporation shall have power to purchase and maintain insurance:

(1) To indemnify the corporation for any obligation which it incurs as a result of the indemnification of directors and officers under the provisions of this article, and

(2) To indemnify directors and officers in instances in which they may be indemnified by the corporation under the provisions of this article, and

(3) To indemnify directors and officers in instances in which they may not otherwise be indemnified by the corporation under the provisions of this article provided the contract of insurance covering such directors and officers provides, in a manner acceptable to the superintendent of insurance, for a retention amount and for co-insurance.

(b) No insurance under paragraph (a) may provide for any payment, other than cost of defense, to or on behalf of any director or officer:

(1) if a judgment or other final adjudication adverse to the insured director or officer establishes that his acts of active and deliberate dishonesty were material to the cause of action so adjudicated, or that he personally gained in fact a financial profit or other advantage to which he was not legally entitled, or

(2) in relation to any risk the insurance of which is prohibited under the insurance law of this state.

(c) Insurance under any or all subparagraphs of paragraph (a) may be included in a single contract or supplement thereto. Retrospective rated contracts are prohibited.

(d) The corporation shall, within the time and to the persons provided in paragraph (c) of section 725 (Other provisions affecting indemnification of directors or officers), mail a statement in respect of any insurance it has purchased or renewed under this section, specifying the insurance carrier, date of the contract, cost of the insurance, corporate positions insured, and a statement explaining all sums, not previously reported in a statement to shareholders, paid under any indemnification insurance contract.

(e) This section is the public policy of this state to spread the risk of corporate management, notwithstanding any other general or special law of this state or of any other jurisdiction including the federal government.

§ 801. Right to amend certificate of incorporation.

(a) A corporation may amend its certificate of incorporation, from time to time, in any and as many respects as may be desired, if such amendment contains only such provisions as might be lawfully contained in an original certificate of incorporation filed at the time of making such amendment.

(b) In particular, and without limitation upon such general power of amendment, a corporation may amend its certificate of incorporaion, from time to time, so as:

(1) To change its corporate name.

(2) To enlarge, limit or otherwise change its corporate purposes.

(3) To specify or change the location of the office of the corporation.

(4) To specify or change the post office address to which the secretary of state shall mail a copy of any process against the corporation served upon him.

(5) To make, revoke or change the designation of a registered agent, or to specify or change the address of its registered agent.

(6) To extend the duration of the corporation or, if the corporation ceased to exist because of the expiration of the duration specified in its certificate of incorporation, to revive its existence.

(7) To increase or decrease the aggregate number of shares, or shares of any class or series, with or without par value, which the corporation shall have authority to issue.

(8) To remove from authorized shares any class of shares, or any shares of any class, whether issued or unissued.

(9) To increase the par value of any authorized shares of any class with par value, whether issued or unissued.

(10) To reduce the par value of any authorized shares of any class with par value, whether issued or unissued.

(11) To change any authorized shares, with or without par value, whether issued or unissued, into a different number of shares of the same class or into the same or a different number of shares of any one or more classes or any series thereof, either with or without par value.

(12) To fix, change or abolish the designation of any authorized class or any series thereof or any of the relative rights, preferences and limitations of any shares of any authorized class or any series thereof, whether issued or unissued, including any provisions in respect of any undeclared dividends, whether or not cumulative or accrued, or the redemption of any shares, or any sinking fund for the redemption or purchase of any shares, or any preemptive right to acquire shares or other securities.

(13) As to the shares of any preferred class, then or theretofore authorized, which may be issued in series, to grant authority to the board or to change or revoke the authority of the board to establish and designate series and to fix the number of shares and the relative rights, preferences and limitation as between series.

(14) To strike out, change or add any provision, not inconsistent with this chapter or any other statute, relating to the business of the corporation, its affairs, its rights or powers, or the rights or powers of its shareholders, directors or officers, including any provision which under this chapter is required or permitted to be set forth in the by-laws, except that a certificate of amendment may not be filed wherein the duration of the corporation shall be reduced.

(c) A corporation created by special act may accomplish any or all amendments permitted in this article, in the manner and subject to the conditions provided in this article.

§ 802. Reduction of stated capital by amendment.

(a) A corporation may reduce its stated capital by an amendment of its certificate of incorporation under section 801 (Right to amend certificate of incorporation) which:

(1) Reduces the par value of any issued shares with par value.

(2) Changes issued shares under subparagraph (b) (11) of section 801 that results in a reduction of stated capital.

(3) Removes from authorized shares, shares that have been issued, reacquired and cancelled by the corporation.

(b) This section shall not prevent a corporation from reducing its stated capital in any other manner permitted by this chapter.

§ 803. Authorization of amendment or change.

(a) Amendment or change of the certificate of incorporation may be authorized by vote of the board followed by vote of the holders of a majority of all outstanding shares entitled to vote thereon at a meeting of shareholders.

(b) Alternatively, any one or more of the following changes may be authorized by or pursuant to authorization of the board:

(1) To specify or change the location of the corporation's office.

(2) To specify or change the post office address to which the secretary of state shall mail a copy of any process against the corporation served upon him.

(3) To make, revoke or change the designation of a registered agent, or to specify or change the address of its registered agent.

(c) This section shall not alter the vote required under any other section for the authorization of an amendment referred to therein, nor alter the authority of the board to authorize amendments under any other section.

§ 804. Class voting on amendment.

(a) Notwithstanding any provision in the certificate of incorporation, the holders of shares of a class or series shall be entitled to vote and to vote as a class upon the authorization of an amendment and, in addition to the authorization of the amendment by vote of the holders of a majority of all outstanding shares entitled to vote thereon, the amendment shall be authorized by vote of the holders of a majority of all outstanding shares of the class or series when a proposed amendment would:

(1) Exclude or limit their right to vote on any matter, except as such right may be limited by voting rights given to new shares then being authorized of any existing or new class or series.

(2) Change their shares under subparagraphs (b) (10), (11) or (12) of section 801 (Right to amend certificate of incorporation) or provide that their shares may be converted into shares of any other class or into shares of any other series of the same class, or alter the terms or conditions upon which their shares are convertible or change the shares issuable upon conversion of their shares, if such action would adversely affect such holders, or

(3) Subordinate their rights, by authorizing shares having preferences which would be in any respect superior to their rights.

(b) If any proposed amendment referred to in paragraph (a) would adversely affect or subordinate the rights of the holders of shares of only one or more series of any class, but not the entire class, then only the holders of each series whose rights would be adversely affected or subordinated shall be considered a separate class for the purpose of this section.

§ 805. Certificate of amendment, contents.

(a) To accomplish any amendment, a certificate of amendment, entitled "Certificate of amendment of the certificate of incorporation of . . . . (name of corporation) under section 805 of the Business Corporation Law," shall be signed, verified and delivered to the department of state. It shall set forth:

(1) The name of the corporation and, if it has been changed, the name under which it was formed.

(2) The date its certificate of incorporation was filed by the department of state.

(3) Each amendment effected thereby, setting forth the subject matter of each provision of the certificate of incorporation which is to be amended or eliminated and the full text of the provision or provisions, if any, which are to be substituted or added.

(4) If an amendment provides for a change of shares, the number, par value and class of issued shares changed, the number, par value and class of issued shares resulting from such change, the number, par value and class of unissued shares changed, the number, par value and class of unissued shares resulting from such change and the terms of each such change. If an amendment makes two or more such changes, a like statement shall be included in respect to each change.

(5) If any amendment reduces stated capital, then a statement of the manner in which the same is effected and the amounts from which and to which stated capital is reduced.

(6) The manner in which the amendment of the certificate of incorporation was authorized.

(b) Any number of amendments or changes may be included in one certificate under this section. Such certificate may also include any amendments or changes permitted by other sections and in that case the certificate shall set forth any additional statement required by any other section specifying the contents of a certificate to effect such amendment or change.

(c) In the case of a change of shares, the shares resulting from such change, shall upon the filing of the certificate of amendment, be deemed substituted for the shares changed, in accordance with the stated terms of change.

§ 805-A. Certificate of change; contents.

(a) Any one or more of the changes authorized by subdivision (b) of section 803 (Authorization of amendment or change) may be accomplished by filing a certificate which shall be entitled "Certificate of change of . . . . (name of corporation) under section 805-A of the Business Corporation Law" and shall be signed, verified and delivered to the department of state. It shall set forth:

(1) The name of the corporation, and if it has been changed, the name under which it was formed.

(2) The date its certificate of incorporation was filed by the department of state.

(3) Each change effected thereby.

(4) The manner in which the change was authorized.

(b) A certificate of change which changes only the post office address to which the secretary of state shall mail a copy of any process against a corporation served upon him or the address of the registered agent, provided such address being changed is the address of a person, partnership or other corporation whose address, as agent, is the address to be changed or who has been designated as registered agent for such corporation, may be signed, verified and delivered to the department of state by such agent. The certificate of change shall set forth the statements required under subparagraph (a) (1), (2) and (3) of this section; that a notice of the proposed change was mailed to the corporation by the party signing the certificate not less than thirty days prior to the date of delivery to the department and that such corporation has not objected thereto; and that the party signing the certificate is the agent of such corporation to whose address the secretary of state is required to mail copies of process or the registered agent, if such be the case. A certificate signed, verified and delivered under this paragraph shall not be deemed to effect a change of location of the office of the corporation in whose behalf such certificate is filed.

§ 806. Provisions as to certain proceedings.

(a) The department of state shall not file a certificate of amendment reviving the existence of a corporation unless the consent of the state tax commission to the revival is delivered to the department. If the name of the corporation being revived is not available under section 301 (Corporate name; general) for use by a corporation then being formed under this chapter, the certificate of amendment shall change the name to one which is available for such use.

(b) The following provisions shall apply to amendments and changes under this article, except under section 808 (Reorganization under act of congress):

(1) The stated capital in respect of any shares without par value resulting from a change of issued shares shall be the amount of stated capital in respect of the shares changed or, if such stated capital is reduced by the amendment, the reduced amount stated in the certificate of amendment. No corporation shall change issued shares into both shares with par value and shares without par value unless the stated capital in respect of the shares so changed or, if such stated capital is reduced by the amendment, the reduced amount of stated capital stated in the certificate of amendment, exceeds the par value of the shares with par value resulting from such change; and the amount of such excess shall be the stated capital in respect of the shares without par value resulting from such change.

(2) No corporation shall increase the aggregate par value of its issued shares with par value, unless, after giving effect to such increase, the stated capital is at least equal to the amount required by subparagraph (a) (12) of section 102 (Definitions).

(3) No reduction of stated capital shall be made by amendment unless after such reduction the stated capital exceeds the aggregate preferential amount payable upon involuntary liquidation upon all issued shares having preferential rights in assets plus the par value of all other issued shares with par value.

(4) Any changes that may be made in the relative rights, preferences and limitations of the authorized shares of any class by any certificate of amendment which does not eliminate such shares from authorized shares or change them into shares of another class, shall not for the purpose of any statute or rule of law effect an issue of a new class of shares.

(5) No amendment or change shall affect any existing cause of action in favor of or against the corporation, or any pending suit to which it shall be a party, or the existing rights of persons other than shareholders; and in the event the corporate name shall be changed, no suit brought by or against the corporation under its former name shall abate for that reason.

(6) A holder of any adversely affected shares who does not vote for or consent in writing to the taking of such action shall, subject to and by complying with the provision of section 623 (Procedure to enforce shareholder's right to receive payment for shares), have the right to dissent and to receive payment for such shares, if the certificate of amendment (A) alters or abolishes

any preferential right of such shares having preferences; or (B) creates, alters or abolishes any provision or right in respect of the redemption of such shares or any sinking fund for the redemption or purchase of such shares; or (C) alters or abolishes any preemptive right of such holder to acquire shares or other securities; or (D) excludes or limits the right of such holder to vote on any matter, except as such right may be limited by the voting rights given to new shares then being authorized of any existing or new class.

§ 807. **Restated certificate of incorporation.**

(a) A corporation, when authorized by the board, may restate in a single certificate the text of its certificate of incorporation without making any amendment or change thereby, except that it may include any one or more of the amendments or changes which may be authorized by the board without a vote of shareholders under this chapter. Alternatively, a corporation may restate in a single certificate the text of its certificate of incorporation as amended thereby to effect any one or more of the amendments or changes authorized by this chapter, when authorized by the required vote of the holders of shares entitled to vote thereon.

(b) A restated certificate of incorporation entitled "Restated certificate of incorporation of . . . . (name of corporation) under section 807 of the Business Corporation Law", shall be signed, verified and delivered to the department of state. It shall set forth:

(1) The name of the corporation and, if it has been changed, the name under which it was formed.

(2) The date its certificate of incorporation was filed by the department of state.

(3) If the restated certificate restates the text of the certificate of incorporation without making any amendment or change, then a statement that the text of the certificate of incorporation is thereby restated without amendment or change to read as therein set forth in full.

(4) If the restated certificate restates the text of the certificate of incorporation as amended or changed thereby, then a statement that the certificate of incorporation is amended or changed to effect one or more of the amendments or changes authorized by this chapter, specifying each such amendment or change and that the text of the certificate of incorporation is thereby restated as amended or changed to read as therein set forth in full.

(5) If an amendment, effected by the restated certificate, provides for a change of issued shares, the number and kind of shares changed, the number and kind of shares resulting from such change and the terms of change. If any amendment makes two or more such changes, a like statement shall be included in respect to each such change.

(6) If the restated certificate contains an amendment which effects a reduction of stated capital, then a statement of the manner in which the same is effected and the amounts from which and to which stated capital is reduced.

(7) The manner in which the restatement of the certificate of incorporation was authorized.

(c) A restated certificate need not include statements as to the incorporator or incorporators, the original subscribers for shares or the first directors.

(d) Any amendment or change under this section shall be subject to any other section, not inconsistent with this section, which would be applicable if a separate certificate were filed to effect such amendment or change.

(e) Notwithstanding that the corporation would be required by any statute to secure from any state official, department, board, agency or other body, any consent or approval to the filing of its certificate of incorporation or a certificate of amendment, such consent or approval shall not be required with respect to the restated certificate if such certificate makes no amendment and if any previously required consent or approval had been secured.

(f) Upon filing by the department, the original certificate of incorporation shall be superseded and the restated certificate of incorporation, including any amendments and changes made thereby, shall be the certificate of incorporation of the corporation.

§ 808. Reorganization under act of congress.

(a) Whenever a plan of reorganization of a corporation has been confirmed by a decree or order of a court in proceedings under any applicable act of congress relating to reorganization of corporations, the corporation shall have authority, without action of its shareholders or board, to put into effect and carry out the plan and decree and orders of the court relative thereto, and take any proceeding and any action for which provision is made in any statute governing the corporation or for which provision is or might be made in its certificate of incorporation or by-laws and which is provided for in such plan or directed by any such decree or order.

(b) Such authority may be exercised, and such proceedings and actions may be taken, as may be directed by any such decree or order, by the trustee or trustees of such corporation appointed in the reorganization proceedings, or if none is acting, by any person or persons designated or appointed for the purpose by any such decree or order, with like effects as if exercised and taken by unanimous action of the board and shareholders of the corporation.

(c) Any certificate, required or permitted by law to be filed or recorded to accomplish any corporate purpose, shall be signed, and verified or acknowledged, under any such decree or order, by such trustee or trustees or the person or persons referred to in paragraph (b), and shall certify that provision for such certificate is contained in the plan of reorganization or in a decree or order of the court relative thereto, and that the plan has been confirmed, as provided in an applicable act of congress, specified in the certificate, with the title and venue of the proceeding and the date when the decree or order confirming the plan was made, and such certificate shall be delivered to the department of state.

(d) A shareholder of any such corporation shall have no right to receive payment for his shares and only such rights, if any, as are provided in the plan of reorganization.

(e) Notwithstanding section 504 (Consideration and payment for shares), such corporation may, after the confirmation of such plan, issue its shares, bonds and other securities for the consideration specified in the plan of reorganization and may issue warrants or other optional rights for the purchase of shares upon such terms and conditions as may be set forth in such plan.

(f) If after the filing of any such certificate by the department of state the decree or order of confirmation of the plan of reorganization is reversed or vacated or such plan is modified, such other or further certificates shall be executed and delivered to the department of state as may be required to conform to the plan of reorganization as finally confirmed or to the decree or order as finally made.

(g) Except as otherwise provided in this section, no certificate filed by the department of state hereunder shall confer on any corporation any powers other than those permitted to be conferred on a corporation formed under this chapter.

(h) If, in any proceeding under any applicable act of congress relating to reorganization of corporations, a decree or order provides for the formation of a new domestic corporation or for the authorization of a new foreign corporation to do business in this state under a name the same as or similar to that of the corporation being reorganized, the certificate of incorporation of the new domestic corporation or the application of the new foreign corporation shall set forth that it is being delivered pursuant to such decree or order and be endorsed with the consent of the court having jurisdiction of the proceeding. After such certificate of incorporation or application has been filed, the corporation being reorganized shall not continue the use of its name except in connection with the reorganization proceeding and as may be necessary to adjust and wind up its affairs, and thirty days after such filing, the reorganized domestic corporation shall be automatically dissolved or the authority of the reorganized foreign corporation to transact business in this state shall cease. To the extent that the adjustment and winding up of the affairs of such dissolved corporation is not accomplished as a part of the proceeding or prescribed by the decree or order of such court, it shall proceed in accordance with the provisions of Article 10 (Non-judicial dissolution).

(i) This section shall not relieve any corporation from securing from any state official, department, board, agency or other body, any consent or approval required by any statute.

§ 901. Power of merger or consolidation.

(a) Two or more domestic corporations may, as provided in this chapter:

(1) Merge into a single corporation which shall be one of the constituent corporations; or

(2) Consolidate into a single corporation which shall be a new corporation to be formed pursuant to the consolidation.

(b) Whenever used in this article:

(1) "Merger" means a procedure of the character described in subparagraph (a) (1).

(2) "Consolidation" means a procedure of the character described in subparagraph (a) (2).

(3) "Constituent corporation" means an existing corporation that is participating in the merger or consolidation with one or more other corporations.

(4) "Suriviving corporation" means the constituent corporation into which one or more other constituent corporations are merged.

(5) "Consolidated corporation" means the new corporation into which two or more constituent corporations are consolidated.

§ 902. Plan of merger or consolidation.

(a) The board of each corporation proposing to participate in a merger or consolidation under section 901 (Power of merger or consolidation) shall adopt a plan of merger or consolidation, setting forth:

(1) The name of each constituent corporation and, if the name of any of them has been changed, the name under which it was formed; and the name of the surviving corporation, or the name, or the method of determining it, of the consolidated corporation.

(2) As to each constituent corporation, the designation and number of outstanding shares of each class and series, specifying the classes and series entitled to vote and further specifying each class and series, if any, entitled to vote as a class; and if the number of any such shares is subject to change prior to the effective date of the merger or consolidation, the manner in which such change may occur.

(3) The terms and conditions of the proposed merger or consolidation, including the manner and basis of converting the shares of each constituent corporation into shares, bonds or other securities of the surviving or consolidated corporation, or the cash or other consideration to be paid or delivered in exchange for shares of each constituent corporation, or a combination thereof.

(4) In case of merger, a statement of any amendments or changes in the certificate of incorporation of the surviving corporation to be effected by such merger; in case of consolidation, all statements required to be included in a certificate of incorporation for a corporation formed under this chapter, except statements as to facts not available at the time the plan of consolidation is adopted by the board.

(5) Such other provisions with respect to the proposed merger or consolidation as the board considers necessary or desirable.

§ 903. Authorization by shareholders.

(a) The board of each constituent corporation, upon adopting such plan of merger or consolidation, shall submit such plan to a vote of shareholders in accordance with the following:

(1) Notice of meeting shall be given to each shareholder of record, as of the record date fixed pursuant to section 604 (Fixing record date), whether or not entitled to vote. A copy of the plan of merger or consolidation or an outline of the material features of the plan shall accompany such notice.

(2) The plan of merger or consolidation shall be adopted at a meeting of shareholders by vote of the holders of two-thirds of all outstanding shares entitled to vote thereon. Notwithstanding any provision in the certificate of incorporation, the holders of shares of a class or series shall be entitled to vote and to vote as a class if the plan of merger or consolidation contains any provision which, if contained in an amendment to the certificate of incorporation, would entitle the holders of shares of such class or series to vote and to vote as a class thereon. In such case, in addition to the authorization of the merger or consolidation by vote of the holders of two-thirds of all outstanding shares entitled to vote thereon, the merger or consolidation shall be authorized by vote of the holders of a majority of all outstanding shares of each such class or series.

(b) Notwithstanding shareholder authorization and at any time prior to the filing of the certificate of merger or consolidation, the plan of merger or consolidation may be abandoned pursuant to a provision for such abandonment, if any, contained in the plan of merger or consolidation.

§ 904. Certificate of merger or consolidation; contents.

(a) After adoption of the plan of merger or consolidation by the board and shareholders of each constituent corporation, unless the merger or consolidation is abandoned in accordance with paragraph (b) of section 903 (Authorization by shareholders), a certificate of merger or consolidation, entitled "Certificate of merger (or consolidation) of .... and .... into .... (names of corporations) under section 904 of the Business Corporation Law", shall be signed and verified on behalf of each constituent corporation and delivered to the department of state. It shall set forth:

(1) The statements required by subparagraphs (a) (1), (2) and (4) of section 902 (Plan of merger or consolidation).

(2) The effective date of the merger or consolidation if other than the date of filing of the certificate of merger or consolidation by the department of state.

(3) In the case of consolidation, any statement required to be included in a certificate of incorporation for a corporation formed under this chapter but which was omitted under subparagraph (a) (4) of section 902.

(4) The date when the certificate of incorporation of each constituent corporation was filed by the department of state.

(5) The manner in which the merger or consolidation was authorized with respect to each constituent corporation.

(b) The surviving or consolidated corporation shall thereafter cause a copy of such certificate, certified by the department of state, to be filed in the office of the clerk of each county in which the office of a constituent corporation, other than the surviving corporation, is located, and in the office of the official who is the recording officer of each county in this state in which real property of a constituent corporation, other than the surviving corporation, is situated.

§ 905. Merger of subsidiary corporation.

(a) Any domestic corporation owning at least ninety percent of the outstanding shares of each class of another domestic corporation or corporations may merge such other corporation or corporations into itself without the authorization of the shareholders of any such corporations. Its board shall adopt a plan of merger, setting forth:

(1) The name of each subsidiary corporation to be merged and the name of the surviving corporation, and if the name of any of them has been changed, the name under which it was formed.

(2) The designation and number of outstanding shares of each class of each subsidiary corporation to be merged and the number of such shares of each class owned by the surviving corporation; and if the number of any such shares is subject to change prior to the effective date of the merger, the manner in which such change may occur.

(3) The terms and conditions of the proposed merger, including the manner and basis of converting the shares of each subsidiary corporation to be merged not owned by the surviving corporation into shares, bonds or other securities of the surviving corporation, or the cash or other consideration to be paid or delivered in exchange for shares of each such subsidiary corporation, or a combination thereof.

(4) Such other provisions with respect to the proposed merger as the board considers necessary or desirable.

(b) A copy of such plan of merger or an outline of the material features thereof shall be given, personally or by mail, to all holders of shares of each subsidiary corporation to be merged not owned by the surviving corporation, unless the giving of such copy or outline has been waived by such holders.

(c) A certificate of merger, entitled "Certificate of merger of . . . . into . . . . (names of corporations) under section 905 of the Business Corporation Law", shall be signed, verified and delivered to the department of state by the surviving corporation. If the surviving corporation does not own all shares of each subsidiary corporation to be merged, such certificate shall be delivered not less than thirty days after the giving of a copy or outline of the material features of the plan of merger to shareholders of each such subsidiary corporation, or at any time after the waiving thereof by the holders of all of the outstanding shares of each such subsidiary corporation not owned by the surviving corporation. The certificate shall set forth:

(1) The statements required by subparagraphs (a) (1) and (2) of this section.

(2) The effective date of the merger if other than the date of filing of the certificate of merger by the department of state.

(3) The date when the certificate of incorporation of each constituent corporation was filed by the department of state.

(4) A statement that the plan of merger was adopted by the board of directors of the surviving corporation.

(5) If the surviving corporation does not own all the shares of each subsidiary corporation to be merged, either the date of the giving to holders of shares of each such subsidiary corporation not owned by the surviving corporation of a copy of the plan of merger or an outline of the material features thereof, or a statement that the giving of such copy or outline has been waived, if such is the case.

(d) The surviving corporation shall thereafter cause a copy of such certificate, certified by the department of state, to be filed in the office of the clerk of each county in which the office of a constituent corporaton, other than the surviving corporaton, is located, and in the office of the official who is the recording officer of each county in this state in which real property of a constituent corporation, other than the surviving corporation, is situated.

(e) The right of merger granted by this section to certain corporations shall not preclude the exercise by such corporations of any other right of merger or consolidation under this article.

§ 906. Effect of merger or consolidation.

(a) Upon the filing of the certificate of merger or consolidation by the department of state or on such date subsequent thereto, not to exceed thirty days, as shall be set forth in such certificate, the merger or consolidation shall be effected.

(b) When such merger or consolidation has been effected:

(1) Such surviving or consolidated corporation shall thereafter, consistently with its certificate of incorporation as altered or established by the merger or consolidation, possess all the rights, privileges, immunities, powers and purposes of each of the constituent corporations.

(2) All the property, real and personal, including subscriptions to shares, causes of action and every other asset of each of the constituent corporations, shall vest in such surviving or consolidated corporation without further act or deed.

(3) The surviving or consolidated corporation shall assume and be liable for all the liabilities, obligations and penalties of each of the constituent corporations. No liability or obligation due or to become due, claim or demand for any cause existing against any such corporation, or any shareholder, officer or director thereof, shall be released or impaired by such merger or consolidation. No action or proceeding, whether civil or criminal, then pending by or against any such constituent corporation, or any shareholder, officer or director thereof, shall abate or be discontinued by such merger or consolidation, but may be enforced, prosecuted, settled or compromised as if such merger or consolidation had not occurred, or such surviving or consolidated corporation may be substituted in such action or special proceeding in place of any constituent corporation.

(4) In the case of a merger, the certificate of incorporation of the surviving corporation shall be automatically amended to the extent, if any, that changes in its certificate of incorporation are set forth in the plan of merger; and, in the case of a consolidation, the statements set forth in the certificate of consolidation and which are required or permitted to be set forth in a certificate of incorporation of a corporation formed under this chapter shall be its certificate of incorporation.

§ 907. Merger or consolidation of domestic and foreign corporations.

(a) One or more foreign corporations and one or more domestic corporations may be merged or consolidated into a corporation of this state or of another jurisdiction, if such merger or consolidation is permitted by the laws of the jurisdiction under which each such foreign corporation is incorporated. With respect to such merger or consolidation, any reference in paragraph (b) of section 901 (Power of merger or consolidation) to a corporation shall, unless the context otherwise requires, include both domestic and foreign corporations.

(b) With respect to procedure, including the requirement of shareholder authorization, each domestic corporation shall comply with the provisions of this chapter relating to merger or consolidation of domestic corporations, and each foreign corporation shall comply with the applicable provisions of the law of the jurisdiction under which it is incorporated.

(c) The procedure for the merger of a subsidiary corporation or corporations under section 905 (Merger or subsidiary corporation) shall be available where either a subsidiary corporation or the corporation owning at least ninety percent of the outstanding shares of each class of a subsidiary is a foreign corporation, and such merger is permitted by the laws of the jurisdiction under which such foreign corporation is incorporated.

(d) If the surviving or consolidated corporation is, or is to be, a domestic corporation, a certificate of merger or consolidation shall be signed, verified and delivered to the department of state as provided in section 904 (Certificate of merger or consolidation; contents) or 905 (Merger of subsidiary corporation), as the case may be. In addition to the matters specified in such sections, the certificate shall set forth as to each constituent foreign corporation the jurisdiction and date of its incorporation and the date when its application for authority to do business in this state was filed by the department of state, and its fictitious name used in this state pursuant to article thirteen of this chapter, if applicable, or, if no such application has been filed, a statement to such effect.

(e) If the surviving or consolidated corporation is, or is to be, formed under the law of any jurisdiction other than this state:

(1) It shall comply with the provisions of this chapter relating to foreign corporations if it is to do business in this state.

(2) It shall deliver to the department of state a certificate, entitled "Certificate of merger (or consolidation) of . . . . and . . . . into . . . . (names of corporations) under section 907 of the Business Corporation Law", which shall be signed and verified on behalf of the surviving corporation in the case of a merger of a subsidiary corporation or corporations under paragraph (c), and in every other case on behalf of each constituent domestic and foreign corporation. It shall set forth:

(A) If the procedure for the merger or consolidation of a constituent domestic corporation was effected in compliance with sections 902 (Plan of merger or consolidation) and 903 (Authorization by shareholders), the following:

(i) The statements required by subparagraphs (a) (1) and (2) of section 902.

(ii) The effective date of the merger or consolidation if other than the date of filing of the certificate of merger or consolidation by the department of state.

(iii) The manner in which the merger or consolidation was authorized with respect to each constituent domestic corporation and that the merger or consolidation is permitted by the laws of the jurisdiction of each constituent foreign corporation and is in compliance therewith.

(B) If the procedure for the merger of a subsidiary domestic corporation was effected in compliance with section 905, the following:

(i) The statements required by subparagraphs (a) (1) and (2) of section 905.

(ii) The effective date of the merger if other than the date of filing of the certificate of merger by the department of state.

(iii) If the surviving foreign corporation does not own all the shares of a subsidiary domestic corporation being merged, either the date of the giving to holders of shares of each subsidiary domestic corporation not owned by the surviving foreign corporation of a copy of the plan of merger or an outline of the material features thereof, or a statement that the giving of such copy or outline has been wavied, if such is the case.

(iv) That the merger is permitted by the laws of the jurisdiction of each constituent foreign corporation and is in compliance therewith.

(C) The jurisdiction and date of incorporation of the surviving or consolidated foreign corporation, the date when its application for authority to do business in this state was filed by the department of state, and its fictitious name used in this state pursuant to article thirteen of this chapter, if applicable, or, if no such application has been filed, a statement to such effect and that it is not to do business in this state until an application for such authority shall have been filed by such department.

(D) The date when the certificate of incorporation of each constituent domestic corporation was filed by the department of state and the jurisdiction and date of incorporation of each constituent foreign corporation, other than the surviving or consolidated foreign corporation, and, in the case of such corporation authorized to do business in this state, the date when its application for authority was filed by the department of state.

(E) An agreement that the surviving or consolidated foreign corporation may be served with process in this state in any action or special proceeding for the enforcement of any liability or obligation of any domestic corporation or of any foreign corporation, previously amenable to suit in this state, which is a constituent corporation in such merger or consolidation, and for the enforcement, as provided in this chapter, of the right of shareholders of any constituent domestic corporation to receive payment for their shares against the surviving or consolidated corporation.

(F) An agreement that, subject to the provisions of section 623 (Procedure to enforce shareholder's right to receive payment for shares), the surviving or consolidated foreign corporation will promptly pay to the shareholders of each constituent domestic corporation the amount, if any, to which they shall be entitled under the provisions of this chapter relating to the right of shareholders to receive payment for their shares.

(G) A designation of the secretary of state as its agent upon whom process against it may be served in the manner set forth in paragraph (b) of section 306 (Service of process), in any action or special proceeding and a post office address, within or without this state, to which the secretary of state shall mail a copy of any process against it served upon him. Such post office address shall supersede any prior address designated as the address to which process shall be mailed.

(f) The department of state shall not file a certificate delivered to it under subparagraph (e) (2) unless the consent of the state tax commission to the merger or consolidation is attached thereto.

(g) Upon the filing of the certificate of merger or consolidation by the department of state or on such date subsequent thereto, not to exceed ninety days, as shall be set forth in such certificate, the merger or consolidation shall be effected.

(h) The surviving or consolidated domestic or foreign corporation shall thereafter cause a copy of such certificate, certified by the department of state, to be filed in the office of the clerk of each county in which the office of a constituent corporation, other than the surviving corporation, is located, and in the office of the official who is the recording officer of each county in this state in which real property of a constituent corporation, other than the surviving corporation, is situated.

(i) If the surviving or consolidated corporation is, or is to be, formed under the law of this state, the effect of such merger or consolidation shall be the same as in the case of the merger or consolidation of domestic corporations under section 906 (Effect of merger or consolidation). If the surviving or consolidated corporation is, or is to be, incorporated under the law of any jurisdiction other than this state, the effect of such merger or consolidation shall be the same as in the case of the merger or consolidation of domestic corporations, except in so far as the law of such other jurisdiction provides otherwise.

§ 908. Guarantee authorized by shareholders.

A guarantee may be given by a corporation, although not in furtherance of its corporate purposes, when authorized at a meeting of shareholders by vote of the holders of two-thirds of all outstanding shares entitled to vote thereon. If authorized by a like vote, such guarantee may be secured by a mortgage or pledge of, or the creation of a security interest in, all or any part of the corporate property, or any interest therein, wherever situated.

§ 909. Sale, lease, exchange or other disposition of assets.

(a) A sale, lease, exchange or other disposition of all or substantially all the assets of a corporation, if not made in the usual or regular course of the business actually conducted by such corporation, shall be authorized only in accordance with the following procedure:

(1) The board shall authorize the proposed sale, lease, exchange or other disposition and direct its submission to a vote of shareholders.

(2) Notice of meeting shall be given to each shareholder of record, whether or not entitled to vote.

(3) The shareholders shall approve such sale, lease, exchange or other disposition and may fix, or may authorize the board to fix, any of the terms and conditions thereof and the consideration to be received by the corporation therefor, which may consist in whole or in part of cash or other property, real or personal, including shares, bonds or other securities of any other domestic or foreign corporation or corporations, by vote at a meeting of shareholders of the holders of two-thirds of all outstanding shares entitled to vote thereon.

(b) A recital in a deed, lease or other instrument of conveyance executed by a corporation to the effect that the property described therein does not constitute all or substantially all of the assets of the corporation, or that the disposition of the property affected by said instrument was made in the usual or regular course of business of the corporation, or that the shareholders have duly authorized such disposition, shall be presumptive evidence of the fact so recited.

(c) An action to set aside a deed, lease or other instrument of conveyance executed by a corporation affecting real property or real and personal property may not be maintained for failure to comply with the requirements of paragraph (a) unless the action is commenced and a notice of pendency of action is filed within one year after such conveyance, lease or other instrument is recorded or within six months after this subdivision takes effect, whichever date occurs later.

(d) Whenever a transaction of the character described in paragraph (a) involves a sale, lease, exchange or other disposition of all or substantially all the assets of the corporation, including its name, to a new corporation formed under the same name as the existing corporation, upon the expiration of thirty days from the filing of the certificate of incorporation of the new corporation, with the consent of the state tax commission attached, the existing corporation shall be automatically dissolved, unless, before the end of such thirty-day period, such corporation has changed its name. The adjustment and winding up of the affairs of such dissolved corporation shall proceed in accordance with the provisions of article 10 (Non-judicial dissolution).

(e) The certificate of incorporation of a corporation formed under the authority of paragraph (d) shall set forth the name of the existing corporation, the date when its certificate of incorporation was filed by the department of state, and that the shareholders of such corporation have authorized the sale, lease, exchange or other disposition of all or substantially all the assets of such corporation, including its name, to the new corporation to be formed under the same name as the existing corporation.

(f) Notwithstanding shareholder approval, the board may abandon the proposed sale, lease, exchange or other disposition without further action by the shareholders, subject to the rights, if any, of third parties under any contract relating thereto.

§ 910. Right of shareholder to receive payment for shares upon merger, consolidation or sale, lease, exchange or other disposition of assets.

(a) A shareholder of a domestic corporation shall, subject to and by complying with section 623 (Procedure to enforce shareholder's right to receive payment for shares), have the right to receive payment of the fair value of his shares and the other rights and benefits provided by such section, in the following cases:

(1) Any shareholder entitled to vote who does not assent to the taking of an action specified in subparagraphs (A) and (B).

(A) Any plan of merger or consolidation to which the corporation is a party, except that the right to receive payment of the fair value of his shares shall not be available:

(i) To a shareholder of the surviving corporation in a merger authorized by section 905 (Merger of subsidiary corporation), or paragraph (c) of section 907 (Merger or consolidation of domestic and foreign corporations); and

(ii) To a shareholder of the surviving corporation in a merger authorized by this article, other than a merger specified in subparagraph (i), unless such merger effects one or more of the changes specified in subparagraph (b) (6) of section 806 (Provisions as to certain proceedings) in the rights of the shares held by such shareholder.

(B) Any sale, lease, exchange or other disposition of all or substantially all of the assets of a corporation which requires shareholder approval under section 909 (Sale, lease, exchange or other disposition of assets) other than a transaction wholly for cash where the shareholders' approval thereof is conditioned upon the dissolution of the corporation and the distribution of substantially all of its net assets to the shareholders in accordance with their respective interests within one year after the date of such transaction.

(C) Any share exchange authorized by section 913 in which the corporation is participating as a subject corporation; except that the right to receive payment of the fair value of his shares shall not be available to a shareholder whose shares have not been acquired in the exchange.

(2) Any shareholder of the subsidiary corporation in a merger authorized by section 905 or paragraph (c) of section 907, or in a share exchange authorized by paragraph (g) of section 913, who files with the corporation a written notice of election to dissent as provided in paragraph (c) of section 623.

§ 911. Mortgage or pledge of, or security interest in, corporate property.

The board may authorize any mortgage or pledge of, or the creation of a security interest in, all or any part of the corporate property, or any interest therein, wherever situated. Unless the certificate of incorporation provides otherwise, no vote or consent of shareholders shall be required to approve such action by the board.

§ 912. Requirements relating to certain business combinations.

(a) For the purposes of this section:

(1) "Affiliate" means a person that directly, or indirectly through one or more intermediaries, controls, or is controlled by, or is under common control with, a specified person.

(2) "Announcement date", when used in reference to any business combination, means the date of the first public announcement of the final, definitive proposal for such business combination.

(3) "Associate", when used to indicate a relationship with any person, means (A) any corporation or organization of which such person is an officer or partner or is, directly or indirectly, the beneficial owner of ten percent or more of any class of voting stock, (B) any trust or other estate in which such person has a substantial beneficial interest or as to which such person serves as trustee or in a similar fiduciary capacity, and (C) any relative or spouse of such person, or any relative of such spouse, who has the same home as such person.

(4) "Beneficial owner", when used with respect to any stock, means a person:

(A) that, individually or with or through any of its affiliates or associates, beneficially owns such stock, directly or indirectly; or

(B) that, individually or with or through any of its affiliates or associates, has (i) the right to acquire such stock (whether such right is exercisable immediately or only after the passage of time), pursuant to any agreement, arrangement or understanding (whether or not in writing), or upon the exercise of conversion rights, exchange rights, warrants or options, or otherwise; provided, however, that a person shall not be deemed the beneficial owner of stock tendered pursuant to a tender or exchange offer made by such person or any of such person's affiliates or associates until such tendered stock is accepted for purchase or exchange; or (ii) the right to vote such stock pursuant to any agreement, arrangement or understanding (whether or not in writing); provided, however, that a person shall not be deemed the beneficial owner of any stock under this item if the agreement, arrangement or understanding to vote such stock (X) arises solely from a revocable proxy or consent given in response to a proxy or consent solicitation made in accordance with the applicable rules and regulations under the Exchange Act and (Y) is not then reportable on a Schedule 13D under the Exchange Act (or any comparable or successor report); or

(C) that has any agreement, arrangement or understanding (whether or not in writing), for the purpose of acquiring, holding, voting (except voting pursuant to a revocable proxy or consent as described in item (ii) of clause (B) of this subparagraph), or disposing of such stock with any other person that beneficially owns, or whose affiliates or associates beneficially own, directly or indirectly, such stock.

(5) "Business combination", when used in reference to any resident domestic corporation and any interested shareholder of such resident domestic corporation, means:

(A) any merger or consolidation of such resident domestic corporation or any subsidiary of such resident domestic corporation with (i) such interested shareholder or (ii) any other corporation (whether or not itself an interested shareholder of such resident domestic corporation) which is, or after such merger or consolidation would be, an affiliate or associate of such interested shareholder;

(B) any sale, lease, exchange, mortgage, pledge, transfer or other disposition (in one transaction or a series of transactions) to or with such interested shareholder or any affiliate or associate of such interested shareholder of assets of such resident domestic corporation or any subsidiary of such resident domestic corporation (i) having an aggregate market value equal to ten percent or more of the aggregate market value of all the assets, determined on a consolidated basis, of such resident domestic corporation, (ii) having an aggregate market value equal to ten percent or more of the aggregate market value of all the outstanding stock of such resident domestic corporation, or (iii) representing ten percent or more of the earning power or net income, determined on a consolidated basis, of such resident domestic corporation;

(C) the issuance or transfer by such resident domestic corporation or any subsidiary of such resident domestic corporation (in one transaction or a series of transactions) of any stock of such resident domestic corporation or any subsidiary of such resident domestic corporation which has an aggregate market value equal to five percent or more of the aggregate market value of all the outstanding stock of such resident domestic corporation to such interested shareholder or any affiliate or associate of such interested shareholder except pursuant to the exercise of warrants or rights to purchase stock offered, or a dividend or distribution paid or made, pro rata to all shareholders of such resident domestic corporation;

(D) the adoption of any plan or proposal for the liquidation or dissolution of such resident domestic corporation proposed by, or pursuant to any agreement, arrangement or understanding (whether or not in writing) with, such interested shareholder or any affiliate or associate of such interested shareholder;

(E) any reclassification of securities (including, without limitation, any stock split, stock dividend, or other distribution of stock in respect of stock, or any reverse stock split), or recapitalization of such resident domestic corporation, or any merger or consolidation of such resident domestic corporation with any subsidiary of such resident domestic corporation, or any other transaction (whether or not with or into or otherwise involving such interested shareholder), proposed by, or pursuant to any agreement, arrangement or understanding (whether or not in writing) with, such interested shareholder or any affiliate or associate of such interested shareholder, which has the effect, directly or indirectly, of increasing the proportionate share of the outstanding shares of any class or series of voting stock or securities convertible into voting stock of such resident domestic corporation or any subsidiary of such resident domestic corporation which is directly or indirectly owned by such interested shareholder or any affiliate or associate of such interested shareholder, except as a result of immaterial changes due to fractional share adjustments; or

(F) any receipt by such interested shareholder or any affiliate or associate of such interested shareholder of the benefit, directly or indirectly (except proportionately as a shareholder of such resident domestic corporation) of any loans, advances, guarantees, pledges or other financial assistance or any tax credits or other tax advantages provided by or through such resident domestic corporation.

(6) "Common stock" means any stock other than preferred stock.

(7) "Consummation date", with respect to any business combination, means the date of consummation of such business combination, or, in the case of a business combination as to which a shareholder vote is taken, the later of the business day prior to the vote of twenty days prior to the date of consummation of such business combination.

(8) "Control", including the terms "controlling", "controlled by" and "under common control with", means the possession, directly or indirectly, of the power to direct or cause the direction of the management and policies of a person, whether through the ownership of voting stock, by contract, or otherwise. A person's beneficial ownership of ten percent or more of a corporation's outstanding voting stock shall create a presumption that such person has control of usch corporation. Notwithstanding the foregoing, a person shall not be deemed to have control of a corporation if such person holds voting stock, in good faith and not for the purpose of circumventing this section, as an agent, bank, broker, nominee, custodian or trustee for one or more beneficial owners who do not individually or as a group have control of such corporation.

(9) "Exchange Act" means the Act of Congress known as the Securities Exchange Act of 1934, as the same has been or hereafter may be amended from time to time.

(10) "Interested shareholder", when used in reference to any resident domestic corporation, means any person (other than such resident domestic corporation or any subsidiary of such resident domestic corporation) that

(A) (i) is the beneficial owner, directly or indirectly, of twenty percent or more of the outstanding voting stock of such resident domestic corporation; or

(ii) is an affiliate or associate of such resident domestic corporation and at any time within the five-year period immediatley prior to the date in question was the beneficial owner, directly or indirectly, of twenty percent or more of the then outstanding voting stock of such resident domestic corporation; provided that

(B) for the purpose of determining whether a person is an interested shareholder, the number of shares of voting stock of such resident domestic corporation deemed to be outstanding shall include shares deemed to be beneficially owned by the person through application of subparagraph four of this paragraph but shall not include any other unissued shares of voting stock of such resident domestic corporation which may be issuable pursuant to any agreement, arrangement or understanding, or upon exercise of conversion rights, warrants or options, or otherwise.

(11) "Market value", when used in reference to stock or property of any resident domestic corporation, means:

(A) in the case of stock, the highest closing sale price during the thirty-day period immediately preceding the date in question of a share of such stock on the composite tape for New York stock exchange-listed stocks, or, if such stock is not quoted on such composite tape or if such stock is not listed on such exchange, on the principal United States securities exchange registered under the Exchange Act on which such stock is listed, or, if such stock is not listed on any such exchange, the highest closing bid quotation with respect to a share of such stock during the thirty-day period preceding the date in question on the National Association of Securities Dealers, Inc. Automated Quotations System or any system then in use, or if no such quotations are available, the fair market value on the date in question of a share of such stock as determined by the board of directors of such resident domestic corporation in good faith; and

(B) in the case of property other than cash or stock, the fair market value of such property on the date in question as determined by the board of directors of such resident domestic corporation in good faith.

(12) "Preferred stock" means any class or series of stock of a resident domestic corporation which under the by-laws or certificate of incorporation of such resident domestic corporation is entitled to receive payment of dividends prior to any payment of dividends on some other class or series of stock, or is entitled in the event of any voluntary liquidation, dissolution or winding up of the resident domestic corporation to receive payment or distribution of a preferential amount before any payments or distributions are received by some other class or series of stock.

(13) "Resident domestic corporation" means an issuer of voting stock which:

(A) is organized under the laws of this state and has its principal executive offices and significant business operations located in this state; and

(B) has at least ten perent of its voting stock owned beneficially by residents of this state. For purposes of this section, the residence of a partnership, unincorporated association, trust or similar organization shall be the principal office of such organization.

No resident domestic corporation, which is organized under the laws of this state, shall cease to be a resident domestic corporation by reason of events occurring or actions taken while such resident domestic corporation is subject to the provisions of this section.

(14) "Stock" means:

(A) any stock or similar security, any certificate of interest, any participation in any profit sharing agreement, any voting trust certificate, or any certificate of deposit for stock; and

(B) any security convertible, with or without consideration, into stock, or any warrant, call or other option or privilege of buying stock without being bound to do so, or any other security carrying any right to acquire, subscribe or to purchase stock.

(15) "Stock acquisition date", with respect to any person and any resident domestic corporation, means the date that such person first becomes an interested shareholder of such resident domestic corporation.

(16) "Subsidiary" of any resident domestic corporation means any other corporation of which voting stock, having a majority of the outstanding voting stock of such other corporation, is owned, directly or indirectly, by such resident domestic corporation.

(17) "Voting stock" means shares of capital stock of a corporation entitled to vote generally in the election of directors.

(b) Notwithstanding anything to the contrary contained in this chapter (except the provisions of paragraph (d) of this section), no resident domestic corporation shall engage in any business combination with any interested shareholder of such resident domestic corporation for a period of five years following such interested shareholder's stock acquisition date unless such business combination or the purchase of stock made by such interested shareholder on such interested shareholder's stock acquisition date is approved by the board of directors of such resident domestic corporation prior to such interested shareholder's stock acquisition date. If a good faith proposal is made in writing to the board of directors of such resident domestic corporation regarding a business combination, the board of directors shall respond, in writing, within thirty days or such shorter period, if any, as may be required by the Exchange Act, setting forth its reasons for its decision regarding such proposal. If a good faith proposal to purchase stock is made in writing to the board of directors of such resident domestic corporation, the board of directors, unless it responds affirmatively in writing within thirty days or such shorter period, if any, as may be required by the Exchange Act, shall be deemed to have disapproved such stock purchase.

(c) Notwithstanding anything to the contrary contained in this chapter (except the provisions of paragraphs (b) and (d) of this section), no resident domestic corporation shall engage at any time in any business combination with any interested shareholder of such resident domestic corporation other than a business combination specified in any one of subparagraph (1), (2) or (3):

(1) A business combination approved by the board of directors of such resident domestic corporation prior to such interested shareholder's stock acquisition date, or where the purchase of stock made by such interested shareholder on such interested shareholder's stock acquisition date had been approved by the board of directors of such resident domestic corporation prior to such interested shareholder's stock acquisition date.

(2) A business combination approved by the affirmative vote of the holders of a majority of the outstanding voting stock not beneficially owned by such interested shareholder or any affiliate or associate of such interested shareholder at a meeting called for such purpose no earlier than five years after such interested shareholder's stock acquisition date.

(3) A business combination that meets all of the following conditions:

(A) The aggregate amount of the cash and the market value as of the consummation date of consideration other than cash to be received per share by holders of outstanding shares of common stock of such resident domestic corporation in such business combination is at least equal to the higher of the following:

(i) the highest per share price paid by such interested shareholder at a time when he was the beneficial owner, directly or indirectly, of five percent or more of the outstanding voting stock of such resident domestic corporation, for any shares of common stock of the same class or series acquired by it (X) within the five-year period immediately prior to the announcement date with respect to such business combination, or (Y) within the five-year period immediately prior to, or in, the transaction in which such interested shareholder became an interested shareholder, whichever is higher; plus, in either case, interest compounded annually from the earliest date on which such highest per share acquisition price was paid through the consummation date at the rate for one-year United States treasury obligations from time to time in effect; less the aggregate amount of any cash dividends paid, and the market value of any dividends paid other than in cash, per share of common stock since such earliest date, up to the amount of such interest; and

(ii) the market value per share of common stock on the announcement date with respect to such business combination or on such interested shareholder's stock acquisition date, whichever is higher; plus interest compounded annually from such date through the consummation date at the rate for one-year United States treasury obligations from time to time in effect; less the aggregate amount of any cash dividends paid, and the market value of any dividends paid other than in cash, per share of common stock since such date, up to the amount of such interest.

(B) The aggregate amount of the cash and the market value as of the consummation date of consideration other than cash to be received per share by holders of outstanding shares of any class or series of stock, other than common stock, of such resident domestic corporation is at least equal to the highest of the following (whether or not such interested shareholder has previously acquired any shares of such class or series of stock):

(i) the highest per share price paid by such interested shareholder at a time when he was the beneficial owner, directly or indirectly, of five percent or more of the outstanding voting stock of such resident domestic corporation, for any shares of such class or series of stock acquired by it (X) within the five-year period immediately prior to the announcement date with respect to such business combination, or (Y) within the five-year period immediately prior to, or in, the transaction in which such interested shareholder became an interested shareholder, whichever is higher; plus, in either case, interest compounded annually from the earliest date on which such highest per share acquisition price was paid through the consummation date at the rate for one-year United States treasury obligations from time to time in effect; less the aggregate amount of any cash dividends paid, and the market value of any dividends paid other than in cash, per share of such class or series of stock since such earliest date, up to the amount of such interest;

(ii) the highest preferential amount per share to which the holders of shares of such class or series of stock are entitled in the event of any voluntary liquidation, dissolution or winding up of such resident domestic corporation, plus the aggregate amount of any dividends declared or due as to which such holders are entitled prior to payment of dividends on some other class or series of stock (unless the aggregate amount of such dividends is included in such preferential amount); and

(iii) the market value per share of such class or series of stock on the announcement date with respect to such business combination or on such interested shareholder's stock acquisition date, whichever is higher; plus interest compounded annually from such date through the consummation date at the rate for one-year United States treasury obligations from time to time in effect; less the aggregate amount of any cash dividends paid, and the market value of any dividends paid other than in cash, per share of such class or series of stock since such date, up to the amount of such interest.

(C) The consideration to be received by holders of a particular class or series of outstanding stock (including common stock) of such resident domestic corporation in such business combination is in cash or in the same form as the interested shareholder has used to acquire the largest number of shares of such class or series of stock previously acquired by it, and such consideration shall be distributed promptly.

(D) The holders of all outstanding shares of stock of such resident domestic corporation not beneficially owned by such interested shareholder immediately prior to the consummation of such business combination are entitled to receive in such business combination cash or other consideration for such shares in compliance with clauses (A), (B) and (C) of this subparagraph.

(E) After such interested shareholder's stock acquisition date and prior to the consummation date with respect to such business combination, such interested shareholder has not become the beneficial owner of any additional shares of voting stock of such resident domestic corporation except:

(i) as part of the transaction which resulted in such interested shareholder becoming an interested shareholder;

(ii) by virtue of proportionate stock splits, stock dividends or other distributions of stock in respect of stock not constituting a business combination under clause (E) of subparagraph five of paragraph (a) of this section;

(iii) through a business combination meeting all of the conditions of paragraph (b) of this section and this paragraph; or

(iv) through purchase by such interested shareholder at any price which, if such price had been paid in an otherwise permissible business combination the announcement date and consummation date of which were the date of such purchase, would have satisfied the requirements of clauses (A), (B) and (C) of this subparagraph.

(d) The provisions of this section shall not apply:

(1) to any business combination of a resident domestic corporation that does not have a class of voting stock registered with the Securities and Exchange Commission pursuant to section twelve of the Exchange Act, unless the certificate of incorporation provides otherwise; or

(2) to any business combination of a resident domestic corporation whose certificate of incorporation has been amended to provide that such resident domestic corporation shall be subject to the provisions of this section, which did not have a class of voting stock registered with the Securities and Exchange Commission pursuant to section twelve of the Exchange Act on the effective date to such amendment, and which is a business combination with an interested shareholder whose stock acquisition date is prior to the effective date of such amendment; or

(3) to any business combination of a resident domestic corporation (i) the original certificate of incorporation of which contains a provision expressly electing not to be governed by this section, or (ii) which adopts an amendment to such resident domestic corporation's by-laws prior to March thirty-first, nineteen hundred eighty-six, expressly electing not to be governed by this section, or (iii) which adopts an amendment to such resident domestic corporation's by-laws, approved by the affirmative vote of the holders, other than interested shareholders and their affiliates and associates, of a majority of the outstanding voting stock of such resident domestic corporation, excluding the voting stock of interested shareholders and their affiliates and associates, expressly electing not to be governed by this section, provided that such amendment to the by-laws shall not be effective until eighteen months after such vote of such resident domestic corporation's shareholders and shall not apply to any business combination of such resident domestic corporation with an interested shareholder whose stock acquisition date is on or prior to the effective date of such amendment; or

(4) to any business combination of a resident domestic corporation with an interested shareholder of such resident domestic corporation which became an interested shareholder inadvertently, if such interested shareholder (i) as soon as practicable, divests itself of a sufficient amount of the voting stock of such resident domestic corporation so that it no longer is the beneficial owner, directly or indirectly, of twenty percent or more of the outstanding voting stock of such resident domestic corporation, and (ii) would not at any time within the five-year period preceding the announcement date with respect to such business combination have been an interested shareholder but for such inadvertent acquisition.

(5) to any business combination with an interested shareholder who was the beneficial owner, directly or indirectly, of five per cent or more of the outstanding voting stock of such resident domestic corporation on October thirtieth, nineteen hundred eighty-five, and remained so to such interested shareholder's stock acquisition date.

§ 913. Share exchanges.

(a)(1) Two domestic corporations may, as provided in this section, participate in the consummation of a plan for binding share exchanges.

(2) Whenever used in this article:

(A) "Acquiring corporation" means a corporation that is participating in a procedure pursuant to which such corporation is acquiring all of the outstanding shares of one or more classes of a subject corporation.

(B) "Subject corporation" means a corporation that is participating in a procedure pursuant to which all of the outstanding shares of one or more classes of such corporation are being acquired by an acquiring corporation.

(b) The board of the acquiring corporation and the board of the subject corporation shall adopt a plan of exchange, setting forth:

(1) The name of the acquiring corporation and the name of the subject corporation, and, if the name of either of them has been changed, the name under which it was formed;

(2) As to the acquiring corporation and the subject corporation, the designation and number of outstanding shares of each class and series, specifying the classes and series entitled to vote and further specifying each class and series, if any, entitled to vote as a class; and, if the number of any such shares is subject to change prior to the effective date of the exchange, the manner in which such change may occur;

(3) The terms and conditions of the proposed exchange, including the manner and basis of exchanging the shares to be acquired for shares, bonds or other securities of the acquiring corporation, or the cash or other consideration to be paid or delivered in exchange for such shares to be acquired, or a combination thereof; and

(4) Such other provisions with respect to the proposed exchange as the board considers necessary or desirable.

(c) The board of the subject corporation, upon adopting the plan of exchange, shall submit such plan, except as provided in paragraph (g) of this section, to a vote of shareholders in accordance with the following:

(1) Notice of meeting shall be given to each shareholder of record, as of the record date fixed pursuant to section 604 (Fixing record date), whether or not entitled to vote. A copy of the plan of exchange or an outline of the material features of the plan shall accompany such notice.

(2) The plan of exchange shall be adopted at a meeting of shareholders by vote of the holders of two-thirds of all outstanding shares entitled to vote thereon. Notwithstanding any provision in the certificate of incorporation, the holders of shares of a class or series shall be entitled to vote

and to vote as a class if the plan of exchange contains any provision which, if contained in an amendment to the certificate of incorporation, would entitle the holders of shares of such class or series to vote and to vote as a class thereon, or if the shares of such class or series are to be exchanged pursuant to the plan of exchange. In such case, in addition to the authorization of the exchange by vote of the holders of two-thirds of all outstanding shares entitled to vote thereon, the exchange shall be authorized by vote of the holders of a majority of all outstanding shares of each such class or series. Notwithstanding shareholder authorization and at any time prior to the filing of the certificate of exchange, the plan of exchange may be abandoned pursuant to a provision for such abandonment, if any, contained in the plan of exchange.

(d) After adoption of the plan of exchange by the board of the acquiring corporation and the board of the subject corporation and by the shareholders of the subject corporation entitled to vote thereon, unless the exchange is abandoned in accordance with paragraph (c), a certificate of exchange, entitled "Certificate of exchange of shares of . . . , subject corporation, for shares of . . . , acquiring corporation, or other consideration, under section 913 of the Business Corporation Law", shall be signed and verified on behalf of each corporation and delivered to the department of state. It shall set forth:

(1) the statements required by subparagraphs (1) and (2) of paragraph (b) of this section;

(2) the effective date of the exchange if other than the date of filing of the certificate of exchange by the department of state;

(3) the date when the certificate of incorporation of each corporation was filed by the department of state;

(4) the designation of the shares to be acquired by the acquiring corporation and a statement of the consideration for such shares; and

(5) the manner in which the exchange was authorized with respect to each corporation.

(e) Upon the filing of the certificate of exchange by the department of state or on such date subsequent thereto, not to exceed thirty days, as shall be set forth in such certificate, the exchange shall be effected. When such exchange has been effected, ownership of the shares to be acquired pursuant to the plan of exchange shall vest in the acquiring corporation, whether or not the certificates for such shares have been surrendered for exchange, and the acquiring corporation shall be entitled to have new certificates registered in its name or at its direction. Shareholders whose shares have been so acquired shall become entitled to the shares, bonds or other securities of the acquiring corporation, or the cash or other consideration, required to be paid or delivered in exchange for such shares pursuant to the plan. Subject to any terms of the plan regarding surrender of certificates theretofore evidencing the shares so acquired and regarding whether such certificates shall thereafter evidence securities of the acquiring corporation, such certificates shall thereafter evidence only the right to receive the consideration required to be paid or delivered in exchange for such shares purusant to the plan or, in the case of dissenting shareholders, their rights under section 910 (Right of shareholder to receive payment for shares upon merger or consolidation, or sale, lease, exchange or other disposition of assets, or share exchange) and section 623 (Procedure to enforce shareholder's right to receive payment for shares).

(f)(1) A foreign corporation and a domestic corporation may participate in a share exchange, but, if the subject corporation is a foreign corporation, only if such exchange is permitted by the laws of the jurisdiction under which such foreign corporation is incorporated. With respect to such exchange, any reference in subparagraph (2) of paragraph (a) of this section to a corporation shall, unless the context otherwise requires, include both domestic and foreign corporations, and the provisions of paragraphs (b), (c), (d) and (e) of this section shall apply, except to the extent otherwise provided in this paragraph.

(2) With respect to procedure, including the requirement of shareholder authorization, a domestic corporation shall comply with the provisions of this chapter relating to share exchanges in which domestic corporations are participating, and a foreign corporation shall comply with the applicable provisions of the law of the jurisdiction under which it is incorporated.

(3) If the subject corporation is a foreign corporation, the certificate of exchange shall set forth, in addition to the matters specified in paragraph (d), the jurisdiction and date of incorporation of such corporation and a statement that the exchange is permitted by the laws of the jurisdiction of such corporation and is in compliance therewith.

(g)(1) Any corporation owning at least ninety percent of the outstanding common shares, having full voting rights, of another corporation may acquire by exchange the remainder of such outstanding common shares, without the authorization of the shareholders of any such corporation and with the effect provided for in paragraph (e) of this section. The board of the acquiring corporation shall adopt a plan of exchange, setting forth the matters specified in paragraph (b) of this section. A copy of such plan of exchange or an outline of the material features thereof shall be given, personally or by mail, to all holders of shares of the subject corporation that are not owned by the acquiring corporation, unless the giving of such copy or outline has been waived by such holders.

(2) A certificate of exchange, entitled "Certificate of exchange of shares of . . . , subject corporation, for shares of . . . , acquiring corporation, or other consideration, under paragraph (g) of section 913 of the Business Corporation Law" and complying with the provisions of paragraph (d) and, if applicable, subparagraph (3) of paragraph (f) shall be signed, verified and delivered to the department of state by the acquiring corporation, but not less than thirty days after the giving of a copy or outline of the material features of the plan of exchange to shareholders of the subject corporation, or at any time after the waiving thereof by the holders of all the outstanding shares of the subject corporation not owned by the acquiring corporation.

(3) The right of exchange of shares granted by this paragraph to certain corporations shall not preclude the exercise by such corporations of any other right of exchange under this article.

(4) The procedure for the exchange of shares of a subject corporation under this paragraph (g) of this section shall be available where either the subject corporation or the acquiring corporation is a foreign corporation, and, in case the subject corporation is a foreign corporation, where such exchange is permitted by the laws of the jurisdiction under which such foreign corporation is incorporated.

(h) This section does not limit the power of a domestic or foreign corporation to acquire all or part of the shares of one or more classes of another domestic or foreign corporation by means of a voluntary exchange or otherwise.

(i)(1) A binding share exchange pursuant to this section shall constitute a "business combination" pursuant to section nine hundred twelve of this chapter (Requirements relating to certain business combinations) if the subject corporation is a "resident domestic corporation" and the acquiring corporation is an "interested shareholder" of the subject corporation, as such terms are defined in section nine hundred twelve of this chapter.

(2) With respect to convertible securities and other securities evidencing a right to acquire shares of a subject corporation, a binding share exchange pursuant to this section shall have the same effect on the rights of the holders of such securities as a merger of the subject corporation.

§ 1001. Authorization of dissolution.

A corporation may be dissolved under this article. Such dissolution shall be authorized at a meeting of shareholders by the vote of the holders of two-thirds of all outstanding shares entitled to vote thereon, except as otherwise provided under section 1002 (Dissolution under provision in certificate of incorporation).

§ 1002. Dissolution under provision in certificate of incorporation.

(a) The certificate of incorporation may contain a provision that any shareholder, or the holders of any specified number or proportion of shares, or of any specified number or proportion of shares of any class or series thereof, may require the dissolution of the corporation at will or upon the occurrence of a specified event. If the certificate of incorporation contains such a provision, a certificate of dissolution under section 1003 (Certificate of dissolution; contents) may be signed, verified and delivered to the department of state as provided in section 104 (Certificate; requirements, signing, filing, effectiveness) when authorized by a holder or holders of the number or proportion of shares specified in such provision, given in such manner as may be specified therein, or if no manner is specified therein, when authorized on written consent signed by such holder or holders; or such certificate may be signed, verified and delivered to the department by such holder or holders or by such of them as are designated by them.

(b) An amendment of the certificate of incorporation which adds a provision permitted by this section, or which changes or strikes out such a provision, shall be authorized at a meeting of shareholders by vote of all outstanding shares, whether or not otherwise entitled to vote on any amendment, or of such lesser proportion of shares and of such class or series of shares, but not less than a majority of all outstanding shares entitled to vote on any amendment, as may be provided specifically in the certificate of incorporation for adding, changing or striking out a provision permitted by this section.

(c) If the certificate of incorporation of any corporation contains a provision authorized by this section, the existence of such provision shall be noted conspicuously on the face or back of every certificate for shares issued by such corporation.

§ 1003. Certificate of dissolution; contents.

(a) A certificate of dissolution, entitled "Certificate of dissolution of . . . . (name of corporation) under section 1003 of the Business Corporation Law", shall be signed, verified and delivered to the department of state. It shall be set forth:

(1) The name of the corporation and, if its name has been changed, the name under which it was formed.

(2) The date its certificate of incorporation was filed by the department of state.

(3) The name and address of each of its officers and directors.

(4) That the corporation elects to dissolve.

(5) The manner in which the dissolution was authorized.

§ 1004. Certificate of dissolution; filing.

The department shall not file such certificate unless the consent of the state tax commission to the dissolution is attached thereto. Upon such filing, the corporation is dissolved.

§ 1005. Procedure after dissolution.

(a) After dissolution:

(1) The corporation shall carry on no business except for the purpose of winding up its affairs.

(2) The corporation shall proceed to wind up its affairs, with power to fulfill or discharge its contracts, collect its assets, sell its assets for cash at public or private sale, discharge or pay its liabilities, and do all other acts appropriate to liquidate its business.

(3) After paying or adequately providing for the payment of its liabilities:

(A) The corporation, if authorized at a meeting of shareholders by a vote of the holders of a majority of all outstanding shares entitled to vote thereon may sell its remaining assets, or any part thereof, for shares, bonds or other securities or partly for cash and partly for shares, bonds or other securities, and distribute the same among the shareholders according to their respective rights. In the case of sale under this subparagraph where the consideration is in whole or in part other than cash, any shareholder, entitled to vote thereon, who does not vote for or consent in writing to such sale, shall, subject to and by complying with the provisions of section 623 (Procedure to enforce shareholder's right to receive payment for shares), have the right to receive payment for his shares. Section 909 (Sale, lease, exchange or other dispostion of assets) is not applicable to a sale of assets under this paragraph.

(B) The corporation, whether or not it has made a sale under subparagraph (A), may distribute any remaining assets, in cash or in kind or partly each, among its shareholders according to their respective rights.

(b) When there are no shareholders, upon dissolution all subscriptions for shares shall be cancelled and all obligations of the corporation to issue shares or of the subscribers to pay their subscriptions shall terminate, except for such payments as may be required to enable the corporation to pay its liabilities.

(c) Upon the winding up of the affairs of the corporation, any assets distributable to a creditor or shareholder who is unknown or cannot be found, or who is under disability and for whom there is no legal representative, shall be paid to the state comptroller as abandoned property within six months from the date fixed for the payment of the final liquidating distribution, and be subject to the provisions of the abandoned property law.

§ 1006. Corporate action and survival of remedies after dissolution.

(a) A dissolved corporation, its directors, officers and shareholders may continue to function for the purpose of winding up the affairs of the corporation in the same manner as if the dissolution had not taken place, except as otherwise provided in this chapter or by court order. In particular, and without limiting the generality of the foregoing:

(1) The directors of a dissolved corporation shall not be deemed to be trustees of its assets; title to such assets shall not vest in them, but shall remain in the corporation until transferred by it in its corporate name.

(2) Dissolution shall not change quorum or voting requirements for the board or shareholders, or provisions regarding election, appointment, resignation or removal of, or filling vacancies among, directors or officers, or provisions regarding amendment or repeal of by-laws or adoption of new by-laws.

(3) Shares may be transferred and determinations of shareholders for any purpose may be made without closing the record of shareholders until such time, if any, as such record may be closed, and either the board or the shareholders may close it.

(4) The corporation may sue or be sued in all courts and participate in actions and proceedings, whether judicial, administrative, arbitrative or otherwise, in its corporate name, and process may be served by or upon it.

(b) The dissolution of a corporation shall not affect any remedy available to or against such corporation, its directors, officers, or shareholders for any right or claim existing or any liability incurred before such dissolution, except as provided in sections 1007 (Notice to creditors; filing or barring claims) or 1008 (Jurisdiction of supreme court to supervise dissolution and liquidation).

§ 1007. Notice to creditors; filing or barring claims.

(a) At any time after dissolution, the corporation may give a notice requiring all creditors and claimants, including any with unliquidated or contingent claims and any with whom the corporation has unfulfilled contracts, to present their claims in writing and in detail at a specified place and by a specified day, which shall not be less than six months after the first publication of such notice. Such notice shall be published at least once a week for two successive weeks in a newspaper of general circulation in the county in which the office of the corporation was located at the date of dissolution. On or before the date of the first publication of such notice, the corporation shall mail a copy thereof, postage prepaid and addressed to his last known address, to each person believed to be a creditor of or claimant against the corporation whose name and address are known to or can with due diligence be ascertained by the corporation. The giving of such notice shall not constitute a recognition that any person is a proper creditor or claimant, and shall not revive or make valid, or operate as a recognition of the validity of, or a waiver of any defense or counterclaim in respect of any claim against the corporation, its assets, directors, officers or shareholders, which has been barred by any statute of limitations or become invalid by any cause, or in respect of which the corporation, its directors, officers or shareholders, has any defense or counterclaim.

(b) Any claims which shall have been filed as provided in such notice and which shall be disputed by the corporation may be submitted for determination to the supreme court under section 1008 (Jurisdiction of supreme court to supervise dissolution and liquidation). A claim filed by the trustee or paying agent for the holders of bonds or coupons shall have the same effect as if filed by the holder of any such bond or coupon. Any person whose claim is, at the date of the first publication of such notice, barred by any statute of limitations is not a creditor or claimant entitled to any notice under this section or section 1008. The claim of any such person and all other claims which are not timely filed as provided in such notice except claims which are the subject of litigation on the date of the first publication of such notice, and all claims which are so filed but are disallowed by the court under section 1008, shall be forever barred as against the corporation, its assets, directors, officers and shareholders, except to such extent, if any, as the court may allow them against any remaining assets of the corporation in the case of a creditor who shows satisfactory reason for his failure to file his claim as so provided. If the court requires a further notice under section 1008, any reference to a notice in this section shall, to the extent that the court so orders, mean such further notice, except that a claim which has been filed in accordance with a notice under this section need not be refiled under such further notice.

(c) Notwithstanding this section and section 1008, tax claims and other claims of this state and of the United States shall not be required to be filed under those sections, and such claims shall not be barred because not so filed, and distribution of the assets of the corporation, or any part thereof, may be deferred until determination of any such claims.

(d) Laborer's wages shall be preferred claims and entitled to payment before any other creditors out of the assets of the corporation in excess of valid prior liens or encumbrances.

§ 1008. Jurisdiction of supreme court to supervise dissolution and liquidation.

(a) At any time after the filing of a certificate of dissolution under this article the supreme court in the judicial district where the office of the corporation was located at the date of its dissolution, in a special proceeding instituted under this section, upon the petition of the corporation, or, in a situation approved by the court, upon the petition of a creditor, claimant, director, officer, shareholder, subscriber for shares, incorporator or the attorney-general, may suspend or annul the dissolution or continue the liquidation of the corporation under the supervision of the court and may make all such orders as it may deem proper in all matters in connection with the dissolution or the winding up of the affairs of the corporation, and in particular, and without limitation of the generality thereof, in respect of the following:

(1) The determination of the validity of the authorization of the dissolution of the corporation and of the execution and delivery of the certificate of dissolution under this article.

(2) The adequacy of the notice given to creditors and claimants and if it is determined to have been inadequate, the requirement of such further notice as the court may deem proper.

(3) The determination of the validity and amount or invalidity of any claims which have been presented to the corporation.

(4) The barring of all creditors and claimants who have not timely filed claims as provided in any such notice, or whose claims have been disallowed by the court, as against the corporation, its assets, directors, officers and shareholders.

(5) The determination and enforcement of the liability of any director, officer, shareholder or subscriber for shares, to the corporation or for the liabilities of the corporation.

(6) The payment, satisfaction or compromise of claims against the corporation, the retention of assets for such purpose, and the determination of the adequacy of provisions made for payment of the liabilities of the corporation.

(7) The disposition or destruction of records, documents and papers of the corporation.

(8) The appointment and removal of a receiver under article 12 (Receivership) who may be a director, officer or shareholder of the corporation.

(9) The issuance of injunctions for one or more of the purposes and as provided in section 1115 (Injunction).

(10) The return of subscription payments to subscribers for shares, and the making of distributions, in cash or in kind or partly each, to the shareholders.

(11) The payment to the state comptroller, as abandoned property, of assets under paragraph (c) of section 1005 (Procedure after dissolution).

(b) Orders under this section may be entered ex parte, except that if such special proceeding was not instituted upon petition of the corporation, notice shall be given to the corporation in such manner as the court may direct. Notice shall be given to such other persons interested, and in such manner, as the court may deem proper, of any hearings and of the entry of any orders on such matters as the court shall deem proper. All orders made by the court under this section shall be binding upon the attorney-general, the corporation, its officers, directors, shareholders, subscribers for shares, incorporators, creditors and claimants.

(c) (1) Simultaneously with the institution of such special proceeding for annulment of the dissolution, the petitioner shall apply to the department of state to reserve the corporation name to the corporation. If such name shall not be available for use, the petitioner forthwith upon being notified thereof shall apply to such department for the reservation of another and available name and any judgment or order of annulment made in such proceeding shall order and direct the petitioner to execute a certificate of change of the corporate name to such other name.

(2) The clerk of the court, or such other person as the court may direct, shall transmit a certified copy of the judgment or order of annulment of the dissolution, together with the certificate of change of corporate name in the appropriate case, to the department of state, and a certified copy of such judgment or order to the clerk of the county in which the office of the corporation was located on the date of the dissolution. Upon filing by the department of state, the annulment of dissolution shall be effected.

§ 1009. Applicability to dissolution under other provisions.

The provisions of sections 1005 (Procedure after dissolution), 1006 (Corporate action and survival of remedies after dissolution), 1007 (Notice to creditors; filing or barring claims) and 1008 (Jurisdiction of supreme court to supervise dissolution and liquidation) shall apply to a corporation dissolved by expiration of its period of duration or under section two hundred three-a of the tax law.

§ 1101. Attorney-general's action for judicial dissolution.

(a) The attorney-general may bring an action for the dissolution of a corporation upon one or more of the following grounds:

(1) That the corporation procured its formation through fraudulent misrepresentation or concealment of a material fact.

(2) That the corporation has exceeded the authority conferred upon it by law, or has violated any provision of law whereby it has forfeited its charter, or carried on, conducted or transacted its business in a persistently fraudulent or illegal manner, or by the abuse of its powers contrary to the public policy of the state has become liable to be dissolved.

(b) An action under this section is triable by jury as a matter of right.

(c) The enumeration in paragraph (a) of grounds for dissolution shall not exclude actions or special proceedings by the attorney-general or other state officials for the annulment or dissolution of a corporation for other causes as provided in this chapter or in any other statute of this state.

§ 1102. Directors' petition for judicial dissolution.

If a majority of the board adopts a resolution that finds that the assets of a corporation are not sufficient to discharge its liabilities or that a dissolution will be beneficial to the shareholders, it may present a petition for its dissolution.

§ 1103. Shareholders' petition for judicial dissolution.

(a) If the shareholders of a corporation adopt a resolution stating that they find that its assets are not sufficient to discharge its liabilities, or that they deem a dissolution to be beneficial to the shareholders, the shareholders or such of them as are designated for that purpose in such resolution may present a petition for its dissolution.

(b) A shareholders' meeting to consider such a resolution may be called, notwithstanding any provision in the certificate of incorporation, by the holders of ten percent of all outstanding shares entitled to vote thereon, or if the certificate of incorporation authorizes a lesser proportion of shares to call the meeting, by such lesser proportion. A meeting under this paragraph may not be called more often than once in any period of twelve consecutive months.

(c) Such a resolution may be adopted at a meeting of shareholders by vote of the holders of a majority of all oustanding shares entitled to vote thereon or if the certificate of incorporation requires a greater proportion of votes to adopt such a resolution, by such greater proportion.

§ 1104. Petition in case of deadlock among directors or shareholders.

(a) Except as otherwise provided in the certificate of incorporation under section 613 (Limitations on right to vote), the holders of one-half of all outstanding shares of a corporation entitled to vote in an election of directors may present a petition for dissolution on one or more of the following grounds:

    (1) That the directors are so divided respecting the management of the corporation's affairs that the votes required for action by the board cannot be obtained.

    (2) That the shareholders are so divided that the votes required for the election of directors cannot be obtained.

    (3) That there is internal dissension and two or more factions of shareholders are so divided that dissolution would be beneficial to the shareholders.

(b) If the certificate of incorporation provides that the proportion of votes required for action by the board, or the proportion of votes of shareholders required for election of directors, shall be greater than that otherwise required by this chapter, such a petition may be presented by the holders of more than one-third of all outstanding shares entitled to vote on non-judicial dissolution under section 1001 (Authorization of dissolution).

(c) Notwithstanding any provision in the certificate of incorporation, any holder of shares entitled to vote at an election of directors of a corporation, may present a petition for its dissolution on the ground that the shareholders are so divided that they have failed, for a period which includes at least two consecutive annual meeting dates, to elect successors to directors whose terms have expired or would have expired upon the election and qualification of their successors.

§ 1104–a. Petition for judicial dissolution under special circumstances.

(a) The holders of twenty percent or more of all outstanding shares of a corporation, other than a corporation registered as an investment company under an act of Congress entitled "Investment Company Act of 1940", no shares of which are listed on a national securities exchange or regularly quoted in an over-the-counter market by one or more members of a national or an affiliated securities association, who are entitled to vote in an election of directors may present a petition of dissolution on one or more of the following grounds:

    (1) The directors or those in control of the corporation have been guilty of illegal, fraudulent or oppressive actions toward the complaining shareholders;

    (2) The proprety or assets of the corporation are being looted, wasted, or diverted for non-corporate purposes by its directors, officers or those in control of the corporation.

(b) The court, in determining whether to proceed with involuntary dissolution pursuant to this section, shall take into account:

    (1) Whether liquidation of the corporation is the only feasible means whereby the petitioners may reasonably expect to obtain a fair return on their investment; and

    (2) Whether liquidation of the corporation is reasonably necessary for the protection of the rights and interests of any substantial number of shareholders or of the petitioners.

§ 1105. Contents of petition for judicial dissolution.

A petition for dissolution shall specify the section or sections of this article under which it is authorized and state the reasons why the corporation should be dissolved. It shall be verified by the petitioner or by one of the petitioners.

§ 1106. Order to show cause; issuance; publication, service, filing.

(a) Upon the presentation of such a petition, the court shall make an order requiring the corporation and all persons interested in the corporation to show cause before it, or before a referee designated in the order, at a time and place therein specified, not less than four weeks after the granting of the order, why the corporation should not be dissolved. In connection therewith, the court may order the corporation, its officers and directors, to furnish the court with a schedule of all information, known or ascertainable with due diligence by them, deemed pertinent by the court, including a statement of the corporate assets and liabilities, and the name and address of each shareholder and of each creditor and claimant, including any with unliquidated or contingent claims and any with whom the corporation has unfulfilled contracts.

(b) A copy of the order to show cause shall be published as prescribed therein, at least once in each of the three weeks before the time appointed for the hearing thereon, in one or more newspapers, specified in the order, of general circulation in the county in which the office of the corporation is located at the date of the order.

(c) A copy of the order to show cause shall be served upon the state tax commission and the corporation and upon each person named in the petition, or in any schedule provided for in paragraph (a), as a shareholder, creditor or claimant, except upon a person whose address is stated to be unknown, and cannot with due diligence be ascertained by the corporation. The service shall be made personally, at least ten days before the time appointed for the hearing, or by mailing a copy of the order, postage prepaid, at least twenty days before the time so appointed, addressed to the person to be served at his last known address.

(d) A copy of the order to show cause and the petition shall be filed, within ten days after the order is entered, with the clerk of the county where the office of the corporation is located at the date of the order. A copy of each schedule furnished to the court under this section shall, within ten days thereafter, be filed with such clerk.

(e) Publication, service and filing provided for in this section shall be effected by the corporation or such other persons as the court may order.

§ 1107. Amending papers.

At any stage, before final order, the court may grant an order amending the petition or any other paper filed in the action or special proceeding, with like effect as though originally filed as amended, or otherwise as the court may direct.

§ 1108. Referee.

If a referee was not designated in the order to show cause, the court, in its discretion, may appoint a referee when or after the order is returnable. The court may at any time appoint a successor referee.

§ 1109. Hearing and decision.

At the time and place specified in the order to show cause, or at any other time and place to which the hearing is adjourned, the court or the referee shall hear the allegations and proofs of the parties and determine the facts. The decision of the court or the report of the referee shall be made and filed with the clerk of the court with all convenient speed.

§ 1110. Application for final order.

When the hearing is before a referee, a motion for a final order must be made to the court upon notice to each party to the action or special proceeding who has appeared therein. The notice of motion may be served as prescribed for the service of papers upon an attorney in an action in such court. When the hearing is before the court, a motion for a final order may be made at the hearing or at such time and upon such notice as the court prescribes.

§ 1111. Judgment or final order of dissolution.

(a) In an action or special proceeding under this article if, in the court's discretion, it shall appear that the corporation should be dissolved, it shall make a judgment or final order dissolving the corporation.

(b) In making its decision, the court shall take into consideration the following criteria:

(1) In an action brought by the attorney-general, the interest of the public is of paramount importance.

(2) In a special proceeding brought by directors or shareholders, the benefit to the shareholders of a dissolution is of paramount importance.

(3) In a special proceeding brought under section 1104 (Petition in case of deadlock among directors or shareholders) or section 1104-a (Petition for judicial dissolution under special circumstances) dissolution is not to be denied merely because it is found that the corporate business has been or could be conducted at a profit.

(c) If the judgment or final order shall provide for a dissolution of the corporation, the court may, in its discretion, provide therein for the distribution of the property of the corporation to those entitled thereto according to their respective rights.

(d) The clerk of the court or such other person as the court may direct shall transmit certified copies of the judgment or final order of dissolution to the department of state and to the clerk of the county in which the office of the corporation was located at the date of the judgment or order. Upon filing by the department of state, the corporation shall be dissolved.

(e) The corporation shall promptly thereafter transmit a certified copy of the judgment or final order to the clerk of each other county in which its certificate of incorporation was filed.

§ 1112. Venue.

An action or special proceeding under this article shall be brought in the supreme court in the judicial district in which the office of the corporation is located at the time of the service on the corporation of a summons in such action or of the presentation to the court of the petition in such special proceeding.

§ 1113. Preservation of assets; appointment of receiver.

At any stage of an action or special proceeding under this article, the court may, in its discretion, make all such orders as it may deem proper in connection with preserving the property and carrying on the business of the corporation, including the appointment and removal of a receiver under article 12 (Receivership), who may be a director, officer or shareholder of the corporation.

§ 1114. Certain sales, transfers, security interests and judgments void.

A sale, mortgage, conveyance or other transfer of, or the creation of a security interest in, any property of a corporation made, without prior approval of the court, after service upon the corporation of a summons in an action, or of an order to show cause in a special proceeding, under this article in payment of or as security for an existing or prior debt or for any other or for no consideration, or a judgment thereafter rendered against the corporation by confession or upon the acceptance of any offer, shall be void as against such persons and to such extent, if any, as the court shall determine.

§ 1115. Injunction.

(a) At any stage of an action or special proceeding under this article, the court may, in its discretion, grant an injunction, effective during the pendency of the action or special proceeding or such shorter period as it may specify in the injunction, for one or more of the following purposes:

(1) Restraining the corporation and its directors and officers from transacting any unauthorized business and from exercising any corporate powers, except by permission of the court.

(2) Restraining the corporation and its directors and officers from collecting or receiving any debt or other property of the corporation, and from paying out or otherwise transferring or delivering any property of the corporation, except by permission of the court.

(3) Restraining the creditors of the corporation from beginning any action against the corporation, or from taking any proceedings in an action theretofore commenced, except by permission of the court. Such injunction shall have the same effect and be subject to the same provisions of law as if each creditor upon whom it is served was named therein.

§ 1116. Discontinuance of action or special proceeding.

An action or special proceeding for the dissolution of a corporation may be discontinued at any stage when it is established that the cause for dissolution did not exist or no longer exists. In such event, the court shall dismiss the action or special proceeding and direct any receiver to redeliver to the corporation all its remaining property.

§ 1117. Aplicability of other provisions.

(a) Subject to the provisions of this article, the provisions of sections 1005 (Procedure after dissolution), 1006 (Corporate action and survival of remedies after dissolution), 1007 (Notice to creditors; filing or barring claims) and 1008 (Jurisdiction of supreme court to supervise dissolution and liquidation) shall apply to a corporation dissolved under this article.

(b) Any orders provided for in section 1008, may be made at any stage of an action or special proceeding for dissolution of a corporation under this article, and if the corporation is dissolved under this article, the court may retain jurisdiction for the purpose of making such orders, after the dissolution, in such action or special proceeding. The court may also make such orders in separate special proceedings, as provided in section 1008.

(c) Notice to creditors and claimants, provided for in section 1007, may also be given, by order of the court, at any stage of an action or special proceeding for dissolution of a corporation under this article.

§ 1118. Purchase of a petitioner's shares; valuation.

(a) In any proceeding brought pursuant to section eleven hundred four-a of this chapter, any other shareholder or shareholders or the corporation may, at any time within ninety days after the filing of such petition or at such later time as the court in its discretion may allow, elect to purchase the shares owned by the petitioners at their fair value and upon such terms and conditions as may be approved by the court, including the conditions of paragraph (c) herein. An election pursuant to this section shall be irrevocable unless the court, in its discretion, for just and equitable considerations, determines that such election be revocable.

(b) If one or more shareholders or the corporation elect to purchase the shares owned by the petitioner but are unable to agree with the petitioner upon the fair value of such shares, the court, upon the application of such prospective purchaser or purchasers or the petitioner, shall stay the proceedings brought pursuant to section 1104–a of this chapter and determine the fair value of the petitioner's shares as of the day prior to the date on which such petition was filed, exclusive of any element of value arising from such filing. In determining the fair value of the petitioner's shares, the court, in its discretion, may award interest from the date the petition is filed to the date of payment for the petitioner's share at an equitable rate upon judicially determined fair value of his shares.

(c) In connection with any election to purchase pursuant to this section:

(1) If such election is made beyond ninety days after the filing of the petition, and the court allows such petition, the court, in its discretion, may award the petitioner his reasonable expenses incurred in the proceeding prior to such election, including reasonable attorneys' fees;

(2) The court, in its discretion, may require, at any time prior to the actual purchase of petitioner's shares, the posting of a bond or other acceptable security in an amount sufficient to secure petitioner for the fair value of his shares.

§ 1201. Action by judgment creditor for sequestration.

Where final judgment for a sum of money has been rendered against a corporation, and an execution issued thereupon to the sheriff of the county where the corporation does its general business, or where its office is located, has been returned wholly or partly unsatisfied, the judgment creditor may maintain an action to procure a judgment sequestrating the property of the corporation and providing for a distribution thereof.

§ 1202. Appointment of receiver of property of a domestic or foreign corporation.

(a) A receiver of the property of a corporation can be appointed only by the court, and in one of the following cases:

(1) An action or special proceeding brought under article 10 (Non-judicial dissolution) or 11 (Judicial dissolution).

(2) An action under section 1201 (Action by judgment creditor for sequestration).

(3) An action brought by the attorney-general or by a shareholder to preserve the assets of a corporation, which has no officer within this state qualified to administer them.

(4) An action to preserve the assets in this state, of any kind, tangible or intangible, of a foreign corporation which has been dissolved, nationalized or its authority or existence otherwise terminated or cancelled in the jurisdiction of its incorporation or which has ceased to do business, brought by any creditor or shareholder of such corporation or by one on whose behalf an order of attachment against the property of such corporation has been issued.

(b) A receiver shall be subject to the control of the court at all times and may be removed by the court at any time.

(c) All actions or special proceedings brought by or against a receiver shall have a preference upon the calenders of all courts next in order to actions or special proceedings brought by the people of the state of New York.

§ 1203. Temporary and permanent receiver.

(a) At any stage before final judgment or final order in an action or special proceeding brought under this article, the court may appoint one or more receivers of the property of the corporation or of the property in this state of a foreign corporation against which an action has been brought under subparagraph (a) (4) of section 1202 (Appointment of receiver of property of a domestic or foreign corporation). Notice of an application for the appointment of a receiver shall be given to the attorney-general and to such other persons and in such manner as the court directs. The determination by the court of the necessity or advisability of appointing a receiver or an attorney for a receiver, and the allowance of expenses, commissions or compensation to the receiver or his attorney, shall be subject to review on appeal. This provision shall not affect any other right to review on appeal.

(b) A receiver appointed by or under a final judgment or order in an action or special proceeding, or a temporary receiver who is continued by the final judgment or order, is a permanent receiver. The court may confer upon a temporary receiver the powers, and subject him to the duties of a permanent receiver, or so much thereof as it deems proper.

§ 1204. Oath and security.

• • • •

§ 1205. Designation of depositories by court.

• • • •

§ 1206. Powers of permanent receiver.

(a) A permanent receiver, upon qualifying under section 1204 (Oath and security), shall be vested with title to all the property of the corporation wherever situated or of the property in this state of a foreign corporation against which an action or special proceeding has been brought under subparagraph (a) (4) of section 1202 (Appointment of receiver of property of a domestic or foreign corporation), for the benefit of the creditors and shareholders of the corporation.

(b) A permanent receiver shall have the power:

(1) To sue in his own name or otherwise for the recovery of the property, debts and causes of action of the corporation. No set-off or counterclaim shall be allowed in any such action for any demand unless it was owing by the corporation to the defendant before the commencement of the action or special proceeding in which the receiver was appointed or unless it shall have been incurred by the receiver subsequent to his appointment.

(2) To sell at public or private sale all the property vested in him, in such manner and on such terms and conditions as the court shall direct, and to make necessary transfers and conveyances thereof.

(3) To examine on oath, to be administered by him, any person concerning any matter pertaining to or affecting the receivership.

(4) To settle or compound any demands by or against the receivership.

(c) When more than one receiver is appointed, all provisions in this article in reference to one receiver shall apply to them.

(d) When more than one receiver is appointed, the debts and property of the corporation may be collected and received by any of them; when more than two receivers are appointed, the powers and rights conferred on them may be exercised by any two.

(e) When more than one receiver is appointed, the survivor or survivors of such receivers shall have all the powers and right of the receivers.

§ 1207. Duties of receiver upon appointment.

(a) Upon appointment and qualification, a receiver shall have the following duties:

(1) To give immediate notice of his appointment by publication once a week for two successive weeks in two newspapers of general circulation in the county where the office of the corporation is located or, in the case of a foreign corporation against which an action has been brought under subparagraph (a) (4) of section 1202 (Appointment of receiver of property of a domestic or foreign corporation), in a newspaper of general circulation as directed by the court, requiring:

(A) All persons indebted to the corporation to render an account of all debts owing by them to the corporation and to pay the same to the receiver at a specified place and by a specified day.

(B) All persons having in their possession any property of the corporation to deliver the same to the receiver at the specified place and by the specified day.

(C) All creditors and claimants, including any with unliquidated or contingent claims and any with whom the corporation has unfulfilled contracts, to present their claims to the receiver in writing and in detail at a specified place and by a specified day, which shall not be less than six months after the first publication of such notice. Whenever a receiver is appointed in dissolution proceedings under article 10 (Non-judicial dissolution) or article 11 (Judicial dissolution), section 1007 (Notice to creditors; filing or barring claims) shall apply and shall control the giving of notice to creditors and claimants and the filing and barring of claims.

(2) To call a general meeting of the creditors of the corporation within four months from the date of his appointment by a notice to be published as directed in subparagraph (a) (1), setting forth the time and place of such meeting, which time shall be not more than two months, nor less than one month after the first publication of such notice. At such meeting, or at an adjournment thereof, the receiver shall present a statement of all accounts and demands for and against the corporation, its subsisting contracts, and the money and other assets in his hands.

(3) To keep true books of account of all moneys received and expended by him as receiver, which books shall be open for inspection at reasonable times by creditors or other persons interested therein. On or before the first day of February in each year, for the preceding calendar year, and at such other times as the court shall direct, the receiver shall file with the clerk of the court by which he was appointed a verified statement showing the assets received, the disposition thereof, the money on hand, all payments made, specifying the persons to whom paid and the purpose of the payments, the amount necessary to be retained to meet necessary expenses and claims against the receiver, and the distributive share in the remainder of each person interested therein. A copy of such statement shall be served by the receiver upon the attorney-general within five days after the filing thereof.

§ 1208. Penalty for concealing property from receiver.

Any persons having possession of property belonging to the corporation, who shall wrongfully withhold such property from the receiver after the day specified in the notice given under section 1207 (Duties of receiver upon appointment), shall forfeit to the receiver double the value of such property, and the same may be recovered in an action by the receiver.

§ 1209. Recovery of assets.

(a) Whenever a receiver, by verified petition to the supreme court at a special term held in the judicial district in which he was appointed shall show that he has good reason to believe that any person has in his possession or under his control, or has wrongfully concealed, withheld or disposed of, any property of the corporation, or that any person can testify concerning such facts, the court, with or without notice, shall make an order requiring such person to appear before the court or a referee, at a time and place designated, and submit to an examination concerning such facts. In such order, or at any time thereafter, in its discretion, the court may enjoin and restrain such person from disposing of any property of the corporation in his possession or under his control.

(b) In any examination under such order, the court may confer immunity in accordance with the provisions of section 50.20 of the criminal procedure law; provided that no immunity shall be conferred except upon twenty-four hours prior written notice to the appropriate district attorney having an official interest therein.

(c) A person so ordered to appear shall be entitled to the same fees and mileage, to be paid at the time of serving the order, as are allowed by law to witnesses subpoenaed to attend and testify in an action in the supreme court, and shall be subject to the same penalties upon failure to appear and testify in obedience to such order as are provided by law in the case of witnesses who fail to obey a subpoena to appear and testify in an action.

(d) A person appearing for examination in obedience to such order shall be sworn, and shall be entitled to be represented on such examination by counsel, and may be cross-examined, or may make a voluntary statement in his own behalf concerning the subject of his examination.

(e) The testimony taken under such order shall be signed and sworn to by the person examined, and be filed in the office of the clerk of the county where the action or proceeding is pending. If it shall appear that any person is wrongfully concealing or withholding, or has in his possession or under his control, any property of the corporation, on notice to him, the court may make an order requiring him forthwith to deliver it to the receiver, subject to the further order of the court.

§ 1210. Order of payment of receiver.

(a) Laborers' wages shall be preferred claims and entitled to payment before any other creditors out of the assets of the corporation in excess of valid prior liens or encumbrances.

(b) The receiver shall subject to any prior liens or encumbrances distribute the residue of the moneys in his hands, among the creditors whose claims have been proved and allowed, as follows:

(1) All debts due by such corporation to the United States, and all debts entitled to a preference under the laws of the United States.

(2) All debts that may be owing by the corporation as trustee.

(3) Judgments against the corporation, to the extent of the value of the real property on which they are liens.

(4) All other creditors, in proportion to their respective demands, without preference to specialty debts.

§ 1211. Final distribution by receiver.

(a) If there remains property of the corporation after the first distribution, the receiver shall, within one year thereafter, make a final distribution among the creditors entitled thereto. Notice that such distribution will be the final distrubution to creditors shall be published once a week for two consecutive weeks in a newspaper of general circulation in the county where the office of the corporation is located.

(b) A creditor or claimant who failed to prove his claim before the first distribution and who proves it before the final one shall receive the sum he would have been entitled to on the first distribution before any further distribution shall be made to other creditors or claimants.

(c) Unless the court shall otherwise direct, no other distribution shall be made thereafter to creditors, except to those having pending actions against the corporation or the receiver.

(d) After the final distribution to creditors, the receiver shall not be answerable to any creditor or claimant, unless his claim shall have been proved before or at the time specified in the notice of the final distribution.

§ 1212. Disposition of moneys retained; surplus; unclaimed distributions.

(a) When any action pending at the time of the final distribution shall be terminated, the receiver shall apply the moneys retained by him to the payment of the amount recovered, and his necessary charges and expenses incurred therein.

(b) After the final distribution to creditors and after deducting his charges and expenses, the receiver shall distribute any surplus among the shareholders of the corporation, in accordance with their respective rights.

(c) Any portion of the assets distributable to a creditor or shareholder who is unknown or cannot be found, or who is under disability and for whom there is no legal representative, shall be paid by the receiver to the state comptroller as abandoned property within six months from the date fixed for the payment of the final liquidating distribution, and be subject to the provisions of the abandoned property law.

§ 1213. Omission or default of receiver.

• • • •

§ 1214. Application by attorney-general for removal of receiver and to close receivership.

(a) Whenever he deems it to be to the advantage of the shareholders, creditors or other persons interested in the assets of any corporation for which a receiver has been appointed, the attorney-general may move:

(1) For an order removing the receiver and appointing another in his stead;

(2) To compel the receiver to account;

(3) For such other and additional orders as may facilitate the closing of the receivership.

§ 1215. Resignation by receiver, filling any vacancy.

• • • •

§ 1216. Final accounting; notice; duty of attorney-general.

• • • •

§ 1217. Commissions.

• • • •

§ 1218. Special provisions relating to actions or special proceedings against foreign corporations.

• • • •

§ 1301. Authorization of foreign corporations.

(a) A foreign corporation shall not do business in this state until it has been authorized to do so as provided in this article. A foreign corporation may be authorized to do in this state any business which may be done lawfully in this state by a domestic corporation, to the extent that it is authorized to do such business in the jurisdiction of its incorporation, but no other business.

(b) Without excluding other activities which may not constitute doing business in this state, a foreign corporation shall not be considered to be doing business in this state, for the purposes of this chapter, by reason of carrying on in this state any one or more of the following activities:

(1) Maintaining or defending any action or proceeding, whether judicial, administrative, arbitrative or otherwise, or effecting settlement thereof or the settlement of claims or disputes.

(2) Holding meetings of its directors or its shareholders.

(3) Maintaining bank accounts.

(4) Maintaining offices or agencies only for the transfer, exchange and registration of its securities, or appointing and maintaining trustees or depositaries with relation to its securities.

(c) The specification in paragraph (b) does not establish a standard for activities which may subject a foreign corporation to service of process under this chapter or any other statute of this state.

(d) A foreign corporation whose corporate name is not acceptable for authorization pursuant to sections 301 and 302 of this chapter, may submit in its application for authority pursuant to section 1304 of this chapter, a fictitious name under which it shall do business in this state. A fictitious name submitted pursuant to this section shall be subject to the provisions of subparagraphs (2) through (9) of paragraph (a) of section 301 and 302 of this chapter. A foreign corporation authorized to do business in this state under a fictitious name purusant to this section, shall use such fictitious name in all of its dealings with the secretary of state and in the conduct of its business in this state. The provisions of section one hundred thirty of the general business law shall not apply to any fictitious name filed by a foreign corporation pursuant to this section, and a filing under section one hundred thirty of the general business law shall not constitute the adoption of a fictitious name.

§ 1302. Application to existing authorized foreign corporations.

Every foreign corporation which on the effective day of this chapter is authorized to do business in this state under a certificate of authority heretofore issued to it by the secretary of state shall continue to have such authority. Such foreign corporation, its shareholders, directors and officers shall have the same rights, franchises and privileges and shall be subject to the same limitations, restrictions, liabilities and penalties as a foreign corporation authorized under this chapter, its shareholders, directors and officers respectively. Reference in this chapter to an application for authority shall, unless the context otherwise requires, include the statement and designation and any amendment thereof required to be filed by the secretary of state under prior statutes to obtain a certificate of authority.

§ 1303. Violations.

The attorney-general may bring an action to restrain a foreign corporation from doing in this state without authority any business for the doing of which it is required to be authorized in this state, or from doing in this state any business not set forth in its application for authority or certificate of amendment filed by the department of state. The attorney-general may bring an action or special proceeding to annul the authority of a foreign corporation doing in this state any business not set forth in its application for authority or certificate of amendment or the authority of which was obtained through fraudulent misrepresentation or concealment of a material fact or to enjoin or annul the authority of any foreign corporation which within this state contrary to law has done or omitted any act which if done by a domestic corporation would be a cause for its dissolution under section 1101 (Attorney-general's action for judicial dissolution) or to annul the authority of a foreign corporation that has been dissolved or had its authority or existence otherwise terminated or cancelled in the jurisdiction of its incorporation. The attorney-general shall deliver a certified copy of the order of annulment to the department of state. Upon the filing thereof by the department of state the authority of the foreign corporation to do business in this state shall be annulled. The secretary of state shall continue as agent of the foreign corporation upon whom process against it may be served in any action or special proceeding based upon any liability or obligation incurred by the foreign corporation within the state prior to the filing of the certified copy of the order of annulment by the department of state.

§ 1304. Application for authority; contents.

(a) A foreign corporation may apply for authority to do business in this state. An application, entitled "Application for authority of . . . . (name of corporation) under section 1304 of the Business Corporation Law", shall be signed and verified by an officer of or attorney-in-fact for the corporation and delivered to the department of state. It shall set forth:

(1) The name of the foreign corporation.

(2) The fictitious name the corporation agrees to use in this state pursuant to section 1301 of this chapter, if applicable.

(3) The jurisdiction and date of its incorporation.

(4) The purpose or purposes for which it is formed, it being sufficient to state, either alone or with other purposes, that the purpose of the corporation is to engage in any lawful act or activity for which corporations may be organized under this chapter, provided that it also state that it is not formed to engage in any act or activity requiring the consent or approval of any state official, department, board, agency or other body without such consent or approval first being obtained. By such statement all lawful acts and activities shall be within the purposes of the corporation, except for express limitations therein or in this chapter, if any.

(5) The county within this state in which its office is to be located.

(6) A designation of the secretary of state as its agent upon whom process against it may be served and the post office address within or without this state to which the secretary of state shall mail a copy of any process against it served upon him.

(7) If it is to have a registered agent, his name and address within this state and a statement that the registered agent is to be its agent upon whom process against it may be served.

(8) A statement that the foreign corporation has not since its incorporation or since the date its authority to do business in this state was last surrendered, engaged in any activity in this state, except as set forth in paragraph (b) of section 1301 (Authorization of foreign corporations), or in lieu thereof the consent of the state tax commission to the filing of the application, which consent shall be attached thereto.

(b) Attached to the application for authority shall be a certificate by an authorized officer of the jurisdiction of its incorporation that the foreign corporation is an existing corporation. If such certificate is in a foreign language, a translation thereof under oath of the translator shall be attached thereto.

§ 1305. Application for authority; effect.

Upon filing by the department of state of the application for authority the foreign corporation shall be authorized to do in this state any business set forth in the application. Such authority shall continue so long as it retains its authority to do such business in the jurisdiction of its incorporation and its authority to do business in this state has not been surrendered, suspended or annulled in accordance with law.

§ 1306. **Powers of authorized foreign corporations.**

An authorized foreign corporation shall have such powers as are permitted by the laws of the jurisdiction of its incorporation but no greater powers than those of a domestic corporation formed for the business set forth in the application for authority.

§ 1307. **Tenure of real property.**

A foreign corporation may acquire and hold real property in this state in furtherance of its corporate purposes and may convey the same by deed or otherwise in the same manner as a domestic corporation.

§ 1308. **Amendments or changes.**

(a) An authorized foreign corporation may amend or change its application for authority from time to time in any and as many of the following respects as may be desired if the amendments contain only such provisions as might be lawfully contained in an application for authority at the time of making such amendment:

(1) To change its corporate name if such change has been effected under the laws of the jurisdiction of its incorporation.

(2) To change its fictitious name filed pursuant to paragraph (d) of section 1301 of this chapter, to another fictitious name, if its true corporate name is not available for use in this state.

(3) To delete its fictitious name filed pursuant to paragraph (d) of section 1301 of this chapter, if its true corporate name is now available for use in this state.

(4) To adopt a fictitious name when the corporate name is changed and is not available in this state.

(5) To enlarge, limit or otherwise change the business which it proposes to do in this state.

(6) To change the location of its office in this state.

(7) To specify or change the post office address to which the secretary of state shall mail a copy of any process against it served upon him.

(8) To make, revoke or change the designation of a registered agent or to specify or change his address.

§ 1309. **Certificate of amendment; contents, effect.**

• • • •

§ 1309-A. **Certificate of change; contents.**

• • • •

§ 1310. **Surrender of authority.**

(a) An authorized foreign corporation may surrender its authority. A certificate, entitled "Certificate of surrender of authority of . . . . (name of corporation) under section 1310 of the Business Corporation Law", shall be signed, verified by an officer of or attorney-in-fact for the foreign corporation or by a trustee, receiver or other liquidator of such corporation, and delivered to the department of state. It shall set forth:

(1) The name of the foreign corporation as it appears on the index of names of existing domestic and authorized foreign corporations of any type or kind in the department of state, division of corporations or, the fictitious name the corporation has agreed to use in this state pursuant to paragraph (d) of section 1301 of this chapter.

(2) The jurisdiction of its incorporation.

(3) The date it was authorized to do business in this state.

(4) That it surrenders its authority to do business in this state.

(5) That it revokes the authority of its registered agent, if any, previously designated and consents that process against it in any action or special proceeding based upon any liability or obligation incurred by it within this state before the filing of the certificate of surrender may be served on the secretary of state after the filing thereof in the manner set forth in paragraph (b) of section 306 (Service of process).

(6) A post office address within or without this state to which the secretary of state shall mail a copy of any process against it served upon him.

(b) The department shall not file such certificate unless the consent of the state tax commission to the surrender of authority is attached thereto.

(c) The authority of the foreign corporation to do business in this state shall terminate on the filing by the department of state of the certificate of surrender of authority.

(d) The post office address specified under paragraph (a) (6) may be changed. A certificate, entitled "Certificate of amendment of certificate of surrender of authority of . . . . (name of corporation) under section 1310 of the Business Corporation Law", shall be signed, verified as provided in paragraph (a) and delivered to the department of state. It shall set forth: . . .

§ 1311. Termination of existence.

When an authorized foreign corporation is dissolved or its authority or existence is otherwise terminated or cancelled in the jurisdiction of its incorporation or when such foreign corporation is merged into or consolidated with another foreign corporation, a certificate of the secretary of state, or official performing the equivalent function as to corporate records, of the jurisdiction of incorporation of such foreign corporation attesting to the occurrence of any such event or a certified copy of an order or decree of a court of such jurisdiction directing the dissolution of such foreign corporation, the termination of its existence or the cancellation of its authority shall be delivered to the department of state. The filing of the certificate, order or decree shall have the same effect as the filing of a certificate of surrender of authority under section 1310 (Surrender of authority). The secretary of state shall continue as agent of the foreign corporation upon whom process against it may be served in the manner set forth in paragraph (b) of section 306 (Service of process), in any action or special proceeding based upon any liability or obligation incurred by the foreign corporation within this state prior to the filing of such certificate, order or decree and he shall promptly cause a copy of any such process to be mailed by registered mail, return receipt requested, to such foreign corporation at the post office address on file in his office specified for such purpose. The post office address may be changed by signing, verifying and delivering to the department of state a certificate of change setting forth the statements required under section 1309–A (Certificate of change; contents) to effect a change in the post office address under subparagraph (a) (4) of section 1308 (Amendments or changes).

§ 1312. Actions or special proceedings by unauthorized foreign corporations.

(a) A foreign corporation doing business in this state without authority shall not maintain any action or special proceeding in this state unless and until such corporation has been authorized to do business in this state and it has paid to the state all fees, penalties and franchise taxes for the years or parts thereof during which it did business in this state without authority. This prohibition shall apply to any successor in interest of such foreign corporation.

(b) The failure of a foreign corporation to obtain authority to do business in this state shall not impair the validity of any contract or act of the foreign corporation or the right of any other party to the contract to maintain any action or special proceeding thereon, and shall not prevent the foreign corporation from defending any action or special proceeding in this state.

§ 1313. **Actions or special proceedings by foreign corporations.**

An action or special proceeding may be maintained by a foreign corporation, in like manner and subject to the same limitations, as an action or special proceeding brought by a domestic corporation, except as otherwise prescribed by statute.

§ 1314. **Actions or special proceedings against foreign corporations.**

(a) An action or special proceeding against a foreign corporation may be maintained by a resident of this state or by a domestic corporation of any type or kind for any cause of action.

(b) Except as otherwise provided in this article, an action or special proceeding against a foreign corporation may be maintained by another foreign corporation of any type or kind or by a nonresident in the following cases only:

(1) Where it is brought to recover damages for the breach of a contract made or to be performed within this state, or relating to property situated within this state at the time of the making of the contract.

(2) Where the subject matter of the litigation is situated within this state.

(3) Where the cause of action arose within this state, except where the object of the action or special proceeding is to affect the title of real property situated outside this state.

(4) Where, in any case not included in the preceding subparagraphs, a non-domiciliary would be subject to the personal jurisdiction of the courts of this state under section 302 of the civil practice law and rules.

(5) Where the defendant is a foreign corporation doing business or authorized to do business in this state.

(c) Paragraph (b) does not apply to a corporation which was formed under the laws of the United States and which maintains an office in this state.

§ 1315. **Record of shareholders.**

(a) Any resident of this state who shall have been a shareholder of record, for at least six months immediately preceding his demand, of a foreign corporation doing business in this state, or any resident of this state holding, or thereunto authorized in writing by the holders of, at least five percent of any class of the outstanding shares, upon at least five days' written demand may require such foreign corporation to produce a record of its shareholders setting forth the names and addresses of all shareholders, the number and class of shares held by each and the dates when they respectively became the owners of record thereof and shall have the right to examine in person or by agent or attorney at the office of the foreign corporation in this state or at the office of its transfer agent or registrar in this state or at such other place in the county in this state in which the foreign corporation is doing business as may be designated by the foreign corporation, during the usual business hours, the record of shareholders or an exact copy thereof certified as correct by the corporate officer or agent responsible for keeping or producing such record and to make extracts therefrom. Resident holders of voting trust certificates representing shares of the foreign corporation shall for the purpose of this section be regarded as shareholders.

(b) An examination authorized by paragraph (a) may be denied to such shareholder or other person upon his refusal to furnish to the foreign corporation or its transfer agent or registrar an affidavit that such inspection is not desired for a purpose which is in the interest of a business or object other than the business of the foreign corporation and that such shareholder or other person has not within five years sold or offered for sale any list of shareholders of any corporation of any type or kind, whether or not formed under the laws of this state, or aided or abetted any person in procuring any such record of shareholders of any such purpose.

(c) Upon refusal by the foreign corporation or by an officer or agent of the foreign corporation to produce for examination or to permit an examination of the record of shareholders as herein provided, the person making the demand for production and examination may apply to the supreme court in the judicial district where the office of the foreign corporation within the state is located, upon such notice as the court may direct, for an order directing the foreign corporation, its officer or agent, to show cause why an order should not be granted directing such production and permitting such examination by the applicant. Upon the return day of the order to show cause, the court shall hear the parties summarily, by affidavit or otherwise, and if it appears that the applicant is qualified and entitled to such examination, the court shall grant an order compelling such production for examination and awarding such further relief as to the court may seem just and proper.

(d) Nothing herein contained shall impair the power of courts to compel the production for examination of the books of a foreign corporation. The record of shareholders specified in paragraph (a) shall be prima facie evidence of the facts therein stated in favor of the plaintiff in any action or special proceeding against such foreign corporation or any of its officers, directors or shareholders.

§ 1316. **Voting trust records.**

• • • •

§ 1317. **Liabilities of directors and officers of foreign corporations.**

(a) Except as otherwise provided in this chapter, the directors and officers of a foreign corporation doing business in this state are subject, to the same extent as directors and officers of a domestic corporation, to the provisions of:

(1) Section 719 (Liability of directors in certain cases) except subparagraph (a) (3) thereof, and

(2) Section 720 (Action against directors and officers for misconduct.)

(b) Any liability imposed by paragraph (a) may be enforced in, and such relief granted by, the courts in this state, in the same manner as in the case of a domestic corporation.

§ 1318. **Liability of foreign corporations for failure to disclose required information.**

(a) A foreign corporation doing business in this state shall, in the same manner as a domestic corporation, disclose to its shareholders of record who are residents of this state the information required under paragraph (c) of section 510 (Dividends or other distributions in cash or property), paragraphs (f) and (g) of section 511 (Share distributions and changes), paragraph (d) of section 515 (Reacquired shares), paragraph (c) of section 516 (Reduction of stated capital in certain cases), subparagraph (a) (4) of section 517 (Special provisions relative to surplus and reserves) or paragraph (f) of section 519 (Convertible shares and bonds), and shall be liable as provided in section 520 (Liability for failure to disclose required information) for failure to comply in good faith with these requirements.

(b) For the purposes of this section, an authorized foreign corporation may by board action determine the amount of its earned surplus before the declaration of its first dividend after either (1) the effective date of this chapter or (2) the date of filing of its application for authority under this chapter, whichever is later, and such determination if made in good faith shall be conclusive. Thereafter such foreign corporation may determine the amount or availability of its earned surplus in the same manner as a domestic corporation.

§ 1319. Applicability of other provisions.

(a) In addition to articles 1 (Short title; definitions; application; certificates; miscellaneous), and 3 (Corporate name and service of process) and the other sections of article 13, the following provisions, to the extent provided therein, shall apply to a foreign corporation doing business in this state, its directors, officers and shareholders:

(1) Section 623 (Procedure to enforce shareholder's right to receive payment for shares).

(2) Section 626 (Shareholders' derivative action brought in the right of the corporation to procure a judgment in its favor).

(3) Section 627 (Security for expenses in shareholders' derivative action brought in the right of the corporation to procure a judgment in its favor).

(4) Sections 721 (Exclusivity of statutory provisions for indemnification of directors and officers) through 727 (Insurance for indemnification of directors and officers), inclusive.

(5) Section 808 (Reorganization under act of congress).

(6) Section 907 (Merger or consolidation of domestic and foreign corporations).

§ 1320. Exemption from certain provisions.

• • • •

§ 1501. Definitions.

As used in this article, unless the context otherwise requires, the term:

(a) "licensing authority" means the regents of the university of the state of New York or the state education department, as the case may be, in the case of all professions licensed under title eight of the education law, and the appropriate appellate division of the supreme court in the case of the profession of law.

(b) "Profession" includes any practice as an attorney and counselor-at-law, or as a licensed physician, and those occupations designated in title eight of the education law.

(c) "Professional service" means any type of service to the public which may be lawfully rendered by a member of a profession within the purview of his profession.

(d) "Professional service corporation" means a corporation organized under this article.

(e) "Officer" does not include the secretary or an assistant secretary of a corporation having only one shareholder.

§ 1502. Corporations organized under other provisions of law.

The provisions of this article shall not apply to corporations heretofore or hereafter duly organized under any other provision of law.

§ 1503. Organization.

(a) Notwithstanding any other provision of law, one or more individuals duly authorized by law to render the same professional service within the state may organize, or cause to be organized, a professional service corporation for pecuniary profit under this article for the purpose of rendering the same professional service, except that one or more individuals duly authorized by law to practice professional engineering, architecture, landscape architecture, or land surveying within the state may organize or cause to be organized, a professional service corporation for pecuniary profit under this article for the purpose of rendering such professional services as such individuals are authorized to practice.

(b) The certificate of incorporation of a professional service corporation shall meet the requirements of this chapter and (i) shall state the profession or professions to be practiced by such corporation and the names and residence addresses of all individuals who are to be the original shareholders, directors and officers of such corporation, and (ii) shall have attached thereto a certificate or certificates issued by the licensing authority certifying that each of the proposed shareholders, directors and officers is authorized by law to practice a profession which the corporation is being organized to practice and, if applicable, that one or more of such individuals is authorized to practice each profession which the corporation will be authorized to practice.

(c) A certified copy of the certificate of incorporation and of each amendment thereto shall be filed by the corporation with the licensing authority within thirty days after the filing of such certificate or amendment with the department of state.

(d) A professional service corporation, other than a corporation authorized to practice law, shall be under the supervision of the regents of the university of the state of New York and be subject to disciplinary proceedings and penalties, and its certificate of incorporation shall be subject to suspension, revocation or annulment for cause, in the same manner and to the same extent as is provided with respect to individuals and their licenses, certificates, and registrations in title eight of the education law relating to the applicable profession. Notwithstanding the provisions of this subdivision, a professional service corporation authorized to practice medicine shall be subject to the prehearing procedures and hearing procedures as is provided with respect to individual physicians and their licenses in Title II-A of article two of the public health law.

(e) A corporation authorized to practice law shall be subject to the regulation and control of, and its certificate of incorporation shall be subject to suspension, revocation or annulment for cause by, the appellate division of the supreme court and the court of appeals in the same manner and to the same extent provided in the judiciary law with respect to individual attorneys and counselors-at-law. Such corporation need not qualify for any certification under section four hundred sixty-four of the judiciary law, take an oath of office under section four hundred sixty-six of such law or register under section four hundred sixty-seven of such law.

(f) The order of suspension, revocation or annulment of the certificate of incorporation of a professional service corporation pursuant to subdivisions (e) and (f) of this section shall be effective upon the filing of such order with the department of state.

§ 1504. Rendering of professional service.

(a) No professional service corporation may render professional services except through individuals authorized by law to render such professional services as individuals.

(b) Each final plan and report made or issued by a corporation practicing professional engineering, architecture, landscape architecture or land surveying shall bear the name and seal of one or more professional engineers, architects, landscape architects, or land surveyors, respectively, who are in responsible charge of such plan or report.

(c) Each report, diagnosis, prognosis, and prescription made or issued by a corporation practicing medicine, dentistry, podiatry, optometry, ophthalmic dispensing, veterinary medicine, pharmacy, nursing, physiotherapy or chiropractic shall bear the signature of one or more physicians, dentists, podiatrists, optometrists, ophthalmic dispensers, veterinarians, pharmacists, nurses, physiotherapists, or chiropractors, respectively, who are in responsible charge of such report, diagnosis, prognosis, or prescription.

(d) Each record, transcript, report and hearing report prepared by a corporation practicing certified shorthand reporting shall bear the signature of one or more certified shorthand reporters who are in responsible charge of such record, transcript, report, or hearing report.

(e) Each corporation practicing public accounting or certified public accounting shall maintain records indicating the identity of each public accountant or certified public accountant, respectively, who was responsible for each report or statement which is issued prepared or examined by such corporation.

(f) Each opinion prepared by a corporation practicing law shall bear the signature of one or more attorneys and counsellors-at-law who are in responsible charge of such opinion.

(g) In addition to the requirements in subdivisions (b) through (f), inclusive, each document prepared by a corporation which under the rules, regulations, laws or customs of the applicable profession is required to bear the signature of an individual in responsible charge of such document, shall be signed by one or more such individuals.

§ 1505. Professional relationships and liabilities.

(a) Each shareholder, employee or agent of a professional service corporation shall be personally and fully liable and accountable for any negligent or wrongful act or misconduct committed by him or by any person under his direct supervision and control while rendering professional services on behalf of such corporation.

(b) The relationship of an individual to a professional service corporation with which such individual is associated, whether as shareholder, director, officer, employee or agent, shall not modify or diminish the jurisdiction over him of the licensing authority and in the case of an attorney and counsellor-at-law, the other courts of this state.

§ 1506. Purposes of incorporation.

No professional service corporation shall engage in any business other than the rendering of the professional services for which it was incorporated; provided that such corporation may invest its funds in real estate, mortgages, stocks, bonds or any other type of investments.

§ 1507. Issuance of shares.

A professional service corporation may issue shares only to individuals who are authorized by law to practice in this state a profession which such corporation is authorized to practice and who are or have been engaged in the practice of such profession in such corporation or a predecessor entity, or who will engage in the practice of such profession in such corporation within thirty days of the date such shares are issued. No shareholder of a professional service corporation shall enter into a voting trust agreement, proxy, or any other type agreement vesting in another person, other than another shareholder of the same corporation or a person who would be eligible to become a shareholder if employed by the corporation, the authority to exercise voting power of any or all of his shares. All shares issued, agreements made, or proxies granted in violation of this section shall be void.

§ 1508. Directors and officers.

No individual may be a director or officer of a professional service corporation unless he is authorized by law to practice in this state a profession which such corporation is authorized to practice and is either a shareholder of such corporation or engaged in the practice of his profession in such corporation.

§ 1509. Disqualification of shareholders, directors, officers and employees.

If any shareholder, director, officer or employee of a professional service corporation who has been rendering professional service to the public becomes legally disqualified to practice his profession within this state, he shall sever all employment with, and financial interests (other than interests as a creditor) in, such corporation forthwith or as otherwise provided in section 1510. All provisions of law regulating the rendering of professional services by a person elected or appointed to a public office shall be applicable to a shareholder, director, officer and employee of such corporation in the same manner and to the same extent as if fully set forth herein. Such legal disqualification to practice his profession within this state shall be deemed to constitute an irrevocable offer by the disqualified shareholder to sell his shares to the corporation, pursuant to the provisions of section 1510 or of the certificate of incorporation, by-laws or agreement among the corporation and all shareholders, whichever is applicable. Compliance with the terms of such offer shall be specifically enforceable in the courts of this state. A professional service corporation's failure to enforce compliance with this provision shall constitute a ground for forfeiture of its certificate of incorporation and its dissolution.

§ 1510. Death or disqualification of shareholders.

(a) A professional service corporation shall purchase or redeem the shares of a shareholder in case of his death or disqualification pursuant to the provisions of section 1509, within six months after the appointment of the executor or administrator or other legal representative of the estate of such deceased shareholder, or within six months after such disqualification, at the book value of such shares as of the end of the month immediately preceding the death or disqualification of the shareholder as determined from the books and records of the corporation in accordance with its regular method of accounting. The certificate of incorporation, the by-laws of the corporation or an agreement among the corporation and all shareholders may modify this section by providing for a shorter period of purchase or redemption, of an alternate method of determining the price to be paid for the shares, or both. If the corporation shall fail to purchase or redeem such shares within the required period, a successful plaintiff in an action to recover the purchase price of such shares shall also be awarded reasonable attorney's fees and costs. Limitations on the purchase or redemption of shares set forth in section five hundred thirteen shall not apply to the purchase or redemption of shares pursuant to this section. Nothing herein contained shall prevent a corporation from paying pension benefits or other deferred compensation to or on behalf of a former or deceased officer, director or employee thereof as otherwise permitted by law. The provisions of this section shall not be deemed to require the purchase of the shares of a disqualified shareholder where the period of disqualification is for less than six months, and the shareholder again becomes eligible to practice his profession within six months from the date of disqualification.

(b) Notwithstanding the provisions of subdivision (a), the corporation shall not be required to purchase or redeem the shares of a deceased or disqualified shareholder if such shares, within the time limit prescribed by subdivision (a), are sold or transferred to another professional pursuant to the provisions of section 1511.

§ 1511. Transfer of shares.

No shareholder of a professional service corporation may sell or transfer his shares in such corporation except to another individual who is eligible to have shares issued to him by such corporation or except in trust to another individual who would be eligible to receive shares if he were employed by the corporation. Nothing herein contained shall be construed to prohibit the transfer of shares by operation of law or by court decree. No transferee of shares by operation of law or court decree may vote the shares for any purpose whatsoever except with respect to corporate action under section nine hundred nine and section one thousand one. The restriction in the preceding sentence shall not apply, however, where such transferee would be eligible to have shares issued to him if he were an employee of the corporation and, if there are other shareholders, a majority of such other shareholders shall fail to redeem the shares so transferred, pursuant to section 1510, within sixty days of receiving written notice of such transfer. Any sale or transfer, except by operation of law or court decree or except for a corporation having only one shareholder, may be made only after the same shall have been approved by the board of directors, or at a shareholders' meeting specially called for such purpose by such proportion, not less than a majority, of the outstanding shares as may be provided in the certificate of incorporation or in the by-laws of such professional service corporation. At such shareholders' meeting the shares held by the shareholder proposing to sell or transfer his shares may not be voted or counted for any purpose, unless all shareholders consent that such shares be voted or counted. The certificate of incorporation or the by-laws of the professional service corporation, or the professional service corporation and the shareholders by private agreement, may provide, in lieu of or in addition to the foregoing provisions, for the alienation of shares and may require the redemption or purchase of such shares by such corporation at prices and in a manner specifically set forth therein. The existence of the restrictions on the sale or transfer of shares, as contained in this article and, if applicable, in the certificate of incorporation, by-laws, stock purchase or stock redemption agreement, shall be noted conspicuously on the face or back of every certificate for shares issued by a professional service corporation. Any sale or transfer in violation of such restrictions shall be void.

§ 1512. Corporate name.

(a) Notwithstanding any other provision of law, the name of a professional service corporation may contain any word which, at the time of incorporation, could be used in the name of a partnership practicing a profession which the corporation is authorized to practice, and may not contain any word which could not be used by such a partnership. Provided, however, the name of a professional service corporation may not contain the name of a deceased person unless

(1) such person's name was part of the corporate name at the time of such person's death; or

(2) such person's name was part of the name of an existing partnership and at least two-thirds of such partnership's partners become shareholders of the corporation.

(b) Such corporate name shall end with the words "Professional Corporation" or the abbreviation "P.C." The provisions of paragraph one of subdivision (a) of section three hundred one shall not apply to a professional service corporation.

§ 1513. Business corporation law applicable.

This chapter, except article thirteen and article fifteen–A, shall be applicable to a professional service corporation except to the extent that the provisions thereof conflict with this article. A professional service corporation may consolidate or merge only with another corporation organized under this article or authorized to do business in this state under article fifteen–A of this chapter, and only if all of the professions practiced by such corporations could be practiced by a single corporation organized under this article.

§ 1514. Annual statement.

Each professional service corporation shall, on or before the first day of July of each year, furnish a statement to the licensing authority listing the name and residence address of each shareholder, director and officer of such corporation and certifying that all such individuals are authorized by law in this state to practice a profession which such corporation is authorized to practice. The statement shall be signed by the president or any vice-president of the corporation and attested to by the secretary or any assistant secretary of the corporation.

§ 1515. Regulation of professions.

This article shall not repeal, modify or restrict any provision of the education law or the judiciary law regulating the professions referred to therein except to the extent in conflict herewith.

§ 1516. Corporate mergers, consolidations and other reorganizations.

Notwithstanding any inconsistent provision of this article, a professional service corporation, pursuant to the provisions of article nine of this chapter, may be merged or consolidated with another corporation formed pursuant to the provisions of this chapter or with a foreign corporation, or may be otherwise reorganized, provided that the corporation which survives or which is formed pursuant thereto is a professional service corporation or a foreign professional corporation practicing the same profession or professions in this state or the state of incorporation. The restrictions on the issuance, transfer or sale of shares of a professional service corporation shall be suspended for a period not exceeding thirty days with respect to any issuance, transfer or sale of shares made pursuant to such merger, consolidation or reorganization, provided that (i) no person who would not be eligible to be a shareholder in the absence of this section shall vote the shares of or receive any distribution from such corporation; (ii) after such merger, consolidation or reorganization, any professional service corporation which survives or which is created thereby shall be subject to all of the provisions of this article, and (iii) shares thereafter only may be held by persons who are eligible to receive shares of such professional service corporation. Nothing herein contained shall be construed as permitting the practice of a profession in this state by a corporation which is not incorporated pursuant to the provisions of this article or authorized to do business in this state pursuant to the provisions of article fifteen–A of this chapter. For the purposes of this section, other reorganizations shall be limited to those reorganizations defined in paragraph one of subsection (a) of section three hundred sixty-eight of the internal revenue code.

ARTICLE 15–A—FOREIGN PROFESSIONAL SERVICE CORPORATIONS

§ 1525. Definitions.
§ 1526. Rendering of professional service.
§ 1527. Professional relationships and liabilities.
§ 1528. Foreign professional service corporation.
§ 1529. Business corporation law applicable.
§ 1530. Filing requirements.

§ 1531. **Annual statement.**
§ 1532. **Regulation of professions.**
§ 1533. **Licensing of individuals.**

ARTICLE 16—SECURITY TAKEOVER DISCLOSURE ACT

§ 1600. **Short title.**
This article shall be known as the security takeover disclosure act.

§ 1601. **Definitions.**
As used in this article, the following terms shall have the following meanings:

(a) "Takeover bid" means the acquisition of or offer to acquire by an offeror from an offeree, pursuant to a tender offer or request or invitation for tenders, any equity security of a target company, if after acquisition thereof the offeror would, directly or indirectly, be a beneficial owner of more than five percent of any class of the issued and outstanding equity securities of such target company.

Such term does not include:

(1) Bids made by a dealer for his own account in the ordinary course of his business of buying and selling such security;

(2) An offer to acquire such equity security solely in exchange for other securities, or the acquisition of such equity security pursuant to such offer, for the sole account of the offeror, in good faith and not for the purpose of avoiding this section, and not involving any public offering of such other securities within the meaning of section four of title one of the "Securities Act of 1933", (48 Stat.77, 15 U.S.C. 77 d (2)); as amended;

(3) Any other offer to acquire an equity security, or the acquisition of such equity security pursuant to such offer, for the sole account of the offeror, from not more than fifty offerees, in good faith and not for the purpose of avoiding the provisions of this article;

(4) Any offer or class of offer where, prior to making the offer, the offeror beneficially owns, directly or indirectly, a majority of the voting equity securities of the target company;

(b) "Offeror" means a person who makes, or in any way participates or aids in making, a takeover bid, and includes persons acting jointly or in concert, or who intend to exercise jointly or in concert any voting rights attached to the securities for which such takeover bid is made. An "offeror" includes an issuer of securities whose securities are or are to be the subject of a takeover bid whether or not the issuer, upon acquisition, will become the beneficial owner of such securities. "An offeror" does not include any bank or broker-dealer in securities loaning funds to the offeror in the ordinary course of the business of the bank or broker-dealer in securities and not otherwise participating in the takeover bid, or any bank, broker-dealer in securities, attorney, accountant or consultant furnishing information or advice to an offeror and not otherwise participating in the takeover bid.

(c) "Offeree" means the beneficial owner, residing in this state, of securities which an offeror acquires or offers to acquire in connection with a takeover bid.

(d) "Target company" means a corporation, organized under the laws of this state and having its principal executive offices or significant business operations located within this state.

(e) "Equity security" means any stock, bond, or other obligation of a target company, the holder of which has the right to vote for the election of members of the board of directors, or those exercising a similar function if the target company is not a corporation, of such target company. Equity security includes any security convertible into an equity security, and also includes any right, option or warrant to purchase an equity security.

§ 1602. Disclosure requirement.

(a) No offeror shall make a takeover bid unless as soon as practicable on the date of commencement of the takeover bid he files with the attorney general at his New York city office and delivers to the target company at its principal executive offices a registration statement containing the information required by section sixteen hundred three of this article.

(b) An offeror shall make full and fair disclosure to offerees of the material information set forth in the registration statement filed pursuant to subdivision (a) of this section.

(c) No solicitation or recommendation to the offerees of a target company to accept or reject a takeover bid shall be made by or on behalf of an offeror or a target company unless at the time copies of such solicitation or recommendation are first published, sent or given to such offerees, the person making such solicitation or recommendation has filed copies of the solicitation or recommendation with the attorney general at his New York city office.

§ 1603. Contents of registration statement.

(a) The registration statement required to be filed pursuant to section sixteen hundred two of this article shall include:

1. Copies of all prospectuses, brochures, advertisements, circulars, letters, or other matter by means of which the offeror proposes to disclose to offerees all information material to a decision to accept or reject the offer;

2. The identity and background of all persons on whose behalf the aquisition of any equity security of the target company has been or is to be effected;

3. The exact title and number of shares outstanding of the class of equity securities being sought, the number of such securities being sought and the consideration being offered therefor;

4. The source and amount of funds or other consideration used or to be used in acquiring any equity security, including a statement describing any securities, other than the existing capital stock or long term debt of the offeror, which are being offered in exchange for the equity securities of the target company also including copies of all loan or credit agreements and letters of commitment used or to be used to secure financing for the acquisition of any equity security of the target company;

5. A statement of any plans or proposals which the offeror, upon gaining control, may have to liquidate the target company, sell its assets, effect a merger or consolidation of it, or make any other major change in its business, corporate structure, management personnel, or policies of employment;

6. The number of shares of any equity security of the target company of which each offeror is beneficial or record owner or has a right to acquire, directly or indirectly, together with the name and address of each person defined in this section as an offeror;

7. Particulars as to any contracts, arrangements, or understandings to which an offeror is party with respect to any equity security of the target company, including without limitation transfers of any equity security, joint ventures, loans or option arrangements, puts and calls, guarantees

of loan, guarantees against loss, guarantees of profits, division of losses or profits, or the giving or withholding of proxies, naming the persons with whom such contracts, arrangements, or understandings have been entered into;

8. Complete information on the organization and operations of offeror, including without limitation the year of organization, form of organization, jurisdiction in which it is organized, a description of each class of the offeror's capital stock and of its long term debt, financial statements for the current period and for the three most recent annual accounting periods, a description of pending legal proceedings other than routine litigation to which the offeror or any of its subsidiaries is a party or of which any of their property is the subject, a brief description of the business done and projected by the offeror and its subsidiaries and the general development of such business over the past five years, the names of all directors and executive officers together with biographical summaries of each for the preceding three years to date; and

9. A statement as to the potential impact, if any, of the offeror's plans or proposals on the residents of New York state, including any material change in the location of the target company's offices or business activities within this state; any plant or facility relocation; any plant or facility closings; any significant reduction in the workforce at an individual plant or facility; any other material change in the number, job classification, compensation, or other terms and conditions of employment of persons employed by the target company in this state; any material change in the relationships of the target company with suppliers or customers within this state, or any other material changes in the target company's business, corporate structure, management, personnel or activities which would have a substantial impact on residents of this state;

10. Particulars as to any pension plans; profit sharing plans; savings plans; educational opportunities; relocation adjustments; labor relations records, including violations of the federal national labor relations act, occupational safety and health act of 1970, fair labor standards act, or employee retirement and income security act, as amended, finally adjudicated or settled within five years of the commencement of the takeover bid; earnings and dividend growth; community activities; and charitable, cultural, educational and civic contributions of the offeror;

11. If the offeror is a natural person, information concerning his identity and background, including without limitation financial statements for the current and three preceding years, a description of his business activities and affiliations during that time period, and a description of any pending legal or administrative proceedings, other than routine and immaterial litigation, to which the offeror is a party or of which any of his property is the subject; and

12. If debt securities or preferred stock are either offered in the takeover bid or used as a source of funds in making the takeover bid, the investment rating, if any, by a generally recognized rating service of such debt security or preferred stock.

(b) If any material change occurs in the facts set forth in the registration statement required by subdivision (a) of section sixteen hundred two of this article, the offeror who filed such statement shall promptly notify the attorney general and the target company of such change in writing or by telephone confirmed in writing and shall amend the registration statement to reflect such change promptly but not later than the date such change is first published, sent or given to offerees.

(c) The attorney general may permit the omission of any information required by subdivision (a) of this section to be included in the registration statement if he determines that such information is immaterial or otherwise unnecessary for the protection of offerees.

§ 1604. Enforcement.

(a) The attorney general may conduct such investigation as he deems necessary concerning any takeover bid for the purpose of determining compliance with the requirements of this article. As part of such investigation the attorney general may require persons to file statements in writing and under oath with his office, subpoena witnesses, compel their attendance, examine them under oath and require the production of books, records, documents and papers.

(b) In the event the attorney general determines that any person is violating or about to violate any provision of this article, or any order, rule or regulation issued pursuant thereto, he may seek, in a court of competent jurisdiction, an injunction temporarily or permanently barring that person from making or taking part in or continuing a takeover bid or from taking up or paying for shares tendered by offerees pursuant to a takeover bid, and the court may grant the relief applied for or so much thereof as it may deem proper.

§ 1605. Violations; penalties.

(a) Every person who willfully violates any provision of this article shall be guilty of a class E felony; every person who willfully violates any order, rule or regulation issued pursuant thereto, shall be guilty of a class A misdemeanor.

(b) A violation of any provision of this article shall constitute a fraudulent practice within the meaning of article twenty-three-A of the general business law.

(c) Every person who violates any provision of this article shall be subject to a civil penalty of one thousand dollars per violation if a natural person or ten thousand dollars per violation if a corporation. When the violation is the failure to file a registration statement as required by subdivision (a) of section sixteen hundred two of this article, the failure to file a solicitation or recommendation as required by subdivision (c) of section sixteen hundred two of this article, or the failure to amend such registration statement as required by subdivision (b) of section sixteen hundred three of this article, each business day of non-registration or failure to file a recommendation or solicitation or failure to amend constitutes a separate violation. The penalty imposed by this section shall be cumulative and more than one penalty shall be recoverable in the same action in any court of competent jurisdiction.

§ 1606. Administration.

(a) This article shall be administered by the attorney general and employees designated by him within the department of law. The attorney general is hereby empowered to promulgate, alter, amend or revoke rules and regulations necessary to carry out the purposes of this article.

(b) The attorney general may establish fees for the filing of any registration statement, not to exceed two thousand five hundred dollars, to recover the costs of administering this article. Such fees may vary according to the maximum consideration payable by the offeror for the securities which are the subject of the takeover bid.

§ 1607. Prosecutions and immunity.

(a) The attorney general may prosecute every person charged with the commission of a criminal offense arising from the violation of any provision of this article. In all such proceedings, the attorney general may appear in person or by his deputy before any court of record or any grand jury and exercise all the powers and perform all the duties in respect of such actions or proceedings which the district attorney would otherwise be authorized or required to exercise or perform; or the attorney general may in his discretion transmit evidence, proof and information as to such offense to the district attorney of the county or counties in which the alleged violation has occurred, and every district attorney to whom such evidence, proof and information is so transmitted shall forthwith proceed to prosecute any corporation, company, association, or officer, manager or agent thereof, or any firm or person charged with such violation. In any such proceeding, wherein the attorney general has appeared either in person or by deputy, the district attorney shall only exercise such powers and perform such duties as are required of him by the attorney general or the deputy attorney general so appearing.

(b) Upon any investigation before the attorney general or his deputy or other officer designated by him, or in any criminal proceeding before any court, magistrate or grand jury, pursuant to or for a violation of any of the provisions of this article, the attorney general, his deputy or other officer designated by him, or the court, magistrate or grand jury, may confer immunity in accordance with the provisions of section 50.20 of the criminal procedure law.

§ 1608. **Designation of secretary of state for service.**

(a) Every nonresident offeror, whether or not such offeror has filed a registration statement, except a foreign corporation which has appointed and keeps a resident agent in this state, shall be deemed to have appointed the secretary of state as his agent upon whom may be served any lawful process, authorized by this article, with the same effect as though served upon the offeror personally.

(b) Service of process pursuant to this section shall be accomplished by leaving a copy of the process in the office of the secretary of state, but it shall not be effective unless notice of the service and a copy of the process is sent by certified or registered mail to the nonresident offeror served, at his last known address.

§ 1609. **Fraudulent, deceptive or manipulative practices.**

(a) No person shall make any untrue statement of a material fact or omit to state any material fact necessary in order to make the statements made, in the light of the circumstances under which they are made, not misleading, or engage in any fraudulent, deceptive, or manipulative acts or practices, in connection with any takeover bid or any solicitation of offerees in opposition to or in favor of any such takeover bid.

(b) It shall constitute a violation of this article for any person who is in possession of material information relating to any takeover bid, which information he knows or has reason to know is nonpublic, which he acquired either before or after the commencement of the takeover bid, and which he knows or has reason to know has been acquired directly or indirectly from an offeror, a target company, or any officer, director, partner or employee or any other person acting on behalf of the offeror or target company, to purchase or sell or cause to be purchased or sold, within or from this state, any securities sought or to be sought by such takeover bid or any securities convertible into or exchangeable for any such securities or any option or right to obtain or to dispose of any such securities.

(c) Fraudulent, deceptive or manipulative acts or practices include without limitation those acts and practices proscribed by rules and regulations which the attorney general is hereby empowered to adopt, promulgate, amend and rescind as is necessary to carry out the provisions of this section.

§ 1610. Exclusions.

This article shall not apply when:

(a) The offeror or the target company is a public utility or a public utility holding company as defined in section two of the "Public Utility Holding Company Act of 1935," (49 Stat. 803, 15 U.S.C. 79), as amended, and the takeover bid is subject to approval by the appropriate federal agency as provided in such act;

(b) The offeror or the target company is a bank or a bank holding company as subject to the "Bank Holding Company Act of 1956," (70 Stat. 133, 12 U.S.C. 1841), and subsequent amendments thereto, and the takeover bid is subject to approval by the appropriate federal agency as provided in such act;

(c) The offeror or the target company is a savings and loan holding company as defined in section two of the "Savings and Loan Holding Company Amendments of 1967," (82 Stat. 5, 12 U.S.C. 1730A), as amended, and the takeover bid is subject to approval by the appropriate federal agency as provided in such act;

(d) The offeror and the target company are banks and the offer is part of a merger transaction subject to approval by appropriate federal or state supervisory authorities.

§ 1611. Validity; saving clause.

In the event any provision or application of this article shall be held illegal or invalid for any reason, such holding shall not affect the legality or validity of any other provision or application thereof.

§ 1612. Requirements for certain takeover bids.

If the takeover bid is not subject to the requirements of section 14(d) of the Securities Exchange Act of 1934, 15 U.S.C. §78n(d), the following additional requirements shall apply to the takeover bid:

(a) The takeover bid shall be made on the same terms to all offerees holding the same class or series of securities.

(b) The period of time within which equity securities may be deposited pursuant to a takeover bid shall not be less than thirty business days.

(c) Equity securities deposited pursuant to a takeover bid may be withdrawn at any time until the expiration of thirty business days after the commencement of the takeover bid and at any time after the expiration of sixty-five days from the commencement of the takeover bid, if the shares have not been purchased, and until the expiration of ten business days following the date of commencement of another offeror's takeover bid for the same equity securities if the shares have not been purchased and if the bidder has received notice or otherwise has knowledge of the commencement of such takeover bid.

(d) Where a takeover bid is made for less than all the outstanding equity securities of a class and where a greater number of such securities is deposited pursuant thereto than the offeror is bound or willing to take up and pay for, the securities taken up and paid for by the offeror shall be taken up and paid for as nearly as possible on a pro rata basis, disregarding fractions, according to the number of securities deposited by each shareholder.

(e) Where an offeror increases the consideration offered in a takeover bid, the offeror shall pay the increased consideration for all equity securities accepted, whether such securities have been accepted by the offeror before or after the increase in consideration.

(f)(1) Within ten days of the filing of a registration statement as required by section sixteen hundred two of this article the attorney general may schedule a public hearing or hearings or conduct such investigation as he deems necessary concerning any takeover bid for the purpose of determining compliance with the requirements of this article;

(2) Any such hearing or investigation shall be declared by order of the attorney general;

(3) Any initial hearing shall commence within twenty days of the filing of a registration statement.

(g) In the event the attorney general shall schedule a public hearing or otherwise conduct an investigation pursuant to subdivision (f) of this section, the attorney general may also, in his discretion, issue an order staying the offeror from purchasing or paying for any shares tendered in response to its takeover bid at any time prior to such purchasing or paying for shares tendered. Every person shall comply with every such order.

(h) In the event the attorney general shall issue a stay payment order pursuant to subdivision (g) of this section, the attorney general shall, no later than thirty days from the issuance of such stay payment order, issue an order containing his findings of fact and conclusions of law.

(i) Any stay payment order issued by the attorney general pursuant to subdivision (g) of this section shall automatically expire within sixty days from its issuance except where the attorney general has in his order containing findings of fact and conclusions of law conditioned the purchase and payment for shares tendered upon changes or modifications in the registration statement, in which event any stay payment order shall be vacated by the attorney general after he is satisfied that such changes or modifications have been publicly disseminated to offerees.

(j) The attorney general may apply, on notice to the offeror and the target company, to a court of competent jurisdiction, and such court may grant an application, for good cause, to extend any of the time periods set forth in this section if an extension is necessary for the protection of offerees.

§ 1613. Private right of action.

Any offeree whose equity securities are the subject of a takeover bid and who has been injured by any violation of this article may bring an action in his or her own name to enjoin such unlawful act or practice and to recover actual damages together with reasonable attorney fees in the event the offeree is successful.

APPENDIX 2

Other Relevant Statutes in New York State

General Business Law

§ 130. Filing of certificates by persons conducting business under assumed name or as partners.

1. No person shall hereafter (i) carry on or conduct or transact business in this state under any name or designation other than his or its real name, or (ii) carry on or conduct or transact business in this state as a member of a partnership, unless:

(a) Such person, if other than a corporation, shall file in the office of the clerk of each county in which such business is conducted or transacted a certificate setting forth the name or designation under which and the address within the county at which such business is conducted or transacted, the full name or names of the person or persons conducting or transacting the same, including the names of all partners, with the residence address of each such person, and the age of any person less than eighteen years of age. Each certificate shall be executed and duly acknowledged by the person or, if there be more than one, by all of the persons conducting the business.

(b) Such person, if a corporation, shall file, together with the fees as set forth in subdivision five of this section, in the office of the secretary of state a certificate setting forth the name or designation under which business is carried on or conducted or transacted, its corporate name, the location including number and street, if any, of its principal place of business in the state, the name of each county in which it does business or intends to do business, and the location including number and street, if any, of each place where it carries on or conducts or transacts business in this state. Each certificate shall be executed and duly acknowledged by an officer of the corporation. A corporation which carries on or conducts or transacts business in this state as a member of a partnership shall not be required solely by reason thereof to file the certificate required by this paragraph if the partners shall have filed the certificate required by paragraph (a) of this subdivision.

1-a. As used in this section, unless the context otherwise requires:

(a) "Person" shall mean an individual, partnership, corporation, and unincorporated association;

(b) The "real name" of a corporation shall mean its corporate name as set forth in its certificate of incorporation and any generally accepted, understood or recognizable abbreviations of such corporate name.

(c) The use by a corporation of a divisional, departmental or trade name or designation, in conjunction with the real name of the corporation, shall be deemed to be the use of the real name of the corporation for purposes of this section.

2. (a) No person or persons shall hereafter use or file a certificate for the use of any name or designation to carry on or conduct or transact business in this state which consists of or includes words, or initials and a word or words, which are or appear to be the full name or names, or the initial or intitials and family name of a person or persons, or a colorable simulation thereof, unless:

(1) the words or initials and word or words appearing to be the full name or initials and family name of a person included, are the true full name or the initials and family name of the person or one of the persons conducting the business; or

(2) the words or initials and words so included, which are or appear to be the full name, or the initials and family name, of any person, have a secondary, historic or geographic meaning or connotation apart from that of a name of a person, and the name or designation so used contains a word or words clearly signifying such secondary, historic or geographic meaning or connotation, or is followed by the abbreviation "a.n.", and said secondary, historic or geographic meaning or connotation is stated in the certificate; or

(3) the person or persons conducting the business are successors in interest to the person or persons theretofore using such name or names to carry on or conduct or transact business, in which case the certificate filed shall so state.

(b) In addition to the prohibitions of paragraph (a) of this subdivision, no corporation shall use or file a certificate for the use of any name or designation to carry on or conduct or transact business in this state which consists of or includes a word or words the use of which is prohibited by subparagraphs three through nine of paragraph a of section three hundred one of the business corporation law or subparagraphs three through eight of paragraph a of section three hundred one of the not-for-profit corporation law.

3. Whenever a certificate which has been filed under this section does not accurately set forth the facts required by this section, or within thirty days after there has been a change in such facts, an amended certificate shall be filed which shall identify the original certificate and incorporate the corrections or changes. If such amended certificate is filed for the purpose of adding or withdrawing the name of any person to the original certificate as a person conducting a business or as a partner, such amended certificate must be executed and acknowledged by such person and by any one or more of the other persons named in the original or last amended certificate, unless otherwise provided by an order of the supreme court. Any other amended certificate may be executed and acknowledged by any one or more of the persons named therein as a person conducting the business or as a partner or, in the case of a corporation, by an officer of the corporation.

4. A certified copy of the original certificate, or if an amended certificate has been filed, then of the most recent amended certificate filed shall be conspicuously displayed on the premises at each place in which the business for which the same was filed is conducted.

5. (a) The several county clerks of this state shall keep an alphabetical index of all certificates, provided for herein, together with appropriate notations of the nature of amended certificates and certificates of discontinuance, and for the indexing and filing of such certificates, they shall receive a fee as specified in paragraph two of subdivision (b) of section eight thousand twenty-one of the civil practice law and rules.

(b)(1) The secretary of state shall keep an alphabetical index of all certificates filed by corporations pursuant to subdivision one herein, together with appropriate notations of the nature of amended certificates and certificates of discontinuance; and for the indexing and filing of such certificates, the secretary of state shall receive a fee of twenty-five dollars ($25.00).

(2) The secretary of state shall also collect from each corporation filing on assumed name certificate the fee or fees, as specified in paragraph two of subdivision (b) of section eight thousand twenty-one of the civil practice law and rules, for each county in which the corporation does business or transacts business or intends to do or transact business, as indicated in the certificate. Any fee or fees collected by the secretary of state for filing a certificate or certificates with a county clerk shall be transmitted to such county clerk together with a copy of such certificate or certificates, for indexing and filing as provided above, within ten (10) business days of the last day of the month in which such fees and certificates were received by the secretary of state. The secretary of state shall also transmit to the appropriate county clerk or clerks within such ten-day period a copy of any amended certificates or certificates of discontinuance received by the secretary of state for filing in such counties.

6. A copy of a certificate filed under the provisions of this section, duly certified to by the county clerk or secretary of state in whose office the certificate is filed, shall be presumptive evidence in all courts of this state of the facts therein contained; provided, however, that neither the certificate itself nor the filing thereof shall, for any purpose other than this section, constitute or be construed as an admission by the filing person, or be used as evidence, that such person does or has done business or has carried on, conducted or transacted business in this state or any county therein, or intended to do so.

7. Subdivision one of this section shall not apply to a limited partnership, or to a person who, or a partnership which, has duly filed a certificate of continued use of firm name under article seven of the partnership law, or to a private banker duly authorized by the superintendent of banks to engage in business pursuant to the provisions of the banking law or to a partnership of attorneys and counsellors-at-law engaged in the practice of their profession, and subdivision three of this section shall not apply to such a person or partnership who has filed a certificate of discontinuance under subdivision ten of this section.

8. The failure to comply with the provisions of this section shall in no way affect the rights of third persons, nor shall this section be deemed or construed to limit the liability of partners under the provisions of the partnership law.

8–a. The acceptance of a certificate by the county clerk or the secretary of state for filing pursuant to the provisions of this section shall not be construed to confer any right to or interest in any trade name; nor shall any of the provisions of this section be construed to affect the rights to, or the enforcement of any rights to, any trade name acquired at any time under the common law of this state.

9. Any person or persons carrying on, conducting or transacting business as aforesaid, who knowingly fails to comply with the provisions of this section or who knowingly makes a false statement in a certificate filed thereunder shall be guilty of a misdemeanor. Any person or persons carrying on, conducting or transacting business as aforesaid who fails to comply with the provisions of this section shall be prohibited from maintaining any action or proceeding in any court in this state on any contract, account or transaction made in a name other than its real name until the certificate required by this section has been executed and filed in accordance with the provisions set forth herein.

10. If the business for which a certificate is filed under this section is discontinued, or the conditions under which it is conducted are such that the filing of a certificate in such county or with the secretary of state is no longer required, a certificate of discontinuance may be filed with the county clerk with whom the original certificate was filed or, if a corporation, with the secretary of state, identifying such certificate and also identifying the amended certificate, if any, last previously filed and certifying the facts by reason of which the filing of a certificate is no longer required. The certificate of discontinuance shall be executed and acknowledged in the same manner as an original certificate and shall specify the date on which the discontinuance occurred or the condtions under which the business is conducted changed so that the filing of a certificate is no longer required. The county clerk or, if a corporation, the secretary of state shall note the discontinuance in the index. A certificate of discontinuance shall be executed by a majority of the persons named in the original certificate or the amended certificate last previously filed as persons conducting or transacting the business or as partners or, in the case of a corporation, by an officer of the corporation, provided that if any of them shall be deceased the certificate shall so state and may be executed and acknowledged by a majority of the survivors, or by the executor or administrator of a deceased person named in the original certificate or last previously filed amended certificate as the only person conducting or transacting the business, and provided further that any such signatures may be dispensed with by order of the supreme court.

Penal Law

§ 190.35 Misconduct by corporate official.

A person is guilty of misconduct by corporate official when:

1. Being a director of a stock corporation, he knowingly concurs in any vote or act of the directors of such corporation, or any of them, by which it is intended:

(a) To make a dividend except in the manner provided by law; or

(b) To divide, withdraw or in any manner pay to any stockholder any part of the capital stock of the corporation except in the manner provided by law; or

(c) To discount or receive any note or other evidence of debt in payment of an installment of capital stock actually called in and required to be paid, or with intent to provide the means of making such payment; or

(d) To receive or discount any note or other evidence of debt with intent to enable any stockholder to withdraw any part of the money paid in by him on his stock; or

(e) To apply any portion of the funds of such corporation, directly or indirectly, to the purchase of shares of its own stock, except in the manner provided by law; or

2. Being a director or officer of a stock corporation:

(a) He issues, participates in issuing, or concurs in a vote to issue any increase of its capital stock beyond the amount of the capital stock thereof, duly authorized by or in pursuance of law; or

(b) He sells, or agrees to sell, or is directly or indirectly interested in the sale of any share of stock of such corporation, or in any agreement to sell the same, unless at the time of such sale or agreement he is an actual owner of such share, provided that the foregoing shall not apply to a sale by or on behalf of an underwriter or dealer in connection with a bona fide public offering of shares of stock of such corporation.

Misconduct by corporate official is a class B misdemeanor.

Index

Agreement of Shareholders, 23, 67, 111–12
Amendment of Certificate of Incorporation; *see* Certificate of Incorporation
Attorney General, 30
Authority of Officers; *see* Officers
Authorized Shares, 47

Board of Directors, 104–7
Bonds, 50
Business Judgment Rule, 121
Buy-Sell Agreement; *see* Agreement of Shareholders
By-Laws, 45–46
    Adoption of, 45–46
    Amendment of, 45

Capital, 47–50, 52–54
Capital Stock, 47–49
Capital Surplus, 55
Certificate of Assumed Name, 31–32
Certificate of Authority; *see* Foreign Corporation
Certificate of Dissolution, 187
Certificate of Doing Business, 3–4
Certificate of Incorporation (C/I), 23–26
    Amendment of, 163–64
    Contents, 23–26
    Filing with Secretary of State, 25–26
Certificate of Partnership, 4
Classification of Corporations, 8–10
Close Corporation; *see* Closely Held Corporation

Closely Held Corporation, 10, 110–12, 188
Conflict of Interest, 127–32
Conflict of Name, 23–24, 31–32
Consideration for Shares, 51–52
Consolidation, 166–67
Constituent Corporations, 164–67
Controlling Shareholders, 150, 189
Cooperative Corporation, 9
Corporate Opportunity; *see* Duties of Directors and Officers
Corporate Purposes, 24–25, 41–42
Corporation—Classifications, 8–10
    What Is a Corporation?, 1–2
Corporation Is a Person, 10
County Clerk's Office, 3, 4, 31
Creditors of the Corporation, 12–14, 169–70, 191
Crime, Liability for, 123
Cumulative Voting, 102–3

Deadlock; *see* Dissolution
Declaration of Dividends; *see* Dividends
De facto Corporation, 26
De jure Corporation, 26
Derivative Suit by Shareholders; *see* Shareholder Derivative Suit
Directors, Board of;
    see also Duties of Directors and Officers
    Committee of, 107
    Compensation, 132
    Discretion of, 51, 70, 121
    Dissenting Directors, 127–28
    Liability of, 120–27
    Meetings, 105–6
        Action Taken without a Meeting, 106

        Conference Call, 106
        Quorum, 105
        Voting, 102–3, 104
    Number of Members, 104
    Powers, 106–7
    Qualification of Members, 104
    Removal of Directors, 104–5
    Special Litigation Committee, 149
    Vacancies, 105
    Voting for, 101–3
Dissolution, 187–90
    Attorney General, 188
    Creditors' Claims, 191
    Deadlock, 188–89
    Involuntary, 188–90
    Judicial Proceeding, 188–90
    Liquidation, 190–92
    Oppressive Conduct, 189, 197–201
    Proclamation, 31, 194–97
    Shareholder Rights upon, 191
    Voluntary, 187
    Winding up, 191–92
Dividends, 69–74
    Action to Declare, 70, 78–80
    Cash, 70
    Declaration of, 70–74
    Discretion of Board of Directors, 70
    Legal Restrictions, 70–74
    Liquidating, 73, 191
    Notice Regarding, 74
    Property, 71
    Right to, 70–74
    Stock, 71–73
    Wrongful or Illegal, 73–74
        Liability of Directors, 74
        Liability of Shareholders, 74

Domestic Corporation, 9
Double Taxation of Dividends, 5–6
Duties of Directors and Officers, 119–32
    Care, Duty of, 119
    Compete, Duty not to, 130
    Conflict of Interest, 129
    Corporate Opportunity, 129
    Diligence, Duty of, 120
    Fiduciary Duties, 128–32
    Loyalty, Duty of, 120
    Obedience, Duty of, 120

Earned Surplus, 55–57
Equity Shares, 70–75
Express Authority, 108
Extraordinary Business Decisions, 151–153

Fictitious Name, 31
Fiduciary Duties,
    Officers and Directors, 128–32, 173–74
    Controlling Shareholders, 150–51, 173
Foreign Corporation, 27–30, 34–35
    Doing Business, 28
    Licensing of, 28–29
    Penalties Imposed, 30
    Qualification Procedure, 28–29
    Sanctions for Failure to Qualify, 30
Foreign Corrupt Practices Act, 124
Formation of the Corporation, 23–27
Franchise Tax, 31
Freeze-out, 150–51, 173, 177–81

Guarantee by the Corporation, 152
Guarantee of Corporate Obligation, 12
Historical Background, 1–2

Incorporator, 24
Indemnification of Officers and Directors, 132–33
Individual Proprietor, 3
Insider Trading, 132
Insolvent, 68, 70
Inspection of Books and Records, 75–77, 81–85
    Common Law Right, 75–76
    Rights under B.C.L., 76–77
Inspector of Elections, 101

Joint-Stock Association, 5
Joint Venture, 5

Legal Entity, 1, 10–12
Liability of Directors, 120–28
Liability of Shareholders, 154–55
Limited Liability, 12–14
Limited Partnership, 4–5
Liquidation; *see* Dissolution
Loans to Directors, 120, 153

Management of the Corporation, 99, 106–7, 109, 110–12
Meeting(s),
    Directors, 105–6
    Organization, 44
    Shareholders, 99–102, 115–17
Merger, 163–66
    "Freeze-out", 173, 177–81
    Subsidiary Merger, 165
Minority Shareholders, 150–51, 173, 189
Model Act, 2
Model Close Corporation Act, 10
Mortgage of Corporate Property, 152

Name, Selection of, 23–24
Non-profit Corporation, 8–9
N.Y.S. Tax Commission, 29, 31, 187

Officers, 107–10
    see also, Duties of Directors and Officers
    Authority of, 108–9, 114–15
    Compensation of, 110
    Liability of, 122–23
    Removal of, 110
    Selection of, 107
    Title of Officers, 108
Oppressive Conduct, *see* Dissolution
Organization Meeting of Incorporators, 44

Partnerships, 4–5
Pension and Profit Sharing Plans, 7–8
Personal Guarantee, 12
Piercing the Corporate Veil, 13–17
Powers of the Corporation, 24–25, 41–42
Preemptive Right, 74–75
Pre-Incorporation Agreement; *see* Agreement of Shareholders,
President, 108, 109, 114–15
Professional Corporation, 9
Promoter of the Corporation, 26–27
    Contracts, 27
    Fiduciary Duty, 27
Proxies, 100–1, 106
Purposes, Corporate, 24–25

Quorum, 100, 105

Ratification by Shareholders, 131
Receiver, 192
Registered Agent, 25
Retained Earnings, *see* Earned Surplus
Revaluation Surplus, 55–58
R.I.C.O., 124–25

Salaries Due to Employees-Unpaid Claims, 12
Salaries Paid to Shareholders, 7
Sale of Assets, 169–70, 171
Secretary of the Corporation, 109–10
Secretary of State, 25
Securities Act of 1933, 123–24
Securities and Exchange Commission (S.E.C.), 123–24
Securities Exchange Act of 1934, 123–24
Shareholders
    Agreement; *see* Agreement of Shareholders
    Appraisal Rights, 171–73
    Dissolution, Rights upon, 191
    Dividends, Right to, 69–73
    Examination of Books and Records, 75–77, 81–85
    Liability of, 154–55
    Meetings, 99–101
        Action taken without a Meeting, 104
    Quorum, 100
    Unanimous Written Consent of, 104
    Voting, 101–2
Shareholder's Derivative Suit, 148–50
    Recovery, 150
    Requirements, 149
    Security for Expenses, 150
Shares
    Authorized, 47, 52–53
    Classification of, 47–50
    Common, 48
    Consideration for, 51–52
    Cumulative Preferred, 49
    Equity, 47, 74
    Issuance of, 47, 52–53
    Issued, 53
    No Par Value, 48
    Outstanding, 53
    Participating Preferred, 48
    Par Value, 48
    Payment for, 51–52

Preemptive Rights, 74–75
Preferred, 48
Reacquired, 50, 69
Redemption of, 68
Subscription for, 50–51
Treasury, 50, 69
Voting, 48
Small Corporation; *see* Closely Held Corporation
Sole Proprietorship, 3–4
Stated Capital, 53–54
Stock Certificate, 65–66
    Lost, Destroyed, or Stolen Certificate, 66
Stock Dividend, 71–73
Stock Record Book, 68
Stock Subscription, 50–51
    After Corporation Is Formed, 51
    Before Corporation Is Formed, 50
Subchapter S, 6

Subsidiary Corporation, 165
Surplus, 54–58
    Capital Surplus, 55
    Earned Surplus, 55
    Revaluation Surplus, 55
Surviving Corporation, 165, 167

Takeovers, 167–70, 173–74
Tax Considerations, 5–8
Tender Offer, 167
Torts, Liability for, 122
Transfer of Shares, 66–68
    Bona Fide Purchaser, 66
    Forged or Unauthorized Indorsement, 66
    Manner of, 66–68
    Restrictions on, 67
Treasury Shares, 50, 52, 69

Ultra Vires, 43–44
    Legal Effect of, 43
    Remedies, 43

Unanimous Written Consent of Directors, 106
Unanimous Written Consent of Shareholders, 104
Unfair Competition, 31–32

Violation of Statute Liability for, 120–21, 122, 123–27
Voting
    Agreements, 110–12
    Cumulative, 102–3
    Directors Meetings, 105–6
    Extraordinary Matters, 151–53
    Proxies, 100, 106
    Shareholders Agreements, 110–12
    Shareholders Meetings, 101–2

Watered Stock, 52, 58, 154
Williams Act, 168–69
Winding up; *see* Dissolution